Under the editorship of

DAYTON D. McKEAN

University of Colorado

*

OTHER TITLES IN THE SERIES

The Government of Republican Italy
John Clarke Adams and Paolo Barile

British Parliamentary Democracy
Sydney D. Bailey

The Federal Government of Switzerland
George A. Codding, Jr.

Government and Politics in Israel
Oscar Kraines

Contemporary Government of Germany
Elmer Plischke

In Preparation

Contemporary Government of Japan
Theodore McNelly

The Second Republic of Austria
H. Pierre Secher

Norwegian Democracy
James A. Storing

*

The Indian Political System

*

NORMAN D. PALMER

UNIVERSITY OF PENNSYLVANIA

HOUGHTON MIFFLIN COMPANY · BOSTON

Copyright Acknowledgments

To Harper & Brothers and Jonathan Cape Limited for passages from *The Soul of India* by Amaury de Riencourt. Copyright © 1960 by Amaury de Riencourt. Reprinted by permission of Harper & Brothers and of Jonathan Cape Limited.

To MacDonald & Co. (Publishers) Ltd. for: Sir Percival Griffiths, *The British Impact on India* (1952).

To The Macmillan Company for: Frank Moraes, *India Today* (1960); Planning Commission Government of India, *The New India: Progress Through Democracy* (1958). Reprinted by permission of The Macmillan Company.

To Oxford University Press for: Michael Brecher, *Nehru: A Political Biography* (1959).

To Princeton University Press for: Selig S. Harrison, *India: The Most Dangerous Decades* (1960); V. P. Menon, *The Transfer of Power in India* (1957); and Richard L. Park and Irene Tinker, eds., *Leadership and Political Institutions in India* (1959).

To the University of Pennsylvania Press and Longmans, Green & Co. Limited for: W. H. Morris-Jones, *Parliament in India* (1957).

To Random House, Inc., and Victor Gollancz, Limited for: Vincent Sheean, *Nehru* (1960).

To The John Day Company, Inc. and the Honorable V. K. Krishna Menon for: *The Discovery of India* (1946) by Jawaharlal Nehru. Reprinted by permission of The John Day Company, Inc., and the Honorable V. K. Krishna Menon.

Houghton Mifflin Company

The Riverside Press · *Cambridge, Massachusetts*

PRINTED IN THE U.S.A.

To

Evelyn and Pat

Good Companions During

My Passage to India

CONTENTS

PREFACE

The closing months of the first decade and a half of independence are a particularly appropriate time for a survey of existing and evolving patterns of government and politics in India. Free India can point to substantial achievements in the brief period of its existence, and it has laid solidly the foundations for future progress; but it is a country with massive problems, and "the most dangerous decades," to use Selig Harrison's words, lie ahead. Most of the "tall leaders" who led the independence struggle and who presided over India's destinies in the post-independence years have passed from the scene. Jawaharlal Nehru — the "tallest" of all except Mahatma Gandhi — still carries on with remarkable vigor and wisdom after a generation of heavy responsibilities and dedicated service; but he is in his seventies, and new leaders must gradually take over from him and from others of his generation who are still active in Indian government and society.

India has survived long years of colonial rule and short years of independence. The threats to its survival as a free nation still come from within as well as from without. Its struggle to achieve national unity and political integration by democratic means is threatened by fissiparous and centrifugal tendencies of many kinds. It is fighting a continuing battle against poverty, illiteracy, population pressures, communalism, casteism, linguistic and regional rivalries and differences, and authoritarian patterns of social and political conduct.

For students of politics India is perhaps the most important of all the newer countries of the so-called "underdeveloped world." In view of its long and complex past, its vast population (larger than all of Africa and Latin America combined), and its present position, the special importance of India can be generally recognized without doing an injustice to any other country.

For students of comparative government, political behavior, and international affairs, as well as for those primarily interested in "the politics of the developing areas," India is a particularly significant laboratory of political, economic, and social development and change. It is a static society in progress, with a political system grounded in orthodox and conservative traditions but nevertheless in a process of change. In the strictest sense of the term India has perhaps not yet evolved a real political system at all; but it has a well-established framework of government and law which is a working reality, although to be sure it sometimes operates in peculiar ways and is often strangely affected by nonpolitical forces and developments. One should remember, however, that in India, to a greater degree than in most countries, it is difficult to determine what is political and what is nonpolitical.

Indian politics must be analyzed from the point of view of specialists in many fields of what are usually called the behavioral sciences. It cannot be analyzed simply by applying normal standards of Western political science.

This brief volume presents a fairly comprehensive view of the evolving Indian political system at a critical period of its development. I am well aware of the difficulties of this approach and of my own limitations in undertaking it, but I have persevered because of the importance of the subject and because of the need for a pioneer study of this sort by an American scholar, and I have cherished the hope that such a study may stimulate other American scholars to give more serious attention to the Indian political scene. Although I have had rather extensive experience in India and have for long been a serious student of Indian affairs, I recognize all too well that I do not really know India in all of its dimensions; but even for Jawaharlal Nehru "the discovery of India" has been an endless quest for something which continually eludes him. As Arnold Toynbee has observed: "India is a whole world in herself; she is a society of the same magnitude as our Western society."

For whatever merit this volume may possess I am particularly indebted to many friends whose knowledge of Indian politics and society has aroused my lasting envy and admiration. Among these friends who know India so well I would single out the following for special mention: S. V. Kogekar, Principal of Fergusson College in Poona, A. Appadorai, Director of the Indian School of International Studies in New Delhi, V. K. N. Menon, Director of the Indian Institution of Public Administration in New Delhi, and C. J. Chacko, Head of the Department of Political Science at Delhi University, where I spent a stimulating year as a Visiting Professor; Richard L. Park of the University of Michigan, Selig S. Harrison of *The New Republic* (formerly an Associated Press correspondent in India), Amaury de Riencourt, a profound student of Indian and other civilizations, and W. H. Morris-Jones of Durham University, author of the standard work on the Indian Parliament; and my colleagues of the South Asia Regional Studies Program at the University of Pennsylvania, particularly W. Norman Brown, Holden Furber, Richard D. Lambert, and Wilfred Malenbaum.

Professor Malenbaum was kind enough to let me use the manuscript of his forthcoming book, *Prospects for Indian Development,* to be published by Allen & Unwin in London. Dayton D. McKean, Dean of the Graduate School at the University of Colorado and editor of the series in which this volume appears, and C. Satyapalan, Lecturer in Political Science at S. N. College in Quilon in the South Indian

State of Kerala, read the entire manuscript and made many helpful comments and suggestions. Richard N. Clark of the Houghton Mifflin Company, with his usual astuteness, patience, and aplomb, guided the manuscript through all the stages leading to publication, and he was even able to induce me to cut it substantially because of necessary space limitations. Mary Sutherland Perkins typed the entire manuscript, and Victor Greene was an invaluable research assistant.

To all of these individuals, and to many more whose contribution to this volume was far greater than anyone else can ever know, I express my deepest appreciation.

A briefer treatment of salient aspects of Indian government and politics is presented in five chapters on India which I contributed to George McT. Kahin, editor, *Major Governments of Asia,* published by the Cornell University Press in 1958. Although I deliberately refrained from consulting these chapters, except on certain points of detail, in preparing this longer work, I am happy to record my indebtedness to Professor Kahin and to the Cornell University Press for the opportunity which they afforded me to undertake a selective introduction to the Indian political scene. Portions of Chapter 2 will also appear in another volume, entitled *High School Social Studies Perspectives,* to be published by Houghton Mifflin. Some of the observations in Chapter 8 were first publicly expressed in a lecture at Bryn Mawr College in April, 1960, in a symposium on "Problems in Implementing Economic Planning in Underdeveloped Areas: India." In preparing Chapter 11 I drew freely on several published articles, particularly three in *Current History* (published in the issues of February, 1956, March, 1959, and March, 1961).

In the preparation of this book I was greatly assisted by a grant from the Committee on the Advancement of Research at the University of Pennsylvania.

NORMAN D. PALMER

Leopard Lake
Berwyn, Pennsylvania
August 15, 1961

* 1 *

The Nature of Indian Politics

To a casual Western observer the existing Indian political system may seem to be essentially a Western import. Upon closer view, however, this system begins to lose some of the stamp of undigested foreign borrowing, and to assume forms which are more closely related to India's peculiar traditions, experience, and needs. Beneath familiar forms are unfamiliar practices and attitudes. The Indian political structure is still in the process of becoming, and its final shape is still not so clear as one might first assume. The Indianization of Indian politics is still going on.

In his important study of the Indian Parliament, Professor Morris-Jones warned that in approaching the study of Indian politics the Western student "is well advised to be on his guard. He should not assume, for instance, that institutions with familiar names are necessarily performing wholly familiar functions. He should be ready to detect political trends and forces in what he will be tempted to set aside as non-political movements. He should be prepared to find the behaviour of those who hold apparently familiar political positions conditioned by considerations which he would not normally associate with such places."[1] Hence special consideration should be given to the nonpolitical factors in India, which often will prove to be more potent in shaping Indian political behavior than trends and institutions which are clearly political.

Obviously there are various "levels of politics" in India, as Professor Morris-Jones has noted. Because it is less familiar and less immediately obvious it is particularly important to recognize what Morris-Jones

[1] W. H. Morris-Jones, *Parliament in India* (Philadelphia, 1957), p. 2.

has called "the presence in Indian politics of a manner of political thought and behaviour which it is difficult to regard simply as a local modification of some aspect of Western politics. It draws its inspiration from religious teachings and represents a development of an aspect of Gandhian politics. It leads its own life, alongside and not wholly unconnected with the world of 'normal' politics, but largely independent of it. It is possible to say that it is not politics at all; in that case the Western pattern (of course, with its modifications) is left in sole command as the only pattern of political conduct available. But it seems more in keeping with the facts to allow that it is politics, even if it is of a kind quite distinct from that of modern Europe."[2]

Sources of Indian Political Thought

At the present time India is engaged in a serious search for its own past. To the extent that this search results in excessive glorification of the past and an unobjective approach to it, it has a harmful effect, not least of all in encouraging ultra-nationalism and a rejection of ideas simply because they are not "Indian"; but to the extent that it helps Indians to understand and appreciate their own history and traditions, it is wholesome. Indians are often criticized as being unhistorically minded. In *The Soul of India,* one of the most penetrating interpretations of Indian history, Amaury de Riencourt wrote: "The key to an understanding of Indian culture lies precisely in this total indifference toward history, toward the very process of *time.*"[3] This may have been true in past decades, when the minds of Indians were concentrated on other things, when they were isolated from each other, and when local and regional influences predominated; and it was generally true during the long period of British dominance. But today the Indian people are making a conscious effort to understand their past and to evolve political, economic, and social practices and institutions which are in keeping with their own genius and traditions as well as suitable for modern problems and needs.

India has a long and rather confused history, and doubtless parts of it might well be forgotten; but there are lessons as well as warnings in India's past. Over the centuries many people have come into India from other places, contiguous or remote, and some of these peoples — including the Aryans, the Moguls, and the British — have extended their control over much of the subcontinent. The golden age of Hinduism came many centuries ago, before the beginning of the Christian era. The great classics of ancient India — the Vedas, the Upanishads, the *Ramayana,* the *Mahabharata,* and many others — date

[2] *Ibid.,* p. 37.

[3] Amaury de Riencourt, *The Soul of India* (New York, 1960), p. 15.

from this early period, and they have had a profound influence on patterns of thought and behavior through the centuries.

During the long centuries since the full flowering of Hindu culture and philosophy many other influences have entered the main stream of Indian political thought. Foremost among these have been the impact of Muslim institutions and concepts of administration, which were dominant in India for several centuries, notably during the apogee of Mogul rule in the sixteenth and seventeenth centuries, and of Western ideas and institutions during the past three centuries or more and most strongly during the past century.

"Contemporary Indian political thought, therefore, stems from many sources, Eastern and Western, ancient and modern."[4] For all the efforts of the revivalists of Hindu traditions during the Hindu Renaissance of the late nineteenth and early twentieth centuries, and for all the present emphasis on the rediscovery of India's past, it is difficult to find any continuity between ancient Hindu political thought and the political ideas that move modern India, or to appraise the relative influence of the many streams of thought that have influenced modern India. "Indeed, Indian political thought is probably as diverse as that of the West. In view of the antiquity and the richness of Indian civilization, this should occasion no surprise."[5]

Leaders and Leadership

Considerable insight into the nature of a society may be obtained from a study of the traditions and types of leadership which have characterized it. The leadership principle has been particularly strong in India, reinforced by the traditional aspects of Indian life and social organization. It is reflected in the great classics of the early Hindu period, in the rigidly structured caste system, in the authoritarian patterns which have prevailed throughout the centuries, in the long experience with foreign conquerors and rulers, in the organization of the villages and other units of rural society, in religious practices and groupings.

In modern India leadership has continued to be of surpassing importance. Of special importance are the influence of religious mystics like Ramakrishna, leaders of the Hindu Renaissance like Vivekananda, great literary figures like Tagore, the unique and all-encompassing leadership of Mahatma Gandhi, the work of the men who are trying to carry on the Gandhian spiritual tradition, notably

[4] Norman D. Palmer, "Indian and Western Political Thought: Coalescence or Clash?", *The American Political Science Review,* XLIX (September, 1955), 755.

[5] *Ibid.,* p. 753.

Vinoba Bhave, and the dominant role in the post-Gandhian era of Jawaharlal Nehru.

India has been fortunate in the character and stature of its leaders. Gandhi, Nehru, Vallabhbhai Patel, and in an earlier generation Tagore, Gokhale, and Tilak would rank among the great figures of the past century in any country. One of India's outstanding assets has been what Dr. Paul Appleby has called "extraordinary national leadership."[6]

Many of India's leaders could truly be described as charismatic leaders. These include persons of such diverse character and personality and ideals as Bal Gangadhar Tilak, Mahatma Gandhi, Subhas Chandra Bose, Vinoba Bhave, Chakravarti Rajagopalachari, and Jawaharlal Nehru. Some of these leaders, notably Gandhi and Bhave, have also been characterized as "unconventional" political leaders, although it is difficult to determine what in the Indian political and social environment is conventional and what is unconventional.

Gandhi. Mahatma Gandhi was a master in using nonpolitical methods to achieve political ends. In South Africa he experimented with a technique of nonviolent opposition which he called *satyagraha* — often translated as "soul-force" — which he professed to have borrowed from ancient Indian teachings and from many other sources, including the writings of Tolstoy. Upon his return to India he soon developed the practice of *satyagraha* into the most formidable weapon the British had ever encountered in the national resistance movement. *Satyagraha* is still practiced in India, often in ways of which Gandhi himself would have disapproved.

Gandhi also used fasting most effectively as a political weapon. This practice, too, is occasionally used in independent India. In December, 1952, a respected Telegu leader, Potti Sriramulu, fasted unto death on the issue of a separate Andhra state, and shortly after his death the Government of India yielded to the demand for this new state. In 1956 the Chief Minister of Bombay State, Morarji Desai, went on a fast in consequence of protests and violence in Ahmedabad over the decision to retain Bombay as a bilingual state, with an enlarged area.

Gandhi harked back to ancient themes in developing some of his distinctive concepts and approaches, in what might be called his nonpolitical approach to politics. To him *satyagraha* was an application of the concept of *ahimsa,* meaning nonviolence in more than a physical sense. In his own distinctive way Gandhi proclaimed the intimate relationship of religion and politics, and he often applied ethical concepts to political action. On innumerable occasions he

[6] Paul H. Appleby, *Public Administration in India: Report of a Survey* (Delhi, 1953), p. 3.

referred to the *Bhagavad Gita* as the guide to his political as well as his spiritual life. In his *Autobiography* he wrote that "there is no other God than Truth," and that "my devotion to Truth has drawn me into the field of politics; and I can say without the slightest hesitation, and yet in all humility, that those who say that religion has nothing to do with politics do not know what religion means."[7]

In his teachings and actions Gandhi gave a more positive twist to the *Bhagavad Gita* and to such ancient concepts as *dharma* and *ahimsa,* and in his techniques of *satyagraha* he seemed to fuse Indian and non-Indian concepts into an effective instrument of political action; but he taught his fellow-countrymen to be proud of their own ideals and traditions and to adopt what was good and useful for them from the outside world without being untrue to themselves or to their past. "By persuading them to draw their strength and inspiration from India and cease being magnetized by the West, the Mahatma impregnated the British-created middle class with Indian ideas and ideals. This was his greatest revolution."[8]

Another ethical principle Gandhi attempted to apply to politics was that of the relationship of ends to means: that no ends, however desirable, should be sought by unworthy means. "The basic lesson that Mahatma Gandhi taught us," wrote Jawaharlal Nehru in his report to the All-Indian Congress Committee when he relinquished the office of President of the Congress Party in January, 1955, "was that means govern ends and that we should never adopt wrong means even for right ends." The leaders of independent India often do not follow this lesson (or other lessons Gandhi taught) but they have attempted to adhere to it and they often refer to it as a guide to their action in the domestic or international fields.

Gandhi generally remained somewhat aloof from the Indian National Congress, but he was the dominant figure in the Indian nationalist movement for many years. Many of his acts and teachings which seemed to have the least political significance proved to be the most astute kind of politics. He never held a party or government position, but he was consulted by the British Government and by the leaders of the Indian National Congress on almost all crucial issues.

Gandhi's influence is not particularly manifest in Indian political life today, although spokesmen of nearly all political parties and ideologies frequently refer to him and pay at least lip service to his teachings. Many Indians are distressed because their Government seems to be functioning in ways obviously different from those advocated by "the

[7] M. K. Gandhi, *An Autobiography, or the Story of My Experiments with Truth* (2nd edition, Ahmedabad, 1940), p. 615.

[8] Frank Moraes, *India Today* (New York, 1960), p. 75.

Father of the Nation." Nehru, often called Gandhi's political heir, is particularly sensitive to charges that he is betraying the principles of the man who was his acknowledged master and guide. His defense is that the Government is acutely aware of Gandhi's teachings and is applying them wherever possible. For example, he often refers to the proper relation of ends and means in domestic and foreign policy. But Nehru, who is a political realist as well as an idealist, is frank to confess that it is not possible to conduct the affairs of a large new nation in the complex world of today wholly in accordance with the rather nebulous and often conflicting principles of government and society which Gandhi enunciated.

Because independent India is obviously not being run along Gandhian lines, many observers, in India and elsewhere, insist that the Mahatma has left almost no impact on India today. In a book published in 1960 Frank Moraes, one of India's leading journalists, wrote: "The imprint of Gandhism, built and maintained over three decades, has for all practical purposes vanished within a decade."[9] This conclusion is justified only if it is applied to the more obvious aspects of contemporary Indian politics; it is doubtful that it applies to the spirit in which Indian politics is in fact being carried on; and almost certainly it is not true with respect to Indian life and thought generally. Gandhi gave a new cast to modern India. Without him, the course of the independence struggle would have been very different; without him, independent India would have been a different and less distinctive nation. "Many Indians disagree today with parts of his philosophy. Now that independence has been won, most Indians find it hard or inconvenient to put into practice his concept of non-violence. But much of modern India would be incomprehensible without reference to the profoundly exciting effect of his many-sided idealism."[10]

[9] *Ibid.*, pp. 220–221.

[10] Beatrice Pitney Lamb, *Introduction to India* (Washington, D.C., 1960), pp. 11–12. In March and April, 1959, the Indian Institute of Public Opinion conducted an All-India survey of the Gandhian legacy, and it summarized the rather surprising findings of this survey as follows:

"The extent of awareness of Gandhiji is surprisingly high, being over 90 per cent in urban areas and as much as 80 per cent in rural areas. On the other hand, the extent of this awareness does not imply that there is a clear image in the public mind of the Mahatma's many-sided personality, or that the image has today a concrete application to practical affairs. To the great majority of respondents, he has even ceased to play the role of Mahatma, though in the minds of a small minority — in which women significantly have a notable place — he is venerated as an incarnation of God. He is best known as an outstanding leader of the nationalist movement and as a social reformer. In neither of these is the unique character

Bhave, Narayan, and Kripalani. In one way or another all of the leaders of independent India were influenced by Gandhi. This influence is more apparent in the nonpolitical than in the political realm, but it is by no means absent in Indian politics. After all, the topmost leaders of India today, almost to a man, were followers of Gandhi. Many of Gandhi's followers are active in that wide area of Indian life in which politics and religion seem to mix in peculiar and pervasive ways. Notable among these men are Vinoba Bhave and, in different degrees, Jayaprakash Narayan and Acharya Kripalani.

Bhave, an elderly Gandhian who professes to have no interest in politics as such, is nevertheless one of the strongest political forces in India today. His Bhoodan Yagna movement is leading what Kripalani has called "the greatest revolution since Gandhi." It is a nonviolent revolution, an economic program with a moral and spiritual purpose, which, as Nehru has said, "reaches the minds and hearts of the people." It calls for the sacrificial giving of land and other possessions as a means of spiritual regeneration. "Only in India, one feels, could there be such a movement. . . . It shows how powerful still is the moral force of the Gandhian outlook."[11]

Bhave started his movement in 1951 in the Telengana area of what was then Hyderabad State, and was largely responsible for changing the attitudes of people who only a few years before had participated in or otherwise aided armed Communist uprisings. The highest leaders of the Government of India visit Bhave from time to time, and they go out of their way in showing deference to him.

Narayan, a leading Indian Socialist, sometimes referred to as a possible successor to Nehru, was so profoundly affected by Bhave and the Bhoodan movement that he announced his intention of abandoning politics to devote his life to this cause. In spite of his

---

of his contribution fully realised. . . . Contrary to the indications of large awareness, the range of application of Gandhian doctrines in practice is disappointingly small. Even on an issue like foreign policy, the support enjoyed by the Prime Minister's policy is not connected with Gandhian principles. . . . The survey is limited in scope, but it gives enough of a general picture of a wide, though receding, Gandhian impact, without any corresponding hard core generating continuing impulses under which Gandhian doctrines can renew themselves in every generation."

For a detailed summary of the results of the survey see "An Analysis of the Gandhian Impact on the Indian People," *Monthly Public Opinion Surveys* of the Indian Institute of Public Opinion, Vol. V, Nos. 2 and 3 (November, December, 1959).

[11] Lady Hartog, *India: New Patterns* (London, 1955), p. 34. For an interesting account of Bhave and the Bhoodan Yagna movement see Hallam Tennyson, *India's Walking Saint: The Story of Vinoba Bhave* (New York, 1955).

"retirement" he has continued to be influential in the Praja Socialist Party and to criticize or to give advice to the Government of India, solicited or unsolicited. He has been outspoken in his criticisms of the "soft" policies of the Government on the actions of the Chinese Communists in Tibet and along the Himalayan frontiers. He has advocated closer relations with Pakistan, and he has personally visited Pakistan since the Ayub Khan regime came into power. He advocates some form of "partyless democracy," although he has never defined precisely what he means by this phrase, and he favors "the reconstruction of Indian polity." Without questioning in any way the sincerity of Narayan's dedication to Bhoodan, it may well be that his "retirement" from politics will prove to be the most astute political move he has ever made. He is almost the only Indian leader, aside from Nehru and Bhave, who has a considerable mass following.

For many years Kripalani has been a prominent figure in Indian politics and society. He held high positions in three political parties. He is a former President of the Indian National Congress; he was the founder and head of the Kisan Mazdoor Praja Party (KMPP); and he served as Chairman of the Praja Socialist Party. He is a powerful orator and a brilliant writer. He has long been an independent and rather enigmatic political leader. Strongly influenced by the nonmodern aspects of Gandhi's thought, he has been increasingly restless under the conditions under which Indian politics have been conducted. In 1960 he resigned from the P.S.P., partly because he disagreed with some of its policies and partly, so he said, because he wanted his "freedom" from the demands of day-to-day political activities. In his new role Kripalani, like Narayan, will nominally be out of political life, but he will almost certainly continue to speak frankly on all subjects, political or spiritual, which interest his facile mind.

Nehru. Since the death of Gandhi more than a decade ago Nehru has been without a peer in India. He has been a truly great leader of his country and his people, a charismatic leader, to whom millions of people have looked for the "gift of grace." Personal contacts are of the greatest importance in India, and Nehru, like Gandhi before him, has kept in touch with the people and has established a kind of mystical relationship with them. India is a land where the belief in *darshan* (the beneficial effect of being in the presence of a great man) is strong and pervasive, and Nehru has made the most of this national trait. By his example he has sought to win the loyalty of the Indian masses, not so much to himself as a leader as to the principles for which he stands and to the nation he is trying to build. This is leadership in the highest sense, and India has been fortunate to have a man of Nehru's calibre and orientation at the helm during the formative years of nationhood.

Consciously or unconsciously, however, Nehru has stifled initiative and leadership by others by the dominating, even domineering, position he has held for so long in Indian public life. S. K. Patil, a strong man of the Congress Party who is India's Minister of Food and Agriculture, stated recently, quite bluntly, that while "Nehru is the greatest asset we have because he is just like a banyan tree under whose shade millions take shelter," nevertheless he is also a liability, "because in the shade of that banyan tree, biologically, nothing grows."[12]

India today faces a crisis of leadership that raises grave questions for the future. The generation of outstanding leaders that piloted India to independence along nonviolent lines is fast passing from the scene. One by one the giants of yesterday have gone, and those who are left are well past the peak of their powers and toward the end of their journeys. Nehru, for all his seemingly inexhaustible energy and buoyancy, is over seventy years of age, and the question, "After Nehru, what?" recurs with growing urgency. In all probability the new generation of leaders will be less well educated and much less oriented toward the West; possibly they will achieve a new synthesis between Indian and Western ways and will find new sources of strength in India's traditions and peoples. But they will also be responsible for running a huge state in a complicated world, and they can hardly do this successfully by finding their political, economic, and social views solely in the *Bhagavad Gita,* in the concepts of *sarvodaya,* and in the Bhoodan Yagna movement.

Characteristics of Indian Society

Problems of Social Communication. Indian society is still characterized by a considerable lack of mobility and by the primacy of local interests over larger considerations. Distances, geographical and social, are great in India. Fewer than 30 per cent of the people are literate. Most of the great decisions are made by a small educated elite whose members for the most part speak English, are familiar with Western thought and institutions, hold most of the important positions in business, government, and the professions, and are often out of touch with the masses of the Indian people. Mass illiteracy, social conservatism, geographical distances, extreme localism and a fairly rigid social structure cut off the great majority of the people from effective participation in the political life of the country.

Social communication is difficult in India, and many of the channels of communication commonly available in Western countries are relatively unimportant in the Indian setting. Illiteracy and regional and linguistic differences lessen the influence of such media of mass communication as the press and the radio. Informal channels of

[12] Quoted in *Time,* Dec. 14, 1959, p. 22.

communication are especially important. Like China, India seems to have a most effective "grapevine" method of transmitting information. Personalities are important in Indian life generally, including politics. "The primary form of communication with the masses is still personal contact. Even the use of posters or of simple pamphlets has been found inadequate both by political parties and by the government. In personal contact the visual impression plays a weighted role. . . . Thus visual symbols such as the spinning wheel used by Gandhi are potent carriers of a political message. Thus, too, the technique of an itinerant leader such as Vinoba Bhave takes on added importance. The personality of leaders and their ability to have a direct impact on their audience will doubtless continue to play an outsized role in Indian politics for some time."[13]

Public Opinion and Pressure Groups. In spite of the mass illiteracy and relative lack of social communication, public opinion is potent in India, even though the study of it as a political force is still quite undeveloped.[14] In India, as elsewhere, various publics may be discerned. The most obvious publics are the uneducated many, whose role in influencing public policy is largely negative and general, and the elite few, who control the effective channels of access and who exercise most of the power. Within each of these publics many subdivisions may be found, especially on particular issues. Divisions between North and South, between regional and linguistic groups, between the literate and the illiterate, between villagers and townspeople, between communal and caste groups have a profound effect on political life and behavior.

Pressure groups also are to be found in India, although perhaps to a lesser degree and in different forms from those in Western states. "Three main types of pressure groups may be distinguished in the Indian setting: (1) special-interest organizations of fairly recent origin representing modern bases of social and economic association familiar to the Western observer, such as trade unions and business groups, social welfare agencies, or youth and women's organizations; (2) organizations representing traditional social relationships, such as caste and religious groups, and (3) organizations representing the Gandhian ideological heritage,"[15] such as the Sarva Seva Sangh, the main agency of the Sarvodaya movement, whose outstanding activity

[13] Gene D. Overstreet and Irene Tinker, "Political Dynamics in India" (a paper prepared for the Modern India Project, University of California, March, 1957), pp. 10–11.

[14] The most extensive continuing surveys of public opinion in India are to be found in the *Monthly Public Opinion Surveys* of the Indian Institute of Public Opinion.

[15] Overstreet and Tinker, "Political Dynamics in India," p. 11.

is the Bhoodan Yagna movement of Vinoba Bhave. The exact role of these pressure groups is hard to determine, but they obviously exert considerable influence on particular issues.

New Classes. In traditional Hindu society the classes that mattered were the high-caste Hindus, notably the Brahmans and the Kshatriyas. In Mogul times a new ruling class of Muslims governed the country, but they made relatively little impact on the masses of the people, who were mostly Hindus. The British became a new ruling aristocracy, and they trained and associated with them a group of Western-educated and Western-oriented Indians, who formed a new class in economic and political life, if not so obviously in Indian society generally. This Western-educated group split up into various classes. Some continued to the end as loyal servants of British rule, while others furnished the top leadership of the nationalist movement.

Gandhi raised up another new class of persons of various castes and backgrounds who were more clearly identified with the masses of the people and with Indian traditions and outlook. Some of the surviving members of this new class have apparently sloughed off the Gandhian tradition. Some are trying to continue it.

A different new class may now be emerging, with deeper roots in local and regional society — a class neither as Westernized in education or outlook as the new classes which developed in the days of British rule nor as devoted to India's past traditions as some of the more conservative followers of Gandhi or some of the many thousands of *sadhus* and other "holy men" who presumably devote their lives to nonmaterial things.[16] This new class — perhaps one should say this new generation — may be able to achieve a more satisfactory synthesis of the many values, foreign and indigenous, which compete for the loyalties of Indians today and which cause that "torment in our minds" of which Nehru has spoken. The members of this new class will presumably place greater emphasis on constructive service in building a new India than on the traditional values of renunciation and sacrifice.

Consensus and Synthesis. An interesting problem for exploration would be the extent to which a genuine political consensus exists in India today. The idea of consensus is deeply ingrained in Indian traditions and practices.[17] It is much more in keeping with traditional ways and attitudes than Western concepts such as decision by majority

[16] See Selig S. Harrison, *India: The Most Dangerous Decades* (Princeton, N.J., 1960), pp. 77–95.

[17] For rather different views on the importance of the idea of consensus in Indian political and social life, see Susanne Hoeber Rudolph, "Consensus and Conflict in Indian Politics," *World Politics,* XIII (April, 1961), 385–399, and W. H. Morris-Jones, "The Unhappy Utopia — JP in Wonderland," *The Economic Weekly,* June 25, 1960.

vote. It has been practiced for centuries in village councils and in other groupings at the local level. It has been employed less frequently at the higher levels of social and political organization. For all the traditional emphasis on consensus and for all the current emphasis on India as a unified nation, Indian society today is, as Professor Morris-Jones has pointed out, "a fragmented society, a society with an absence of a basic consensus." This " 'absence of consensus' theme," states Professor Morris-Jones, "has been central to an understanding of modern Indian politics."[18]

Some students of Indian history and politics would insist that a remarkable degree of consensus has existed throughout Indian history and that this consensus still exists on fundamentals. Historically, it arises out of the unifying forces in Indian social and religious life, notably Hinduism and the caste system. At the present time it is reinforced by the common experience and challenge of building a new nation, by the widespread acceptance of the basic decisions which have been made regarding the nature of the new state, including the decision to build a modern secular and democratic state, and above all the decision to establish a "socialist pattern of society." It is also reinforced by an almost unparalleled continuity and quality of national leadership. Undoubtedly Nehru himself, the chief political spokesman for India for a generation and the dominant figure in the Indian scene generally since the assassination of Gandhi early in 1948, has been a great unifying influence, and has done much to develop a high degree of political consensus, even in "a fragmented society."

Among the finest traditions of Indian society have been those of assimilation, tolerance, and synthesis, as illustrated in the two great religions (or religio-philosophical systems) which originated in the Indian subcontinent, Hinduism and Buddhism. These qualities have given a distinctive flavor to Indian life and culture. They help to explain how over the centuries India tolerated and to a large degree absorbed many different racial groups and cultures. Out of the blending of the old and the new, the indigenous and the foreign, a distinctively Indian culture has emerged. To be sure, cultures as divergent from the mainstream of Hindu culture as those of the Muslims and the British were not wholly assimilated, but they did merge with the dominant Hindu strain to form that unique synthesis which is the stamp of the culture of modern India.

"The tradition of India," in the view of a profound student of Indian history, K. M. Panikkar, "has always been one of synthesis . . . a singular ability to absorb the culture of others and assimilate it with-

[18] W. H. Morris-Jones, "The Exploration of Indian Political Life," *Pacific Affairs,* XXXII (December, 1959), 419.

out losing her own identity. It is the synthesis of Aryan and Dravidian that laid the basis of Hindu civilization. . . . The prolonged contact with Islam had profound significance for every aspect of Indian life."[19] India later became the "meeting-ground of the East and the West." Indeed, as G. K. Gokhale observed in 1911 at the Universal Races Conference in London, "whereas the contact of the West with other countries had only been external, in India the West had so to say entered into the very bone and marrow of the East."[20] Arnold Toynbee has pointed out that the Western impact on India was more intimate than on any other part of Asia, although of all the major Asian civilizations the dominant civilization of India, the Hindu, is most alien to the civilization of the West.[21]

The result of "the meeting of East and West" in India is thus summarized by Panikkar, in terms of the assimilation-tolerance-synthesis trilogy:

> . . . the inheritance that India has stepped into is only partly Hindu and Indian. The inheritance from the West is of no less importance in many fields. Modern India does not live under the laws of Manu. Her mental background and equipment, though largely influenced by the persistence of Indian tradition, have been moulded into their present shape by over a hundred years of Western education, extending practically to every field of mental activity. Its social ideals are not what Hindu society had for long cherished, but those assimilated from the West and derived predominantly from the teachings of Western social thinkers. . . . In fact it will be no exaggeration to say that the New Indian State represents . . . ideals and principles which are the results of an effective, even if imperfect, synthesis between the East and the West.[22]

Prospects for Democracy in India

One of the greatest experiments in human history is going on in India today. It is the experiment of many millions of people trying to attain a tolerable standard of existence and decent political, economic, and social institutions in the face of tremendous obstacles from within and from without, and to achieve these goals in a democratic way. There are many forces inside India which tend to pull her in a different direction.

The factors which militate against democracy are indeed formidable.

[19] K. M. Panikkar, *The State and the Citizen* (Bombay, 1956), p. 19.
[20] Quoted in *ibid.*
[21] Arnold Toynbee, *The World and the West* (New York and London, 1953), Chapter III ("India and the West").
[22] Panikkar, *The State and the Citizen,* p. 18.

The Indian political tradition is far more authoritarian than democratic. At no time in her long history was India really united. Prior to 1947 those who most nearly succeeded in unifying India were foreign conquerors, notably the Moguls and the British. The social systems which developed in the Indian subcontinent were varied indeed, but almost without exception they emphasized the group rather than the individual and produced social conflict and immobility. Communalism was a seriously divisive force, especially affecting relations between Hindus and Muslims. The caste system of the Hindus, whatever its utility and justification in past centuries, became rigid and divisive, and those who were outside the pale — the "untouchables" — had hardly any rights at all.

Today untouchability is legally abolished, and most of the leaders of India strongly oppose the excesses of communalism and the caste system; but it is nevertheless true that casteism and communalism[23] are still among the most powerful forces in India, and their influence is generally divisive and undemocratic. "Caste and community are still in everyday life the significant units of social actions with most people [of India]. . . . Casteism and communalism, therefore, continue to influence political activity at every stage from the panchayat right up to Parliament."[24]

It is hard to bring the illiterate masses, living mostly in scattered villages, into active participation in the life of the nation; and until this is achieved such "democracy" as exists will be imposed from above and will be guided by the few. In a country where means as well as ends are so important, can the end of democracy be achieved by essentially undemocratic means?

India is still bedeviled by local and regional loyalties. There is still little real sense of national unity. For a nation in only the second decade of its existence this fact is hardly surprising, but it is an ever-present danger, one of which Nehru and other Indian leaders are acutely aware. The decentralizing tendencies in India are strengthened by linguistic and historical differences and by mutual suspicions. On the one hand, India is still in search of national unity, and centrifugal tendencies are strong; on the other, the Central Government has assumed an increasing amount of authority and power. Thus democracy

[23] Communalism "is the term given in India and Pakistan to the sense of insecurity which any community feels and the accompanying action it takes to protect itself and further its own interests. It is applied in different localities to groups differentiated by religion, language, region, historical origin, occupation. . . . It is above all applied to the ill-feeling existing in Hindu-Muslim relationships." W. Norman Brown, *The United States and India and Pakistan* (Harvard University Press, 1953), pp. 112–113.

[24] "Caste and Politics," *The Radical Humanist,* XXI (April 28, 1957), 211.

is threatened by both centripetal and centrifugal tendencies. India lacks a well-developed party system, and as far as the Central Government is concerned, it has been almost a one-party state. The situation is different in a few of the States, but in most of these exceptional cases the opposition that has developed to the point of effectiveness could hardly be called wholesome from the democratic point of view.

Pressures from without as well as from within place India's experiment in democracy in peril. The general world situation, especially as it affects Asia, is not conducive to genuine democracy. The new nations of Asia need to marshal their limited resources to improve the life conditions of their people. They need time to deal with internal problems of desperate urgency. But the outside world impinges upon them, and makes their task doubly difficult.

India, with one of the lowest standards of living in the world and with a rapidly increasing population, must find ways and means to meet the growing demands of more and more people. If her present leaders, who have deliberately chosen the democratic way, fail to meet these needs, they may be forced to give way to other leaders who will take India along authoritarian paths, in the direction of communalism or some form of totalitarianism. India needs to grow more food, to find ways of providing employment for more people, to deal with the growing problem of the "educated unemployed" in the towns and cities and with the vast amount of underemployment in the countryside, to improve the standards of political life, to identify people generally with the effort at national development, to give them a sense of belonging to the new nation of which they are citizens. A well-established democratic system would be severely tested by these problems, and the Indian system of democracy has not yet developed deep roots.

It is therefore easy to give way to doubts and fears about the suitability of democracy in the Indian environment. Skeptics and prophets of gloom abound, in India and elsewhere. Indians of such diverse background as Narayan, Suniti Kumar Chatterji, and C. Rajagopalachari have expressed the direst forebodings about India's future. Indian newspapers and journals of opinion voice the same refrain. Many foreign observers join in the chorus. These doubts and fears are effectively expressed in two of the most important of the recent books on India by informed and sympathetic foreigners — Amaury de Riencourt's *The Soul of India* and Selig S. Harrison's *India: The Most Dangerous Decades.* Both authors are pessimistic about the prospects for democracy in India, and even of the prospects for India's survival as a nation. They agree that India is in for plenty of trouble in "the most dangerous decades" just ahead; that after Nehru goes India may split up into regional fragments or come under some form of authoritarian control; that, as de Riencourt puts it, "This underlying tendency toward Balkanization is further complicated by the most baffling set of social and economic problems likely to present themselves anywhere in the world";[25] that the center of political life is shifting to regional levels; that, while the caste system is breaking down in certain respects, conflicts between castes are being intensified by party politics, linguistic and regional rivalries, and other current developments.

Fortunately there are many sources of strength in the Indian political environment, and many factors working for democracy. The fact is that India today is a working democracy-in-being, with perhaps the best administrative structure and the most stable government anywhere on the mainland of Asia. An American student of public administration, who made a detailed survey of the operations of the Indian system of government, reached the conclusion that India has made "the most significant political effort of the century, certainly, and the grandest in dimensions, relative to developed resources, in the world's history."[26]

In spite of the diversity of India and the many divisive forces which have stood in the way of political unification in the past, India has shown a basic unity throughout the centuries which has survived invasions and wars and many decentralizing tendencies. This fundamental unity in the midst of diversity is a phenomenon which many astute observers of the Indian scene have sensed and recorded, without ever being able to define it precisely. It is a central theme of Nehru's fascinating book, *The Discovery of India.* It is apparently deeply rooted in the ancient religious and philosophical outlook of the people of India, which has given Indians what G. L. Mehta has called a "synthetic outlook."

In a television interview in London on July 7, 1957, Prime Minister Nehru insisted that India did have a democratic tradition, although he explained that this tradition in centuries past had been manifest largely in villages and other small centers of grass-roots democracy. With relatively few exceptions, the prevailing pattern of control in India, whether under Hindu rulers or Muslim or British conquerors, was authoritarian; but on local levels it is true that Indians have had a long schooling in what might be called primitive democracy. This tradition should not be exaggerated, as many spokesmen of modern India are inclined to do when they write or speak about representative institutions in ancient India or when they glorify the role of the *panchayats* (see

[25] De Riencourt, *The Soul of India,* p. 357.

[26] Paul H. Appleby, Convocation Address, Nagpur University, December, 1952.

page 150) which are now being revived as a base of the democratic system today on the village level. Nevertheless, India can rightly claim traditions which are favorable to the growth of democratic ideas and practices.

The British ruled India undemocratically, which is perhaps the only way that one people can rule over another, long after they had deepened and broadened the institutions of democracy at home; but consciously or unconsciously they trained thousands of Indians in the arts of government and administration. In fact, their impact was so great that the leaders of the Indian nationalist movement adopted the parliamentary system of democracy almost as a matter of course. The contest was not even close.

Many of the leaders of the independence struggle, including Gandhi and Nehru, had been trained in Britain, had become familiar at first hand with the workings of British parliamentary democracy, and had been steeped in the ideas of liberal democracy. Hundreds of others had had some experience with various forms of legislative or administrative bodies which were established during the later phases of British rule. For a century the educational system in India had been patterned along British lines, and those who were exposed to it were more familiar with Western institutions and ideas than they were with their own heritage. The British contributed to India a sound administrative structure and concepts of law and order. Directly or indirectly they also contributed a sense of liberty under law.

The prospects for democracy in India have been immeasurably heightened by the success of the Indian political experiment during the first decade and a half of independence. As has been pointed out, India has been fortunate in its leadership. On the whole, the Constitution is working well. Economic and social changes have for the most part been conducive to greater social mobility and to greater participation by the people in the life of the nation. The Five Year Plans have speeded the process of economic development, and some aspects of them, such as the Community Development Program and the National Extension Service, have had a direct and appreciable impact on millions of people. The basic decisions have been made, and the great task ahead is to preserve past gains and to make independence meaningful for the masses of the people. There is a new spirit in India, a new feeling of self-confidence, a new awakening. More and more Indians are beginning to feel not only that democracy is the right system for India, but that it is becoming well-established and will succeed.

Obviously a critical period is ahead for India, which will have to face this time of crisis under rather unfavorable conditions after its "tall" leaders have passed from the scene. Among the unfavorable conditions which are already clearly discernible are the growing strength of linguistic and other internal divisive forces, the growing doubts of the country's ability to make sufficient progress in economic development, the growing disillusionment of influential groups in Indian society, and the growing doubts about the relative merits of democracy versus authoritarianism in an underdeveloped country. The "key to the Indian crisis," in the opinion of A. M. Rosenthal of the *New York Times,* is to be found in the success or failure of "the attempt of the Government to match the awakening desires of an enormous population and to convince itself and the people that they should resist the attractions of what seem to be the swifter methods of authoritarianism."[27]

The odds against the evolution of a free society in India are very great. It is handicapped by its own traditions, its historical experience, its limited resources, the poverty of its masses, population pressures, and an unfavorable international environment. But there is much in India's traditions and experience which has paved the way for democratic self-government, and the success of its experiment in independence to date and of its development programs are encouraging manifestations of both the will and the capacity to survive as a democratic state. Clearly the Indian experiment is still going on and the outcome is still uncertain.

The Indian revolution has been one of the great revolutions of modern times, and it is still in process. At the opening of the Nangal-Hydel canal, in July, 1954, Prime Minister Nehru said:

> We are the children of the revolution of India. Do not imagine that the revolution in India was not a revolution because it was a peaceful one; it was one of the biggest revolutions in the world.
>
> That revolution is not over, and we have still to continue it. We have finished it in a way in the political sphere. We have to continue it in the social and economic sphere because we cannot remain static.

[27] A. M. Rosenthal, "India's Great Adventure, Ten Years Later," *New York Times Magazine,* Aug. 11, 1957.

* 2 *

Hindus, Moguls, and John Company

Modern India and Pakistan are the product of centuries of evolution and experience of the many different racial groups that have either amalgamated or coexisted in the subcontinent. Special attention must be given to the early Hindu period, for it was then that Hindu culture reached its zenith and that Hindu society, institutions, and beliefs were largely shaped, and to the British period, for this was the time when the impact of Western ideas and institutions had a marked effect on the evolution of modern India and Pakistan.

A Western student of Indian history is constantly baffled by the length and complexity of the story, by the strange intermixture of legend, religion, and history, by the mystical otherworldliness and life negation of the Hindus, by the lack of reliable written records until well into the medieval period, by a long series of invasions, by the rise and fall of innumerable petty kingdoms, "states," and "republics," with little concept of political unity and no actual unity, except to a limited degree in a few scattered periods, by the strange patterns of life and thought that developed in the subcontinent, and by the general lack of a true historical outlook among the Indian people.

The Indian subcontinent was the center of one of the oldest of civilizations. Discoveries in the present century at various places in the Indus Valley, notably at Mohenjo-daro, Kot Diji, and Harappa, have revealed the existence of an advanced urban culture as early as 2500 or perhaps even 3000 B.C. Thus the Harappa culture of the Indus Valley is apparently as old as the civilizations of the Tigris-Euphrates and the Nile Valleys. With the possible exception of China, India has been the center of the oldest continuous civilizations of high level anywhere in the world.

The main periods are three of very unequal length: the Hindu period, beginning with or soon after the Aryans came to India nearly 3,500 years ago and extending until the marked decline of Hindu culture after the tenth or eleventh centuries A.D.; the Muslim period, beginning with the first major invasions by Muslims not long after the death of Mohammed and reaching both its apex and its age of decline under the Moguls; and the British period, lasting about two hundred years from the consolidation of British power in the middle of the eighteenth century until the British withdrawal in 1947. The Harappa culture of the pre-Hindu period, as we have seen, was also of importance, and of course the years since independence, even though only an instant in historical time, are the most important of all for the student of contemporary affairs.

The Hindu Period

We may think of the Hindu period as extending roughly for 1,500 years before and after the beginning of the Christian era. The invasion of the Indo-Aryan people, apparently from south central Asia, in the second millennium B.C. was more of a folk movement than an invasion. The Aryans spread out over much of the western and northern part of the subcontinent. The Dravidians were forced into the south. Over the centuries a good deal of intermixture occurred between Aryans and Dravidians, but even today the dominant racial stock of south India is Dravidian while that of most of the north and west is Aryan.

The two great religio-philosophical systems which developed in the Indian subcontinent, Hinduism and Buddhism, and also Jainism, began to emerge shortly after the coming of the Indo-Aryan peoples. Some practices associated with Hinduism apparently existed in pre-Aryan times, but certainly the effective beginnings of Hinduism, including the Vedic literature, the Sanskrit language, the germs of the caste system, especially Brahmanism, and certain basic concepts and beliefs can be dated from the early Aryan period.

Hinduism. Hinduism is perhaps more philosophy, or metaphysics, than religion in any specific sense, although it may also be used as a term to apply to a wide range of religious beliefs and postures, ranging from something akin to animism to monotheism, with a strong emphasis on pantheism in most instances. Most Hindus do not regard themselves as monotheists, although they do recognize Brahma, the creator, the source of all things, as one of the holy triad of Hinduism, along with Vishnu, the preserver, and Shiva, the destroyer. Vishnu appears in many incarnations (avatars), the most popular of which is in the form of Krishna. Shiva, with his many arms, his many fierce incarnations, and his terrible consort, Kali, has always exercised an irresistible fascination for many Hindus. "The story of Shiva," suggests Frank Moraes, "is symbolic of the emotional and contemplative mosaic which enmeshes Hindu thought and character."[1] Cults dedicated to the worship of Vishnu or Shiva, or their various incarnations, have flourished and still flourish in many parts of India.

Most of the basic beliefs and doctrines of India have their origin in Hindu ideology. Among these are the so-called four ends of life: *artha, karma, dharma,* and *moksha.* It is impossible to give meaningful English equivalents of these terms; they symbolize, respectively, material gain, the pursuit of love and pleasure, duty, and salvation. These concepts have had a central place in Indian thought and action — or inaction.[2] Other concepts, such as *maya,* illusion, and *ahimsa,* nonviolence, are inextricably associated with Hinduism, although *ahimsa,* which Gandhi made one of his motivating doctrines, was emphasized even more in Buddhism and in Jainism. *Ahimsa,* in the opinion of W. Norman Brown, is "the most dynamic concept of Indian ethics since the days of Buddha and Mahavira, 2500 years ago."[3]

Hinduism is also associated with more formal systems of philosophy, stemming many centuries ago from Brahmanism and from the influence of great Hindu philosophers, such as Shankara. The best known of all the formal systems of Hindu philosophy are Nyaya, Vaishesika, Samkhya, Yoga, Mimamsa, and Vedanta. They have all had a profound impact on Indian thought, and in various ways are still influential. This is especially true in the case of Yoga and Vedanta. Yoga — a word which means union — emphasizes the discipline of the body and the mind. Vedanta, stemming from Brahmanism and from the Upanishads, was developed into a system known as Advaita Vedanta, or nondualist Vedanta, several centuries later by Shankara. As Nehru, who professes to be an agnostic, although his traditions are Hindu, has stated, "It is this philosophy which represents the dominant philosophic outlook of Hinduism today."[4]

For a Western student Hinduism offers special problems of understanding and interpretation. It is a most complicated and varied religious-philosophical-metaphysical creed, ranging all the way from

[1] Frank Moraes, *India Today* (New York, 1960), p. 4.

[2] See *Sources of Indian Tradition,* compiled by William Theodore de Bary, Stephen Hay, Royal Weiler, and Andrew Yarrow (New York, 1958), pp. 205–366.

[3] "Indian National Ideals Today," Mary Keatinge Das Memorial Lecture, Columbia University, Nov. 28, 1955.

[4] Jawaharlal Nehru, *The Discovery of India* (New York, 1946), p. 182. See also *Sources of Indian Tradition,* pp. 300–307.

ideas which seem to be without form and almost without substance to some of the most rigid and systematic of philosophical systems. It does not have generally accepted interpreters, and it is one of the most tolerant and absorptive of religions or philosophic systems. Because Hindus believe that while truth is one, there are many roads leading to it, they tend to react negatively to advocates of a proselytizing religion, like Islam or Christianity. It is particularly hard for Westerners to grasp the intricacies of Hinduism, whether it is viewed as an inchoate body of folk beliefs which seem to matter to masses of the Indian people, or as a complicated and subtle pattern of philosophic systems, or as the worship of various cults dedicated to Vishnu, Shiva, or their incarnations. Yet there is no escaping the importance of Hinduism in the Indian experience. As T. Walter Wallbank has pointed out, "Hinduism, or the Hindu way of life, is one of the most important historical ingredients of modern India."[5]

The Caste System. Any study of Hindu society must give special attention to the caste system, one of the most rigid social systems ever evolved in any part of the world. It emerged in India, along with Hinduism itself, many centuries ago, and was chiefly associated with the Indo-Aryan invaders. It developed its distinctive features and its rigidity over the centuries. It became in fact "the central feature of Hindu society. . . . Throughout the centuries the caste system gave Indian society stability, and so partially compensated for the lack of large-scale political genius displayed in much of the Hindu period. . . . Caste was in fact the vehicle in which almost everything of permanent value in Hinduism was carried."[6]

In ancient India four main castes emerged: the Brahmans, the highest caste, the scholars and "priests" of Hinduism; the Kshatriyas, the nobles and warriors, to which most of the rulers of various kingdoms and smaller "states" belonged; the Vaisyas, the merchants and traders; and the Sudras, the workers. Members of the three upper castes were the "Twice-Born," the elite of Hindu society. In one way or another most of the more than 2,000 castes and subcastes in India today have stemmed from the four basic castes, but the pattern has become hopelessly complicated, at least for the outsider.

At the bottom of the social scale were the untouchables, people without caste, although even among this large group there were grades and variations. The untouchables of India became "the largest subordinate racial group in the world";[7] they were subject to all kinds of discrimination, and were forbidden to have any but the most rigidly

[5] T. Walter Wallbank, *A Short History of India and Pakistan* (New York, 1958), p. 37.

[6] Sir Percival Griffiths, *Modern India* (New York, 1957), p. 31.

[7] Louise Ouwerkerk, *The Untouchables of India* (London, 1945), p. 3.

circumscribed dealings with caste Hindus. Even today there are some 50,000,000 untouchables in India. Most of them still live in segregated areas, and do menial tasks. In villages, the strongholds of Hindu orthodoxy, many of the old taboos still exist. But untouchability is now officially illegal, and untouchables have more opportunities than they have ever enjoyed in the past. Today a few untouchables occupy high positions in government and the professions. Untouchables are given special opportunities in schools and certain professions; but they are still untouchables, and will so remain until a profound change sets in in the minds of the caste Hindus.

The caste system itself is still a powerful influence in India, although it is changing rapidly. Along with the joint family system,[8] another traditional Hindu institution, it determines the patterns of life of most Hindus: how they will live, what they will eat, whom they will marry, what professions they will enter, what societal obligations they must accept. Gandhi, although strongly opposed to untouchability, saw some social values in the caste system; but many of the leaders of modern India believe that it has no place in the contemporary world. Nehru himself, a high caste Brahman of Kashmiri descent, has stated flatly that "in the social organization of today it has no place left," and that the "aristocratic approach based on traditionalism" on which it was based "has to change completely, for it is wholly opposed to modern conditions and the democratic ideal."[9]

Buddhism and Jainism. Buddhism, with its emphasis on "the noble eightfold path" to *nirvana,* was an offshoot of Hinduism. Siddhartha Gautama, who became known as the Buddha ("the enlightened one"), was a Kshatriya, son of a ruler of a territory near Nepal, who lived in the sixth and fifth centuries B.C. At the age of 29 he renounced a life of ease, spent many years as a hermit and wanderer, and finally attained "the great enlightenment." Buddhism

---

The term "untouchable" has virtually disappeared from the Indian vocabulary, although untouchability has by no means disappeared from Indian life. Many Indians seem to feel that when foreigners refer to the "untouchables" they reflect a rather disparaging attitude toward India generally. The official designation of the untouchables is "Scheduled Castes." Gandhi referred to them as "Harijans," meaning "Children of God."

[8] The joint family system is a traditional larger family unit within the Hindu caste framework. "Within the caste the traditional unit has been the 'joint family,' which consists of a man, his wife (or wives), and all his descendants except the married females, living in a common household, the earnings of each member being in some measure the property of all. . . . This system has largely broken down in modern India as the economic structure has been changing." W. Norman Brown, *The United States and India and Pakistan,* (Harvard University Press, 1953), pp. 32–33.

[9] Nehru, *Discovery of India,* p. 532.

flourished in India for centuries, reaching its height at the time of the Mauryan emperors Asoka and Mahendra in the third century B.C. Eventually it almost died out in the region of its origin, but it spread to Tibet, China, Korea, Japan, much of Southeast Asia, and Ceylon, and it is still a powerful force in all of these areas today.

Jainism, another offshoot of Hinduism, was founded, according to Jainist tradition, by twenty-four Tirthankanas, of whom Mahavira — an historical figure who was an older contemporary of the Buddha — was the last. Jainism emphasizes asceticism and self-discipline. Each *yati* (ascetic) must take five vows: to injure no living thing, to speak the truth, to abstain from stealing, to renounce all worldly goods, and to practice sexual continence. This ascetic religious system never attracted large numbers of followers, but it exercised an influence in India far out of keeping with its numbers. Gandhi, for example, was profoundly influenced by it. Today there are perhaps 1,500,000 Jains in India.[10]

The Classics of Hinduism. The great classics of Hinduism, as well as of Buddhism and Jainism, date from the Hindu period. Most of the Hindu literature was written in Sanskrit; most of the Buddhist writings were in Pali or Prakrit; most of the Jainist tracts were in Prakrit. The best known and most important of Hindu classics are the Vedas, the Upanishads, and the epics. The Vedas, the sacred scriptures of Hinduism, date back to a time shortly after the coming of the Aryans; they were apparently written in Vedic, a parent language of Sanskrit. The oldest and most famous of the Vedas is the *Rig Veda,* some one thousand hymns of praise of different gods, often called the oldest of all the great works of literature and religion known to man. The Upanishads, poetic dialogues on metaphysics, were written after the Vedas, and are in part derived from these earlier classics; they were the source of the major systems of Hindu philosophy, and therefore have been of continuing importance.

The two great Sanskrit epics are, of course, the *Mahabharata* and the *Ramayana,* apparently composed sometime between 200 B.C. and 200 A.D. The *Mahabharata* is perhaps the world's longest epic, a fabulous account of dynastic struggles, with all kinds of subplots and moralizing. In the course of the account of a great battle between the Pandavas and the Kauravas the philosophical discourse on right action and duty which is known as the *Bhagavad Gita* appears. The *Bhavagad Gita* is perhaps the most famous piece of Hindu literature. Every student of Indian civilization should read and try to understand this little gem of Hinduism.

The other great epic, the *Ramayana,* is far shorter and more unified than the *Mahabharata.* It tells of the adventures of Rama, who allied

[10] See *Sources of Indian Tradition,* pp. 45–202.

himself with Hanuman, king of the monkeys, and fought a mighty war in Ceylon. When he was restored to his Indian kingdom, he subjected his wife, Sita, to various ordeals to test her virtue. The *Ramayana* has been an inexhaustible source of legends, dramas, and popular folk tales throughout the centuries.

Hindu Political Thought and Institutions. Most of this ancient literature is essentially religious in character, and contains little which would normally be classed as political thought; but the Arthasastra and Nitisastra literature, notably Kautilya's *Arthasastra* and the Manu-samhita, the laws of Manu, the most influential Hindu legal work, and the Santiparvan of the *Mahabharata,* "provide material which can clearly be labeled political thought as distinct from philosophy in general."[11] Ancient Indian political thought "deals with many subjects which have bulked large in the political theory of the Western world. Among these are the nature and origin of the state, types of states, the relation of state and society, the forms of government, the origin of kingship, the duties of kings, royal authority and its limitations, power politics, diplomacy and administration. Perhaps we should also include theories of the state of nature, the social contract, and sovereignty, possibly even international law. Conflicting theories of international relations can be found in ancient India as well as in the modern world. The doctrine of *mandala* or circle of states was a kind of Hindu theory of the balance of power, and the doctrine of *sarvabhauma* suggests modern theories of world federation or a world state."[12] There seems to be rather general agreement that *dharma* is the central concept of Hindu political thought; indeed, Radhakrishnan has called it the most important concept in Indian thought generally. *Dharma* cannot be defined precisely, but it refers to a man's moral obligations or duty. "In the context of the *dharmashastras* (or Hindu Political Science) the word *dharma* came to mean 'the privileges, duties and obligations of a man, his standard of conduct as a member of the Aryan community, as a member of one of the castes, as a person in a particular stage of life.' "[13] Thus "*dharma* is relative to time, place, circumstances, sex, age, temperament, vocation." Everyone has his *dharma.*

Another basic Hindu political concept is that of the *saptanga,* or the "seven limbs" of the state. These are *svamin* or sovereign, *amatya*

[11] Norman D. Palmer, "Indian and Western Political Thought: Coalescence or Clash?", *The American Political Science Review,* XLIX (September, 1955), 755. See also A. S. Altekar, *State and Government in Ancient India* (Benares, 1949), pp. 1–3.

[12] Palmer, "Indian and Western Political Thought," p. 755.

[13] K. P. Mukerji, *The State* (Madras, 1952), p. 327. See Appendix I (pp. 321–346), "The Hindu Conception of Dharma." See also Sarvepalli Radhakrishnan, *Indian Philosophy* (New York, 1922), I, 52; and Nehru, *Discovery of India,* p. 77.

or minister, *janapada* or *rastra* referring to territory with people, *durga* or fortress, *kosa* or treasury, *danda* or *bala* meaning sceptre or army, and *mitra* or friends or allies. This doctrine of *saptanga,* in the opinion of Benoy Kumar Sarkar, "constitutes the basis of all political speculation among the Hindu philosophers."[14]

The political systems and institutions which emerged in the Hindu period were varied and complex. Apparently the prevailing pattern was that of monarchy in various forms; rulers, usually Kshatriyas, often claimed to rule by right, but they were usually subject to certain sanctions, including even a kind of right of rebellion if they abused their power. There were some germs of "democratic" practices in ancient India, chiefly in the existence of a number of so-called republics, the institution of the *panchayat* (council) in many Indian villages, and the recognition of the obligations of the rulers to act in the interests of the people; but, in spite of a strong tendency today to claim that democracy has always been congenial to the Hindu tradition, there was little that could truly be called democratic in ancient India. The dominant tradition was authoritarian.

Ancient India was never brought entirely under a single political state. Two great dynasties, the Mauryan from the fourth to the second century B.C. and the Gupta from the fourth to the sixth centuries A.D., extended their sway over a large part of the subcontinent, except the far south; and one later ruler, Harsha, who reigned over an important north Indian kingdom for more than fifty years in the seventh century, was successful in extending some measure of control over a substantial part of the subcontinent. Kautilya, the author of the classic of Arthasastra writings, was apparently a minister at the court of Chandragupta, the founder of the Mauryan Empire. Kautilya has been called "not only a kingmaker, but also . . . the greatest Indian exponent of the art of government, the duties of kings, ministers, and officials, and the methods of diplomacy."[15] His *Arthasastra* is a very practical manual of statecraft and administration, which has often been compared with Machiavelli's *The Prince*. The most famous of the Mauryan rulers was the great Asoka, who ruled in the third century B.C. Asoka, of course, is known as one of the great rulers of history. He is particularly renowned because after long campaigns of conquest he turned to the arts of peace; he became a devout Buddhist, and devoted himself to the welfare of his subjects. The best known of Gupta rulers was Chandragupta II, who reigned in the late fourth and early fifth centuries A.D. He extended his empire over most of north

[14] Benoy Kumar Sarkar, *The Political Institutions and Theories of the Hindus* (Leipzig, 1922), p. 167.

[15] J. F. Fleet, Introductory Note in *Kautilya's Arthasastra,* trans. by R. Shamasastry (4th edition, Mysore, 1951) p. v.

India, from his great capital at Pataliputra, in what is now Bihar State. The Gupta period was the golden age of Hindu culture, as exemplified by the dramas and other works of Kalidasa, the cave paintings at Ajanta, and the cultural contributions of several great universities, the most famous of which was Nalanda, whose scholars later played a large part in spreading Indian culture abroad.

Contacts with China and Southeast Asia. Throughout the centuries India has experienced many waves of invasions by peoples of varying racial and cultural characteristics who came into the subcontinent through the mountain passes in the west-northwest. Some of these invasions, such as those by Alexander the Great and by many bands of marauders from inner Asia, were brief and left relatively little impact. Others, notably those of the Aryan peoples over many decades, had a profound effect upon the racial composition and civilization of India. All of the major invading groups which remained in India mingled with the peoples they found there, and were absorbed into the dominant Hindu culture. Thus from its earliest history India was affected by developments from outside its borders.

In the early centuries of the Christian era fairly extensive contacts developed with China and with Southeast Asia. Buddhist monks and traders traveled by various hazardous overland routes or by equally dangerous routes by sea to China, and hundreds of Chinese pilgrims and scholars came to India. "It is a striking fact," observes Amaury de Riencourt, "that in all relations between the two Civilizations, the Chinese was always the recipient and the Indian the donor."[16]

From this time, also, dates the great Indian impact on Southeast Asia, so great that it is sometimes referred to as "the Indianization of Southeast Asia" and the area itself is often called "Greater India." "From the first to the ninth centuries A.D., from the zenith of Indian Civilization to its petrifaction, four great waves of colonization hit the southeast, every one of them organized by some powerful South Indian state." These waves of organized colonization were supplemented by the work of Buddhist monks, by a flourishing commerce, and by individual settlements. "Since racial admixture between natives and Indians was carried out over a number of centuries, a great many elements of Indian civilization entered quite naturally into the Southeast Asian blood stream and became an organic part of Southeast Asia. Between the second and fifth centuries A.D., Indian kingdoms were founded in Malaya, Cambodia, Vietnam, Sumatra, Java, Bali, and Borneo. Everywhere, Indian influence prevailed over the Chinese, and for evident reasons: an undoubted cultural superiority owing to much greater philosophic and religious insight (China itself fell under the spell of Buddhism), and also to a far more flexible script. Further-

[16] Amaury de Riencourt, *The Soul of India* (New York, 1960), p. 141.

more, Indian Civilization respected the political autonomy of its colonies and the cultural freedom of all its units, and, on the whole, worked through peaceful penetration." The mighty empires that arose in Southeast Asia a few centuries later — including the Sailendra and Majapahit Empires and the kingdoms of the Khmers and of Champa — reflected Indian influence. Today "all over Southeast Asia tremendous ruins are strewn, testifying to the immense influence of Indian Civilization." More important, Indian influence, dating back to this early period, and accentuated by modern contacts and immigration, can be found throughout most of Southeast Asia today, with the exception of Vietnam, where Chinese influences predominate.[17]

Hindu India in Decline. After the Gupta period Indian influence continued in Southeast Asia, but in India itself the great days of the Hindu era were over. "The Indian political world went back to its anarchic medley of quarreling states and countless dynasties, many of which are forever lost to history, because Indians kept no historical records and reports from foreign travelers were lacking."[18] In the north, which had been the center of most of the important Hindu empires, only one empire, that of Harsha in the seventh century, seems to have rivaled the mighty empires of the past; and we would know little even about the great Harsha had it not been for the fact that the famous Chinese pilgrim, Hsuan Tsang, left voluminous records of his work. The center of power and of culture shifted to the south, which had been the source of the colonizing efforts in Southeast Asia. There important empires rose, flourished, and declined even after the Gupta period. Notable among these were the Pallavas and the Cholas. But the general picture was one of near anarchy. "What India lacked was political unity and social solidarity. Her leaders counted by hundreds; her energy was frittered away in petty squabbles between the various states. She may correctly be described during this period as merely a geographical expression."[19]

To the extent that it was held together at all, Indian society survived because of the unifying force of Hinduism as a philosophic and cultural force, and of the caste system, and because of the persistence of those institutions of local government which over the centuries had provided some element of stability and protection and even of popular expression amid the tendencies toward absolutism or anarchy.

Thus far Hindu India had been able, for all its lack of unity and fissiparous tendencies, to absorb foreign invaders and to survive its political weaknesses. From the thirteenth century on it was faced with

[17] *Ibid.*, pp. 142, 159, 161.

[18] *Ibid.*, p. 142.

[19] Iswari Prasad, quoted in Sir Percival Griffiths, *The British Impact on India* (London, 1952), p. 29.

its greatest internal and external challenges, arising from the unwelcome necessity of dealing with foreign invaders more powerful than any that had yet come into India and that, unlike their many predecessors, could not be absorbed into the basic Hindu life-stream, and from the equally unwelcome necessity of making fundamental adaptations to the modern world. For a time it seemed that Hindu India might disappear under these powerful new and alien pressures. It is a remarkable tribute to the basic strength and staying power of the ideas and institutions that developed in the heyday of the Hindu period that Hindu traditions are still strong, indeed predominant, in modern India, although the impact of the Muslims and the West is very manifest.

The Muslim Period

The Muslim period was of much shorter duration than the long era of Hindu ascendancy, and its impact was much less profound; but the millions of Muslims in India and Pakistan today — the largest concentration of the followers of Islam to be found anywhere in the world — look to it as the golden age. It did mark the beginning of a new era in Indian history, during which large numbers of Muslim invaders came into the subcontinent, established themselves as rulers of most of the area, developed a great political and administrative system under the Moguls, converted hundreds of thousands of Hindus, and co-existed rather than amalgamated with the Hindu majority.

Islam and Hinduism represented not only two different religions, but two different civilizations and ways of life. Muslims came to India as invaders and conquerors. In the great days of the Delhi Sultanate and even more of the Mogul Empire they were definitely the dominant political force in India, as far as overall control was concerned. Their impact on local government and institutions even in those parts of the subcontinent over which they ruled was slight, and their impact on the masses of the people was even less, although many Hindus were converted to Islam by force or persuasion. Most of the more than 100,000,000 Muslims in India and Pakistan today are descendants not of Muslim invaders or rulers but of converted Hindus. Thus was introduced the greatest of all the communal problems that have bedeviled the subcontinent and that in a sense laid the basis for a separate existence which eventually culminated in the partition of the subcontinent and the formation of the Islamic state of Pakistan.

Before the Moguls. Followers of the new religion of Islam appeared in Sind as early as the eighth century. In the late tenth and early eleventh centuries the great Afghan ruler, Mahmud of Ghazni, made many destructive raids into India, and maintained control for some time of much of western India. In 1206 an Afghan general founded the Delhi Sultanate, which at the height of its power in the late thirteenth and early fourteenth centuries ruled over a large part of India, except Kashmir and the extreme south. In 1398 Tamerlane or Timur, a Mongol conqueror who claimed to be a descendant of Genghis Khan, sacked Delhi and ended the Delhi Sultanate; and although the Sultanate was revived in the middle of the fifteenth century and lasted for another seventy-five years, it never regained its former influence.

"For five hundred years the Muslims failed to build up a stable polity . . . and in general the early Muslims in India displayed no more constructive political genius than had their Hindu predecessors."[20] For a time in the fourteenth, fifteenth, and sixteenth centuries the Hindu Empire of Vijayanagar, which at the height of its power controlled nearly all of India south of the Krishna River, seemed to present a formidable challenge to the growing Muslim power; but the forces of Vijayanagar were defeated by Muslim armies in 1565, and the capital of the Empire was destroyed. By this time the most powerful of all the Muslim rulers were strongly entrenched in the north. In 1526 a descendant of Tamerlane, Baber, captured Delhi and founded the Mogul (or Moghul or Mughal) Empire.

The Moguls. The greatest of the Mogul rulers, Akbar (1556–1605), was a contemporary of Queen Elizabeth of England, and had an even longer reign over a much larger empire; in his time the Mogul Empire was probably stronger and more important than was England under Elizabeth. Next to Asoka, Akbar is the best known of all the rulers of India. He fought many wars to consolidate his great empire; he developed an effective administrative system; although he was himself illiterate, he made his courts at Delhi, Fatehpur Sikri, and Agra centers of culture and learning, as well as of architectural magnificence; he was remarkably tolerant of all religions, and spokesmen of many faiths — Hindus, Parsis, Jains, Jesuits, as well as Muslims — explained and defended their beliefs at his court; he even tried, unsuccessfully, to develop a new religion, the *Din-i-Ilahi,* which would be a synthesis of Islam and other faiths.

Mogul administration in the time of Akbar, according to Sir Percival Griffiths, had five main characteristics. It was "in origin a foreign domination. . . . Akbar was as much a non-Indian by birth and early training as were Clive and Hastings." It was a "complete despotism," in which "the emperor's will was law in the most literal sense." It was established along military lines, and "even officials employed wholly in civil duties were graded in the military hierarchy." Akbar himself said that "a monarch should be ever intent on conquest lest his neighbors rise against him," and this aim of conquest "necessarily conditioned his organisation of the system of government." A fifth characteristic

[20] Griffiths, *The British Impact on India,* p. 30.

of the Mogul Empire "was the complete absence of an hereditary aristocracy." This had unfortunate effects when lesser men than Akbar were emperors, but in the days of the Great Mogul it "gave Akbar a free hand to refashion administration in a scientific manner."[21]

Akbar perceived that even he, with all his power and might, had to depend upon many people to govern his vast empire, populated mostly by non-Muslims. For this reason he made friends with powerful Rajputs, who had resisted Muslim inroads for decades, and he enlisted the services of thousands of Hindus. Some of his wives, chief officials, and military commanders were Hindus. Unfortunately his successors — Jehangir, Shah Jehan, and Aurangzeb — were lesser men, lacking his ability, integrity, prestige, and tolerance. Although the Mogul empire reached its greatest extent under Shah Jehan and Aurangzeb, it decayed because of internal difficulties caused by inefficient rule and religious intolerance and because of the growing challenge from the Sikhs and the Marathas. The Sikh religion was founded by Nanak, the first *guru,* shortly before the beginnings of Mogul rule, and the tenth and last *guru,* Govind Singh, was a contemporary of Aurangzeb. So was the great Maratha leader, Shivaji, who declared his independence of the Mogul empire and from his capital in Poona launched a number of expeditions against the Moguls and conquered a considerable part of central India.

The Mogul Empire really came to an end after the death of Aurangzeb in 1707, but theoretically it continued until 1862, under a series of puppet emperors. Its weaknesses became more and more apparent after the strong hand of Akbar was removed. "The Mogul Empire," Vincent Smith observed, "like all Asian despotisms, had shallow roots. Its existence depended mainly on the personal character of the reigning autocrat and on the degree of his military power. It lacked popular support, the strength based on patriotic feeling, and on the stability founded upon ancient tradition."[22]

The British Period to 1857: In the Days of "John Company"

For the past four and a half centuries and more the people of India have been subject to the growing impact of the West, at a time when the ancient glories of the subcontinent, save for the brief days of Mogul power, were fading and when Asia generally was falling behind the West in technological and political development. During this long pe-

[21] Griffiths, *The British Impact on India,* pp. 123–127. Griffiths has two excellent chapters on Mogul administration (pp. 122–142). See also Sir Jadunath Sarkar, *Mughal Administration* (Calcutta, 1935).

[22] Vincent Smith, *The Oxford History of India* (2nd edition, London, 1923), p. 465.

riod, which a distinguished Indian scholar-diplomat, K. M. Panikkar, has called "the Vasco da Gama epoch of Asian history," a new India emerged under the impact of the West, especially of the British, which in turn produced various kinds of Indian responses.

For some two centuries the Western contacts with India were relatively few and inconsequential, confined largely to the efforts of Portuguese, Spanish, French, and British explorers, and trading companies, chiefly British and French.

The Consolidation of British Control in India. The most important of all the trading companies was the British East India Company. Formed in 1600, the Company was at first concerned only with trade and commerce, and had only limited contacts with India, chiefly through the ports of Calcutta, Madras, and Bombay. Gradually, however, faced with the necessity of dealing with pirates, protecting its interests in India, and competing with other trading companies, the Company became involved in political and military activities, which in time made it in fact the leading power in India. As early as 1687, during the reign of Aurangzeb, the Directors of the Company instructed their chief representative in Madras "to establish such a politie of civil and military power, and create and secure such a large revenue to secure both . . . as may be the foundation of a large, well grounded, secure English dominion in India for all time to come."[23] "In 1715 the Company sent an embassy to the Mogul court and wrested from the weak ruler extensive privileges throughout the Empire, including the right to trade in Bengal free of all duties, to rent additional territory around Calcutta, and the right to coin money in Bombay and to circulate it throughout India. The *firman* of 1716–1717 became known as the 'Magna Charta' of the Company, the major step in the establishment of this new type of politico-commercial power on Indian soil."[24]

Even though the central power of the Moguls was weakening, the British East India Company did not have a clear field for its expanding activities. Other possible successors to the Moguls were also active in the early eighteenth century, notably the French, the Muslim rulers of the states of Mysore and Hyderabad, the Marathas, and the Sikhs, with powerful invaders from Persia and Afghanistan also constituting no small threat. One by one, however, the British eliminated or cut down the power of their chief rivals.

The struggle between the British and the French in India in the early eighteenth century was a phase of the overall struggle between the two powers, which was waged on the European continent, in North Amer-

[23] Quoted in R. C. Majumdar, H. C. Raychaudhuri, and K. Datta, *An Advanced History of India* (London, 1946), p. 639.

[24] De Riencourt, *The Soul of India,* p. 199.

ica, and on the high seas, as well as in India. The French East India Company, formed by Colbert in 1664, established trading posts in Pondicherry, Chandernagore, and elsewhere in Bengal and along the Coromandel coast. For a time, under the brilliant and determined Dupleix, it threatened to oust the British from South India. This threat was finally eliminated by Robert Clive, an official of the British East India Company, through a combination of military operations and wily diplomacy, during the Indian phase of the Seven Years War, which, among other results, ended effective French influence in India.

Effective control by the Company may be dated from the decisive triumph over the French, acknowledged in the Treaty of Paris of 1763, and the granting of the *diwan* — the right of collecting revenues — for Bengal, Bihar, and Orissa to the Company by the Mogul emperor in 1765. The work of Clive was continued by the famous Warren Hastings, who was Governor-General from 1774 to 1784, and by Lord Wellesley, who may in a sense be regarded as the first true British imperialist in India.[25]

One of the first acts of Lord Wellesley as Governor-General (1798–1805) was to enter into an alliance with the Nizam of Hyderabad and the Peshwa, the Brahman chief minister of the Maratha Confederacy, against Tipu Sultan, ruler of Mysore, who was defeated and killed in 1798. "By the beginning of the nineteenth century British forces were maintained in Mysore, Hyderabad and Oudh, and either in this way or by direct rule Britain controlled large areas of India."[26] By brilliant campaigns and by profiting from internal conflicts among member states of the Maratha Confederacy, Lord Wellesley effectively broke the power of the Marathas and forced them to enter into the British system of subsidiary alliances. Further campaigns against some Maratha rulers were necessary over a decade later. This time the Marathas were finally defeated, the Peshwa was deposed, the main Maratha rulers were brought within the orbit of the British alliance system, and a great deal of territory was ceded to the British East India Company.

In the 1840's the Sikhs, who had established firm control and a proud military tradition in the Punjab, took the initiative against the British. After two Sikh wars they were decisively defeated and the Punjab was added to the territories under the direct control of "John Company." In 1856, during the Governor-Generalship of Lord Dalhousie, the vast kingdom of Oudh was also annexed.

Thus by the middle of the nineteenth century most of India was controlled by the British — either directly by the British East India Company or indirectly through the system of alliances and resident agents

[25] Griffiths, *The British Impact on India,* p. 88.
[26] *Ibid.,* p. 90.

in a multitude of princely States. Many of the former Indian States were annexed by the Company under the doctrine of lapse, especially during the Governor-Generalship of Lord Dalhousie.

"John Company" and the British Government. When the political power of the British East India Company was solidly established, the British Parliament began to exercise an increasing degree of interest and control over its activities, although until 1868 the British Government left the major task of governance in India to the Company. The Regulating Act of 1773 was the first of a long series of acts of the British Parliament which set the limits for the operations of the Company. The Amending Act of 1781 provided that all dispatches from the Company concerning political and certain other matters had to be submitted to the British Government. Some of the leading orators in the Parliament, in a day of great orators, turned their fire on the Company — on the alleged patronage, corruption, perfidy, greed, and ill-gotten gains. Fox called the Company's administration "a system of despotism unmatched in all the histories of the world." Burke in 1784 denounced the Company as "one of the most corrupt and destructive tyrannies that probably ever existed in the world."

Pitt's India Act of 1784 and a series of supplementary measures in the decade that followed established a clear chain of control through the British Parliament and the Board of Control to the Governor-General and Council of Bengal to the Governors and Councils of the Bombay and Madras Presidencies. Several Charter Acts progressively whittled down the other powers of the East India Company. The most important of these was the Charter Act of 1833, which put an end to the commercial activities of the Company, leaving it as a purely administrative body, and which gave more power to the Governor-General and Council.

The East India Company was in effect the successor to Mogul rule in India. Consciously and unconsciously it served as the agent of British imperialism in what later became "the brightest jewel in the British Crown." Thus its activities profoundly affected the course of Indian life and development, for good and for ill. It is impossible even to chronicle the many steps which were taken by the various representatives of the Company, from Robert Clive and Warren Hastings to Lord Dalhousie, over a period of nearly a century; it is even more impossible to assay the effects of the steps which were taken and of the impact of "John Company" on the Indian scene.

Consider, for example, the actions of Lord William Bentinck, who was Governor-General from 1828 to 1835. Some of the reforms which he sponsored were of a truly spectacular nature, striking directly at long-established practices; notable among these reforms were the abolition of suttee (the practice of widow-burning), the suppression of thuggee (ritual strangling by worshippers of the goddess Kali), and efforts to end the practice of female infanticide. Other measures taken by Bentinck attracted less attention, but were perhaps equally noteworthy. These included many administrative reforms, reduction in the costs of government, stricter supervision of the Indian States. The Charter Act of 1833 was passed while Bentinck was Governor-General.

Perhaps the most far-reaching of all Lord Bentinck's reforms was the decision to adopt English as the medium of instruction in Indian education. This represented a great victory of the "Anglicists" over the "Orientalists" in England. Lord Macaulay, then Law Minister in the Board of Control for Indian affairs, was the leader in the movement to make English the medium of instruction in India and thereby, as Macaulay said, to train a class of Indians who would be "Indian in blood and color, but English in taste, in opinion, in morals and in intellect," and who would be faithful allies of the British in governing India.

For more than a century this policy was a brilliant success. Generation after generation of Westernized Indians served as "clerks" and lesser civil servants in British employ, and made it possible for the British to run a vast country with remarkably few English troops and officials. In the long run, of course, the Westernized Indians, trained in English and in Western ways, were the leaders of the movement for independence from the British. In a dim way Macaulay foresaw this eventuality, but he did not shrink from it. "When it comes," he declared, "it will be the proudest day in English history."

The long-run significance of this decision has been clearly stated by Amaury de Riencourt:

> From 1835 on, European learning through the medium of the English language was patronized by the Anglo-Indian government and revolutionized the whole educational system of India with far-reaching effects on the social and political structure of Indian society. The first result, of course, was to widen the great gap between the small English-educated classes and the great illiterate or vernacular-educated masses. The gap was also widened between the Hindu middle classes and the Hindu upper classes, who remained faithful to their traditional learning, and the Indian Muslims, who remained aloof from Western education altogether. . . . Yet, for all its defects, it is this education and the use of the English tongue that gave actual coherent *unity* to India. If this had not happened, if the British, in a more diabolic mood, had concentrated on developing the vernaculars, there is no doubt that there would not have been *one* Indian nationalism, but *several*.[27]

The British Impact on India. One of the most important and gen-

[27] De Riencourt, *The Soul of India,* pp. 252, 290.

erally unfortunate results of the domination of India by a trading company turned imperial ruler, supported by British power, was the virtual destruction of the economic institutions on which Indian society had been based, including village communities, the system of landholding, and cooperative associations and industries. As a result of British policies in England and in India and of the prevailing economic philosophy in Britain, a flourishing Indian trade and commerce virtually collapsed, and the growing middle class collapsed also. The effects on the system of landholding were equally disastrous.

The Permanent Settlement of Bengal and subsequent measures in other parts of India interposed a new class of middlemen, who had come into existence in Mogul times, between the state and the farmers. These middlemen, generally known as *zamindars,* collected land revenue and paid agreed-upon amounts to the state. In time they became in effect hereditary landowners; they dominated the land system of most of India for more than a century and a half, until the system which they represented was largely ended by acts of the independent Government of India and the constituent States. Even today the influences of the *zamindari* system are still manifest. The earlier systems of landholding and revenue collection have never been fully revived, although some efforts, patterned to some degree after the ancient institutions, are being made.

The British impact on India was more profound than that of any of the previous invaders since the coming of the Aryans; "through their new-found political power, they were able to carry out a profound social transformation through redistribution of economic power."[28] Modern India reflects the profundity of this impact; but it also reflects the tremendous staying power of old institutions and traditions, especially in the social and religious or philosophical realms.

By the beginning of the second half of the nineteenth century it seemed that the British had established a pattern of control that would endure for a long, long time, and that they had brought a new India into being. But the century that followed began with a major uprising against the British, witnessed the consolidation and nadir of British rule and the rise of an increasingly powerful independence movement, and ended with the independence of India and Pakistan. The British set in motion forces which were more powerful than they themselves realized, and it is these forces, rather than the British policies and influence, which really created modern India.

[28] *Ibid.*, p. 209.

* 3 *

The British Century

Approximately a century elapsed between the zenith of the power of the British East India Company during the Governor-Generalship of Lord Dalhousie (1848–1856) and the end of British rule in India in 1947. The beginning of this century was highlighted by the "Mutiny" of 1857 and the assumption of direct control of India by the British Government in the following year. The century ended with the withdrawal of the British and the independence of two new states in the subcontinent, India and Pakistan. The great events of the century were the consolidation of British rule, which resulted in the establishment of a pattern of colonial administration probably more highly developed than that in any other colonial area at any time; the increasing association of Indians in the work of government, below the policy-making level; various steps in the direction of self-government, from the Indian Councils Act of 1861 to the Government of India Act of 1935; the rise of a strong nationalist movement, led by the Indian National Congress and, on the Muslim side, by the Muslim League; and eventually, with increasing concessions by the British and increasingly successful techniques of resistance by the Indians, under Mahatma Gandhi, the last days of British rule in India.

The century prior to 1947, therefore, witnessed new techniques of colonial control and new techniques of resistance to that rule. It may properly be called the British century, for the British did govern India in this period in a real sense; but while it witnessed the apogee of British power in India, it also marked the final phases of the British part of the Indian story. The British impact on India, however, did not end with independence in 1947.

The "Mutiny" and Its Consequences

In conventional histories of India by British or other foreign writers the "Sepoy Mutiny" of 1857 is presented as an uprising of disaffected

Indian "Sepoys" (Indian soldiers in British employ), chiefly in a few cities and cantonments in north India, caused by the unfortunate incident of the greased cartridges, which offended Muslims and Hindus alike (though for different reasons), limited in scope and operations, and suppressed after a few months' desultory fighting without undue difficulty. Today, in both India and Pakistan, the "Mutiny" is described rather generally as "the War of Independence," and any suggestions that it was not this in fact are usually resented. In *The Discovery of India,* written several years before independence, Nehru himself declared: "It was much more than a military mutiny, and it spread rapidly and assumed the character of a popular rebellion and a war of Indian independence."[1]

Unquestionably the "Mutiny" was prompted by causes much more deep-seated than revulsion against the use of greased cartridges, and it led to many significant results. It was in fact a watershed in modern Indian history. According to one perceptive Indian writer it was prompted basically by a "revulsion against western influence." "The repeated annexation of territories by a foreign power, the spread of western modes of education and new ideas of life — all combined revealed to the Hindu mind a consistent effort to substitute a western for a Hindu civilisation."[2] The British position in India was never the same after the "Mutiny," although for a time it seemed that British rule was never more firmly entrenched.

Two of the most immediately significant results were the end of the East India Company, and the assumption of direct control by the British Government. These momentous changes were incorporated in the Act for the Better Government of India, which received the Royal assent on August 2, 1858. The main responsibility for the government of India was vested in a parliamentary minister, the Secretary of State for India, assisted by an advisory Council for India. All the powers of the East India Company, and all the military forces of the Company, were transferred to the Crown.

An even older, and once even more powerful, institution also came to an end shortly after the "Mutiny." This was the Mogul Empire, which theoretically existed until the death of the last of the "emperors," Bahadur Shah II, in 1862, although it had of course long been "the shade of a shadow of a shade." The British had allowed successors of Akbar and Aurangzeb to retain the title of Emperor, but some years before the "Mutiny" the British Government decided that after the death of Bahadur Shah II "the imperial rank should no longer be rec-

[1] Jawaharlal Nehru, *The Discovery of India* (New York, 1946), p. 324.
[2] S. N. Ray, "The Sepoy Mutiny of 1857," *The Radical Humanist,* XXI (May 12, 1957), 237.

ognized." So ended the Mogul Empire. Some twenty years later, however, a different kind of imperial rank was recognized, with great fanfare. By the Royal Titles Bill of 1876, sponsored by Benjamin Disraeli, Queen Victoria was made "Empress of India."

Other consequences of the "Mutiny" were less obvious but perhaps even more significant. Actually, many of the new developments in India after 1857 were occasioned not so much by the "Mutiny" itself as by the changing circumstances, in England, India, and the world as a whole, which helped to account for the many significant developments in British-Indian relations during the "British Century." Certainly, for various reasons, relations between British and Indians became more distant after 1857, even though British rule was more efficient and more extensive and probably more benevolent, and even though increasing numbers of Indians were associated with the administration of the subcontinent. The British were particularly careful that the ratio of British to Indian troops in the British Indian Army should never again be such as to make possible another formidable uprising. They were careful to keep Indians in lesser positions in administration, and to keep them out of policy-making positions. They were likewise careful to keep Muslims out of positions of trust and responsibility, for they remembered the seemingly uncooperative attitude of Muslims in the past, and they believed that Muslims had been involved out of proportion to their numbers in the uprising of 1857.

The Pattern of British Rule

During the ninety years of direct rule in India the British developed an effective administrative system, patterned after the system evolved during the earlier century of "Double Government." There is particular value in an understanding of how India was governed by the British, because the system developed by the British has been in large measure continued by the Indians themselves since independence.

In the heyday of British rule all of India was controlled either directly or indirectly by the British authorities. The subcontinent was divided into two main parts: British India, and the India of the princely States. Since there were 562 of these princely States at the time of partition, some as large as major states of Western Europe (notably Jammu and Kashmir, Hyderabad, and Mysore), and since they existed in all parts of the subcontinent and covered nearly two-fifths of the total area, a political map of India prior to partition looked like a piece of crazy quiltwork. In each of the princely States the British had a resident, who was usually the effective source of power, although to the fullest extent possible every deference was paid to the prerogatives and pomp and customary privileges of the hereditary rulers, especially to major potentates like the Maharajas of Jammu and Kashmir and of Mysore or the Nizam of Hyderabad.

British India was divided into provinces, of which there were eleven at the time of independence in 1947. The main centers of British rule were in Calcutta, Madras, and Bombay. The Governor-General, called also the Viceroy when he was acting on behalf of the British Crown, maintained headquarters in Calcutta until the early 1920's, when the capital of British India was moved to the new city of New Delhi, now the capital of independent India. The Viceroy was responsible to the Secretary of State for India, who headed the India Office in Westminster, and through him to the Cabinet and the British Parliament. After the establishment of direct telegraph communications between England and India in 1870, the administration of affairs in India was subject to more direct and effective control from London.

The provinces of British India, which were very large in size and which often embraced more people than in most of the independent states of the world, were divided for purposes of administration into divisions, districts, and subdistricts usually called *tahsils* or *talukas*. The district was the most important of these administrative units, and the officer in charge, usually known simply as the District Officer, but sometimes also called the District Magistrate or the Collector, was the key man in the whole system of local administration. Most members of the Indian Civil Service served for a time as District Officers. As the various titles given to him suggest, he had many functions, both official and unofficial. Officially, he was charged with the overall tasks of administering the affairs of his district, with the preservation of law and order, the dispensing of justice, and the collection of revenue. He represented the British Government in rural India. Unofficially, his duties and symbolic importance were even greater. He was the physical embodiment and symbol of the British Raj; he was the man to whom the people looked for protection, guidance, and advice.[3] He symbolized the power and splendor of the British Raj, as well as the unwelcome aspects of all-powerful and all-pervasive government. Of all the British representatives in India he had the closest contacts with the Indian masses. In the latter days of the British period more and more Indians, usually Indian members of the I.C.S., served as District Officers, thereby gaining valuable experience in the administration of their own country.

The British always ruled India with remarkably few administrators, military personnel, and others from the home country. Hundreds of Englishmen, often of England's most distinguished families, served in

[3] See R. Carstairs, *The Little World of an Indian District Officer* (London, 1912).

India during the British century and before — as political representatives and advisers, as members of the top ranks in the Indian Civil Service, as officers and soldiers in the British Indian Army. These were the men who built and maintained an empire, the men of whom Kipling wrote, the "guardians" whom Philip Woodruff has described.[4] Their services, sufferings, privileged existence, and experiences on the frontiers of empire in India have been told in innumerable memoirs, monographs, novels, and other writings. Less well-known are the services, sacrifices, and contributions of the far larger numbers of Indians who helped Britain govern a mighty empire.

Particularly noteworthy was the Indian Civil Service, the "steel frame" of British administration in India, which gained for itself a well-deserved reputation as perhaps the finest and most incorruptible civil service in the world. Members of the I.C.S., carefully recruited and trained, and held up to the highest standards of efficiency and integrity, manned most of the key administrative posts in India in British days. They were often criticized for developing a spirit of elitism and an exaggerated sense of their own importance, but no one could deny that they measured up impressively to the responsibilities entrusted to them.

From its establishment in the eighteenth century until well into the twentieth century few Indians were recruited for the I.C.S. As late as 1892 only 21 of the 992 members of this Service were Indians; in 1903 only 94 out of 1307 I.C.S. Officers were Indians. Toward the end of the British period, however, the number of Indians in the I.C.S. increased greatly, so that eventually they outnumbered the British members. Several hundred non-British I.C.S. Officers were available to India at the time of independence, and somewhat less than 200 to Pakistan. These men did yeoman service in carrying on the work of government and administration in the early stages of nation-building. Today the ranks of the former I.C.S. Officers have been thinned by death, resignation, and transfer to other duties; but even today those former I.C.S. Officers who are still in active service in India or Pakistan hold key positions in central and local administration, in diplomacy, and in various trouble-shooting roles. They are still the most professional of the professionals in the subcontinent.

Steps Toward Self-Government: From 1861 to 1892

At the beginning of the British century little thought had been given by the British to any future for their Indian empire other than its in-

[4] See Philip Woodruff (pseud. of Philip Mason), *The Men Who Ruled India.* Vol. I, *The Founders of Modern India* (London, 1953). Vol. II, *The Guardians* (London, 1954). See also John Masters, *Bugles and a Tiger* (New York, 1956).

definite continuation, and few Indians seemed to be opposed to this objective. Even though the objective was clear, however, the British found it advisable, both for external and internal reasons, to associate increasing numbers of Indians with the work of administration and to make concessions looking toward greater self-government of the Indian realm. Thus the steps toward self-government during the British century did much to determine the course and nature of British rule and they helped to prepare Indians for the assumption of full political responsibility in 1947. The fact that this was not the objective in the beginning is perhaps of only incidental importance.

The story of the steps toward self-government during the British century is a complicated one, involving a few major landmarks, innumerable lesser steps, and a bewildering variety of men, motives, and events. The major landmarks were at least six, three in the latter half of the nineteenth century which prepared the way for the even greater ones in the first half of the twentieth. These were: the Indian Councils Act of 1861; the increased attention to local government symbolized by and stemming from Lord Ripon's famous Resolution on Local Self Government of 1882; the Indian Councils Act of 1893; the Morley-Minto Reforms of 1909; the Montagu-Chelmsford Reforms of 1918 and the Government of India Act of 1919; and the Government of India Act of 1935. Some knowledge of the nature and significance of these major landmarks is essential to an understanding of the government and politics of independent India.

The Indian Councils Act of 1861 enlarged the Council of the Governor-General and the Council of the Governor of each Presidency (Calcutta, Madras, and Bombay) for purposes of legislation, although the Governor-General was empowered to veto any measures proposed by the enlarged Council, and the general authority of the British Crown and Parliament was strictly preserved. Even before 1858 the executive and legislative authority in India was vested in the Governor-General-in-Council. In 1853 six members were added to the Council for legislative purposes. This change has been described as marking "the modest beginning of a parliamentary system in India."[5] The enlarged Council was known as the Legislative Council, although it had no independent powers. While it was a limited measure, the broad significance of the Act of 1861 should not be overlooked. It established the framework within which the Government of India functioned in the following decades. A year after its passage three Indians were appointed to the Legislative Council as non-official members, the first Indians to be associated with the higher councils of the Government of India in the British period.

[5] R. C. Mazumdar, H. C. Raychaudhuri, and K. Datta, *An Advanced History of India* (London, 1946), p. 849.

Before the 1880's "the principle of local self-government had been put into practice only in the cities of Calcutta and Bombay, and in a few of the towns of the Central Provinces and North-Western Provinces. Elsewhere, although a framework of local administration and local taxation existed, control was firmly in the hands of servants of the government." Lord Ripon, a liberal-minded Viceroy, was responsible for the famous Resolution on Local Self-Government of May 18, 1882, which set forth "the general principles which were to govern the future development of local representative institutions" in India.[6] The purpose of the resolution was clearly stated: "It is not primarily with a view to improvement in administration that this measure is put forward and supported," although "in course of time, as local knowledge and local interest are brought to bear more freely upon local administration, improved efficiency will follow." Instead, "it is chiefly designed as an instrument of political and popular education," and as an outlet for the talents and ambitions of the growing numbers of educated Indians. The resolution advocated the development of Local Boards in subdivisions of districts, both urban and rural, with a majority of elected nonofficial members wherever possible. Even when these Local Boards were established, however, they were still under the supervision on District Boards, which in turn were largely controlled by the District Officers, who served as chairmen.

Shortly after the issuance of the resolution, Local Self-Government Acts were passed in several of the provinces of British India to give effect to the recommendations in the resolution; but in general progress in the direction of genuine local self-government, especially at the subdistrict level, was disappointingly slow. Nearly a quarter of a century later G. K. Gokhale observed that local government "still remains all over the country where it was placed by Lord Ripon a quarter of a century ago, and in some places it has even been pushed back."[7] The Report of the Royal Commission upon Decentralisation in 1909, which has been called "the watershed in the history of local government" in India, made recommendations similar to those of the Resolution of 1882, but again the results were disappointing.

The Indian Councils Act of 1892 was the result of expressions of dissatisfaction by the Indian National Congress and liberal spokesmen in India and in England over the operations of the Legislative Councils as provided for in the Indian Councils Act of 1861. It increased the

[6] Hugh Tinker, *The Foundations of Local Self-Government in India, Pakistan and Burma* (London, 1954), pp. 42, 44. For the text of the Resolution on Local Self-Government of 1882 see P. Mukherji, ed., *Indian Constitutional Documents* (Calcutta, 1918), Vol. I, pp. 638–651.

[7] *Collected Speeches of the Hon. G. K. Gokhale* (Madras, n.d.), Appendix, p. 149.

* The Development of Self

	CENTRAL	GOVERNMENT
	EXECUTIVE	LEGISLATURE
1861 Indian Councils Act	Viceroy Council of 5 all British	Legislative Council 12 government officials, British 6 non-officials, appointed, British & Indian
1909 Morley-Minto Reforms	Viceroy Council of 7 1 Indian 6 British	Legislative Council 27 *elected* members, Indian 36 government officials, British 5 non-officials, appointed, Indian
1919 Montagu-Chelmsford Reforms	Viceroy Council of 7 3 Indians 4 British	Council of State (Upper House) 34 elected members: 32 Indian, 2 British 20 government officials: 3 Indian, 17 British 6 non-officials: 5 Indian, British
1935 Government of India Act	(*The provisions of the 1935 Act, which would have federated British India with the Indian States ruled by the Princes, never came into force.*)	Legislative Assembly (Lower House) 105 elected members: 97 Indian, 8 British 26 govt. officials: 5–10 Indian, 21–16 British 14 non-officials: Indian
1946 First All-Indian Viceroy's Council	Viceroy Council of 14 all Indian, representing major Indian parties	Council of State and Legislative Assembly (practically as above)
1947		INDIAN INDEPEN

;overnment in British India

PROVINCIAL GOVERNMENTS EXECUTIVE	LEGISLATURE	
;overnor	Legislative Council at least half the members appointed non-officials, mostly Indian	**1861** Indian Councils Act
;overnor Executive Council including 1 Indian	Legislative Council some elected members, who with non-official appointees outnumbered government officials	**1909** Morley-Minto Reforms
(Dyarchy) ;overnor Executive Council Indians and British; some portfolios transferred to Indians	Legislative Councils with a majority of elected members	**1919** Montagu-Chelmsford Reforms
(Provincial autonomy) ;overnor All-Indian Council in charge of all portfolios	Legislatures with a majority of elected members; in some provinces a Legislative Assembly and a Legislative Council	**1935** Government of India Act
As above; 1935 rights continue		**1946** First All-Indian Viceroy's Council
NCE ACT		**1947**

Courtesy British Information Services

number of members in the Central and provincial Legislative Councils, and it provided that the nomination of nonofficial members should be on the basis of recommendations by the Calcutta Chamber of Commerce and the nonofficial members of the Legislative Councils of Madras, Bengal, and Bombay Presidencies, and the North-Western Province, in the case of the Governor-General's Council, and by local bodies such as the municipalities and chambers of commerce in the case of Governors' councils. "In this (indirect) acceptance of the principle of election lies the momentous character of the change made by the Indian Councils Act of 1892." The Act also enlarged the powers of the Legislative Councils. Thus while the Act of 1892 "was not meant to mark the beginnings of [a] parliamentary system" in India, "nevertheless, it is a definite milestone on the road that led to the establishment of parliamentary government later on."[8]

Steps Toward Self-Government: From 1892 to 1918

From 1899 to 1905 Lord Curzon, one of the greatest of British colonial administrators, was Governor-General of India. A man of great energy and organizing skill, he ran the Government of India with a firm hand. Even today some of the tangible evidences of his great contributions are still manifest. But he was also an imperious and autocratic man, and he alienated his superior authorities in England and influential elements in Indian society alike. Two of his acts provoked widespread resistance in India. These were his attempt to strengthen state control and responsibility for university education through the Indian Universities Act of 1904, and the partition of Bengal in 1905. His successor, Lord Minto, was a man of very different type, who cooperated with the Secretary of State for India, the famous liberal statesman and author, Lord Morley, in a series of reforms. The Morley-Minto Reforms were embodied in the Indian Councils Act of 1909 and the rules and regulations promulgated in implementation of this Act. They also included the appointment of two Indians to the Council of the Secretary of State for India, and of the first Indian Law Member of the Viceroy's Executive Council.

The Indian Councils Act of 1909 greatly expanded the membership and functions of the Legislative Councils in India. It also empowered the Governor-General to create Executive Councils for the Governors in the larger provinces and to enlarge the Executive Councils that already existed in Madras and Bombay. Members of the Legislative Councils continued to be of three main types: officials, nominated nonofficials, and elected nonofficials. The electorates created by the

[8] J. P. Suda, *Indian Constitutional Development and National Movement* (Meerut, 1951), Vol. I, pp. 31–32.

regulations under the Act were divided into three main classes: general, class, and special.[9]

These regulations introduced for the first time the principle of communalism into official Indian political life, by providing for separate electorates for Muslims. In one sense this was a factor which had already existed for a long time, and therefore only the official recognition was new; in another sense, it was an additional divisive factor in Indian politics, generally accepted by the British authorities after 1909, which had all kinds of unfortunate consequences and which undoubtedly helped to pave the way for the eventual division of the subcontinent and the creation of the Islamic state of Pakistan. In October, 1906, in response to a hint conveyed through the Private Secretary to the Viceroy, a deputation of leading Muslims, led by the Aga Khan, waited upon the Viceroy, Lord Minto, at Simla and presented him with a carefully prepared Address. The Address asked for separate Muslim electorates, and outlined an elaborate scheme of Muslim representation. It based its request on the ground that "the position accorded to the Mohammedan community, in any kind of representation, direct or indirect, and in all other ways affecting their status and influence, should be commensurate not only with their numerical strength, but also with their practical importance and the value of the contribution which they make to the defence of the Empire" and with due regard to "the position they occupied in India a little more than a hundred years ago." Lord Minto expressed his sympathy with this request, which in effect amounted to an official acceptance of the principle of communal representation.

While the germs of later concessions were embodied in the Indian Councils Act of 1909, the intention of its framers and supporters was to make certain limited concessions to Indian sentiment without in any way affecting the predominant position of the British rulers. In a speech in the House of Lords when the Act was being considered, Lord Morley said: "If it could be said that this chapter of reforms led directly or indirectly to the establishment of a parliamentary system in India, I for one would have nothing to do with it." Three years later Lord Crew, then Secretary of State for India, confirmed this position by asserting that "the experiment of extending a measure of self-government practically free from parliamentary control to a race not our own is one which cannot be tried." Yet only five years

[9] Of the 27 elected members of the Viceroy's Legislative Council 13 were to be elected by general electorates, mostly nonofficial members of the provincial Legislative Councils, 6 by special landowners' constituencies in six provinces, 6 by Muslim constituencies, and 2 by special electorates, one each by the Chambers of Commerce of Bombay and Bengal.

later, on August 20, 1917, another Secretary of State for India, Edwin Samuel Montagu, in an historic pronouncement declared that the aim of the British Government was "the progressive realisation of responsible government in India."

What were the reasons for this significant change in British policy and outlook? They are to be found in many developments between the years 1909 and 1917, including the dissatisfaction of most Indians with the aftermath of the Morley-Minto reforms, the agitation of the Indian National Congress and the Home Rule movement, and, above all, the consequences of World War I for India. During the war the British were particularly concerned with securing the cooperation of Indians in the war effort, and the Indians expected and even demanded further concessions from the British as the price of such cooperation.

On August 20, 1917, Mr. Montagu made a statement in the House of Commons which became "the basis of all subsequent legislation by the British Parliament in relation to India."[10] The statement included the following significant declaration:

> The policy of His Majesty's Government, with which the Government of India are in complete accord, is that of the increasing association of Indians in every branch of the administration and the gradual development of self-governing institutions with a view to the progressive realisation of responsible government in India as an integral part of the British Empire. . . . I would add that progress in this policy can only be achieved by stages. The British Government and the Government of India, on whom the responsibility lies for the welfare and advancement of the Indian peoples, must be the judges of the time and measure of each advance, and they must be guided by the co-operation received from those upon whom new opportunities of service will thus be conferred and by the extent to which it is found that confidence can be reposed in their sense of responsibility.[11]

The Secretary of State for India also announced that he would soon go to India at the head of a mission, for purposes of consultation and

[10] Suda, *Indian Constitutional Development,* p. 125.

[11] *Report on Indian Constitutional Reforms, 1918* (Montagu-Chelmsford Report), p. 1. Since Mr. Montagu made it clear that "the British Government and the Government of India . . . must be the judges of the time and measure of each advance," and that India would remain "an integral part of the British Empire," it is obvious that he used the terms "responsible government" and "self-governing institutions" in a much more limited sense than they have come to signify in contemporary Western political science. An American political scientist, for example, would use the term "responsible government" in the sense of answerable, and he would equate "self-governing institutions" or "self-government" with political independence.

enquiry. After consultations with the Viceroy, Lord Chelmsford, and other officials and with some influential Indian spokesmen, investigations of prevailing conditions in India, and consideration of several proposals for reforms, the Montagu mission, on July 8, 1918, issued the Report on Indian Constitutional Reforms. The Report was popularly referred to as the Montagu-Chelmsford or the Montford Report. It accepted the principle of Montagu's declaration of August, 1917, that the aim should be "the progressive realisation of responsible government in India." It laid down four fundamental objectives for future constitutional advance: (1) "popular control in local bodies and the largest possible independence for them of outside control"; (2) establishment in the provinces, in which "the earlier steps towards the progressive realization of responsible government should be taken," of "the largest measure of independence . . . of the Government of India which is compatible with the due discharge by the latter of its own responsibilities"; (3) enlargement of the membership and functions of the Indian Legislative Council and increase of its representative element; and (4) relaxation of the control of Parliament and the Secretary of State for India over the Government of India and the provincial governments.[12]

Government of India Act of 1919

On the basis of the Montford Report, and the recommendations of three committees set up to complete its work, the Government of India Act of 1919 was drafted. This act is a major landmark along the road to self-government in India. It made significant changes in the machinery for the government of India, both in London and in India. It reduced the number of members of the India Council, a group of advisers to the Secretary of State for India, and it provided for the transfer of some of the Secretary's functions to a new official, to be known as the High Commissioner for India. It also increased the degree of Parliamentary control over the administration of Indian affairs. In India it radically modified the nature of the central legislative body, providing for a new legislature of two chambers, a Council of State and an Indian Legislative Assembly, to be made more representative than the previous unicameral Indian Legislative Council. The Council of State was to consist of 60 members, 34 of whom were to be elected — 20 by general electorates, 3 by European Chambers of Commerce, and 11 by communal electorates. Of the 144 members of the Indian Legislative Assembly, 103 were to be elected — 51 by general constituencies, 32 by communal constituencies, and 20 by special constituencies. The new central legislature was given a wide field of activity, but the Governor-General, still directly responsible

[12] *Ibid.*, p. 123.

to the Secretary of State for India and the British Parliament, exercised a veto power over any of its enactments.

Since the federal provisions of the Government of India Act of 1935 were never put into effect, the central executive and legislature in India as determined by the Act of 1919 continued to function until the Indian Independence Act of 1947.

In the provinces of British India the Government of India Act of 1919 introduced changes which were so novel in character that they are of continuing interest to students of government. These took the form of a dual system of government known as "dyarchy."[13] Provincial subjects were divided into two classes — the "Reserved" and the "Transferred." Reserved subjects, including finance, land revenue, justice, and police, remained the responsibility of the Governor, acting as the representative of the British Government. Responsibility for transferred subjects, including local self-government, education, health, and public works, was entrusted to the voters of the provinces, through the Legislative Councils, which were enlarged in membership and functions and made more representative of various communities and interests. Thus "the government of each Governor's Province was divided into two parts — the Governor in Council in charge of the 'Reserved Departments' and the Governor acting with Ministers in charge of the 'Transferred Departments' — each part accountable to separate and distinct sets of people — the British electors in the one case and the provincial voters in the other."[14]

"Dyarchy was not only a novel but also a clumsy experiment in constitution-making," and it is hardly surprising that in the unfavorable environment which existed in India in 1919 and after it proved to be a failure. "It was a failure in the sense that the objective for the sake of which it was introduced was not realized; there was no real transfer of power to the people, no genuine responsible government even in the limited sphere of transferred subjects. The absence of stable political parties, the presence in the legislatures of a large bloc of officials and nominated non-officials, and of persons returned from communal and special constituencies, the joint purse, the powers of the Governor to override the advice given by the ministers, the rights of the services: all these factors combined together to prevent the growth of responsible government in the provinces."[15]

[13] See Lionel Curtis, *Dyarchy* (Oxford, 1920); A. Appadorai, *Dyarchy in Practice* (London, 1937); and "Kerala Putra" (pseud. of K. M. Panikkar), *The Working of Dyarchy in India* (Bombay, 1928).

[14] Gurmukh Nihal Singh, *Landmarks in Indian Constitutional and National Development*, Vol. I, 1600 to 1919 (3rd edition, Delhi, 1952), pp. 293–294.

[15] Suda, *Indian Constitutional Development*, pp. 173, 181–182.

Another consequence of the Montagu-Chelmsford Reforms was the improvement of the machinery for cooperation between British India and the Indian States. Relations between the British and the rulers of the Indian States had gone through many stages in the previous century and a half, ranging from noninterference to a policy of "subordinate isolation." While paying considerable deference to the princes, the British Government left no doubt that it was the paramount power in all of India. Its general position was thus summarized in the Montagu-Chelmsford Report: "The States are guaranteed security from without; the Paramount Power acts for them in relation to foreign powers and other States, and it intervenes when the internal peace of their territories is seriously threatened."[16] The report recommended the creation of a permanent "Council of Princes," with "a small Standing Committee to which the Viceroy of the Political Department might refer." The Government of India Act of 1919 contained no provisions regarding the Indian States, but the recommendations of the Montford Report were not forgotten. Its proposals were considered at a Conference of the Ruling Princes in January, 1919, and a more definite scheme, based on the proposals, and sponsored by the Viceroy and the Secretary of State for India, at another Conference of Princes in November, 1919. The decision to constitute the Chamber of Princes was announced by Royal Proclamation, and the Duke of Connaught formally inaugurated the Chamber in February, 1921.

The Simon Commission and the Round Table Conferences

The Government of India Act of 1919 provided for a review of the political situation in India every ten years. Well before that time, in November, 1927, the Governor-General, Lord Irwin, announced the appointment of an Indian Statutory Commission, under the chairmanship of Sir John Simon. Although the Commission, composed exclusively of Englishmen, visited India twice, and made every effort to discharge its duties faithfully, its work was greatly hampered by the hostile reception it received in India. It was boycotted not only by the Indian National Congress but also by almost all sections of Indian opinion, including the Indian Liberals. Its report was not released until May, 1930. By this time the situation in India had changed, and few people paid much attention to the Commission's recommendations, which included provincial autonomy, with safeguards, and the possibility at some future date of a federal constitution which would embrace both British India and the Indian States.

Doubtless the Simon Report deserved a better fate. R. Coupland described it as "the most complete study of the Indian problem that

[16] *Report on Indian Constitutional Reforms, 1918,* p. 190.

had yet been made."[17] Many of its recommendations were eventually incorporated into the Government of India Act of 1935. But C. F. Andrews expressed the prevailing view in India when he said that it dealt more "with that old India which I knew when I first went out nearly thirty years ago, before the national movement had started; it shows little understanding of the Young India which we see rising to-day on the tide of national upheaval."[18]

While trying to justify the exclusion of Indians from membership in the Simon Commission, Lord Birkenhead, Secretary of State for India, had challenged Indians of varying shades of opinion to produce an agreed-upon proposal for constitutional reform. Indian leaders accepted this challenge, and organized an All-Parties Conference in 1928. This Conference appointed a subcommittee under the chairmanship of Motilal Nehru, father of Jawaharlal Nehru, with a distinguished membership representing different groups in the Indian National Congress, the Liberals, and some Muslims, to draft a constitution. The Nehru Report recommended full responsible government for India along the lines of the self-governing Dominions as "the next immediate step," and left some scope for those who wanted to insist on complete independence as the immediate goal.[19] Although it was endorsed by the All-Parties Conference in August, 1928, it encountered considerable opposition in some of the affiliated organizations. The Muslim League, in particular, was divided in its attitude. Some of its members wanted to reject the report completely, on the ground that it was slanted in favor of Hindus and did not accept the views of the League. Even within the Congress some younger members, led by Subhas Chandra Bose and Jawaharlal Nehru, were reluctant to endorse any recommendation which did not demand complete independence. After the intervention of Mahatma Gandhi, the Congress agreed on a resolution promising to "adopt the Constitution if it is accepted in its entirety by the British Parliament on or before the 31st of December, 1929." Otherwise the Congress announced its intention to organize a campaign of nonviolent noncooperation.

On October 31, 1929, Lord Irwin issued a proclamation, containing the following commitment: "I am authorised on behalf of His Majesty's Government to state clearly that in their judgment it is implicit in the declaration of 1917 that the natural issue of India's constitutional progress . . . is the attainment of Dominion Status." The proclamation also announced that a Round Table Conference would be held in

[17] See R. Coupland, *The Indian Problem* (New York, 1944), Vol. I, Chapter VIII, "The Simon Report," pp. 97–112.

[18] C. F. Andrews, *India and the Simon Report* (London, 1930), p. 40.

[19] See *All Parties Conference, 1928: Report of the Committee Appointed by the Conference to Determine the Principles of the Constitution for India* (Allahabad, 1928).

London soon after the publication of the Simon Report to consider the recommendations of that Report and other proposals for Indian constitutional reform.

Events were moving toward a showdown between the Indian National Congress and the British Government. At the annual session of the Congress in 1930, held in Lahore, Mahatma Gandhi moved a resolution which declared: "This Congress . . . declares that the word Swaraj in . . . the Congress constitution shall mean Complete Independence . . . This Congress authorises the All India Congress Committee, whenever it deems fit, to launch upon a programme of civil disobedience." In March and early April Gandhi made his famous salt march, which was the signal to start a massive civil disobedience campaign. When the First Round Table Conference met in London in November, 1930, Gandhi and thousands of Congress supporters were in jail. Fifty-seven nominated delegates from British India and sixteen representing the Indian States attended the Conference. Upon its conclusion in mid-January, 1931, the British Prime Minister issued a declaration of policy, favoring "the advance of India through the new Constitution to full responsibility for her own Government," and pledging to take steps to enlist the cooperation of those who were engaged in civil disobedience. Shortly thereafter the leaders of the movement were released from jail. Gandhi thereupon entered into negotiations with Lord Irwin, which led in March to a settlement known as the Gandhi-Irwin Pact. Gandhi agreed to suspend the civil disobedience campaign in return for certain concessions from the British. This pact was quite unpopular with the younger group in the Congress, but it was ratified at a meeting of the Congress in Karachi.

Gandhi attended the Second Round Table Conference in the latter part of 1931, as the sole representative of the Congress. It proved to be a trying experience for him; in fact, he himself described it as a "long, slow agony." The representatives of the British Government and of various communal interests in India joined in postponing consideration of basic questions, such as the communal problem, and spent endless hours in considering minor matters. Gandhi returned to India in a melancholy frame of mind, and found that the situation had deteriorated even during his short absence. The British authorities took the initiative in preventing a renewal of civil disobedience by arresting thousands of Congressmen; by the end of April all of the top leaders and nearly 70,000 persons, including more than 5,300 women, were in prison. In the autumn Gandhi embarked on his most famous — and nearly fatal — fast in successful protest against a proposal by the British Government to create separate electorates for the untouchables. In May, 1933, he was released from prison just as he started another fast. On his release he advised the suspension of the civil disobedience campaign, and after another period of imprisonment he recommended the abandonment of individual civil disobedience as well.

In November–December, 1932, while the Congress leaders were in prison, a Third Round Table Conference was convened. After this session, which was even boycotted by the British Labor Party, the British Government issued new proposals for India in a White Paper. These proposals were disappointing to Indians. They were made even less satisfactory after the deliberations of a Joint Committee of the British Parliament, which considered the Indian problem for eighteen months. Out of these deliberations came the Government of India Act of 1935, the last and most important of the great landmarks along the road to self-government and eventual independence for India.

Government of India Act of 1935

Briefly stated, the Act of 1935 may be regarded as a constitution for a federal state in India, in which both British India and the Indian States would be joined. It abolished dyarchy in the provinces, and provided instead for provincial autonomy and full responsible government. It envisioned a kind of dyarchy at the Centre,* with some of the central subjects to be administered by the Governor-General with the advice and assistance of his ministers, responsible to the Central Legislature, and other subjects to be administered by him subject to the overall control of the British Crown.

The federation provided for in the Act of 1935 was a most peculiar one. Since it was never really established, it is impossible to say whether it would have been a workable arrangement. However, it served as a model for the federal state which India established in the Constitution of 1950. There is a striking similarity between the Government of India Act of 1935 and the Indian Constitution of 1950. It is a remarkable political fact that the major legislative contribution of the British to the government of India, a contribution which was widely criticized and in large part rejected by Indians at the time of its passage, should have been so largely accepted fifteen years later by independent India, just free from British rule.

According to the Act of 1935, the federation of India was to consist of the eleven Governor's provinces and the six Chief Commissioner's Provinces which constituted British India and those Indian States whose rulers agreed to accede to it. The federation was to be brought into being only when and if the rulers of Indian States representing not less than half the total population of the States and entitled to not less than

* In India the Central Government is almost invariably referred to as the "Centre," and this common usage is adopted in this volume.

half of the total number of seats alloted to the States in the upper chamber of the federal legislature had agreed to join the federation.

In dealing with four federal subjects, namely foreign relations, defense, ecclesiastical affairs, and tribal areas, the Governor-General would be responsible only to the Secretary of State for India and the British Parliament; he would not be constitutionally bound to consult his ministers at all. For the remaining federal subjects he was to act after consultation with the Council of Ministers, but in many instances even here he was not bound to accept the advice of the ministers. He was empowered to appoint the ministers, in consultation with the leader of the majority group in the House of Assembly. He could dismiss the ministers at his pleasure, although they were also responsible to the legislature. He would still have a wide variety of discretionary powers and special responsibilities.

The federal legislature was to consist of the British sovereign, represented by the Governor-General, and two Houses to be known as the Council of States and the House of Assembly. The Council of States was to be composed of 156 representatives of British India, 150 of whom were to be elected on a class or communal basis, and not less than 52 nor more than 104 representatives of the Indian States, nominated by the rulers. The House of Assembly was to consist of 250 representatives of British India, 105 to be elected from general constituencies, and the remainder from class and special constituencies, all through a system of indirect election, and not more than 125 representatives of the Indian States, to be nominated by the rulers. The powers of the federal legislature, while extensive, were severely limited by the control which the Viceroy, as the representative of the British Crown, was to have over it.

In the provinces the Act of 1935 provided for a considerable measure of autonomy and responsible government, instead of the system of dyarchy introduced by the Government of India Act of 1919. The executive of a province was to consist of a Governor and a Council of Ministers responsible to a legislature. Six of the provinces were to have bicameral legislatures, and the rest a single chamber to be known as the Legislative Assembly. Of the 1585 seats provided for in the Legislative Assemblies, 959 were general seats (including 151 reserved for scheduled tribes and classes), 482 were Mohammedan seats, and the remainder were reserved for other class and communal and special groups. When elections were held for the Legislative Assemblies in 1937, some 35,000,000 people, including more than 6,000,000 women, were given the right to vote — a fivefold increase over any previous franchise in India.

As in any federal constitution, the distribution of powers between the central government and the constituent units of the federation was a matter of great interest and delicacy. The Act of 1935 spelled out these powers in great detail, and in a most ingenious way. It attempted to place all possible subjects of legislation in one of three lists: a Federal List, a Provincial List, and a Concurrent List. The 59 subjects on the Federal List included defense, external affairs, central finance, central communications, and customs. Among the 54 subjects on the Provincial List were justice, police, land tenure and acquisition, local self-government, public health, education, agriculture, provincial finance, and tolls. Both the federal and provincial legislatures were empowered to pass legislation relating to any subjects on the Concurrent List, which included 26 subjects, such as criminal and civil procedure, control of the professions, and labor matters.

The Act of 1935 also made certain changes in the "Home" Government of India to conform with the grants of additional political power to the proposed new Indian federation and its constituent units. A notable change was the abolition of the India Council, which had been in existence as an advisory body to the Secretary of State for India since 1858.

Most federations have been formed by agreement among smaller political units and their representatives. The federation envisioned in the Government of India Act of 1935 was proposed by the British Government, and represented the concessions which that Government was willing to make, or felt obliged to make, to public opinion at home, to the Indian nationalist leaders, to spokesmen of Indian communal groups, and to the rulers of the Indian States.

In India the Government of India Act of 1935 received a frigid reception. If it had been enacted a generation before, it would have been hailed as a welcome step along the road to self-government. In the temper of the mid-1930's, with the nationalist movement a growing force and with new forces in the Indian scene, the Act was regarded as wrongly motivated and inadequately conceived. The Indian National Congress, the Muslim League, and other parties were hostile to it, though for different reasons. Jawaharlal Nehru, in *The Discovery of India,* written in 1944 while he was confined in a British prison, reflected the Congress attitude toward the Act:

> This provided for some kind of provincial autonomy and a federal structure, but there were so many reservations and checks that both political and economic power continued to be concentrated in the hands of the British government. Indeed in some ways it confirmed and enlarged the powers of an executive responsible solely to that government. The federal structure was so envisaged

> as to make any real advance impossible, and no loophole was left for the representatives of the Indian people to interfere with or modify the system of British-controlled administration. . . . The act strengthened the alliance between the British government and the princes, landlords, and other reactionary elements in India. . . . The whole complicated structure of government remained as it was.[20]

Since the federal provisions of the Act could not be put into effect because of the reluctance of the Indian princes, the British Government decided to proceed with the implementation of those provisions relating to responsible government in the provinces, and it announced that general elections would be held early in 1937 for the members of the provincial legislature. After considerable debate the Congress decided to participate in the elections, as did the Muslim League.

The Congress scored a notable success in the elections, winning clear majorities in six provinces, and pluralities in three other provinces. After these electoral successes the Congress leaders announced that they would not approve the formation of Congress ministries "unless the leader of the Congress party in the Legislature is satisfied and able to state publicly that the Governor will not use his special powers of interference or set aside the advice of ministers in regard to their constitutional activities." Not until June 21, 1937, did the Governor-General make a public statement which was regarded as satisfactory on this point to the Congress. Soon afterwards Congress ministries were formed in eight provinces. The Congress created considerable resentment on the part of the Muslim League and certain minority groups by deciding against participation in coalition ministries in provinces where no party had a clear majority, and by refusing to include non-Congressmen in the cabinets in provinces where they had a majority.

On the whole, the Congress ministries made a creditable record while they shared the responsibilities of administration in most of the provinces of British India. Coupland's evaluation was well-deserved: "Taken as a whole the record of its Ministers was one in which the Congress could take reasonable pride. Its leaders had shown that they could act as well as talk, administer as well as agitate, and among them and their followers there was a genuine ardour for social reform."[21] The Congress experience in provincial responsibility,

[20] Nehru, *The Discovery of India,* pp. 368–369.

[21] R. Coupland, *India: A Restatement* (London, 1945), pp. 160–162. For a detailed analysis of the record of the Congress and non-Congress governments in the provinces in the period 1937–1939, see Coupland, *The Indian Problem,* Vol. II, pp. 22–157.

however, was short-lived. In October, 1939, on instructions from the party's high command, all the Congress ministries resigned on the war issue, which led to a definite parting of the ways between the main wing of the nationalist movement and the British Government.[22]

The Transfer of Power

Protracted negotiations between British representatives and spokesmen of the Indian National Congress failed to find a way out of the impasse that had developed over fundamentally different approaches to the issue of participation in the war. In August, 1940, the Viceroy pledged that the British Government, after the war, would agree to convene a representative body to frame a new constitution for India, and he appealed for such unity in India "as would enable her to make the fullest possible contribution in the world struggle against tyranny and aggression." The Congress view was that it was impossible to co-operate in any "world struggle against tyranny and aggression" when India was not free and when it was faced with "an arrogant imperialism which is indistinguishable from Fascist authoritarianism," to use the language of a resolution of the Congress Working Committee in December, 1941. In the meantime the Muslim League had issued its Lahore resolution in 1940, demanding a separate Pakistan, and the Indian Communists, after denouncing the "imperialist war," changed their position completely, in conformity with the international party line, after the Nazi assault on the Soviet Union in June, 1941.

In March–April, 1942, Sir Stafford Cripps, known as a friend of India, came to India to investigate ways and means of giving effect to the British offer of August, 1940. In late March he issued some general proposals, and in a broadcast on March 30 he said: "Let us enter upon this primary task of the defence of India in the now sure knowledge that when we emerge from the fire and the travail of war it will be to build a free India upon foundations wrought by the Indian

[22] Many Indians at the time and subsequently thought that the resignation of the Congress ministries was a serious mistake. V. P. Menon has stated this view most forcefully: "Had it [the Congress] not resigned from its position of vantage in the provinces the course of Indian history might have been very different. By resigning, it showed a lamentable lack of foresight and political wisdom. There was little chance of its being put out of office; the British Government would surely have hesitated to incur the odium of dismissing ministries which had the overwhelming support of the people. Nor could it have resisted a unanimous demand for a change at the Centre, a demand which would have been all the more irresistible after the entry of Japan into the war. In any case, it is clear that, but for the resignation of the Congress, Jinnah and the Muslim League would never have attained the position they did." V. P. Menon, *The Transfer of Power in India* (Princeton, N.J., 1957), p. 152.

people themselves." Neither the Congress nor the Muslim League would accept his proposals, and Sir Stafford abruptly terminated his negotiations and admitted failure. Shortly thereafter the Congress high command, following Gandhi's advice, demanded an immediate end to British rule, and threatened "a mass struggle on non-violent lines on the widest possible scale" if this demand was not met. The reply of the British Government was to imprison Gandhi, Nehru, and virtually all the important leaders of the Congress, and to declare that the Congress committees were unlawful associations.

At the end of the war, therefore, the prospects for agreement of the British and the Congress for the peaceful transfer of power seemed to be remote. Yet within two years not only was basic agreement reached on objectives but the complicated details for interim arrangements and final independence were worked out among all major factions, and India and Pakistan began their ventures as independent nations.[23] This remarkable achievement in liquidation and rebirth required a high level of statesmanship and forbearance on all sides, especially on the part of the new Labor Government and the Parliament in Britain and on the part of responsible leaders of Indian opinion in the Congress, the Muslim League, and elsewhere.

In June, 1945, after extended negotiations in India and England, the new Viceroy, Lord Wavell, broadcast proposals "to ease the present political situation and to advance India towards her goal of full self-government." He announced his intention to hold a political conference at Simla, to which twenty-one Indian leaders would be invited. The Simla Conference did bring together representatives of all the major political groups in India, but it did not produce a meeting of minds. The Viceroy himself described it as a failure. "The Simla Conference," as V. P. Menon has observed, "afforded a last opportunity to the forces of nationalism to fight a rear-guard action to preserve the integrity of the country, and when the battle was lost the waves of communalism quickly engulfed it. Only the Hobson's choice of partition was left."[24]

Soon after this unhappy event a Labor Government came into power in Britain and World War II ended with the surrender of Japan. These developments created a more favorable atmosphere for determining India's political future, and also made the need of some lasting solution even more urgent. On September 16, 1945, the

[23] For the details of the developments in 1945–1947 leading to the transfer of power, see *ibid.* and E. W. R. Lumby, *The Transfer of Power in India, 1945–7* (New York, 1954).

[24] Menon, *The Transfer of Power in India,* p. 215. Menon devotes an entire chapter to the Simla Conference of 1945 (Chapter VIII, pp. 182–215).

Viceroy announced that elections to the central and provincial legislatures would be held during the winter, and that he would "convene as soon as possible a constitution-making body." Elections to the central Legislative Assembly were held in late 1945, and resulted in decisive victories for the Congress and the Muslim League, proving that they "were the only parties that counted in the country."[25] This fact was confirmed in elections to provincial legislatures, which were held early in 1946. As a result of the provincial elections Congress ministries were formed in six provinces. The Muslim League did not fare so well, but it did form ministries in Bengal and Sind.

In January, 1946, a British Parliamentary Delegation of ten members visited India, and received a cordial welcome. In March a British Cabinet Mission, consisting of Lord Pethick-Lawrence, Secretary of State for India, Sir Stafford Cripps, President of the Board of Trade, and A. V. Alexander, First Lord of the Admiralty, came to India to confer with Indian leaders and to consider various proposals for the solution of the "Indian problem." After several meetings with Gandhi, Maulana Azad, Jinnah, and other Indian leaders, the members of the Mission invited representatives of the Congress and the Muslim League to confer with them at Simla. The conference was held in May, but served only to dramatize the gulf that existed between the Congress and the Muslim League. Since it could not bring the main parties into agreement, the Cabinet Mission issued its own proposals. Rejecting the demand of the Muslim League for partition, the Mission proposed a Union of India, embracing both British India and the Indian States, with a Constituent Assembly consisting of representatives of the provincial legislatures and divided into three sections.

After further negotiations both the Congress and the Muslim League accepted the Cabinet Mission plan, with many conditions and reservations. Later the League, charging that the Mission had "played into the hands of the Congress," revoked its acceptance of the plan, and raised again the demand for a separate Pakistan. The League did participate in the elections for members of the Constituent Assembly, and won all but five of the seats alloted to Muslims. The Congress won all the general seats save nine.

The British Government decided to go ahead with its interim plans, even without the cooperation of the Muslim League. On August 6, 1946, the Viceroy invited Nehru to form an interim Government. This Government was sworn in on September 2nd. In mid-October the Muslim League reversed its previous decision, and agreed to participate, chiefly in order to prevent the Congress from consolidating its position to the detriment of the League's interests. When the Viceroy issued

[25] *Ibid.*, p. 226.

invitations for the first meeting of the Constituent Assembly, however, Jinnah announced that the League would not participate. In spite of the League's refusal, the Constituent Assembly met on December 9th. Dr. Rajendra Prasad, later President of the Republic of India, was elected President. Nehru immediately introduced an important "Objectives Resolution," which envisaged the Indian Union as "an independent Sovereign Republic." The Congress insisted that the League should either participate in the Constituent Assembly, or withdraw its representatives from the interim Government.

Confronted with this dilemma, the British Labor Government made a momentous decision. On February 20, 1947, Prime Minister Attlee announced in the British Parliament that the Government intended to take the necessary steps to transfer power into Indian hands by June, 1948. If no agreement had been reached among the Indian parties by that time, his Government would then consider whether it would transfer power "as a whole to some form of central Government for British India, or in some areas to the existing provincial Governments, or in such other way as may seem most reasonable and in the best interests of the Indian people." The Prime Minister also announced that Lord Mountbatten would go to India as Viceroy, charged with the task of implementing the historic decision. This announcement was generally hailed in India and in Britain, although in both countries there were those who greeted it with the direst forebodings. In the debate on the announcement in the House of Commons, former Prime Minister Winston Churchill made his famous and, fortunately, ill-founded prophecy: "In handing over the Government of India to these so-called political classes we are handing over to men of straw of whom in a few years no trace will remain."

Lord Mountbatten arrived in India on March 22, 1947. He quickly concluded that the date for the transfer of power should be moved up, and that the decision between one or two states should be referred to the Indians themselves. On June 3 the British Government's new plan was announced in London and New Delhi. It provided for the handing over of power before the end of the year to one or two governments, each to have Dominion Status. In broadcasts over All-India Radio that evening Nehru, Jinnah, and the Sikh leader Baldev Singh joined with the Viceroy in explaining and endorsing the new plan, although Nehru, at least, did so with a heavy heart.

Less than two and a half months elapsed between the announcement of the British Government's plan for the final transfer of power and the inauguration of the new nations of India and Pakistan. In this short time, in an atmosphere of growing tension and under a spirit of great urgency, was carried out what Lord Birdwood called "the greatest political and military operation in history."[26] "There was so much to be done within such a limited time. The verdicts of the provinces had to be ascertained; parliamentary legislation had to be hurried through; if partition were decided upon, the administrative services and armed forces had to be divided, assets and liabilities to be apportioned and the boundaries in the disputed areas to be settled — all these tasks had to be carried through more or less simultaneously."[27]

When the results of the decisions in the crucial provinces, obtained by votes in the legislative assemblies or by referenda or other ways, became known, there was no longer any doubt that the subcontinent would emerge from its long period of dependence as two nations, not one. In effect East Bengal, West Punjab, Sind, Baluchistan and the North-West Frontier Province voted for Pakistan. Once this basic decision had been confirmed, the Indian Independence Bill was introduced in the House of Commons on July 4. Although it was properly labeled by the Secretary of State for India as "a Bill unique in the history of legislation in this country," it was passed by the House of Commons on July 15 and by the House of Lords on the following day, and received the Royal Assent on July 18. On August 14 the necessary adaptations of the Government of India Act of 1935 were put into effect by the India (Provisional Constitution) Order, 1947. "By August 15th the rulers of all the States geographically contiguous to India, with the exception of Hyderabad, Junagadh and one or two States in Kathiawar with Muslim rulers, had signed the Instrument of Accession and the Standstill Agreement. The fundamental unity of the country having been ensured, India became one federation with the provinces and the States as integral parts."[28]

India was not one, but two new states. On August 15 both India and Pakistan officially became Dominions. In Karachi, the capital of the new Islamic state of Pakistan, Jinnah was sworn in as Governor-General and Liaquat Ali Khan as Prime Minister. In New Delhi, Lord Mountbatten, having given up his post as British Viceroy, was sworn in as Governor-General of free India, and he in turn swore in a new Cabinet, headed by Nehru. The British century was over. The destiny of India was henceforth primarily in Indian hands.

[26] Lord Birdwood, *India and Pakistan: A Continent Decides* (New York, 1954), p. 34.
[27] Menon, *The Transfer of Power in India,* p. 387.
[28] *Ibid.,* p. 413.

* 4 *

Toward Independence: The Nationalist Movement

Along with the organizing skill and the military power which enabled the British to conquer and to rule India for many decades came the ideas which eventually liberated it. "British imperialism in India had two contradictory sets of features. In some respects, it had a revolutionary character. In others it was reactionary in the extreme. But in both its phases, British rule encouraged and provoked the rise and development of the nationalist struggle for justice and independence."[1]

While the British were consolidating their power in India, they were also, unwittingly, laying the bases for Indian independence. Their contributions were manifold: political, administrative, legal, economic, social, cultural, educational, and psychological. Politically, they assumed effective power in India at a very low period in Indian history, when the Mogul dynasty was hardly more than a shell of its former self, when the Hindu revivalism under the Marathas had fallen far short of its avowed goals, when other Western powers, notably France, were rivals for trade and influence in the subcontinent. They gave India a greater degree of national unity and solidarity and a better form of government than it had ever enjoyed, save perhaps during a few periods in the long course of Indian history. Administratively, the British developed a pattern of rule which is still followed in its basic outlines by free India. This administrative system extended through British India, even to the village level, and indirectly it affected the princely States as well. By associating Indians in increasing numbers

[1] Santosh Trikha, *Political Parties in India* (unpublished doctoral dissertation, University of Saugar, Sagar, India, 1955), p. 56.

in the administrative services, the British helped to train generations of capable administrators. Legally, they gave India something close to a uniform code of justice, a revolutionary departure indeed from the previous patterns of regional and local "justice" and communal differences. They also gave India a concept of liberty under law. Economically, they destroyed the base of existence of village India, and they undoubtedly "milked" India for British ends, but they introduced new forms of land tenure, they tied the country together economically as well as politically, they helped to create new economic classes and interests, and they developed systems of trade and finance which have prevailed to the present day. Socially, they helped to ameliorate some of the worst abuses of the strongly intrenched caste system, and they created new standards and practices of social behavior. Culturally, they brought India into contact with the West, and helped India to rediscover its own past as well as the riches of other cultures. Educationally, they made great progress in achieving the objective recommended by Lord Macaulay in his famous Minute of 1835: "to form a class who may be interpreters between us and the millions whom we govern; a class of persons, Indian in blood and colour, but English in taste, in opinions, in morals, and in intellect."[2] The existing educational system in India is largely constructed along British lines, with certain concessions to the advocates of a *sarvodaya* society, the demands of champions of linguistic reforms, the goals of free, compulsory education on a mass scale, and the needs of an independent state in the modern world. Psychologically, the British were themselves victims of a kind of superiority complex which gave them great confidence and prestige but which often blinded them to the real conditions and attitudes of the Indians whom they ruled. Conversely, the Indian reaction to British superiority was a blend of inferiority complexes, an aping of their rulers, resentment of foreign rule, Hindu or Muslim revivalism, esoteric movements of many kinds, and a determination to take their future into their own hands.

Whatever the British may have contributed to India, and however successful they may have been in training many generations of Indians to help them rule the subcontinent, there was always a fundamental conflict of interests between Britain and India. Briefly stated, the British were interested in ruling India primarily for British interests, which by a process of rationalization they often interpreted as being India's best interests as well; whereas the Indians were primarily

[2] Thomas Babington Macaulay, *Prose and Poetry* (Cambridge, Mass., 1952), p. 729. See also *Sources of Indian Tradition,* compiled by Wm. T. de Bary, Stephen Hay, Royal Weiler, and Andrew Yarrow (New York, 1958), pp. 596–601.

concerned with Indian interests, whether they accepted British rule as the best thing for them or whether they espoused the cause of independence. This basic conflict of interests explains many developments in the modern history of India. As Toynbee has pointed out, the Western impact on India was closer than that on any other part of Asia, but the gulf between Western civilization and the predominant Hindu civilization of India was very great.[3] The Indian acceptance of British rule, except among a relatively few individuals, was always a tentative and rather negative one; and the Indian response to this rule took many forms.

Characteristics of Indian Nationalism

One of the most vigorous Indian responses was the rise of an increasingly effective and popular nationalist movement. As an organized movement, nationalism in India dates from the latter half — and indeed from the last fifteen years — of the nineteenth century; but it had its roots in certain movements and in the work of certain individuals of the early nineteenth century.

To be sure, some Indian writers have claimed a much earlier origin for Indian nationalism,[4] and there are indeed many evidences in India's past of the existence of conditions and attitudes which have entered into the complex phenomenon of modern nationalism. Other precursors of nationalism in India might be sought on a regional level, for many parts of the subcontinent have traditions of ancient power and glory which can easily be fused into a nationalist movement. The Marathas are an outstanding example, for they cherish the memory of a great leader — Shivaji, a mighty Maratha chieftain of the seventeenth century — and of days of greatness in the late seventeenth and early eighteenth century when Maratha power dominated a large part of western and central India.[5]

Some of the features of Indian nationalism are common to nationalist movements and feelings everywhere; others are characteristic of Asian nationalism; others are peculiar to India itself. The nationalist movement in India was a political movement with strong economic,

[3] Arnold Toynbee, *The World and the West* (London, 1953), Chapter III, "India and the West."

[4] See Radhakumud Mookerji, *Nationalism in Hindu Culture* (London, 1921), pp. 50, 51, 52.

[5] In 1784 Warren Hastings wrote: "The Marathahs possess, alone of all the people of Hindostan and Deccan, a principle of national attachment, which is strongly impressed on the minds of all individuals of the nation, and would probably unite their chiefs, as in one common cause, if any great danger were to threaten the general state." Quoted in Jawaharlal Nehru, *The Discovery of India* (New York, 1946), p. 270.

social, and religious aspects. It was essentially a creation of and a reaction against foreign rule. It was a movement of protest which eventually became a movement of revolt. Before 1885 it lacked effective organization and focus. After that date the Indian National Congress was the spearhead of the nationalist movement.

The first leaders of the Congress were moderates steeped in the traditions of Western liberalism. They favored the continuance of British rule, and concentrated on relatively mild requests for greater participation of Indians in the political life of the country. Shortly after the turn of the century the leadership of the Congress was divided between moderates and an increasingly influential and vocal group of more militant nationalists, sometimes called extremists. These new leaders were more critical of British rule and more militant in their demands.

During the period of World War I the moderates and extremists cooperated more closely, but shortly thereafter the Congress came under the domination of Mahatma Gandhi, who remained the most powerful voice in the nationalist movement from that time until the achievement of Indian independence. Under Gandhi the Congress, which had been largely a movement of intellectuals, with some broadening of leadership and support under the extremists, became a genuine mass movement. It also embraced more radical elements, and included in its ranks socialists of all hues, peasants and workers organizations, the Radical Humanists, and even Communists. By the 1930's the Congress was flatly demanding complete independence, although it was not clear on the timetable for achieving that goal. Most of the Congress leaders were in fact surprised when the British actually did set a date for independence, and even more surprised when the British moved up that date and transferred power completely and with considerable grace.

Nationalism is a complex phenomenon wherever it is encountered, but in India it was particularly complex because of the environment in which it arose and because of the many forces, internal and external, which affected it. In the nineteenth and twentieth centuries India experienced a great reawakening, produced no doubt by the Western impact upon it, and by the search to find its own identity in a changing situation. Nationalism was powerfully stimulated by the work of many persons and organizations whose efforts were directed to the rediscovery and revitalization of the past and to the preservation of basic ideals and faiths. Even movements which were essentially nonpolitical and even reactionary in their fundamental outlook contributed to the development of a nationalist upsurge. A very powerful impetus was given by the Ramakrishna movement, inspired by one of the great religious mystics of modern India and organized and developed by his leading disciple, Vivekananda, who preached that India should undertake a spiritual conquest of the world. Vivekananda was also associated with the Hindu Renaissance of the late nineteenth and early twentieth centuries, which contributed in various ways to the growth of nationalism.

Nationalism eventually permeated all sections of the subcontinent, but for some time it was confined largely to British India. Most of the early leaders of the nationalist movement were Bengalis or Marathas. Bengal, the homeland of Surendranath Banerjea, Vivekananda, Aurobindo Ghose, C. R. Das, Rabindranath Tagore, and a host of other great leaders of modern India, had a long tradition of both intellectual and revolutionary activity. There the contacts with the British were longest and closest, for Calcutta was the main center of British rule in India throughout most of the British period. The British ruled with the cooperation of hundreds of Bengalis who were trained for administrative service; but the British never did win over the Bengalis, and after the partition of Bengal that province became a head center of disaffection and nationalist agitation, sometimes taking extreme forms. The experience in Maharashtra was quite different. Although Bombay was another center of British power, the Marathas had a proud tradition of independence from both Mogul and British control, based on the successes which they achieved against Aurungzeb and their continued resistance to British encroachments until the early years of the nineteenth century. They cherished memories, based in part on chauvinistic exaggeration, of the great days when they controlled a large part of western India and when they seemed to have a chance to extend their influence still farther, at least until the British became the dominant power in the subcontinent. Some of the greatest leaders of Indian nationalism, including Pherozshah Mehta, Ranade, Gokhale and Tilak, were Maharashtrians; the last three were all Chitpavan Brahmans. This fact is a reminder of the special role of the Brahmans in the nationalist movement, although the greatest of all modern Indians, Mahatma Gandhi, did not belong to this caste. Gandhi was also neither a Bengali nor a Maharashtrian. He was a member of the Vaisya or merchant caste and was a Gujerati from Saurashtra.

The nationalist movement in India was always dominated by Hindus. This is certainly not surprising, for the great majority of Indians were Hindus. Moreover, under the British the Muslims lost much of their former position and influence, and the Hindus benefited more from the opportunities opened up by the British to enter the trades, professions, and governmental and educational service. Muslims were further alienated by the many evidences that in the minds of some of the nationalist leaders the struggle for *swaraj* in its various forms was linked with a revival or reaffirmation of Hinduism. Vivekananda advocated a revival of Hindu virtues and Tilak gave a strong Hindu cast to all of his efforts. Even Gandhi was suspect by many Muslims; while he made Hindu-Muslim unity a major plank in his program, he spoke of the need for a *ram rajya* — a Hindu conception of an ideal kingly rule; he opposed partition and the establishment of a separate Muslim state, and he was, after all, a Hindu. Many Muslims were active in the nationalist movement; some, like Maulana Azad, held high positions in the Indian National Congress and later in the government of independent India. But the majority of the Muslims of India remained aloof from the Congress, especially at the beginning of its activities, when their great leader, Sir Syed Ahmad Khan, advised them to have no part in it, and in the years just preceding independence, when the Muslim League captured the allegiance of most of them. In short, while there was a kind of all-India nationalism, at least in the negative sense of opposition to foreign rule and of the demand of "India for the Indians," it would be more accurate to refer to two types of nationalism in India — Hindu nationalism, headed by the Congress, and Muslim nationalism, eventually led by the Muslim League.

The greatest spokesmen of Indian nationalism in its final phases constantly sought to promote what Jawaharlal Nehru called a "real or Indian nationalism" — "something quite apart from these two religious and communal varieties" (Hindu and Muslim).[6] They were ardent nationalists in the sense that they wanted freedom for their country, freedom from foreign rule, and economic, social, and human freedom as well. But they also had a world outlook which was almost nonnational, or even antinational. "It is surprising," wrote Nehru in *The Discovery of India,* "how internationally minded we grew in spite of our intense nationalism. No other nationalist movement in a subject country came anywhere near this."[7] Tagore denounced the evils of modern nationalism, and in one of his best-known poems, included in his Nobel Prize-winning volume, *Gitanjali,* he expressed the hope that his country would awake into a "heaven of freedom" "where the world has not been broken up into fragments by narrow domestic walls." Gandhi declared: "I do want to think in terms of the whole world. . . . I want the cultures of all lands to be blown about my house as freely as possible." Nehru warned that nationalism "is a narrowing creed," and he insisted that "we seek no narrow

[6] Jawaharlal Nehru, *Glimpses of World History* (4th edition, London, 1949), p. 720.

[7] Nehru, *The Discovery of India,* p. 427.

nationalism." All three of these great nationalist leaders were bent on freeing India not only from the British yoke but, as Gandhi once declared, "from any yoke whatsoever." Yet all of the nationalist leaders of India came gradually to accept the view that political independence for India was an essential step, if only the first step, toward the kind of freedom which they envisaged for their country and their people.

Thus nationalism, both as a negative and as a positive force, did much to gain independence for India and to shape the India of today. It was a major force in the India of the nineteenth and twentieth centuries. In *The Discovery of India* Nehru wrote: "Nationalism was and is inevitable in the India of my day; it is a natural and healthy growth. For any subject country national freedom must be the first and dominant urge; for India with her intense sense of individuality and a past heritage, it was doubly so."[8]

Main Stages of the Nationalist Movement

The story of the nationalist movement in India may be divided into five stages, with the terminal dates of each succeeding stage being 1885, 1905–1907, 1919–1920, 1934–1935, and 1947, respectively. An analysis of each of these stages will throw some light on the historical evolution of the struggle for independence and on the characteristics of Indian nationalism.

1. The Formative Stage, to 1885. Until recently the beginnings of the Indian nationalist movement were usually dated from the founding of the Indian National Congress in 1885. Now more attention is being given to the formative period of Indian nationalism, prior to 1885. Among the highlights of this period are the manifold activities of Raja Ram Mohan Roy in the early nineteenth century; the contributions of a number of other liberal reformers, especially in Bengal and Maharashtra; the influence of a large number of politico-religious organizations, such as the Brahmo Samaj and the Arya Samaj; British policies such as the introduction of a British pattern of education; the beginnings of the association of Indians in the civil service; the first Indian Councils Acts; the circumstances leading to the transfer of power in India from the British East India Company to the British Government itself; the "Mutiny" of 1857 and its aftermath; the growing feelings on the part of certain British and Indian leaders of the need for an organization to serve the dual purpose of siphoning off mounting Indian unrest and of presenting to the British authorities the just grievances of the Indians and their desire for greater representation in political and economic affairs; the formation

[8] *Ibid.*, pp. 40–41.

of several societies, notably the Calcutta Indian Association, which were in effect precursors of the Indian National Congress; and the early efforts of many persons, including Surendranath Banerjea and Dadabhai Naoroji, who were to become prominent leaders of the Congress in its early phases.

Raja Ram Mohan Roy (1772–1833) is often called not only "the Father of Indian Nationalism" but also "the Father of Modern India." A man of universal interests and tremendous energy, Ram Mohan Roy acquired a remarkable knowledge of both Western and Indian civilization. After a successful career in the Bengal Civil Service, Roy retired at the age of 42 to devote his energies to his political and other interests. An admirer of the liberal ideas of the West and of the teachings of Christ, he also saw much value in the lessons of the Vedas and in India's past; but he found many things to criticize in both Western and Eastern civilization. He was critical of such Indian practices or institutions as the caste system, child marriage, and widow-burning. He believed that British rule was a good thing for India, and he hoped that his fellow-countrymen would take advantage of the opportunities afforded them by the British. He founded and edited newspapers in Bengali, English, and Persian, and he established several secondary schools. In 1838 he organized the Brahmo Samaj (Society of God), a society which "was to exercise a deep influence on the intellectual, social, and religious life of India,"[9] and which has been described as "the pioneer of the nationalist movement."[10]

Many other organizations founded well before 1885 contributed directly or indirectly to the development of a spirit of nationalism. Prominent among these were the British India Society (1843), the British Indian Association (1851), the associations organized in Bombay, Madras, and Calcutta to present representations to the British Government at the time of the renewal of the Charter of the East India Company in 1853, and the Arya Samaj, founded in Bombay in 1875 by Dayananda Saraswati. Dayananda, "the Luther of India," regarded the Vedas as infallible, and the Arya Samaj, with its slogan of "Back to the Vedas," advocated a kind of militant Hinduism which alienated Muslims and many Hindus as well; but many nationalist leaders were associated with it, and its contributions to the cause of Indian nationalism have continued until the present day.

The "Mutiny" of 1857 also contributed to the growth of Indian nationalism, although, as has been noted, it was far from being a nationalist uprising. Before 1857, as Dr. R. C. Majumdar, one of

[9] *Sources of Indian Tradition,* p. 572.

[10] A. R. Desai, *Social Background of Indian Nationalism* (London, 1948), p. 265.

India's leading historians, has pointed out, India "had not yet developed any general idea of either conscious nationalism or true patriotism."[11] After the "Mutiny" the nationalist idea was promoted by many individuals and organizations, and within two decades it began to take on institutional form.

The immediate precursor and "true prototype" of the Indian National Congress was the Calcutta Indian Association, founded in 1876. Its leading spirit was Surendranath Banerjea, whose dismissal from the Indian Civil Service led him to devote the remainder of a long life to "redressing our wrongs and protecting our rights, personal and collective." A powerful orator, Banerjea made three highly successful lecture tours in various parts of India — in 1877, 1878, and 1884. At the All-India Durbar in Delhi in 1877, convened by the Governor-General, Lord Lytton, to celebrate the conferring of the title of Empress of India on Queen Victoria, representatives of Indian organizations advanced the idea of a national organization of Indians to voice the sentiments of the Indian people. This idea intrigued Surendranath Banerjea, who attended this Durbar, and was apparently taken up by the Calcutta Indian Association. Under the auspices of the Association a National Conference was held in Calcutta in 1883. This was "the first effort of its kind in India" and "must be regarded as the true forerunner of the Congress of 1885."[12]

Other Indians who were soon to play a prominent part in the work of the Indian National Congress began their active work in the 1870's and early 1880's. By the year 1870 Dadabhai Naoroji, who was later known as the grand old man of the Indian nationalist movement and who was the first Indian to be elected to the British Parliament, had formulated his famous theory of "economic drain" as a result of British rule and foreign exploitation. "It was this theory of economic drain which may be considered to have laid the foundation for the political agitation of Indians from 1885 onwards."[13] It profoundly influenced the thinking of several generations of Indians and it is still widely held, even by eminent Indian economists. Before 1885, also, Justice Ranade began his life-long work for economic and social reforms and "laid the foundations of what later came to be called Indian political economy."[14] Naoroji and Ranade differed in their outlook and in their policies. Ranade espoused views which appealed

[11] Quoted in the *Radical Humanist,* XXI (June 30, 1957), 319.

[12] Nandalal Chatterji, "The Forgotten Precursor of the Indian National Congress," *Journal of Indian History,* XXXVI (April, 1958), 13.

[13] From an unpublished précis of S. D. Javadekar, *Adhunik Bharat* (*Modern India*), a treatise in Marathi, p. 13. See also William R. Smith, *Nationalism and Reform in India* (New Haven, 1938), p. 140.

[14] Précis of *Adhunik Bharat,* p. 13.

to the moderates in the Indian nationalist movement, whereas Naoroji's approach, a more direct and critical one, found favor with the group which is often referred to as the extremists.

The beginnings of Muslim nationalism can also be traced to the years prior to 1885. In part this took the form of harking back to the great days of Muslim rule in India, when the Moguls were at the height of their power. In part it was a reaction against the difficulties which the Muslims experienced after the consolidation of British rule and particularly after they failed to hold their own with Hindus in the economic and political field. They suffered further as a result of the "Mutiny," for which the British Government held them in large measure responsible. Yet in the years following the "Mutiny," when Muslim fortunes and spirits seemed to be at a low ebb, a change in their political, if not economic, status set in.

The leading spirit in this Muslim revival was Sir Syed Ahmad Khan (1817–1898), who urged his fellow-Muslims to overcome their superstitions and bigotry, to cease feeling sorry for themselves, to work for their moral and material improvement, and to cling to the fundamentals of their faith while at the same time preparing themselves more adequately for the demands and needs of the contemporary world. Two cardinal points in his creed were cooperation with the British and a preservation of Muslim identity against the Hindus. He did much to reconcile the Muslims to British rule, and to remove British suspicions and contempt of Indian Muslims. He advised the Muslims to remain aloof from the Indian National Congress, on the ground that it would inevitably come under Hindu domination. In the circumstances of India he argued that the Muslims could not identify themselves with the Hindus, but must instead seek their own salvation along different lines. Sir Syed believed that the best way to preserve the Muslim way of life was for the Muslims to become better educated. This included education in Western culture as well as in the Indian and Islamic past. In 1877 he founded the Anglo-Oriental College at Aligarh, which later developed into the Muslim University. The Aligarh movement, of which Sir Syed was the moving spirit, contributed to the regeneration of the Muslims in India and laid the basis for a more active Muslim political movement at a later period.

2. The Indian National Congress: Moderates versus Extremists. In 1885 the nationalist movement entered its second and more organized phase with the founding of the Indian National Congress. From that date until 1947 the Congress was the chief voice of Indian nationalism. Almost all of the prominent spokesmen of nationalism were at one time associated with it.

The British authorities in India looked with favor upon the new organization. One of its chief founders was an Englishman, Allan Octavian Hume, and several Englishmen and one Englishwoman (Mrs. Annie Besant, the famous theosophist) were Presidents of the Congress. Hume conceived of the Congress as a means of channeling the growing discontent in the subcontinent in a constructive way. Lord Dufferin, then Viceroy in India, gave his blessing to the movement. The object of the Congress was not at first separation from Great Britain, but continued association with it; the views of the Congress were presented in moderate terms, and they were confined largely to requests for administrative reforms and for the greater participation of Indians in the British-controlled administration and in local and national elective bodies. Surendranath Banerjea, one of the early leaders of the Congress, declared as late as 1895: "It is not severance that we look forward to — but unification, permanent embodiment as an integral part of that great Empire that has given the rest of the world the models of free institutions."[15]

During the first two decades of its existence the Congress was under the direction of Indian liberals who were English-educated and admirers of Western ideas and institutions, and it drew its support from a small but influential group of the intelligentsia and the commercial classes. Among its early leaders were Dadabhai Naoroji (1825–1917), Surendranath Banerjea (1848–1926), Justice M. G. Ranade (1842–1901), and Pherozshah Mehta (1845–1915). Toward the end of this period the leading figure in the Congress was G. K. Gokhale (1866–1915), a disciple of Ranade, who devoted his life to the public service. For some years, until his death in 1915, Gokhale maintained his position of leadership of the Congress, save for the years when the extremist group in the Congress had the upper hand. In 1885 he joined the Deccan Education Society, and he taught for several years at Fergusson College in Poona, which the Society established in the year in which he became associated with it. In 1905 he founded the Servants of India Society, an organization dedicated to the public welfare, which Gandhi once tried in vain to enter. Gandhi, however, regarded Gokhale as his "political *guru.*" For the last thirteen years of his life Gokhale was a member of the Imperial Legislative Council. While he believed in cooperation with the British and in a policy of gradualism, he did not hesitate to criticize British policies. His annual speeches on the imperial budget in the Imperial Legislative Council

[15] From Presidential Address to the Indian National Congress in 1895; quoted in Desai, *Social Background of Indian Nationalism,* p. 294. See *The Speeches and Writings of Hon. Surendranath Banerjea* (Madras, 1927), pp. 93–96.

were brilliant exposés of the economic shortcomings of British rule.

From the 1890's on more and more criticisms of the British were voiced in Congress ranks and a number of events occurred which tended to create a rift between the Congress and the Government. Notable among these events were certain policies of the British authorities and the rise of a more extremist group within the Congress. The partition of Bengal and several other developments in 1905–1907 widened the rift and ushered in a more militant phase of Indian nationalism. The British authorities tried to curb the activities of the Congress, and they warned against the consequences of what they regarded as growing radicalism within Congress ranks. Apparently they believed that their policies and warnings were bearing fruit in a weakening of the Congress. In 1900 Lord Curzon wrote to the Secretary of State for India: "The Congress is tottering to its fall, and one of my great ambitions while in India is to assist it to a peaceful demise."

While the policy of the British Government toward the Congress was hardening, the control of the liberals within the organization was being challenged by a younger but very active group of more militant nationalists. This group drew its chief support from Bengal, Maharashtra, and the Punjab. In Bengal the leaders were Bepin Chandra Pal and Aurobindo Ghose, in the Punjab the chief leader was Lala Lajpat Rai, and in Maharashtra the more militant school of nationalism was led by Bal Gangadhar Tilak. The movement in Bengal was strongly colored by the religious mysticism of the great Hindu mystic, Ramakrishna, especially as interpreted by his greatest disciple, Swami Vivekananda.

Tilak turned to India's past for inspiration, and he sought to induce a spirit of pride and self-respect in his fellow-countrymen. He revived the cult of Shivaji (the great Maratha warrior of the seventeenth century) and the Ganapati festivals, and used these for political purposes. Later, during his years of exile and confinement in Mandalay (1908–1914), he wrote a lengthy commentary on the *Bhagavad Gita,* in which he reinterpreted that great Indian classic as preaching a philosophy of political and religious action.

The British journalist, Valentine Chirol, called Tilak "the Father of Indian Unrest." Undoubtedly the policies which he championed were twisted by more extremist followers into a philosophy of justifiable violence, and his own attitude toward the many acts of violence which agitated Bengal after 1908 was always rather paradoxical. But he was not himself an apostle of violence. He was a spokesman of the extremist or nationalist group within the nationalist movement which emphasized the political struggle rather than social and economic reforms, which distrusted the British rather than believed in the importance of cooperating with the foreign rulers, and which advocated stronger pressures than the moderates were willing to endorse. "Political rights," argued Tilak, "will have to be fought for. The Moderates think that these can be won by permission. We think that they can be got by strong pressure." He held that the so-called extremists were not in fact very extreme. He brought the demand for *swaraj* squarely into the center of the nationalist agitation. In ringing words, quoted over and over again throughout India, he declared: "Swaraj is my birthright and I will have it." He was perhaps the first nationalist leader who had a great appeal to the masses of the people. In a sense he foreshadowed the great work of Mahatma Gandhi in this respect. He is still referred to today by the name by which he was best known during his lifetime: "Lokamanya" — "Honored by the People."[16]

Tilak and others in the extremist group preached a kind of Hindu revivalism which gave new life to the nationalist movement, but which at the same time further alienated many Muslims from the movement. The separation of Muslim from Hindu nationalism became more marked as a result of the formation of the Muslim League in 1906, the famous deputation of Muslim spokesmen, led by the Aga Khan, to the Viceroy in 1906 in order to petition the British authorities for separate electorates for Muslims in elections, and the endorsement of the principle of separate electorates in the Morley-Minto reforms of 1909.

3. The Era of Gokhale and Tilak. Thus the third period of Indian nationalism was ushered in by agitation, extremism, and separatism. At the annual session of the Indian National Congress in 1905 a nationalist party was formed within the Congress, under the leadership of Tilak, with strong support from Lala Lajpat Rai and B. C. Pal — a triumvirate popularly referred to as Lal-Bal-Pal, or the "national trinity." At the 1906 Congress session Dadabhai Naoroji, then 80 years old, exhorted leaders of both moderate and extremist groups to work together for the goal of *swaraj*. But this was not to be. At the historic session of the Congress at Surat in 1907 Tilak and Aurobindo Ghose led a movement of the extremists to gain control of the Congress; this effort failed, amid scenes of wild disorder, and for several years thereafter the control of the Congress remained in the hands of the moderates.

This was a low period in the nationalist movement as a whole. The extremists were accused of complicity in various acts of violence, and their chief leaders were removed or retired from active political

[16] See M. A. Buch, *Rise and Growth of Indian Militant Nationalism* (Baroda, 1940); D. V. Tahmankar, *Lokamanya Tilak* (London, 1956); *Sources of Indian Tradition,* pp. 717–724.

life. In 1908 Tilak was tried and sentenced to six years of confinement in Mandalay. Lala Lajpat Rai was deported from the Punjab. Aurobindo Ghose was imprisoned briefly for alleged complicity in the terrorism that was flaring up in Bengal, and after his release he was a changed man. In 1910 he abandoned Bengal and his wife, and retired to the French possession of Pondicherry, where he spent the remaining forty years of his life.

A very different Bengali voice — that of Rabindranath Tagore — was heard in protest against the wave of violence in Bengal. In disgust at the terrorism in his native province Tagore virtually withdrew from political activity. He continued to write stirring poems and other works which made him at once one of the greatest apostles of Indian nationalism and one of the greatest critics of modern nationalism. Later, in the Gandhian era, he again played a more direct role in the nationalist movement.

The position of the extremists, greatly weakened by the arrest or retirement of their chief leaders, was made more difficult by British concessions, including the Morley-Minto reforms and the abolition of the partition of Bengal in 1911. However, for some five years after the return of Tilak from Burma in 1914 the extremists were in the ascendancy, although even Tilak seemed to be more moderate than in former days. From the time of his return, and particularly from 1915, when he became more active again and when his great rival, Gokhale, died, until his death in 1920 he was the unquestioned leader of the nationalist movement.

During the years of the First World War the movement gained strength and cohesion. The 1915 session of the Congress passed a compromise resolution which paved the way for Tilak and his followers to re-enter the national organization. At the 1916 session in Lucknow the reunion of moderates and extremists was consolidated. Another important development at the Lucknow Congress was the endorsement of the so-called "Lucknow Pact," for cooperation between the Congress and the Muslim League.

As Tilak had observed many years before, "the Extremists of today will be Moderates tomorrow." Moderates, extremists, and Muslims could unite on the demand for a large measure of self-government after the war. The extremists, to be sure, also developed other organizations, notably the Home Rule Leagues, in which Tilak and Mrs. Annie Besant were particularly active. A campaign of *swadeshi*[17]

[17] Swadeshi: a Hindi word derived from Sanskrit, meaning "home-made." Refers to the "buy home goods movement," a kind of economic boycott which the Indian National Congress used effectively in its resistance to British rule, especially in the Gandhian era.

and of national education was also launched. Some of the liberals in the Congress, feeling unhappy with the more radical trend in the main nationalist party, seceded and formed the Liberal Federation. Within the Congress Tilak formed a Congress Democratic Party to agitate for self-government through a policy of "responsive cooperation."

The British Government made sweeping concessions to Indian demands in the Montagu-Chelmsford Reforms of 1918 and the Government of India Act of 1919. The National Congress in 1919 passed a resolution labeling these reforms as "inadequate, unsatisfactory and disappointing," and urging the British Parliament to "take early steps to establish full Responsible Government in India in accordance with the principles of self-determination." However, the resolution also declared that "Pending such introduction, the Congress trusts that, so far as may be possible, the people will so work the Reforms as to secure an early establishment of full Responsible Government."

Dissatisfaction with the "inadequate, unsatisfactory, and disappointing" British concessions was deepened by tensions arising from various repressive acts and policies of the British authorities. Among these were the notorious Rowlatt Acts, the arrest of Mrs. Besant and other Congress leaders (Mrs. Besant was elected President of the Congress in 1917, while she was still interned), the shooting of several hundred Indians in Amritsar in April, 1919, on the orders of the British General, Dyer (the Jallianwala Bagh massacre), and the alleged failure of the British to redeem their wartime pledges to India. Moreover, the nationalist movement soon was given greater depth and a new direction under its greatest leader, Mahatma Gandhi.

4. The Gandhian Era. In 1915 Mohandas Karamchand Gandhi returned to India after twenty years in South Africa. In South Africa, where he had gone upon completing several years of study in England (where he was admitted to the bar), he developed ideas and a philosophy of action which represented his own individualistic blend of Western and Indian ideas and practices. Notable among these were his concepts of *satyagraha,* which he often translated loosely as "soul-force," his emphasis on the doctrine of *ahimsa,* or nonviolence, and his theories of the relation of ends and means. For some months after his return to India he traveled about the country and observed conditions at first hand. Then he began to take an active part in the independence movement, through the Congress and the Home Rule Leagues, and through limited experiments in the technique with which his name is forever associated — that of nonviolent noncooperation.

After the death of Tilak in 1920 Gandhi became the unquestioned leader of the nationalist movement, although some other nationalist leaders, Hindu as well as Muslim, did not approve of his methods and although he sometimes openly disagreed with Congress policies. But whether his advice was followed at a given time or not, and whether he was in the forefront of the nationalist struggle or in prison or in "retirement," he gave the struggle the imprint of his powerful personality. Gandhi had the courage of his convictions, and he won a following among the masses of the people that is unparalleled in the long course of Indian history. He gave a new direction and a new purpose to the nationalist struggle. It is impossible to exaggerate his contributions, not only to the nationalist cause but to the rebirth of modern India in far more than a political sense.

The Congress might have lost much of its momentum if it had not come under the influence of a man who was big enough to bring the different factions together and to give the movement a mass base, a new technique of political action, and a deeper meaning. Gandhi taught that *swaraj* should be the goal, and *satyagraha* the means, but first the people of India should understand the means and be worthy of the goal. "The English have not taken India," Gandhi declared; "we have given it to them. . . . It is Swaraj when we learn to rule ourselves." Again he wrote: "Our noncooperation is a retirement within ourselves. . . . In order to be fit to save others, we must try to save ourselves. Indian nationalism is not exclusive, nor aggressive, nor destructive. It is health-giving, religious, and therefore humanitarian."[18]

The fourth phase of Indian nationalism, from 1919–1920 to 1934–1935, witnessed three major campaigns of nonviolent noncooperation along the lines recommended by Gandhi. It also saw the end of the loose alliance between the Congress and the Muslim League, after the Khilafat issue (see page 239) had ceased to have much significance, considerable dissatisfaction within the Congress with some of Gandhi's techniques, and efforts by the British Government to find another formula for making further concessions to India in the light of growing nationalist pressures and the unsatisfactory working of the experiment in dyarchy under the Government of India Act of 1919.

Shortly after his return from South Africa, Gandhi gave an effective demonstration of his technique of civil disobedience. When he was ordered to leave a district in Bihar where he was investigating the conditions of workers on indigo plantations, he refused to obey the

[18] Quoted in *Sources of Indian Tradition,* pp. 809, 822. The first statement is from Gandhi's *Hind Swaraj,* written in 1909, the second from a reply to Tagore which originally appeared in Gandhi's weekly magazine, *Young India.*

order, was arrested, and pleaded guilty at his trial. So great was the outcry over his arrest that he was released without punishment. In 1919, when the British imposed restrictions upon civil liberties, Gandhi asked the people of India to join in a campaign of nonviolent non-cooperation. This advice was endorsed by the Indian National Congress in the following year, and was launched in 1921. For a time the campaign seemed to go well, even though thousands of Indians were imprisoned for their nonviolent resistance; but when some Congress followers resorted to violence, Gandhi called off the whole campaign, saying that he had made a "Himalayan miscalculation" in believing that the people of India were ready for this new form of resistance. Many of the Congressmen who had been imprisoned as a result of the campaign, including the young Jawaharlal Nehru, disapproved of Gandhi's action, but it was endorsed by the Working Committee of the Congress. In March, 1922, shortly after the civil disobedience campaign had been suspended, Gandhi was arrested on charges of sedition, and sentenced to six years' imprisonment. He was released two years later.

With Gandhi in prison the nationalist struggle lost much of its focus. Even after his release in 1924 the controversies inside the Congress continued. Communal tensions became more serious, and socialist and Communist groups and several working class organizations arose outside of the Congress. A number of prominent Congress leaders, including C. R. Das, Motilal Nehru (the father of Jawaharlal Nehru), and Vithalbhai Patel, formed a Swaraj Party to press for the immediate achievement of Dominion status for India. This party was for a time given charge of much of the political work of the Congress. Under its influence the historic Madras session of the Congress in 1927, for the first time, and over Gandhi's objections, passed a resolution declaring that independence was the goal of the Congress. In 1928 a committee of the Congress, headed by Motilal Nehru, outlined a scheme of constitutional government. This report was not approved by Gandhi; for different reasons it was attacked from other sources, including the Muslims, who objected to its stand against separate electorates and who claimed that it was a Hindu document, and a group of younger men within the Congress, including Motilal's son, Jawaharlal, and Subhas Chandra Bose, who demanded immediate independence as a goal. The Congress session in Lahore in 1930 adopted a resolution defining *swaraj* as complete independence, and adopting January 26th as "Independence Day." It is no mere coincidence that the Constitution of the Republic of India became effective twenty years later on the same day, which is celebrated each year in independent India as "Republic Day."

Gandhi's salt march in 1930 ushered in the second mass campaign of civil disobedience and demonstrated the driving power of his techniques of peaceful noncooperation. The Mahatma selected the simple act of making salt from the sea, in defiance of British laws, because the salt tax affected almost every Indian villager. "As the independence movement is essentially for the poorest in the land," he explained, "the beginning will be made with this evil." As a result of his decision salt, as Nehru said, "suddenly became a mysterious word, a word of power." On April 6, 1930, after a 24-day march of 240 miles from Ahmedabad to Dandi, Gandhi defied the British by taking a small amount of salt from the sea. At first he was not arrested, although thousands of his fellow-*satyagrahis* were; but in early May, after he had notified the Viceroy that he intended to lead a raid on a government salt depot, he too was taken into custody. Even though nearly 100,000 Indians were imprisoned, the civil disobedience campaign went on. Thousands of humble people engaged in passive resistance activities, and they kept their discipline in spite of *lathi*[19] charges of the police and other forceful measures against them.

In January, 1931, Gandhi and the members of the Working Committee of the Congress were released, and two months later Gandhi reached an agreement with the Viceroy, Lord Irwin, which led to the suspension of the noncooperation campaign and to Gandhi's participation in the Second Round Table Conference in London in late 1931 as the sole representative of the Congress. From his point of view the conference was a complete failure. Upon his return to India he found that many Congress leaders were back in jail. In January, 1933, he was again arrested. Shortly thereafter he began a "fast unto death" against a British decision to grant separate electorates for untouchables. The fast ended a week later when the British Government reversed its decision.

With this dramatic demonstration of the power of *satyagraha* a third mass movement of civil disobedience gained momentum. By April, 1933, 120,000 Indians were in jail. In May Gandhi embarked on another fast, which soon led to his release. A short time later he suspended the noncooperation campaign. This action was criticized by many leaders of the Congress, some of whom were becoming dissatisfied with the methods which Gandhi was using in shaping the nationalist movement. Subhas Chandra Bose and Vithalbhai Patel, who were in Europe at the time, declared in a joint statement: "We are clearly of the opinion that Mr. Gandhi as a political leader has failed. The time has come for a radical reorganization of the Congress of a new principle, with a new method, for which a new leader is

[19] A lathi is a wooden stave, six to eight feet long, shod with metal, used by the police in India, especially in British days.

essential." Gandhi resigned his membership in the Congress because of the growing criticisms of his leadership.

5. The Achievement of Independence. Thus the fourth period in the history of Indian nationalism ended with the Congress Party at a rather low ebb, after spectacular victories in the nonviolent noncooperation campaigns, with the British Government capping real concessions to Indian demands with the Government of India Act of 1935. But by this time the nationalist movement, thanks largely to Gandhi, had won mass support. It had even stimulated some political consciousness in the Indian States. It was no longer directed toward an increasing measure of self-government within the British Empire. The goal now was complete independence.

Since the early 1920's, and especially after the return of Jinnah from several years' residence in England in 1934, Muslim nationalism had been developing apart from the main nationalist movement. Most politically conscious Muslims had tended to accept the view of Sir Syed Ahmad Khan, that the Muslims of India should remain aloof from the Congress and should look to their own interests. The formation of the Muslim League in 1906 and the granting of separate electorates in the Morley-Minto reforms of 1909 tended to emphasize the political as well as the social and religious distinctiveness of the Indian Muslims. In Mohammad Ali Jinnah they found an able leader.

Gradually the idea developed that wherever possible the Muslims should have a separate political status, within or without the British Empire. Much of the credit for this idea goes to the great Muslim poet-philosopher of the subcontinent, Muhammad Iqbal. In his presidential address at the 1930 session of the Muslim League Iqbal said: "I would like to see the Punjab, North-West Frontier Province, Sind and Baluchistan, amalgamated into a single state. Self-government within the British Empire or without the British Empire, the formation of a consolidated North-West Indian Muslim State appears to me to be the final destiny of the Muslims at least of North-West India." Iqbal made no suggestions for the parts of Bengal which contained a Muslim majority.

The establishment of Congress governments in most of the provinces in 1937 was only one of the developments of the late 1930's which strengthened the Muslim League and which led it to demand a separate Muslim state. The League Congress in Lahore in 1940 passed an historic resolution, placing the League on record for the first time in favor of a separate state of Pakistan. Even then the boundaries of the proposed new state remained to be defined.

During World War II the League profited from the favors bestowed upon it by the British, because its position regarding the war was, from the British viewpoint, far more sympathetic and cooperative than was that of the Congress, which opposed the war effort. While the leading Congressmen spent most of the war years in jail, the leaders of the Muslim League were able to pursue their ends with little competition. After the war the League was in a relatively impregnable position, so that Pakistan became in fact the price of independence.

The leaders of the Congress and the Muslim League differed fundamentally regarding the nature of Indian society and the kind of political system which should be established with the withdrawal of the British. The Congress was dedicated to what later came to be called the idea of the secular state, whereas the spokesmen of the League, faithful to the principles of Islam, argued that religion and politics could not be separated. They also charged that the Congress was a Hindu organization in which the Muslims would never be given a fair voice. In 1937 Jinnah declared, with reference to the failure of the Congress to associate Muslims with their provincial ministries: "On the very threshold of what little power and responsibility is given, the majority community have clearly shown their hand that Hindustan is for the Hindus." Jinnah became an advocate of a theory that had been held by other prominent Muslims before him, namely that the Muslims of India were not just a minority group but were in fact a separate "nation." In his presidential address at the Lahore session of the Muslim League in 1940, which adopted the Pakistan resolution, Jinnah asserted: "Mussalmans are a nation according to any definition of a nation and they must have their homeland, their territory and their state." This "two-nations" theory was anathema to the leaders of the Congress, and above all to Mahatma Gandhi, who once wrote: "The 'two-nations' theory is an untruth . . . Hindus and Muslims of India are not two nations. . . . My whole soul rebels against the idea that Hinduism and Islam represent two antagonistic cultures and doctrines."

By the time the Muslim League had come out flatly for Pakistan the Congress was locked in a basic struggle with the British Government over the issue of India's proper role during World War II. When, upon the outbreak of the war in Europe in September, 1939, the British Government declared that India too was at war with the Axis powers, the Congress strongly protested. At this time it was again under the strong influence of Mahatma Gandhi. In 1939 Subhas Chandra Bose had been elected President of the Congress over a candidate supported by Gandhi; but most of the members of the Working Committee resigned after this election, and Bose, unable to reach an agreement with Gandhi, resigned the presidency. Subsequently he formed the Forward Bloc within the Congress, but soon he left India, to reappear in Nazi Germany and later in Japan and Southeast Asia, where he became identified with the puppet Indian government established with the support of the Japanese, and with the Indian National Army.

The Congress protest against involvement in World War II was contrary to the advice of Nehru and other Congress leaders, but it was a reflection of Gandhi's whole approach. Gandhi argued that India could cooperate with the British in a fight for freedom only if it were granted freedom immediately. Otherwise it must withhold its support. This position of the Congress greatly hampered the British and Allied operations in the Asian theater, and led to increasingly strained relations between the British authorities and the Congress. The impasse became complete with the passage of the "Quit India" resolution in 1942. Most of the Congress leaders spent the rest of the months of the war in prison. Gandhi himself was released in 1944 because of ill health, but Nehru and most of the Congress leaders were kept in confinement until a few weeks before V–E Day.

Independence came to India shortly after World War II. The main questions in the immediate postwar period were the time of the granting of independence and the circumstances under which it should be granted. The nationalist leaders had to prepare themselves to face the responsibilities of freedom, rather than to continue to fight the British. In 1947 the only alternatives seemed to be partition or continuance of British rule. Two independent nations came into existence on the Indian subcontinent, which had never achieved real unity during the entire course of its long history, and which had come closest to this unity under foreign rule.

The winning of independence came about as a result of many developments, in India and elsewhere. Certainly the nationalist movement in India placed increasing pressure upon the British. "The eventual achievement of Indian independence in 1947 was the outcome of a combination of circumstances — probably the most important being the weakening effect of two world wars on Britain's power and prestige in Asia — but the presence of a disciplined political organization under a revered leader greatly facilitated the transfer of power."[20] Power was transferred to two nations instead of one, because the Muslims of India chose not to identify themselves with the main nationalist movement. After 1947 the basic problems facing both new nations were the consolidation of independence, making that independence meaningful, learning how to co-exist with each other, and how to exist in the world of the mid-twentieth century.

[20] *Sources of Indian Tradition,* p. 802.

5

The Nature of the Indian State: The Basic Decisions

India paid a heavy price for independence. In the final stages the hopes for freedom were jeopardized not by the opposition of the British but by the widening gulf between the Indian National Congress and the Muslim League. Because of this communal rift two new nations emerged, not one, and unhappily from the beginning of their independent existence these new nations were at odds with each other.

Even today, at least in India, many of those who were involved in the freedom struggle look back on the months prior to independence and wonder whether partition could have been avoided, or what the consequences would have been in the long run if they had refused to pay this price for independence. In a much-discussed book, published posthumously, the most famous of all the Muslims who cast their lot with India, Maulana Abul Kamal Azad, wrote: "If we had remained steadfast and refused to accept partition, I am confident that a safer and more glorious future would have awaited us."[1] This would almost certainly have delayed India's independence indefinitely, but apparently the Maulana, at least in retrospect, would have regarded the postponement with equanimity. Lord Wavell, the Governor-General prior to Lord Mountbatten, had in fact recommended that the British should not set a date for their withdrawal, and when the new Labor Prime

[1] Maulana Abul Kamal Azad, *India Wins Freedom* (Calcutta, 1959), p. 226.

Minister, Clement Attlee, did not agree, Lord Wavell resigned. "Looking at the events after ten years," mused Maulana Azad, "I sometimes wonder who was right. . . . Perhaps history will decide that the wiser policy would have been to follow Lord Wavell's advice."[2] Instead, in February, 1947, the British Government announced a definite date for independence, and then in June, on Lord Mountbatten's advice, moved the date up to August 15th of that same year. By this time most of the leaders of the Congress had accepted the inevitability of partition, although their hearts were heavy.

Thus the demand for a separate Pakistan, which the Muslim League had first officially made in 1940, was granted. In view of the separate paths and ways of life of Hindus and Muslims over the centuries, and especially in view of the events of the decade prior to independence, including the increasing hold of the Muslim League on the Muslims of the subcontinent and the growing feeling of most Muslims that they would fare badly in a Hindu-dominated state, there was probably, in the last days, no choice other than partition. Even if the British had stayed on for a longer time, it is doubtful that the Muslim League could have been reconciled to a single Indian state, and other problems would have arisen as well.

V. P. Menon has summarized clearly the major considerations which led most of the leaders of the Congress to acquiesce in partition:

> The Congress had accepted the division of the country on two considerations. In the first place, it was clear from the unyielding attitude of the Muslim League that a united India would either be delayed or could only be won at the cost of a civil war. Secondly, it was hoped that the establishment of a separate Muslim state would finally settle the communal problem which had for so long bedevilled Indian politics and thwarted all progressive aspirations, that India and Pakistan would thereafter live in peaceful relations with each other, and that all men of goodwill on either side would be free to concentrate on improving the economic conditions of the common people.[3]

The Aftermath of Partition

The aftermath of partition was also bitter. Instead of averting a communal struggle, the division of the subcontinent occasioned one of the major internal disasters of modern times. Hundreds of thousands of people on both sides of the new frontiers, especially in the divided Punjab, were massacred. The rejoicing over independence soon gave way to horror over the murders, riotings, and innumerable lesser acts

[2] *Ibid.*, pp. 177–178.

[3] V. P. Menon, *The Transfer of Power in India* (Princeton, N.J., 1957), p. 440.

of violence, accompanied by a mass uprooting of people who, abandoning most of their worldly possessions, moved from one side of the frontier to the other, under hazardous and trying conditions, often involving loss of life and harassments of all kinds. By June, 1948, some five and a half million Hindus and Sikhs had crossed from West Pakistan into India, and about an equal number of Muslims had moved the other way. This mass movement of people created a major refugee problem, which has never been fully resolved, especially since the movement of refugees has continued in both directions ever since, although on a lesser scale.

Lord Mountbatten and nearly all responsible leaders of the National Congress and the Muslim League were confident that the dislocation which would inevitably accompany partition could be kept under control and that there would be no major acts of violence or undue suffering.[4] They could not have been more wrong. Even today memories of the horrors of the weeks following partition are etched into the hearts of those who lived through those trying times. Indians certainly did not foresee such a tragedy. At a press conference in February, 1959, Nehru said: "When we decided on partition I do not think any of us ever thought that there would be this terror of mutual killing after partition. It was in a sense to avoid that we decided on partition. So we paid a double price for it, first, you might say politically, ideologically; second, the actual thing happened that we tried to avoid."

After a few weeks the worst excesses were over, and the new Government of India began to bring the situation under control. Thus at the very outset it faced and overcame a major crisis. As V. P. Menon has recalled:

> The communal holocaust, the two-way exodus of refugees, their protection and the rehabilitation of those who had come to India — all these provided the Government of India, at a time when the administrative machinery was already out of joint as a result of partition, with a task which was as stupendous as any nation ever had to face. If in its initial stages the situation had not been controlled with vigour, the consequences would have brought down the Government itself.[5]

[4] As V. P. Menon wrote, many years later: "It is true that the situation was full of fear and foreboding; but we had not expected to be so quickly and so thoroughly disillusioned." Menon, *The Transfer of Power in India,* pp. 417–418. Maulana Azad records that on May 14, 1947 Lord Mountbatten told Gandhi: "At least on this one question I shall give you complete assurance. I shall see to it that there is no bloodshed and riot." *India Wins Freedom,* p. 190.

[5] Menon, *The Transfer of Power in India,* p. 434.

Many other developments in the early weeks of independence cast a pall over the new state. Among these two may be singled out for special mention. In October, 1947, tribal raiders moved into Kashmir, and Indian troops were airlifted to Srinagar to drive them back, after the hasty last-minute accession of the Hindu Maharaja of Kashmir to India. In 1948 India and Pakistan nearly came to the brink of war over Kashmir. Although a cease-fire was agreed upon, on January 1, 1949, through the good offices of the United Nations, the Kashmir question has been the major issue in dispute between India and Pakistan ever since.

The second event seemed even more portentous. On January 30, 1948, while he was conducting a prayer meeting on the lawn of the Birla Mansion in New Delhi, Mahatma Gandhi, then 78 years of age, was killed by three bullets fired at close range by a member of the Rashtriya Swayamsevak Sangh (RSS) from Maharashtra, who violently objected to the Mahatma's policy of Hindu-Muslim unity and brotherhood. Thus Gandhi was a victim of the very communal forces which he had fought for so long. It was in a grim way fortunate that his assassin was a communalist Hindu and not a Muslim; for if he had been killed by a Muslim, India might have witnessed another blood bath far greater in horror than that which had darkened the early days of independence. The assassination of "the Father of the Nation" so soon after the nation had been born raised grave doubts about India's future, and plunged the people of India into the darkest despair, mingled with pride in the little man who had been the greatest among them and with determination to remain true to his teachings. Nehru voiced the feelings of his fellow-countrymen when he spoke, in broken tones, over All-India Radio shortly after Gandhi's death:

> Friends and comrades, the light has gone out of our lives and there is darkness everywhere. . . . Our beloved leader, Bapu as we called him, the Father of the Nation, is no more. Perhaps I am wrong to say that. . . . For the light that shone in this country was no ordinary light. The light that has illumined this country for these many many years will illumine this country for many more years, and a thousand years later, that light will still be seen in this country and the world will see it and it will give solace to innumerable hearts.

In a sense, Gandhi had done his work, although its full fruits will not be manifest until and unless many radical changes occur in Indian life and thought. In his last months, he was increasingly disturbed by the many signs that his teachings were being neglected or even ignored. He was distressed by the orgy of communal fury, which ran counter to everything he had fought for, and by all too many evidences that those who were in charge of the destinies of the new nation, mostly his own disciples, were making compromises and following policies of which he could not wholly approve. Gandhi is still one of the most living forces in India today, but one may question the extent to which modern India, in its political, economic, social, or spiritual life, is being true to his high principles and example.

The Integration of the Indian States

When Gandhi passed from the Indian scene, the leaders of the new Government were engrossed in the many tasks of consolidating independence, as well as in problems immediately created by partition, such as the rehabilitation of refugees. Foremost among these were the integration of the Indian States and the work of constitution-making.

The Indian Independence Act of 1947 did not propose a solution for the problem of the Indian States, but it did terminate the paramountcy or suzerainty of the crown over these political units. Legally the States thereupon became independent. But it was obviously absurd to think of the subcontinent divided into two large new independent nations carved out of British India, with one of these nations divided by some thousand miles of the territory, and peppered with scores of other "independent states," ranging in size from Hyderabad and Jammu and Kashmir to a few score areas.

The position of the British Government and of the Indian National Congress on this issue was clear enough. In his speech on the Indian Independence Bill in the House of Commons the British Prime Minister, Mr. Attlee, said: "It is the hope of His Majesty's Government that all the States will in due course find their appropriate place with one or the other Dominion within the British Commonwealth." On July 15, 1947 the All-India Congress Committee categorically rejected the claims of some of the States to independence and the theory of paramountcy. Speaking at this meeting of the A.I.C.C. Nehru declared that the States had only two alternatives: they could join the Indian Union either individually or in groups. "There is no third way out of the situation — third way meaning independence or special relation to a foreign power."

Immediately after the plan to partition the subcontinent and to grant independence on August 15, 1947, was announced by the British Government, the Interim Government decided to set up a States Ministry to handle the problem of the integration of the Indian States. Sardar Vallabhbhai Patel was placed in charge of the States Ministry, and in the next two years or so this determined and influential man, who also served as Deputy Prime Minister until his death in 1951, by a combination of cajolery and firmness not only secured the accession of most of the Indian States to the Union of India but also merged and integrated many of these States and laid the foundations for their full integration into the new Indian nation. "The work accomplished by him at the States' Ministry amounts to a silent revolution. The accession of the States to the Indian Union was secured by peaceful negotiations before August 15, 1947, and in a little over two years after independence the political geography of India was rationalised by the *merger or the consolidation and integration* of the States. . . . India was unified as never before in her history. . . . Sardar Patel may be truly described as the architect of Indian unity."[6] His top lieutenant at the States Ministry, V. P. Menon, many years later wrote a detailed account of *The Story of the Integration of the Indian States,* a book which depicts something of the magnitude, the difficulties, and the brilliant diplomacy of Sardar Patel's great work.[7]

Patel's first act as States Minister was to appeal to all the princely rulers of Indian States in territories contiguous to the India-Union-to-be to accede to the Union in three subjects, foreign relations, defense, and communications. Lord Mountbatten, in an address to the Chamber of Princes on July 25, 1947, made the same appeal. In a remarkable display of cooperation, whatever their misgivings, the Indian Princes responded to these appeals. By August 15, 1947, all but three of the Indian States whose territories were geographically contiguous to the new State of India had acceded to the Indian Union. The three exceptions were significant, particularly since they imposed further strains on the already unhappy relations with Pakistan.

The Muslim ruler of Junagadh, a small state in Kathiawar, near the southeastern frontier of West Pakistan, acceded to Pakistan, and Pakistan accepted the accession, even though the population of the State was predominantly Hindu. Encouraged, no doubt, by outside forces, the people of the State forced the ruler to flee, and in November, 1947, the Muslim Diwan was compelled to invite the Government of India to intervene. Junagadh became a part of the Indian Union after a plebiscite in February, 1948 showed that this was the wish of the overwhelming majority of its people.

Hyderabad, the largest of the Indian States, with a Muslim ruler and a Hindu majority, and entirely surrounded by Indian territory, pre-

[6] N. Srinivasan, *Democratic Government in India* (Calcutta, 1954), p. 108.

[7] V. P. Menon, *The Story of the Integration of the Indian States* (New York, 1956). See also Government of India, Ministry of States, *White Paper on Indian States* (Delhi, 1950).

sented an even more difficult problem. Apparently the Nizam of Hyderabad, one of the world's richest men, desired to maintain an independent status. In November, 1947, he signed a stand-still agreement with the Government of India, but prolonged negotiations failed to persuade him to accede to India. In the meantime disorders broke out inside the State, encouraged by Communists and by a militant Muslim organization known as the Razackers, and raiders from Hyderabad made incursions into Indian territory. In September, 1948, Indian troops were ordered into Hyderabad, and after three days of spasmodic fighting the Nizam capitulated. In November, 1948, he agreed to accede to the Indian Union.

The Maharaja of Kashmir, a Hindu who ruled despotically over a Muslim majority, refused to accede either to Pakistan or to India prior to August 15, 1947, contrary to the advice of Lord Mountbatten. On October 26th he did accede to India, but only because tribal invaders, encouraged by Pakistan, had pushed to within a few miles of Srinagar, the capital of the State, and because the Government of India, to which he appealed for aid, refused, on Lord Mountbatten's advice, to send help unless he acceded to India. The next day the Governor-General of India, Lord Mountbatten, announced that "as soon as law and order have been restored in Kashmir and her soil cleared of the invader, the question of the accession should be settled by a reference to the people." This referendum has never been held, much to Pakistan's chagrin. India and Pakistan nearly became involved in a war over Kashmir in 1948. Since January 1, 1949, a cease-fire has prevailed, and the State has been in fact divided along the cease-fire line. Repeated efforts by representatives of the United Nations and by the U.N. Security Council to work out a plan for the steps leading to a plebiscite which would be acceptable to both India and Pakistan have failed. India now regards the accession of Kashmir as final and irrevocable, and the State is one of the fifteen constituent units of the Indian Republic. Pakistan, of course, has refused to accept this claim, and it still insists that the future of all of Jammu and Kashmir should be determined by a vote of the people.

The peaceful accession of all of the Indian States in the territories embraced in the Indian Union, except Junagadh, Hyderabad, and Kashmir, even before independence, averted what could easily have been a major political crisis. After accession came the equally difficult problem of integration, democratization, and modernization of political units which, save for a few enlightened States such as Mysore, were notoriously backward and even feudal. This task was largely accomplished within two years after independence, again thanks to Sardar Patel and his associates in the States Ministry.

Out of former British India and the India of the princely States a new map of India emerged. Only three Indian States, Hyderabad, Jammu and Kashmir, and Mysore, retained their original form. These large States, plus 275 smaller States which were merged into five State Unions, became the eight Part B States (see page 138) of the Indian Union. Two hundred and sixteen States were merged with the Part A States. Sixty-one others were merged with Part C States. After the reorganization of the States in November, 1956, Hyderabad passed out of existence as a separate unit, and only Mysore and Jammu and Kashmir remained. The boundaries of Mysore were substantially changed, and, of course, a large part of Jammu and Kashmir remained on the Pakistan side of the cease-fire line.

Basic Objectives and Decisions

What was to be the nature of the new Indian state? To what extent would it incorporate some of the ideas and institutions of the ancient past, and to what extent would it be patterned after British and Western models? To what extent would it embody Gandhian ideas and ideals? What type of government would be created? Would it be a democratic state? If so, what form of democracy would be adopted? What would be its orientation in foreign policy? What would be its ideology? These and other questions, basic to the very nature of the state, were answered either before independence or within a short time thereafter. Although they raised fundamental problems of government, most of them were resolved quickly, almost by default, with very little opposition and with very little support for any other alternatives. This is a remarkable fact, reflecting no lack of attention to fundamentals but instead a widespread agreement regarding them. Out of the varied experience of the past came a kind of political consensus which was most impressive, and rather unexpected.

The basic aims and objectives of the new state had been clearly and positively stated many times prior to independence, and they have been reaffirmed on countless occasions since 1947. Jawaharlal Nehru, one of the most eloquent and most loquacious of world leaders, with a great capacity to voice the sentiments of his people and to enunciate basic principles, has often spoken in terms of fundamentals. Two of the most significant statements of aims and objectives were the so-called Objectives Resolution, approved by the Constituent Assembly on January 22, 1947, and the Preamble to the Constitution of 1950.

At the first meeting of the Constituent Assembly, on December 9, 1946, Nehru, then head of the Interim Government, moved the Objectives Resolution, one of the politically significant documents in the history of the independence movement in India. It was especially significant because of the time, the mover, and the contents. Introduced in the very first session of the Constituent Assembly, the nucleus of the Parliament-to-be, it seemed to symbolize the successful conclusion of the struggle for freedom from British rule and the beginning of an independent existence, when the leaders and people of India had to reassess and reaffirm their basic aims and principles and consider seriously the practical problems of government. The fact that it was moved by Nehru, the political spokesman of the New India, was also of great practical and symbolic significance. The nature of the document made it appear to be what it was obviously intended to be, namely a statement of the bases on which the new Indian state would be established. It contained these declarations:

> This Constituent Assembly declares its firm and solemn resolve to proclaim India as an Independent Sovereign Republic and to draw up for her future governance a Constitution,
>
> Wherein all power and authority of the Sovereign Independent India, its constituent parts and organs of government are derived from the people;
>
> Wherein shall be guaranteed and secured to all the people of India justice, social, economic, and political; equality of status, of opportunity, and before the law; freedom of thought, expression, belief, faith, worship, vocation, association, and action, subject to law and public morality; and
>
> Wherein adequate safeguards shall be provided for minorities, backward and tribal areas, and depressed and other backward classes, and
>
> Whereby this ancient land attain its rightful and honoured place in the world and make its full and willing contribution to the promotion of world peace and the welfare of mankind.

The Preamble to the Indian Constitution of 1950 is obviously patterned along the lines of the Objectives Resolution of 1947:

> WE, THE PEOPLE OF INDIA, having solemnly resolved to constitute India into a SOVEREIGN, DEMOCRATIC REPUBLIC and to secure to all its citizens:
>
> JUSTICE, social, economic and political;
>
> LIBERTY of thought, expression, belief, faith, and worship;
>
> EQUALITY of status and of opportunity; and to promote among them all
>
> FRATERNITY assuring the dignity of the individual and the unity of the Nation;
>
> IN OUR CONSTITUENT ASSEMBLY . . . DO HEREBY ADOPT, ENACT AND GIVE TO OURSELVES THIS CONSTITUTION.

Seven of the basic decisions regarding the nature of the new state which were made with due consideration but without significant opposition were: (1) India should be a parliamentary democracy; (2) it should be a federal state; (3) it should be a republic; (4) it should have a written constitution; (5) it should be a member of the Commonwealth; (6) it should be a secular state; and (7) it should be a welfare state.

Parliamentary Democracy in India

As the time of independence approached there was no doubt that the new Indian state would be a democracy, in form if not in spirit. Most of the leaders of India, for more than a century, had been steeped in the principles of nineteenth-century liberal democracy and of twentieth-century socialist democracy. To a certain extent some of these leaders — such as Subhas Chandra Bose and even Gandhi himself — looked elsewhere for the principles on which the future Indian state should be founded, but they could not fashion alternative principles which gained widespread acceptance or even understanding. Undoubtedly, too, Indian leaders were conditioned to favor parliamentary democracy because of their close associations with the British, who over the centuries had evolved the most successful example of this form of democracy.

From the British, educated Indians learned the principles of parliamentary democracy, even though in India British seldom practiced this or any other form of democracy. In fact, almost to the last, prominent Englishmen denied that they considered a parliamentary system either suited to or desirable for India. This was, however, not the prevailing opinion. As the date for independence approached, it was generally assumed, by both Indians and Englishmen, that India would adopt the parliamentary system, and this decision was, in a sense, made long before British and Indian spokesmen turned to the task of drafting the outlines of the new state. Since then its wisdom has seldom been seriously questioned. This is all the more remarkable since the suitability of parliamentary democracy for Asian countries is being questioned in many quarters, by Asian leaders and by foreign students of government alike, and since India's two largest neighbors — Burma temporarily and Pakistan for what seems to be a permanent abandonment — deliberately turned away from parliamentary democracy and announced that it is unsuited to their needs and aspirations.

While parliamentary democracy has been under attack in many quarters, and has broken down in several Asian countries, the leaders of India have repeatedly reaffirmed their dedication to it. Speaking in the Lok Sabha on March 28, 1957, Prime Minister Nehru said:

We chose this system of parliamentary democracy deliberately; we chose it not only because to some extent, we had always thought on those lines previously, but because we thought it was in keeping with our own old traditions, not the old traditions as they were, but adjusted to the new conditions and new surroundings. We chose it — let us give credit where credit is due — because we approved of its functioning in other countries, more especially in the United Kingdom.

Federalism in India

For understandable reasons there is a tremendous interest in the subject of federalism among students and practitioners of the art of government in India. A large new state such as India, faced with the problem of establishing a central authority strong enough to govern a vast area inhabited by millions of people with different historical and linguistic background and interests, almost inevitably has to establish some form of federal structure. The Republic of India is a federation, although it has many distinctive features which seem to modify the essentially federal nature of the state.

Some students of government, Indian and foreign, describe India as a quasi-federal state, and some even regard it as more unitary than federal. G. N. Joshi, a leading authority on the Indian Constitution, holds that "the Union is not strictly a federal polity but a quasi-federal polity with some vital and important elements of unitariness. . . . It is designed to work as a federal government in normal times, but as a unitary government in times of emergency."[8] "It must be remembered," states Professor Suda, "that though India is a federation, her constitution departs from the ideal of a true federation in several vital and significant ways. She is not a genuine federation, but a quasi-federation having several features of a unitary state."[9] Professor Kenneth Wheare, a well-known British authority on federalism, classified India as "a unitary state with subsidiary federal principles rather than a federal state with subsidiary unitary principles."[10] However, as Professor Charles Alexandrowicz, Research Professor of Law at Madras University, points out, the application of such "a rigid definition of the federal principle to various types of existing federations may deprive it of any practical meaning."[11] He argues that India is a true federa-

[8] G. N. Joshi, *The Constitution of India* (3rd edition, London, 1954), p. 32.

[9] J. P. Suda, *Indian Constitutional Development and National Movement* (Meerut, 1951), p. 523.

[10] "India's New Constitution Analyzed," *A.L.J.*, XLVIII, 21; quoted in Alan Gledhill, *The Republic of India* (London, 1951), p. 92.

[11] C. H. Alexandrowicz, "Is India a Federation?", *The International and Comparative Law Quarterly*, III (July, 1954), 402.

tion — although, like all other federations, it has distinctive characteristics — and that it is misleading even to refer to India as a quasi-federation. It is difficult to determine to what extent these differences are merely semantic ones and to what extent they are based on fundamentally different interpretations of the nature of the Indian state.

In any federation the key questions center around the relative roles and powers of the central government and the constituent units. Centralizing tendencies are manifest in all federations under modern conditions. In India the central government was deliberately given rather extraordinary powers, and since independence these powers have been rather freely exercised in a state dedicated to a planned economy and beset by regional and linguistic divisions.

India is an example of an administrative rather than a contractual federation. It was imposed from above, not from below. Its interim constitution was the Government of India Act of 1935, as amended to fit the needs of an independent state. This Act was the brainchild of the British authorities, not of the Indians themselves, and was designed to establish a highly centralized federation with a fair measure of provincial autonomy, always subject to the ultimate control of the paramount power. Its federal features were never implemented, but their influence on the character of the government of independent India is manifest. The Indian Constitution of 1950 was modeled in large part after the Act of 1935.

This Constitution contains a number of provisions which seem to give the Centre such extraordinary powers as to raise questions regarding the federal nature of the Indian state. Article 3 authorizes the central Parliament, presumably by a simple majority, to form new States or to alter the boundaries of any State, without necessarily obtaining the consent of the State or States affected. Under this authority the new State of Andhra was carved out of the States of Madras and Hyderabad in 1953, and the political map of India, especially in the South, was drastically changed by the States Reorganization Act of 1956. Article 248 vests residuary powers in the Indian federation in the Centre, unlike the arrangement in most federations. Article 249 provides that if two-thirds of the members of the Council of States approve, Parliament may "make laws with respect to any matter enumerated in the State List," and specified in a resolution of the Council. Article 254 provides that if any law passed by a State Legislative Assembly is repugnant to a statute of the federal Parliament, the latter shall prevail. Articles 352 to 360 contain the emergency provisions which empower the President in effect to suspend the Constitution and to take over the administration of a State or States of the Indian Union if he is satisfied that there is a threat to the security of the nation, or a breakdown of the constitutional machinery of a

State or States, or a financial emergency. Some commentators maintain that these emergency provisions, stronger than those to be found in any other federal constitution, would transform India from a federal to a unitary state during periods of emergency. It is doubtful, however, whether the basic character of any state can be changed so easily. The essential tests relate to the precise relationships between the Centre and the Indian States.

Many other provisions of the Constitution could be cited in support of the view that the Central Government has in fact such extraordinary authority as to support the view that India is no more than a quasi-federation, at best, or that if it is a federation at all, it has many unitary features. Experience since independence has given further evidence of the central role of the Government of India in New Delhi. With Nehru as the unquestioned leader of the country, and with the Congress Party in a virtually unchallenged position at the Centre, if less so in some of the States, the powers of the Central Government have been augmented by the extraordinary role of a single leader and a single party. Moreover, the overall initiative and control in the fields of economic planning and development, social reform, and fiscal administration, not to mention the usual dominance of the Centre in foreign policy, defense, and communications, in a state dedicated to "the socialist pattern of society" have greatly enhanced the power and prestige of the Centre. In India there has been, and still is, a tendency to look to government for most things, and this usually means the Central Government.

The Constitution of 1950, obviously copying the Government of India Act of 1935, itemizes the powers of the Centre and the States in three lists, a Union List, a State List, and a Concurrent List. Subject to certain qualifications, which give the Central Government a fairly wide area of discretionary authority, the State Legislatures have power to make laws respecting any item on the State List, and to share with the central Parliament in the supervision and control of subjects on the Concurrent List.

In spite of the many evidences of extreme concentration of authority in the Centre — a tendency accentuated by the needs of the welfare state and by the general Indian attitude toward government — there are also many decentralizing tendencies in the Indian state. Dr. Paul Appleby, in his studies of the Indian administrative system, was astounded to discover how much the Centre was dependent on the States for the actual implementation of major national programs and how little real authority the Centre seemed to have in vital areas of policy and administration. "In both the Centre and the States," he wrote in his report on public administration in India, "prevailing structures, except in a few fields . . . provide chiefly for 'co-ordination' rather than for administration." His conclusion in this area of mutual responsibility and power was a rather startling one:

> It is not too unfair, I think, to say that except for the character of its leadership, the new national government of India is given less basic resource in power than any other large and important nation, while at the same time having rather more sense of need and determination to establish programs dealing with matters important to the national interest. The administrative trend is evidently to go still further, to give over to the states some financial resource now in the province of the Centre, to minimize in practice some of the marginal or interpretative zones of power, and to retreat before an opposition state minister's charges of "interference" with the states.[12]

During the debates on the draft Constitution in the Constituent Assembly, Dr. Ambedkar, who was chairman of the drafting committee, declared that the States of the Union of India "are as sovereign in their field which is left to them by the Constitution as the Centre in the field which is assigned to it."[13] This statement seems rather misleading, in view of the extraordinary powers given to the Centre in the Constitution and the dominant role of the Centre in the years since the Constitution went into effect; but, as Dr. Appleby noted, the Centre is dependent to an extraordinary degree on the States for the implementation of many basic decisions and policies, and talk of "decentralization" is in the air. Moreover, the States are the strongholds of the growing opposition to the dominant Congress Party and of the tendencies toward provincialism, regionalism, and lingualism, strengthened by the reorganization of the State boundaries along essentially linguistic lines, which constitute major threats to the unity and even to the survival of the nation. As Benjamin Schoenfeld has pointed out, "The problems which Indian federalism faces stem from the needs of her people to have a central government armed with sufficient powers needed to solve modern economic and political problems on one hand, and the strong sentiments of regionalism found throughout the land."[14]

[12] Paul H. Appleby, *Public Administration in India: Report of a Survey* (Delhi, 1953), pp. 16–17.

[13] *Constituent Assembly Debates,* X, 339.

[14] Benjamin N. Schoenfeld, *Federalism in India* (Washington, D.C., 1960), p. 21. "The broad grants of power in the Centre List, the all-inclusive character of the Concurrent List, the mechanisms for abrogating state control over subjects in the State List, the lack of full legal control over municipalities by the states under the constitution, the gravitation of control under circumstances of emergency and national interest all point to the unitary character of Indian Government. The centrifugal character of Indian political authority is not inherent in the basic or fundamental nature of the constitution, but rather in the policy developed by the national

This is a problem with which almost all federal states are necessarily concerned, but it seems to be an unusually critical one in the case of India.

The Republic of India

The Preamble to the Constitution declares that India is a "sovereign democratic republic." It became a republic only on January 26, 1950, when the Constitution went into effect. From August 15, 1947, until that date it functioned on a kind of interim arrangement, under the Government of India Act of 1935, the Indian Independence Act, and other basic statutes, most of which were originally enacted by the British Parliament and then after independence adapted to the needs of independent India. During this interval the Head of the Union of India, as the federal state was officially known, was a Governor-General, appointed by the British Sovereign on the advice of the Indian Prime Minister. Free India had two Governors-General — Lord Mountbatten, who was also the last of the British Governors-General and C. Rajagopalachari, a veteran leader of the Congress Party. Lord Mountbatten continued on as Governor-General after India became independent, at the urgent request of Nehru and his associates. It is a significant commentary on the attitudes of the leaders of the new state toward Britain that Lord Mountbatten should have been asked to serve in this capacity, and that he and his Government should have agreed to this arrangement. For a time there seemed to be a possibility that Pakistan too would ask him to serve as its Governor-General, but the leaders of Pakistan became rather embittered at Lord Mountbatten, and Mohammed Ali Jinnah decided that he wanted to be Pakistan's first Governor-General, instead of Prime Minister. Lord Mountbatten's services to independent India until his resignation in June, 1948, were great, and were generally recognized and appreciated.

Rajagopalachari, one of Gandhi's closest associates, was the logical choice to be the first Indian Governor-General of the Indian Dominion. He held this office until January 26, 1950, when Dr. Rajendra Prasad, another old Gandhian, who had been President of the Constituent Assembly, was inaugurated as President of the Republic of India.

While there was little opposition in India in the weeks prior to independence to the British proposal that free India should be a Dominion, with a Governor-General as Head of the State and repre-

---

government under a particular administration. When the character of the Indian government is viewed in terms of the socialist objectives of the planned economy which have been an adopted goal in India, then the federal character of that government becomes even more difficult to envisage." *Ibid.*, pp. 14–15.

sentative of the British Crown, the constitution-makers decided, soon after independence, that the new Constitution should make India a republic, with an indirectly elected President as Head of State. The position and powers of the President of the Republic of India are very different from those of the American President, who is the effective as well as the nominal head of the executive branch of the government; they are in fact more similar to those of the British sovereign. But India, a parliamentary democracy, is also a republic, and the Head of the State is an Indian, in no way responsible to the British Crown.

A Written Constitution

While it is true, as Sydney Bailey points out, that "the British Constitution is by no means wholly unwritten," there is no single written document which has the status of organic law and "no marked or clear distinction between laws which are not fundamental or constitutional and laws which are fundamental or constitutional."[15] If India had followed the British precedent, it too would have had no written constitution. A different decision, however, was made, for reasons which seemed to be compelling. The British, departing from their own practice, had given India a kind of written constitution in the Government of India Act of 1935, one of the longest and most involved pieces of legislation ever enacted by the British Parliament. This Act, supplemented by the Indian Independence Act of 1947, another elaborate legislative measure of the British Parliament, with certain essential amending statutes passed by the Constituent Assembly of India, gave the Indian Union a kind of constitution from independence until the Constitution went into effect on January 26, 1950.

The leaders of the Congress Party, and the members of the Constitution drafting committee, were in substantial agreement on India's need for a single written Constitution, which should be the organic law of the Indian Republic and which would spell out clearly the nature of the Republic, the organization and powers and mutual relations of the Centre and the States, the fundamental rights of the citizen, the directive principles of State policy, and many matters which in more established and less divided republics might be left to ordinary law or to custom and convention. In a vast country with little tradition of unity, with people of different historical, racial, cultural, and religious backgrounds, with special problems of communalism, regionalism, lingualism, and casteism, and differing social customs and differing concepts of law and society, it was deemed necessary to spell out the basic principles of the new state in elaborate detail. The resulting

[15] Sydney D. Bailey, *British Parliamentary Democracy* (Boston, 1958), pp. 6, 8.

Constitution, drafted in remarkably short time, showed the obvious influence of these ideas and of the Government of India Act of 1935.[16] It was, in fact, the longest constitutional document in the world.[17] It has served India well during the formative years of the Republic.

India in the Commonwealth

In deciding to make India a republic the leaders of the new state were confronted with the problem of India's continued relationship, if any, with the Commonwealth — or the British Commonwealth of Nations, as it was then generally called — whose members, all having Dominion status, professed loyalty to the British Crown. No precedent existed for a republic within the Commonwealth constellation. Some of the older Dominions seemed to feel that the Commonwealth should remain a smaller and more homogeneous association, and they looked askance at the inclusion of peoples of very different racial and cultural backgrounds, especially at those with antimonarchist views. Many persons in India felt that India should sever all ties with the former ruling power. The decision of the leaders of the Congress Party to join the Commonwealth surprised many, in India and abroad, for Nehru and other Congress spokesmen had often indicated that an independent India would break away completely from the nation which had governed it for so long.

The happier relations between the Indian leaders and the British Government after the end of World War II, and some sober second thoughts of the Indian leaders as they faced the imminent problem of India's role as an independent state, led to the decision to become a Dominion in the Commonwealth, at least for the time being. In October, 1947, when it was already apparent that India would become a republic, the question of continued association with the Commonwealth was discussed at a Commonwealth Prime Ministers meeting in London, and the formula which seemed to be most seriously considered called for multiple citizenship with the King of England as "first citizen" in each Dominion. Since both India and the other members of the Commonwealth wished to find some way to continue the Commonwealth tie after the Indian Republic was established, a formula was agreed upon at a special meeting of the Commonwealth Prime Ministers, held in London in late April, 1949. This formula was announced in an historic declaration:

[16] For valuable insights into the work of constitution-making in India, see B. N. Rau, *India's Constitution in the Making,* edited by B. Shiva Rao (Madras, 1960). B. N. Rau was Constitutional Adviser to the Constituent Assembly.

[17] The official edition of the Indian Constitution runs to more than 250 pages, with another 64 pages of Contents and Index.

> The Government of India have informed the other Governments of the Commonwealth of the intention of the Indian people that under the new constitution which is about to be adopted India shall become a sovereign independent Republic. The Government of India have, however, declared and affirmed India's desire to continue her full membership of the Commonwealth of Nations and her acceptance of the King as the symbol of the free association of its independent member nations and as such the Head of the Commonwealth.
>
> The Governments of the other countries of the Commonwealth, the basis of whose membership of the Commonwealth is not hereby changed, accept and recognize India's continuing membership in accordance with the terms of this Declaration.

Thus by a simple declaration India's continued membership in the Commonwealth was assured. The formula worked out at the Commonwealth Prime Ministers Conference in 1949 is an important step in the evolution of this unique and successful international association. It has since been invoked by other Commonwealth members.

There was some criticism inside India of the decision that the Republic of India should remain within the Commonwealth. "Britain's past relations with India, her imperialism and power politics and the racial discrimination practised in the Dominions were urged against India's association with the Commonwealth. It was pointed out that there were no affinities of race or religion or of language and culture between India and the white members of the Commonwealth to make such association natural and that the decision showed a lack of faith on the part of India in her strength and destiny."[18] It is difficult to evaluate the intensity of these views in India. They are frequently expressed in the press and on the public platform. They were most clearly evident at the time of the Suez crisis of 1956, when Indians so strongly disapproved of the British military action in Egypt that many questions were raised regarding the wisdom of a continuing association with a Western power which would act in such a manner. Even before the Suez crisis "almost every single opposition party in the country was against India's Commonwealth connexion — a phenomenon probably unique in the entire Commonwealth."[19] The fact that India is on bad terms with another member of the Commonwealth, Pakistan, and with a former member, South Africa, also raises doubts among Indians of the value of the Commonwealth tie. Nehru and other Indian leaders, however, are staunch advocates of continued

[18] N. Srinivasan, *Democratic Government in India,* p. 154.

[19] M. S. Rajan, "India and the Commonwealth, 1954–56," *India Quarterly,* XVI (January–March, 1960), 47.

membership in the Commonwealth, which, they argue, in no way compromises their independence or freedom of action and which involves no commitments of any kind, while at the same time it does bring decided advantages to India.

India as a Secular State

In a country inhabited by people with such diverse religious background and beliefs, in which religious factors were interwoven with historical experience to a degree hardly equalled in any other part of the world, it was necessary for the framers of the Constitution to face squarely the question of the role of religion in the new republic. The answer was unequivocal: India should be a secular state, in which every citizen has the right to practice his own faith, and has the same political and social rights as every other citizen, but a state which is neutral in matters of religion and is not organized along religious lines.

Nehru has been a leading champion of the concept of the secular state. Indeed, the creation of India as a secular state may in time come to be accepted as "one of his greatest achievements," to use the words of Chester Bowles.[20] Nehru has a great aversion to the intrusion of religious factors into politics, and he is especially concerned with transforming his country from "a caste-ridden society" in which communalism constitutes a major threat to all the values that he cherishes to "a national State which includes people of all religions and shades of opinion and is essentially secular as a State."[21] "Religion is all right," he has said, "when applied to ethics and morals, but it is not good mixed up with politics."[22]

This statement seems to be in direct contrast to the views of Mahatma Gandhi, whom Nehru himself once described as "essentially a man of religion, a Hindu to the innermost depths of his being."[23] In a famous passage in his *Autobiography* Gandhi wrote: "I can say without the slightest hesitation, and yet in all humility, that those who say that religion has nothing to do with politics do not know what religion means."[24] Gandhi and Nehru, the master and the disciple, approached the problem of the relation between religion and politics from very different angles, but essentially their positions were not so far apart as far as the nature of the Indian state was concerned.

[20] Chester Bowles, *Ambassador's Report* (New York, 1954), p. 104.

[21] Speech at Aligarh in 1948; quoted in Donald E. Smith, *Nehru and Democracy* (Calcutta, 1958), p. 147.

[22] Speech in the Lok Sabha, Sept. 17, 1953.

[23] Jawaharlal Nehru, *The Discovery of India* (New York, 1946), p. 365.

[24] M. K. Gandhi, *An Autobiography, or The Story of My Experiments with Truth* (2nd edition, Ahmedabad, 1948), p. 615.

Gandhi, a deeply religious man, saw merit and truth in all religions, and he "felt that any form of political association based exclusively on adherence to a particular religion was worse than undemocratic."[25] Nehru, who professes himself to be an agnostic, said that "I have no desire to interfere with any person's belief"; but he objects strongly to any efforts to perpetuate "a complete structure of society . . . by giving it religious sanction and authority," and he desires a State which "protects all religions, but does not favour one at the expense of others and does not itself adopt any religion as the State religion." Hence it is easy to understand why both Gandhi and Nehru, though perhaps for different reasons, were so strongly opposed to the whole idea of partition, and why Nehru referred to the decision of the Constituent Assembly in Karachi, in November, 1953, to make Pakistan an Islamic Republic as "a medieval conception, . . . totally opposed to any democratic conception."[26]

Nehru insisted that free India should be a noncommunal, secular state. He boasts of the fact that "Our Constitution is based on this secular conception and gives freedom to all religions."[27] While the

[25] Smith, *Nehru and Democracy,* p. 155.

[26] These four statements may be found in the following sources, respectively: (1) Nehru, *Circular to the Pradesh Congress Committees,* August, 1954; (2) Jawaharlal Nehru, *Glimpses of World History* (New York, 1942), p. 736; (3) *The Hindu* (Madras), July 17, 1951, p. 4; and (4) *The Hindu,* Nov. 16, 1953, p. 1.

[27] Nehru, *Circular to the Pradesh Congress Committees,* August, 1954. "The Government of a country like India," Nehru declared on another occasion, "with many religions that have secured great and devoted followings for generations, can never function satisfactorily in the modern age except on a secular basis." *The Hindu,* Sept. 13, 1950, p. 9. It is difficult to determine to what extent the people of India have truly accepted the idea of a secular state. As Dr. Ambedkar, India's most famous "untouchable," declared in the debates on the draft Constitution in the Constituent Assembly: "The religious conceptions in this country are so vast that they cover every aspect of life from birth to death. There is nothing which is not religious." *Constituent Assembly Debates,* VII, 781. Professor J. P. Suda expressed a point of view which is probably quite widespread among the Hindus of India: "By making India a *secular* state it is not meant that the government or the state becomes anti-religious or irreligious or that it cannot promote the higher or spiritual values of life. All that the phrase means is that the state is absolutely neutral in religious matters. . . . There is . . . one great danger lurking in the idea of a secular Indian state. The genius of our race has been spiritual . . . ancient India struck the note of spiritual greatness and placed before mankind deep and eternal spiritual truths. These truths are preserved in the great epics, the *Ramayan* and the *Mahabharata,* and the *Bhagwad Gita.* If the secular Indian Republic ignores these great treasure-houses of spiritual knowledge, it would do itself great and irreparable injury." Suda, *Indian Constitutional Development and National Movement,* pp. 520, 521–522.

word "secular" does not appear in the Constitution, the principles of secularism are embodied in it, especially in many Articles in Part III, dealing with fundamental rights, and in Article 325, which provided for "one general electoral roll for every territorial constituency," thus abolishing the separate communal electorates which had existed ever since the Morley-Minto Reforms of 1909.

India as a Welfare State

Reflecting the basic orientation and desires of most of the leaders of modern India, and mindful of the Preamble to the Objectives Resolution of December, 1946, the framers of the Indian Constitution incorporated many provisions designed to make India a welfare state. The basic aims of a welfare state were clearly foreshadowed in the Preamble to the Constitution, and in virtually all of Part IV of the Constitution, containing the Directive Principles of State Policy. Article 36 states: "The State shall strive to promote the welfare of the people by securing and protecting as effectively as may be a social order in which justice, social, economic and political, shall inform all the institutions of the national life." Most of the prominent leaders of Indian political life have been and are professed socialists, although it is often difficult to determine exactly what socialism means to them. Gandhi's economic and social views could hardly be subsumed under the term "socialism," although there were undoubtedly many socialist elements in his creed. Nehru has regarded himself as a socialist for many years. He has obviously been influenced by Marxist views, but at the same time he has not identified himself as a Marxist, and he has often attacked communism and the Communists. Only a few staunch conservatives, notably Vallabhbhai Patel and C. Rajagopalachari, have had much influence in the inner circles of the Congress Party. It is perhaps suggestive, however, that Gandhi had frequent associations with Birla, one of India's leading "capitalists," and that there has always been a conservative wing in the Congress Party.

Even most of the so-called conservatives profess support for socialism in one form or another. A common statement in almost all circles in India — sometimes, it is true, made with tongue in cheek — is: "We are all socialists now." Dominant Indian opinion is opposed to capitalism and the "acquisitive society" and is unabashedly in favor of a welfare state. This goal has been clearly stated on innumerable occasions. One of the best known statements was made in a resolution adopted by the Congress Party at its annual session at Avadi in January, 1955:

> In order to realise the object of the Congress . . . and to further the objectives stated in the Preamble and Directive Principles of State Policy of the Constitution of India, planning should take

place with a view to the establishment of a socialistic pattern of society, where the principal means of production are under social ownership or control, production is progressively speeded up and there is equitable distribution of the national wealth.

In subsequent years the Congress reaffirmed the Avadi resolution, and endorsed specific suggestions for implementing it. The word "socialist" is usually used, instead of "socialistic." At its annual session at Indore in January, 1957, the Congress amended its Constitution to read that the object of the Congress is the "establishment in India by peaceful and legitimate means of a Socialist Co-operative Commonwealth."

These, then, were seven vital decisions regarding the basic nature of the Indian state: that India should be a "sovereign democratic republic," to use the language of the Preamble to the Constitution, with a parliamentary system, a federal structure, a written Constitution, associated with the Commonwealth, and dedicated to the conceptions of secularism and of the welfare state. All of these decisions were made with so little debate and discussion that they may almost be regarded as assumptions rather than decisions. It is nevertheless remarkable that there should have been so marked a political consensus on questions which are inherently so controversial and which affected sensitive areas of India's political and social anatomy.

Universal, Direct Suffrage

Two other major decisions were made only after extensive debate and considerable soul-searching, and even today many people, for various reasons, entertain doubts of their wisdom. The first of these decisions was embodied in Article 326 of the Indian Constitution, the first words reading as follows: "The elections to the House of the People and to the Legislative Assembly of every State shall be on the basis of adult suffrage." These innocuous sounding words reflected a bold gamble and a radical departure from previous practice. Even in the elections for the provincial assemblies which were held in 1937 under the Government of India Act of 1935 only some 35,000,000 Indians, all but 6,000,000 being males, were eligible to vote. Prior to that time the electorate had been only about one-fifth as large. Most of the people of India, therefore, had had no previous experience in voting. Moreover, all but a small proportion — certainly less than 20 per cent — were illiterate. What would be the consequences of giving the vote to every adult person over the age of twenty-one, male or female, literate or illiterate?

Under the conditions prevailing in India, the decision to base the Indian democracy on unrestricted, universal, direct adult suffrage was a momentous one, perhaps the boldest decision the framers of the Constitution made. It is still too early to determine whether the gamble in genuine democracy will pay off, but it may be that the future of democracy in India depends on the results of this gamble. The Indian experiment in adult suffrage contrasts favorably with the limitations on the franchise, including an increasing resort to indirect elections, which have been imposed in many other Asian countries which profess to be democratic, including the system of "basic democracies" in Pakistan and of "guided democracy" in Indonesia. It remains to be seen which approach to democracy will prevail in the Asian scene.

States Reorganization Along Linguistic Lines

The second decision, which was taken with grave misgivings, against the known opposition of Nehru and many other leaders of the Congress Party, was the decision to organize the Republic of India essentially along linguistic lines. Ironically, this decision was wholly in keeping with demands of the Indian National Congress, dating back to 1921: "In stimulating linguistic agitation the Congress Party before independence helped to create a monster which now challenges India's existence as a single nation and taxes her Government's ability to maintain law and order."[28] For six years the Government of India resisted mounting demands for the reorganization of the State boundaries to conform more closely to linguistic considerations. Actually, in at least fifteen of the twenty-eight States of India after independence more than 75 per cent of the people spoke a single dominant language, and in Bombay State, with two dominant languages, 76 per cent listed either Marathi or Gujerati as their mother tongue.[29]

But this was not enough to satisfy the champions of linguistic regionalism, especially in the South of India. In 1953 the floodgates of lingualism were opened, and the flood began. In December, 1952, Potti Sriramulu, in a gesture of self-sacrifice which aroused the Telegu-speaking people of north Madras State, fasted unto death in Madras on the issue of a separate state for his people, and shortly afterward the Government of India, against its own desires, promised to create a separate State of Andhra. This new State came into existence in the fall of 1953.

A few weeks later, still under the pressure of linguistic agitation and tensions, the Government appointed a three-man States Re-

[28] Marshall Windmiller, "The Politics of States Reorganization in India: The Case of Bombay," *Far Eastern Survey,* XXV (September, 1956), 129.

[29] See "The Effect of the Territorial Reorganization of India in 1956 on Linguistic Homogeneity and Concentration," *Intelligence Report* (issued by the Office of Intelligence Research, Department of State), No. 7579, Sept. 17, 1957, Table 1.

organization Commission. The Commission took two years to make its report, thus giving time for passions to die down, on the one hand, and for advocates of the linguistic principle to state their case and organize for later activity, on the other. Bearing in mind that its first task was the "preservation and strengthening of the unity and security of India," the Commission warned against excessive deference to linguistic feelings, for "further emphasis on narrow loyalties by equating linguistic regions with political and administrative frontiers must diminish the broader sense of the unity of the country." Nevertheless, the Commission recommended new linguistic states for the South and it warned that "further deferment of a general reorganization will cause dissatisfaction and disappointment."[30] It recommended some changes in the boundaries of Bombay State, but it did not favor the division of Bombay State into two states, in which Marathi and Gujerati were generally spoken. This decision was received with satisfaction by the Gujeratis, but was strongly objected to by many Marathi-speaking people. A Samyukta Maharashtra Samiti (United Maharashtra Committee) was formed to press for a separate State of Maharashtra, including Vidarbha, a predominantly Marathi-speaking section which the Commission proposed to create as a separate State.

After heated debates the Working Committee of the Congress Party endorsed most of the SRC Report, but it proposed an entirely different arrangement in Bombay State. It recommended that this State should be divided into three States of Maharashtra, Gujerat, and Bombay (chiefly the city of Bombay). This recommendation was equally unsatisfactory to Maharashtrians, and embarrassed Congress members from the Maharashtra area, while giving further impetus to the Samyukta Maharashtra Samiti and an excellent opportunity for the Communists to exploit the anti-Congress feeling in this part of India.

In the next few months the Working Committee changed its mind, and when the States Reorganization Bill was introduced into the Parliament, it called for the reorganization of India into fourteen States, with a clearly dominant language in each, with the exception of Bombay, which was to be enlarged instead of divided, and the Punjab, where the main prevailing languages were associated with Hindi. Hindi was the dominant language in Uttar Pradesh, Bihar, and Madhya Pradesh, and languages related to Hindi, namely Rajasthani and Punjabi, were dominant in Rajasthan and the Punjab, respectively. Kashmiri prevailed in the Valley of Kashmir, although other languages were spoken by large numbers of Kashmiris. Each of the other languages officially recognized in the Eighth Schedule of

[30] See *Report of the States Reorganization Commission* (New Delhi, 1955), pp. 45, 229–237.

the Indian Constitution, except Sanskrit, the classical language of Aryan India, Marathi and Gujerati, which shared linguistic importance in different parts of Bombay, and Urdu, closely related to Hindi, was the dominant language in one State, and in only one State. Listed in order of numbers of persons speaking each language as a mother tongue, the coincidence of language and State was as follows: Telegu — Andhra Pradesh; Tamil — Madras; Bengali — West Bengal; Kannada —Mysore; Malayalam — Kerala; Oriya — Orissa; Assamese — Assam.

Having in effect conceded the essentially linguistic basis of States reorganization, the Indian Government found that its decision was generally welcomed in most of the country, but definitely unpopular in linguistically frustrated Bombay and the Punjab. The feelings of the Marathi- and Gujerati-speaking peoples of still united Bombay were expressed in agitations and violence, and in remarkable electoral successes of candidates supported by the Mahagujerat Janata Parishad in Gujerat and the Samyukta Maharashtra Samiti in Maharashtra in the general elections in 1957.

The demands for separate States of Gujerat and Maharashtra would not die down, and at length, on May 1, 1960, the Government of India, reflecting the surrender of the Congress Party on this issue, officially divided Bombay State into these two States, to bring the number of Indian States to fifteen. This action in effect signified as complete a concession to the linguistic principle as seemed to be possible, except perhaps in the Punjab, where the linguistic issue was complicated by the fact that the two main languages, Hindi and Punjabi, were linguistically similar, and by the added fact that the members of the militant Sikh organization, the Akali Dal, were demanding a separate Sikh State (some even demanded an independent Sikhistan).

The entire agitation over linguistic States demonstrated that the Congress had opened a Pandora's box indeed when it championed the principle of the reorganization of India on a linguistic basis, and it stimulated the divisive forces in India to such an extent as to raise doubts about the capacity of free India to survive as a unified State dedicated to the democratic way.[31] Whereas most of the other basic decisions regarding the nature of the Indian state have tended to give meaning and reality to the concept of a democratic India, the reluctant concessions to linguistic demands have revealed the strength of regional as against national loyalties.

[31] These doubts have been effectively expressed and documented in a number of excellent books, written by both Indians and non-Indians. See, for example, C. Rajagopalachari, *Our Democracy* (Madras, 1957); Selig S. Harrison, *India: The Most Dangerous Decades* (Princeton, N.J., 1960); and Amaury de Riencourt, *The Soul of India* (New York, 1960).

* 6 *

The Central Government

New Delhi, the capital of India since the early 1920's, is a British-built city next to historic old Delhi, and it contains many physical and intangible reminders of the days of British rule. As the capital of independent India, it is expanding rapidly, as the governmental apparatus of the vast new country expands. Some of the buildings which house the ministries and other units of government, notably the Secretariat buildings, the domed Rashtrapati Bhavan, once the residence of the Governor-General and now of the President of India, and the vast circular Parliament building nearby, are very British and, as some think, rather un-Indian. New Delhi is now full of modern buildings which accommodate agencies of the Executive branch of the Government or other governmental needs. Notable among these are some structures which are not used for the Executive departments, including the imposing new Supreme Court building and the modernistic structures rising in the spacious diplomatic enclave, among them the new United States Embassy, perhaps the most discussed diplomatic structure in the world. Many more functionally designed new buildings provide quarters for governmental agencies and personnel.

The Government of India today is a vast, sprawling bureaucracy, centered in New Delhi but reaching out to the remotest village. Most of the people on the government rolls are lesser government servants, who do routine work for very low salaries, and peons, who run errands, do odd jobs, sit outside of office doors, and presumably enhance the prestige of the persons for whom they work. At the apex of the structure are the top civil servants, mostly members of the Indian Administrative Service, with a few active members of the old Indian Civil Service in key positions of central or State administration or in the diplomatic service, and at the very top the Ministers, the members

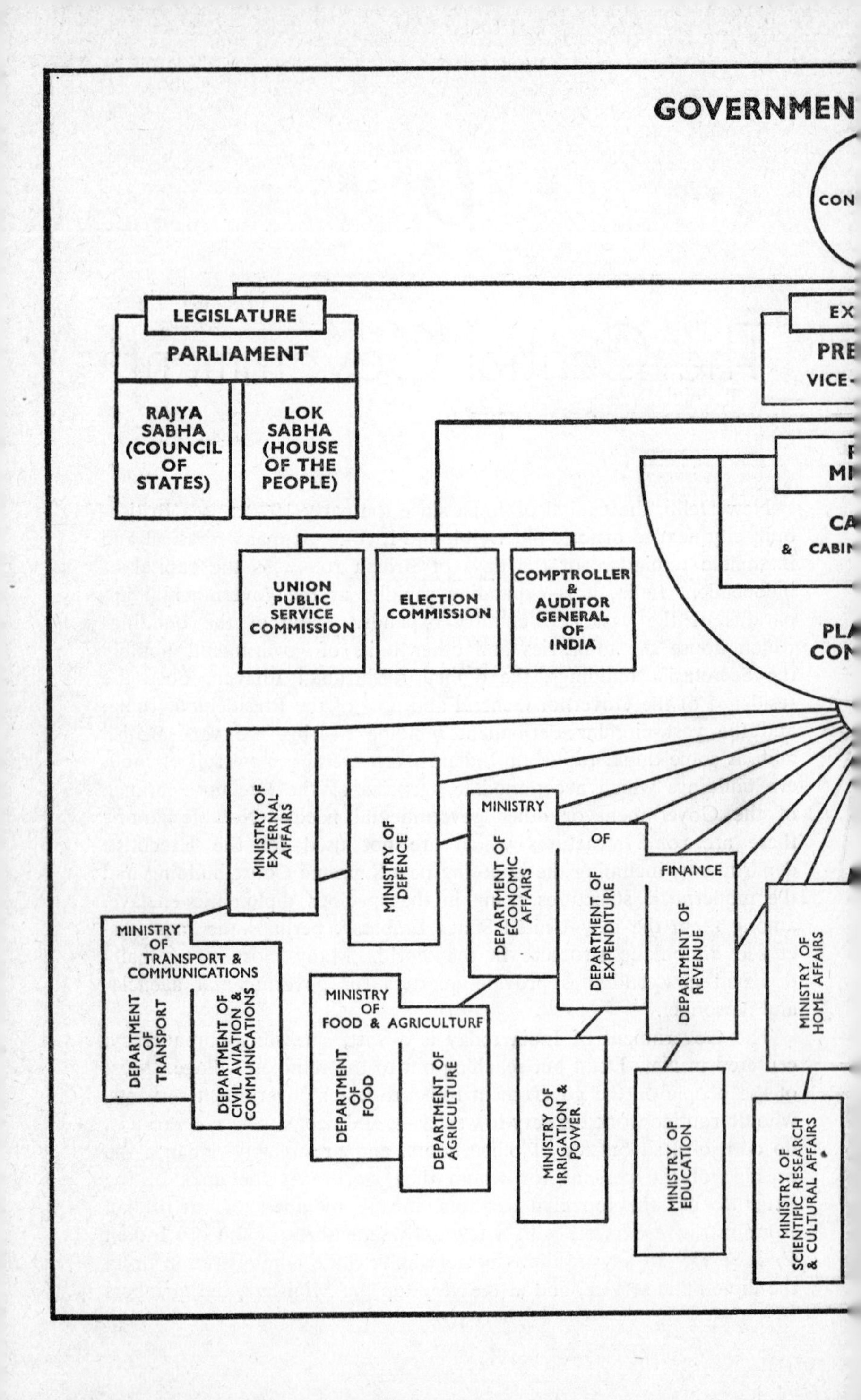
GOVERNMEN
CON
LEGISLATURE
PARLIAMENT
RAJYA SABHA (COUNCIL OF STATES)
LOK SABHA (HOUSE OF THE PEOPLE)
EX
PRE
VICE-
MI
CA
& CABIN
UNION PUBLIC SERVICE COMMISSION
ELECTION COMMISSION
COMPTROLLER & AUDITOR GENERAL OF INDIA
PLA
CON
MINISTRY OF EXTERNAL AFFAIRS
MINISTRY OF DEFENCE
MINISTRY OF FINANCE
DEPARTMENT OF ECONOMIC AFFAIRS
DEPARTMENT OF EXPENDITURE
DEPARTMENT OF REVENUE
MINISTRY OF HOME AFFAIRS
MINISTRY OF TRANSPORT & COMMUNICATIONS
DEPARTMENT OF TRANSPORT
DEPARTMENT OF CIVIL AVIATION & COMMUNICATIONS
MINISTRY OF FOOD & AGRICULTURF
DEPARTMENT OF FOOD
DEPARTMENT OF AGRICULTURE
MINISTRY OF IRRIGATION & POWER
MINISTRY OF EDUCATION
MINISTRY OF SCIENTIFIC RESEARCH & CULTURAL AFFAIRS

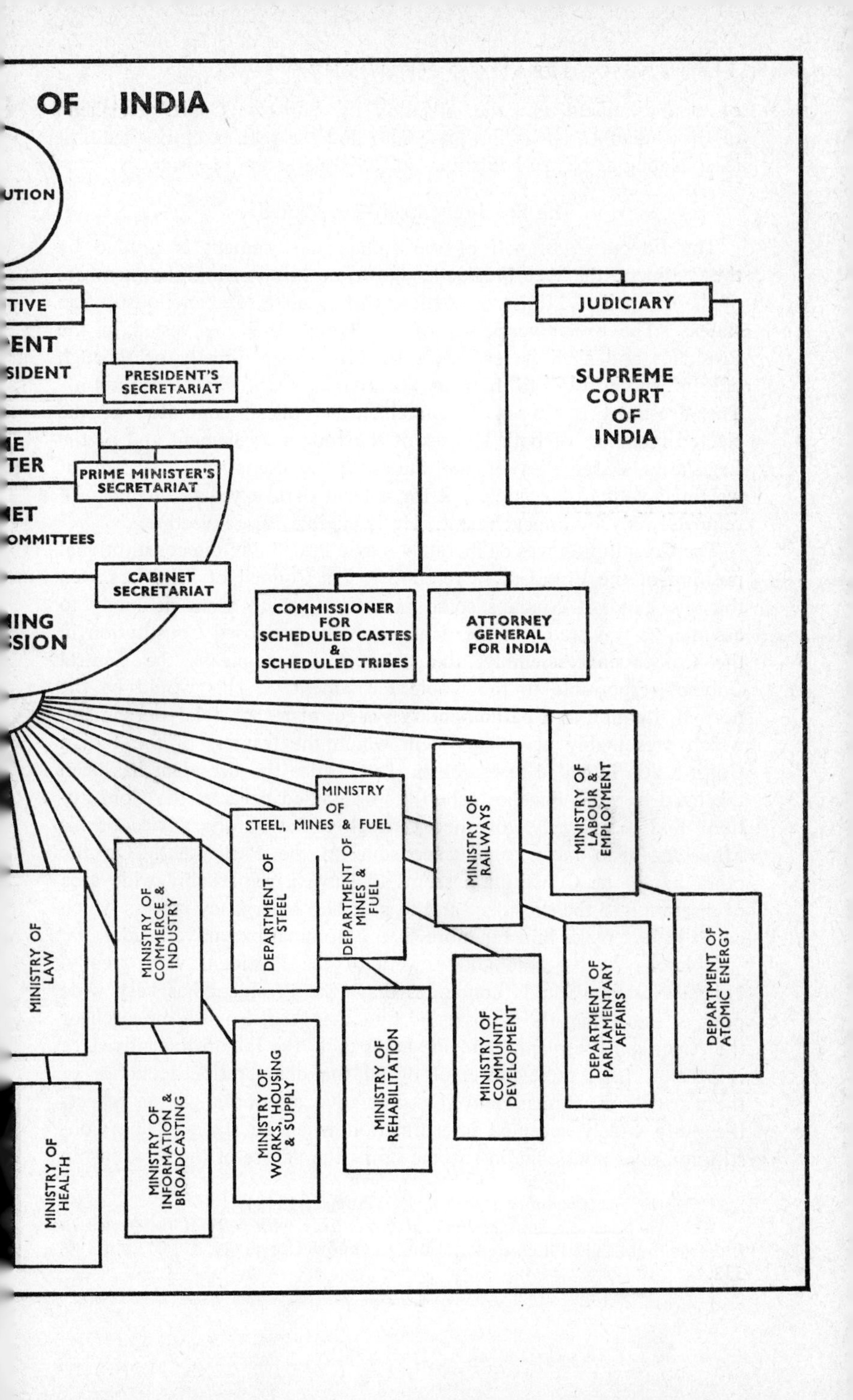

OF INDIA
JUDICIARY
SUPREME COURT OF INDIA
PRESIDENT'S SECRETARIAT
PRIME MINISTER'S SECRETARIAT
CABINET SECRETARIAT
COMMISSIONER FOR SCHEDULED CASTES & SCHEDULED TRIBES
ATTORNEY GENERAL FOR INDIA
MINISTRY OF STEEL, MINES & FUEL
DEPARTMENT OF STEEL
DEPARTMENT OF MINES & FUEL
MINISTRY OF RAILWAYS
MINISTRY OF LABOUR & EMPLOYMENT
MINISTRY OF LAW
MINISTRY OF COMMERCE & INDUSTRY
DEPARTMENT OF ATOMIC ENERGY
DEPARTMENT OF PARLIAMENTARY AFFAIRS
MINISTRY OF COMMUNITY DEVELOPMENT
MINISTRY OF REHABILITATION
MINISTRY OF WORKS, HOUSING & SUPPLY
MINISTRY OF INFORMATION & BROADCASTING
MINISTRY OF HEALTH

of the Parliament, and the judges of the Supreme Court. The head of the Indian Union is the President, and the real executive head, at least as long as Nehru holds that office, is the Prime Minister.

The President and Vice President

The Executive Branch of the Indian Government is headed by the President, the Vice President, the Prime Minister and the members of the Council of Ministers. Article 53 (1) of the Indian Constitution states: "The executive power of the Union shall be vested in the President and shall be exercised by him either directly or through officers subordinate to him in accordance with this Constitution." The President is chosen by an electoral college composed of the elected members of both Houses of the Indian Parliament and of the Legislative Assemblies of the States, by a complicated system of weighted voting. He is elected for a term of five years, and may be removed only by impeachment. He is eligible for re-election.

The Constitution was deliberately vague in defining the constitutional position of the President in relation to his Council of Ministers. On the one hand, it contains some provisions which seem definitely to assume, as was stated in the debates on the proposed Constitution in the Constituent Assembly, that "the President means the Central Cabinet responsible to the whole Parliament."[1] This would be the normal situation in a parliamentary system of responsible government, which presumably was the system which the framers of the Indian Constitution intended to establish. In practice the President has been the head of what Bagehot called "the dignified parts of the Constitution" and has largely governed through and with the advice of his Ministers, who have been responsible to the Parliament. On the other hand, the Constitution seems to leave a remarkably wide area of discretion to the President and to give him emergency powers which could in fact make him far more than a nominal executive head.

Opinions on the role and powers of the President vary greatly. Udaya Narayan Shukla concludes that "the President has very wide powers, more than those possessed by either [the] English monarch or the American President," and she holds that "the Indian Executive . . . is perhaps [the] most powerful of all the democratic executives of the world."[2] R. Ramaswamy, a senior advocate of Bangalore, reflects the more widely accepted interpretation when he states: "The Constitution does not define in specific terms the nature of the relationship

[1] *Constituent Assembly Debates,* IX (Aug. 3, 1949), 150.

[2] Udaya Narayan Shukla, *Federal Executives with Special Reference to India* (unpublished Ph.D. dissertation, Lucknow University, 1956), pp. 296, 332.

between the President and the Council of Ministers. But there are clear indications available in the provisions of the Constitution as to what the framers of it intended that relationship to be. And if we consider all the relevant provisions as an integral whole, the conclusion, I think, seems clear that the constitutional relationship created by the new constitution between the President and the Council of Ministers will be substantially analogous to the position the King of Great Britain occupies *vis-à-vis* the British Cabinet. In other words, the President of India will be a constitutional head who has only the right to be kept informed of and to express his views upon the many questions which arise within the Union orbit of activity but who cannot override the advice tendered to him by his ministers relative to any action he has to take as executive head of the Union."[3] Professor D. N. Banerjee concurs. The President of India, he argues, "occupies in the Indian constitutional system the same position as the Crown does in the English Constitution."[4]

In addition to the normal executive powers, which he exercises on the advice of the Prime Minister and the Council of Ministers, the President of India has certain legislative powers, such as various kinds of veto and the power to issue ordinances while Parliament is not sitting, some important financial powers, although his sphere in the financial field is quite limited, and some extraordinary emergency powers.

In cases of grave emergency the President is authorized to issue a proclamation and to take such measures as he deems necessary, within the provisions of the Constitution, to deal with the emergency situations. These emergency powers are spelled out in great detail in the Constitution (Articles 352–360). The President may assume emergency powers in three situations: (1) if a threat to the security of India, "whether by war or external aggression or internal disturbance," has arisen; (2) if a situation has developed in a State which makes it impossible for the constitutional machinery in that State to operate; or (3) if the financial stability or credit of India or any part of it is threatened. In each instance the President is nominally sole judge of the existence of an emergency, although presumably he will act as an agent of the Government and not on his own discretion. He must lay each proclamation issued under the emergency provisions

[3] M. Ramaswamy, "The Constitutional Position of the President of the Indian Republic," *The Canadian Bar Review,* June–July, 1950, p. 649.

[4] D. N. Banerjee, "The Growth of Parliamentary Government in India, 1919–1950," *Parliamentary Affairs,* IX (Spring, 1956), 172. See also D. N. Banerjee, "The Indian Presidency," *The Political Quarterly,* January–March, 1955.

of the Constitution before Parliament, and no proclamation may remain in effect for more than two months unless it has been approved by the Parliament. Even then, no emergency situation may be maintained for more than six months at a time, and in no event may it be extended beyond a period of three years.

Many students of Indian government believe that because of the emergency powers bestowed upon him under the Constitution, the President of India is far more than a nominal head of state. The test here, as elsewhere, is whether the President can exercise these powers at his own discretion, or whether he acts only on the advice of responsible ministers. In practice, in accordance with the intent of the framers of the Constitution, the President has used his emergency powers only when requested to do so by the Prime Minister.

These powers have been invoked in five important instances: in the Punjab in 1951–52 for a period of ten months, in PEPSU (Patiala and East Punjab States Union) in 1953–54 for approximately one year, in Andhra in 1954 for four months, in Travancore-Cochin for eleven months in 1956–57, and in Kerala (comprising substantially the same territorial area as the former State of Travancore-Cochin) in 1959–60 for about six months.[5] A detailed study of each of these cases would show that the President's emergency powers are extensive, that they have been exercised with firmness but with discretion, that they provide real safeguards against the collapse of state administration, and that they have not thus far been abused, although the danger of abuse is always present.

Grave reservations have been expressed regarding the emergency provisions of the Constitution. During the debates in the Constituent Assembly H. V. Kamath declared: "I have ransacked most of the constitutions of the democratic countries of the World . . . and I can find no parallel to this chapter of emergency provisions in any of the other constitutions of democratic countries in the world. The closest approximation to my mind is reached in the Weimar Constitution of the Third Reich which was destroyed by Hitler taking advantage of this very provision contained in that constitution."[6] C. V. H. Rao has expressed the opinion that the "peculiar constitutional provisions relating to the President" can be used as "a communist stepping stone for [the] establishment of dictatorship" and that "the combination of an adventurous Prime Minister and a complacent or unscrupulous President" (or vice versa) "could certainly subvert parliamentary

[5] See Kishore K. Koticha, "Presidential Intervention under Article 356 of the Constitution of India," *Journal of the Indian Law Institute,* II (October–December, 1959), 125–133; especially the chart on p. 126.

[6] *Constituent Assembly Debates,* IX (Aug. 2, 1949), 104.

democracy."[7] Professor Suda has asserted flatly that "by declaring an emergency the President can transform the federal constitution into unitary. Such a power of converting a federal into a unitary state is not to be found in any other federal constitution."[8]

The reasons for including the emergency provisions in the Constitution are clear. The framers of the Constitution, for all their doubts and reservations, felt that the central government of the new and weak state which had just come into being had to be given sufficient authority to deal with emergency situations arising from internal disorders and divisions or from external dangers. The riots and murders and general dislocation which accompanied partition, and the strained relations with Pakistan arising from the tension over Kashmir and a variety of other unresolved issues, convinced them that such emergencies might indeed arise.

As G. N. Joshi has suggested, "the actual part which a President may play in the decisions" of the Indian Government "will largely depend upon the personal equation."[9] India has been very fortunate in having for its first President Dr. Rajendra Prasad, a beloved elder statesman and old Gandhian, a former President of the Indian National Congress and President of the Constituent Assembly from its inception in late 1947 until he assumed the office of President of the Indian Republic in January, 1950. Dr. Prasad has conceived of his role as a unifying and symbolic one. He has not attempted to take advantage of the ambiguity of the Constitution or of the emergency powers he possesses under the Constitution. He has acted only upon the advice of the Prime Minister, although he has not hesitated to express his views to the Prime Minister. His relations with Nehru have apparently been excellent. Nehru has been the real head of the Indian executive, and Dr. Prasad has always deferred to him; but at the same time Nehru has gone out of his way to confer with the President and to keep him informed, far more than he is required to do under the Constitution. Thus a good precedent has been set, although there is still a danger of a reversion of roles if a strong-minded President and a weak Prime Minister happen to occupy the two top offices. The example of Pakistan, where other conventions were established from the beginning, suggests that "the personal equation" is indeed an important one.

The Vice President of the Republic of India is elected for a term of

[7] C. V. H. Rao, "The President and Parliament," in A. B. Lal, ed., *The Indian Parliament* (Allahabad, 1956), p. 226.

[8] J. P. Suda, *Indian Constitutional Development and National Movement* (Meerut, 1951), p. 575.

[9] G. N. Joshi, *The Constitution of India* (3rd edition, London, 1954), p. 123.

five years by the members of both Houses of Parliament. In the event of a vacancy in the office of President as a result of death, resignation, or removal from office, the Vice President shall act as President, but only until a new President is elected, which must be within a period of six months following the vacancy in that office. The Vice President is also ex officio Chairman of the Council of States.

Obviously the Vice President of India has rather limited functions and almost no real powers, unless he is called upon to act as President; but again much depends on the personal equation. India has had a most distinguished Vice President, Dr. Sarvepalli Radhakrishnan, one of the world's leading philosophers, who has given prestige and dignity to the office. He has presided over the deliberations of the Indian Council of States with grace and charm, and often with wit. While he has not always observed strict parliamentary procedure, his personal influence and prestige have more than compensated for any departures from normal practices. He has been a disinterested adviser, confidant, and friend to Dr. Prasad and Nehru, and to others in high positions in the Government and in Indian life generally. Perhaps this is his greatest contribution.

The Prime Minister and the Council of Ministers

Consecutive paragraphs of Article 75 of the Indian Constitution contain the following provisions regarding the Council of Ministers:

> The Ministers shall hold office during the pleasure of the President. The Council of Ministers shall be collectively responsible to the House of the People.

These and other provisions of the Constitution, plus certain ambiguities and omissions, have led some students of Indian government and politics to suggest that there is some confusion as to the precise role of the Council of Ministers and as to the relation of its head, the Prime Minister, and its members to the President. There is the further question of the real degree of responsibility of the Council to the Parliament. In the light of the political experience under the British and the intent of the framers of the Constitution, however, there can be little doubt that the Constitution was designed to provide India with a genuine system of parliamentary democracy, in which the Council of Ministers would be in fact responsible to the Parliament and in which the Prime Minister would be the *de facto* head of the Indian executive.

In the actual operations of the Government of India under the Constitution the Council of Ministers has functioned with relation to the symbolic head of the State, the President, in a manner which has encouraged respect for the high office of the Presidency without detracting from the real powers of the responsible executive, but it has not been controlled by the Parliament to a degree which would seem desirable in a healthy parliamentary system, and it has been dominated by the Prime Minister to an extraordinary degree.

The reason for the dominance of the Prime Minister is obvious, for the Prime Minister since independence — and even before under the Interim Government — has been Jawaharlal Nehru. Nehru has been much more than Prime Minister of India, important as that role has been; he has been a leader of the Indian "revolution," which he interprets in economic and social as well as in political terms, the political heir of Gandhi, the leader of the dominant political organization, a charismatic leader par excellence, the very symbol of the new India. Important and able men have held ministerial posts, but with the exception of Vallabhbhai Patel, who served as Deputy Prime Minister until his death in 1951, no one has really shared Nehru's authority.

The Council of Ministers is composed of Ministers who are members of the Cabinet, Ministers who are not members of the Cabinet, known as Ministers of State, and Deputy Ministers. The Ministers and Deputy Ministers, of course, head the great departments of the Indian Government. In 1957, for example, the Government was divided into the following ministries and departments: External Affairs, Defense, Finance, Home Affairs, Law, Commerce and Industry, Steel, Mines and Fuel, Railways, Transport and Communication, Labor and Employment, Food and Agriculture, Irrigation and Power, Education and Scientific Research, Health, Information and Broadcasting, Works, Housing and Supply, Rehabilitation and Minority Affairs, and Community Development. Special mention should also be made of the separate departments of Parliamentary Affairs and of Atomic Energy, and of the Planning Commission, which is concerned with one of the most vital aspects of Indian policy, the work of economic planning and development. An analysis of the organization and functions of each of these ministries and agencies would throw much light on the actual scope and work of government in India.[10]

The Indian Parliament

In the vast circular Parliament House in New Delhi, with its scores of marble columns, the Parliament of India sits. This central law-making body consists of the President and two Houses. The Upper

[10] For a detailed description of the organization and functions of the ministries, departments, and other branches of the Government of India, see The Indian Institute of Public Administration, *The Organisation of the Government of India* (Bombay, 1958).

House is known as the Rajya Sabha, or the Council of States, while the Lower House is called the Lok Sabha, or the House of the People. The relations between the two Houses are roughly comparable to those between the British House of Lords and House of Commons. The procedures followed in the Indian Parliament are based on those in the British Parliament.

On the other hand, the Indian Parliament has not achieved in the political system of India a position of such central importance as has the British Parliament in the British parliamentary system. This is due to many factors, including the relative lack of experience of the Indian Parliament and of most of its members, the absence of deeply rooted conventions, the limitations placed upon it under the Constitution, and its actual subordination to the strong personality of the Prime Minister and to the central organs of the Congress Party, which has a top-heavy representation in the legislative body.

The Indian Parliament normally holds two sessions a year. According to the Constitution not more than six months may elapse between sittings.

Council of States. The Council of States is limited in size to 250 members. Twelve of the members are nominated by the President to represent the arts and professions — the Constitution specifically mentions "literature, science, art and social service." Not more than 238 members represent the States. These members are elected by the elected members of the State Legislative Assemblies, with the representation of each State determined roughly in accordance with population. The Council is not subject to dissolution, but approximately one third of its members retire every second year. Some of those whose terms expire are, of course, re-elected. As has been noted, the presiding officer of the Council, acting in an ex officio capacity, is the Vice President of India. When this office is vacant, or when the Vice President is absent, a Deputy Chairman, chosen from among the members of the Council, presides.

Presumably the Council of States is a coordinate branch of the Indian Parliament, but it is in fact much less influential than the House of the People. Professor J. P. Suda calls it "one of the weakest second chambers in the world, weaker than even the House of Lords."[11] As in the British Parliament, all money bills must originate in the House of the People, and in case of doubt whether a measure is a money bill or not the Speaker of the House alone decides. If the two Houses differ on any bill, the differences are resolved in a joint sitting, in which each member of each House has one vote. This obviously gives the advantage to the House of the People, which is twice the

[11] Suda, *Indian Constitutional Development and National Movement,* p. 604.

size of the Council of States. Practically all the members of the Cabinet, including Nehru himself, sit in the House of the People, although occasionally they may meet with the Council of States. The Council does not function effectively as a delaying and revising chamber. It seldom suggests revisions in bills sent to it from the House of the People, and very few of the suggested revisions are adopted by the House. While its members are chosen on a different basis from the members of the Lower House, and while presumably these members represent the States of the Indian Union, there is little difference in age, experience, background, and outlook between members of the two Houses. As Morris-Jones has noted, "Composed of men similar to those who sit in the House of the People, the Council has, not surprisingly, failed to evolve a distinct role for itself."[12]

Most democratic states of the world have bicameral legislatures, but in many of these states there is growing criticism of the upper chamber. In India doubts about the value of the Council of States were voiced even during the debates on the draft Constitution in the Constituent Assembly. On one occasion Dr. Ambedkar, the famous spokesman of the "untouchables" of India who served as chairman of the committee which drafted the Constitution, stated: "I cannot say that I am very strongly prepossessed in favour of a second chamber. To me it is like the Curate's egg — good only in parts."[13] In the opinion of Professor M. P. Sharma "the Council of States does not seem to have been created with any particular purpose beyond bringing the Constitution in line with the prevailing fashion of bicameralism. In our country, the credit of second chambers has at no time been high, and it will not be surprising if the Council of States lives simply to serve as one of the ornamental parts of the Constitution."[14] Many members of the Council have expressed impatience over the limitations imposed upon them, and criticism of the Council seems to be growing. It seems unlikely, however, that it will be abolished.

While it is undoubtedly a weak upper chamber, as are most upper chambers, the Indian Council of States does serve a number of useful functions, although perhaps not as effectively as its advocates expected. While it has not functioned well as a delaying and revising chamber, which presumably should be one of its major contributions, it has been an active body. During the lifetime of India's first Parliament, from 1952 to 1956, the Council of States, in fifteen sessions, dealt with 363 bills. One hundred and one bills — 69 Government bills and 32

[12] W. H. Morris-Jones, *Parliament in India* (Philadelphia, 1957), p. 257. This is by far the most thorough and objective study of the Indian Parliament.

[13] *Constituent Assembly Debates,* VII, 1317.

[14] M. P. Sharma, *The Government of the Indian Republic* (Allahabad, 1951), p. 147.

private members' bills — originated in the Council. Among these were four important social measures — the Hindu Marriage Act, the Hindu Minority and Guardianship Act, the Hindu Succession Act, and the Hindu Adoptions and Maintenance Act — which formed vital parts of the so-called Hindu Code Bill. "The Council of States thus took credit for enacting what might perhaps rightly be claimed to be the most important social reform measures affecting the vast majority of the people of India."[15] During the same fifteen sessions of the Council no less than 12,733 questions were admitted; 6,572 were answered orally, together with 34,839 supplementary questions. Twenty-one Governmental resolutions were adopted in the Council. Forty-one private members' resolutions were discussed, and four were adopted.

The level of discussion and debate in the Council of States has been consistently high. It is a more orderly but no less interesting assembly than the House of the People. Some of the speeches of its members, such as those of Pandit H. H. Kunzru on the Preventive Detention Act in 1952, are worthy of comparison with the best efforts in the House of the People, and really probe to fundamentals. Debates on foreign affairs are frequently held in the Council, and are usually of a high order. This was true of the debates on international developments in August, 1954, and on the Sino-Indian border disputes in 1959.

House of the People. According to the Representation of the People Act of 1950, membership in the House of the People was fixed at no more than 496 members, with all members except nine, at most, to be elected by universal, direct suffrage, and with each member to represent at least 75,000 and no more than 500,000 people. The President was authorized to nominate one member for the Andaman and Nicobar Islands, six members for Jammu and Kashmir (until a regularly constituted Legislative Assembly was set up), and two members for the Anglo-Indian community, if this community received no representation in the regular voting. While the principle of separate electorates was not recognized, certain seats were reserved for a period of ten years for Scheduled Castes, Scheduled Tribes, and the Anglo-Indian community. Membership in the House of the People, which officially became known as the Lok Sabha in 1954, is now limited to 500. The normal life of the House is five years, although it may be dissolved by the President at any time, in accordance with the usual practice in a parliamentary system, and its life may be extended for no more than one year at a time if the President proclaims a national emergency.

The presiding officer of the Lok Sabha is the Speaker. This im-

[15] P. Vijayaraghavan, *Second Chamber of the Indian Legislature* (unpublished Ph.D. dissertation, University of Saugar, 1960), p. 187.

portant office has been held by two able men, G. V. Mavalankar until his death in February, 1956, and then M. Ananthasayanam Ayyangar, who had served as Deputy Speaker. Mavalankar was a great Speaker, one of the ablest in the Commonwealth countries. He had had many years of experience as a presiding officer, and he carried out his duties in the Lok Sabha with firmness, efficiency, and studied fairness. He was highly respected, not only by the Congress members of the House — he had been identified with the Congress Party — but by the opposition M. P.'s as well. Ayyangar is a different kind of person, less firm and formidable but in his own way effective. He too had had extensive experience as a presiding officer, in the Legislative Assembly in his native state of Madras as well as in the Lok Sabha. The present Deputy Speaker, Hukam Singh, is a quiet, gentlemanly Sikh, a lawyer and judge by profession, who is a former President of the Akali Dal, the main Sikh political organization.

1. *Committees of the House.* Much of the work of the Lok Sabha is done through various committees. From the time of their introduction into the Central Legislative Assembly in 1922, until March, 1952, the various central legislative bodies which functioned under British rule or after independence had a well-developed system of advisory standing committees. After the first general elections in 1951–52 the Nehru government decided that standing committees should be abolished. In reply to criticism of this decision the Prime Minister "explained that these committees had been formed in quite different conditions and that they would now have 'no meaning.' They belonged to a different system of institutions from those now in existence, and in any case they had proved of little use in recent years."[16]

Although standing committees do not exist in name, the House of the People does rely upon various kinds of committees for the discharge of much of its day-to-day work. These committees fall into three categories: (1) general committees concerned primarily with the organization and powers of the House, such as the Committee on Rules, the Business Advisory Committee, and the Committee on Government Assurances; (2) legislative committees, chiefly select committees appointed for the consideration of particular bills and committees on petitions, resolutions, and subordinate legislation; and (3) the finance committees, notably the powerful Committees on Public Accounts and on Estimates.

The Committee on Government Assurances, established in December, 1953, appears to be "a wholly Indian invention." Its terms of

[16] Morris-Jones, *Parliament in India,* p. 310. See also Norman D. Palmer and Irene Tinker, "Decision Making in the Indian Parliament," in Richard L. Park and Irene Tinker, eds., *Leadership and Political Institutions in India* (Princeton, N.J., 1959), pp. 122–123.

reference are sweeping ones: "The functions of the Committee are to scrutinise the assurances, promises and undertakings, etc., given by Ministers from time to time on the floor of the House and to report on (a) the extent to which such assurances have been implemented; and (b) where implemented, whether such implementations have taken place in the minimum time necessary for the purpose." The rationale of this unique committee is thus explained by Professor N. Srinivasan:

> It is common experience that when criticised Governments are profuse in their assurances that mistakes pointed out will not be repeated, that reparation would be made for any injuries and wrongs complained of and that steps would be taken to implement some particular policy. But no means or machinery exist in democratic countries to enforce the fulfilment of such assurances other than the continued interest of private members. The Committee on Government Assurances . . . is an attempt to provide such machinery.[17]

Because there is a considerable body of delegated legislation in India, the work of the Committee on Subordinate Legislation, also established in December, 1953, is particularly important. The main function of the Committee is to study all such delegated legislation and to report to the Lok Sabha "whether the powers delegated by Parliament have been properly exercised within the framework of the statute delegating such powers."

The Public Accounts Committee not only checks the audit reports of the Comptroller and Auditor General and other records and operations for technical irregularities, but it also is interested in any evidences of waste, corruption, inefficiency, or operational deficiencies in the conduct of the nation's financial affairs. It is thus "Parliament's watchdog and guardian of the people against official negligence or corruption." Its reports are important documents.

According to the Rules of Procedure of the Lok Sabha the function of the Estimates Committee is to "examine such of the estimates as may seem fit to the Committee and to report what, if any, economies consistent with the policy underlying these estimates may be effected therein, and to suggest the form in which the estimates shall be presented to Parliament." The Committee has taken a broad view of its functions, and has not hesitated to make studies and recommendations affecting the whole field of administrative organization and policy. For this reason its many substantial reports have been more than technical studies. Some of these reports, such as the ninth report on "Administrative, Financial and Other Reforms," have been major

[17] N. Srinivasan, *Democratic Government in India* (Calcutta, 1954), pp. 260–261.

contributions to public administration in India. W. H. Morris-Jones has called attention to the broader contributions of the Committee:

> To a very real extent, this type of committee, inspired as it is by the idea not simply of economy nor even of efficiency alone but also of acting as a check against an oppressive or arbitrary executive, achieves a special significance as a substitute for a real Opposition. Indeed, it may well be that in an underdeveloped country — in which there is a wide measure of agreement not only on goals but also on methods — this kind of arrangement may be more suitable. . . . Finally, it must be noted that the Estimates Committee, perhaps more than the Public Accounts Committee, performs two tasks of quite special importance in India. In the first place, it is a most valuable training-ground for members of the House. . . . In the second place, the reports of the Committee have a great educative value inside the House and also outside. They can help greatly to build up that layer of informed public opinion which is so urgently needed if the gap between rulers and ruled is to be closed.[18]

2. *Procedure in the House.* Within the broad framework of powers and responsibilities specified in the Constitution the Parliament of India functions according to rules of procedure which are similar to those in the British Parliament. A bill is introduced in the House of the People through the usual British procedure of three readings, with the first reading largely by title only, the second the stage of debate and detailed consideration, and the third a general discussion usually leading to a vote, by viva voce or by division. Between the first and second readings a bill may be referred to a select committee, although in India this practice is usually followed on important bills only. In the British Parliament more bills are referred to select committees, and consideration by these committees comes after and not before the second reading.

Question time is an important feature of the work of both Houses of the Indian Parliament. It takes place every day during a session in the Lok Sabha and four days a week in the Rajya Sabha. The procedure of the question period is patterned after that followed in the British House of Commons. Hundreds, even thousands, of written questions are filed with the Speaker at every session, and many more oral supplementary questions are entertained. The question period is usually the most interesting and lively part of the meetings of the Parliament. It puts the Ministers and other governmental spokesmen on their merit, and it provides Nehru himself with one of his best opportunities for generalship and for discussion of issues of public interest. It also gives the opposition members of the Parliament their

[18] Morris-Jones, *Parliament in India,* pp. 307–308.

best opportunity to force the Government, backed by an overwhelming majority in the House, to pay some attention to them and to defend itself against criticisms. Twice a week in the House, whenever time permits, a half hour is allotted late in the afternoon for discussions of topics of national importance which have been the subjects of questions.

Most of the bills that are introduced are, of course, Government bills. Very little time is allowed for the introduction of private members' bills, and very few of the private bills that are considered are approved. Opposition members may influence legislation by putting questions in the question period, by participating in debates on Government bills, and by membership on select committees, finance committees and other committees of the House, but they have little chance of pushing through any legislation of their own.

To be officially recognized by the Speaker as an opposition group, a party or coalition of parties must have at least fifty members in the Lok Sabha. No opposition party has come even close to this figure to date, whereas membership in the Congress Party has ranged between 350 and 400 members in a House of approximately 500. When Dr. Shyama Prasad Mookerjee, one of the most powerful parliamentarians India has seen, was a member of the Lok Sabha as leader of the Jan Sangh, he was recognized as leader of a rightist coalition known as the Democratic Nationalist Party, but even this coalition was unable to command fifty seats. The Praja Socialist Party has attempted to form a Parliamentary coalition in order to gain recognition as an official opposition group, but this effort too has not been productive. The largest single opposition group in the Lok Sabha in the present Parliament is the Communist Party, but this party has fewer than thirty members and only a few of its really top leaders, such as S. A. Dange, are M.P.'s.

Powers and Functions of Parliament. The Parliament of India has rather extensive powers and performs a variety of important functions. Its main function, of course, is as India's chief lawmaking body. Its functions in this respect are limited legally by the federal nature of the Indian Republic and by the power of the Supreme Court to declare Parliamentary legislation of most types unconstitutional. It is further limited in an extra-legal way by the degree of real control over it which is exercised by the Prime Minister and the chief organs of the Congress Party. It has some constituent powers. It is authorized by the Constitution, for example, to alter the boundaries of a State, and it has reorganized the Indian States in a major way by ordinary legislation. A majority of the total membership in each House may amend the Constitution, with the President's assent, except in certain vital matters, in which case amendments proposed by the Parliament must receive the assent of at least half of the State legislatures. Since the Council of Ministers, i.e., the *de facto* executive of the Indian Republic, is "collectively responsible to the House of the People," "we can say that it is the character of the House of the People which will determine the character of the government of the day."[19] As we have seen, the House has control over the nation's finances, and in this vital area the Government must therefore obtain the cooperation and approval of the House.

The Indian Parliament is the country's major deliberative body. It is here that important problems of domestic and foreign policy are debated and passed upon, and while much of the discussion is carried on *in camera,* in the councils of the ruling party and in Parliamentary committees, the major issues sooner or later come before the Parliament for public discussion and debate. In spite of the widespread illiteracy and concentration on matters of local concern, increasing interest has been shown in the deliberations of the Parliament. When any important measure is being discussed, crowds of people try to get into the few seats in the gallery of the House of the People or the Council of States, the Parliamentary discussions are printed almost verbatim in leading newspapers, and the Parliament seems to feel stimulated to look upon itself as a true forum for the consideration of major issues of national policy. It serves as a means of ventilating the grievances of the public. Even though the opposition is weak and divided, the value of this function should not be minimized. On some occasions, when public opinion seemed to be well ahead of the Government, this fact has been most effectively dramatized in the Indian Parliament and has eventually had some bearing on Government policy. This was the case immediately after the Russian suppression of the uprising in Hungary in 1956, and after the Chinese suppression of the revolt in Tibet and the Chinese moves along the borders of India in 1959. Generally speaking, however, the opposition has had little success in changing Government policy. As Dr. Lanka Sunderam, a leading Independent M.P., has remarked, "in the Lok Sabha there are few recorded instances when Government has acceded to the demands of the Opposition, and each such measure is something to be cherished."[20]

Undoubtedly Parliament serves a most important function by providing a training ground for national leaders, and by giving such people practical experience in the workings of parliamentary democracy. This is an especially important function in India, where

[19] Suda, *Indian Constitutional Development and National Movement,* p. 602.

[20] Lanka Sunderam, "The Role of An Independent Member," in Lal, ed., *The Indian Parliament,* p. 67.

democracy is not deeply rooted, where the responsibilities of independence are just beginning to be understood, and where relatively inexperienced people are charged with vast responsibilities. In the first Indian Parliament, from 1952 to 1956, more than 55 per cent of the members had had no previous legislative experience.[21] The members of the second Parliament were even more inexperienced.

Language is an added problem in the Parliament. Article 120 of the Constitution states that the business of the Parliament shall be conducted in Hindi or in English, but it also provided that the Speaker could "permit any member who cannot adequately express himself in Hindi or in English to address the House in his mother tongue." This provided an opportunity for a babel of tongues and for mutual incomprehensibility in the proceedings of the Parliament. Most of the M.P.'s can speak English or Hindi, or both, but many of those from the South and from tribal areas and other parts of the country cannot and many of those who can refuse to do so for reasons of local pride or aversion to the idea of using a foreign language or a North Indian tongue.[22]

The conditions under which the Indian M.P.'s have to work impose further handicaps. "They are not only inexperienced; they are also poorly educated, poorly paid, and usually in straitened circumstances. They lack adequate staff assistance, and they receive little help in research and preparation of speeches and reports. Moreover, many M.P.'s do not even make good use of the facilities at their disposal. It is difficult for them to find the time or the opportunity for serious reflection or study; their ways of life as well as their living arrangements make them easy prey for hordes of people who may flock about them at all hours. Often they are out of touch with their constituents, who in any event, if they have any interest in politics at all, are probably more interested in their representatives to local bodies and the state assemblies than in their representatives in far-off New Delhi."[23]

It is difficult to assess the precise role of the Parliament of India in the Indian governmental system. It is the chief lawmaking agency,

[21] Morris-Jones, *Parliament in India,* p. 117 (Table V).

[22] Most of the speeches and other statements in the House of the People are still made in English, but the use of Hindi is growing. During the five sessions of the House from 1952 to 1954 the average number of minutes of Hindi reporting per day varied from 34 to 58. Speeches made in Hindi are published in Hindi, without English translation, but a Hindi edition of the debates is issued, together with an English edition. The distinguished Muslim, Maulana Azad, who was Minister of Education until his death in 1958, always spoke in Urdu in the House, although he also spoke English fluently. See Morris-Jones, *Parliament in India,* pp. 144–146.

[23] Palmer and Tinker, in Park and Tinker, eds., *Leadership and Political Institutions in India,* pp. 135–136.

but it does not really make the basic decisions. Certainly it does not yet play the central role which would be expected in a parliamentary system. Some critics have maintained that it is "no more than Pandit Nehru's *durbar,*" and it is true that the Prime Minister and a handful of leading figures in the Congress Party make most of the basic decisions, which the Parliament, if called upon, will almost automatically approve. The Congress Parliamentary Party, which has such a preponderance of strength in both Houses of the Parliament, is clearly subordinate to major agencies of the Party, notably the Working Committee, and to Nehru himself.

With all of these limitations, however, the Parliament of India, especially the Lok Sabha, has functioned with remarkable effectiveness, and it has established itself as an indispensable part of the governmental machinery. Nehru has been an active participant in its proceedings, and he has paid great deference to it. He has helped to establish strong foundations for the continuance of parliamentary rule in India. Future Prime Ministers, who will be men of lesser stature and influence, will inevitably have to pay even greater attention to the Parliament. "There are abundant reasons to believe that, even in the Congress Party, the support that the Prime Minister enjoys will be subject to the overall consent of Parliament. A major political revolution has thus appeared almost as a convention."[24]

The Supreme Court of India

Unlike the United States, India has a single judicial system, not a system of dual courts, with the Supreme Court at the head of the judicial hierarchy, with High Courts in each of the states, and with district courts and other subordinate courts in the local areas of government. In framing the judicial provisions of the Constitution, special attention was paid to the practice in the United States as well as in Great Britain and other countries, and decisions of the Indian Supreme Court frequently cite decisions of the Supreme Court of the United States.[25] After considerable discussion the framers of the Constitution did not adopt a due process of law clause, along the lines of the American model, but at least two articles of the Constitution use words suggestive of due process. Article 21 declares that "No person shall be deprived of his life or personal liberty except according to procedure established by law," and Article 31 (1) states that "No

[24] "The Stature of Parliament," *The Eastern Economist,* XXXI (Dec. 5, 1958), 849.

[25] "In recent times, the influence of American Constitutional Law and of American political thought is making itself felt increasingly." K. Lipstein, "The Reception of Western Law in India," *International Social Science Bulletin,* IX (1957), 95.

person shall be deprived of his property save by authority of law." In the famous case of *Gopalan v. Madras* the Supreme Court of India rejected a contention that Article 21 was the equivalent of the American due process clause, but Justice William O. Douglas of the United States Supreme Court, who has written a brilliant comparative analysis of the legal systems of India and the United States, has observed: "I discern in Indian judicial decisions a flavor of due process when it comes to questions of substantive law."[26] A preliminary draft of the Constitution contained a provision specifically relating to judicial review, but this was omitted in the final text. There can be no question, however, that judicial review is a significant prerogative of the Indian judiciary, and that the Supreme Court exercises a wide jurisdiction in this area.

According to the Constitution the Supreme Court of India was to consist of a Chief Justice and not more than seven other judges. Parliament was authorized to change the number of judges, and has done so. The present number is ten, in addition to the Chief Justice. The Chief Justice and other judges are appointed by the President of India, "after consultation with such of the Judges of the Supreme Court and of the High Courts in the States as the President may deem necessary," and the Chief Justice "shall always be consulted" in the case of appointments of other members of the highest court.

The Court has three main kinds of jurisdiction: original, appellate, and advisory. Its original jurisdiction extends to any dispute (1) between the Government of India and one or more States; (2) between the Government of India and any State or States, on one side, and one or more States on the other; and (3) between two or more States. Its appellate jurisdiction extends to three types of cases, namely constitutional, civil, and criminal. In these types of cases, under certain conditions, appeals may be made from any High Court to the Supreme Court. The President may refer a question of public importance to the Court for its consideration, and the Court, if it so chooses, may submit an advisory opinion to the President. According to Professor Charles Alexandrowicz, a leading authority on Indian constitutional law, the first advisory opinion of the Indian Supreme Court, dealing with the delegation of legislative authority, "after Gopalan's case is the second fundamental pronouncement of the Court on the Constitution as such."[27]

[26] William O. Douglas, *We the Judges: Studies in American and Indian Constitutional Law from Marshall to Mukherjea* (Garden City, N.Y., 1956), p. 28.

[27] Charles H. Alexandrowicz, *Constitutional Developments in India* (London, 1957), p. 5. For the text of this advisory opinion see Reference under Article 143, 14 *Supreme Court Journal* 527.

Located in the splendid new Supreme Court building in New Delhi, which also houses a magnificent legal library and the Indian Law Institute, an important legal research agency, the Supreme Court of India has won an enviable place for itself in the Indian constitutional system. It has invariably been composed of able judges, and its decisions have been of real importance. This is true in spite of the fact that its sphere of competence can be, and has been, limited by the Indian Parliament and is restricted in certain other ways under the Constitution. Many of its most important judgments on constitutional issues have related to the interpretation of Article 14, guaranteeing equality before the law, Article 19, guaranteeing important freedoms to the individual, and Article 31, regarding property rights. The Preventive Detention Act, first enacted in 1950, and renewed subsequently, has given rise to a number of cases which have come before the Supreme Court. The best known of these cases was that of *Gopalan v. Madras.*[28] A. K. Gopalan, then the leader of the Communists in the House of the People, was arrested and confined under this Act, and he brought legal action for release on the ground that he had been deprived of his rights as a citizen under Articles 14 and 19. The Supreme Court, in a historic decision, which Professor Alexandrowicz has called "the first great pronouncement of the Supreme Court of India on the Constitution generally,"[29] denied Gopalan's claim and upheld the Government's action.

Article 31 of the Constitution provided for compensation for any property "acquired for public purposes," but it apparently gave the Parliament full authority to fix the amount of the compensation. Soon after the Constitution went into effect, various questions arose regarding the propriety and legal authority for land reform programs enacted by some of the States, with the strong encouragement of the federal Government. The Constitution (First Amendment) Act of 1951 modified and clarified Article 31 by stating clearly that no law for the acquisition of property by any State should be declared void on the ground that it was inconsistent with Article 31. A number of Supreme Court cases upheld the claims of former land-holders that their property had been taken from them without just compensation. Nehru maintained that the Supreme Court should not attempt to act as a "third House of Parliament," and the Government pushed through the Constitution (Fourth Amendment) Act in 1955 providing that the question of the reasonableness of the compensation was no longer justiciable. Many Indian and foreign students of Indian constitutional law have criticized this amendment, but others have argued that the amendment was necessary to clarify the intent of the framers of

[28] 1950 *Supreme Court Journal* 174–311.

[29] Alexandrowicz, *Constitutional Developments in India,* p. 5.

Article 31 and to insure that important measures of social reform are not blocked by judicial decisions.[30]

The Public Services

In one respect, at least, India was probably more fortunate than any other formerly dependent territory which has achieved independence. It inherited from the British period an elaborate and well-organized administrative structure and a variety of Imperial Services, manned by well-trained men. At the head of these services was the Indian Civil Service, the "steel frame" of the British Indian administrative system. Even today, although their ranks, never numerous, have been decimated by death, resignation, and assignment to other duties, and although all of the British I.C.S. Officers save one or two have gone, former I.C.S. Officers hold many of the administrative posts of highest responsibility and prestige, both in the Centre and in the States.

The successor to the I.C.S. is the Indian Administrative Service, which has more members and far less prestige than the old Indian Civil Service. Its members are recruited from among the most promising young Indians who hold a university degree, through a system of examinations; they are carefully trained at an in-service training school, now located in Mussoorie; they serve an apprenticeship at the Centre and in the States, including at least one assignment with a District Officer and with increasing frequency with officials of the Community Development Program. After their probationary period they then receive more responsible assignments.

The Public Services of India consist of two broad groups, the Defense Forces and the Civil Services. The Constitution says nothing about the recruitment, training, or conditions of service of members of the armed forces; but many of the officers appointed to the National Defense Academy, the Military College, the Indian Air Force

[30] In his Tagore Law Lectures at the University of Calcutta in July, 1955, Justice Douglas said: "Whatever the cause, the 1955 amendment casts a shadow over every private factory, plant, or other individual enterprise in India. The legislature may now appropriate it at any price it desires — substantial or nominal. There is no review of the reasonableness of the amount of compensation. The result can be just compensation or confiscation — dependent wholly on the mood of the Parliament." Douglas, *We the Judges,* p. 296. Professor Alexandrowicz holds a different view: "It is difficult for the reader of the Fourth Constitutional Amendment Act to escape the conclusion that it simply aims at restoring to some extent what was laid down by the Constituent Assembly but changed by judicial interpretation. . . . The Constitution has in fact not been changed much but rather redrafted in order to reflect better the original intentions of the constitution-makers." Alexandrowicz, *Constitutional Developments in India,* p. 94.

Flying College, and to the commissioned ranks of the Indian Navy are appointed in consultation with the Union Public Service Commission, after examinations conducted by the Commission.

The Civil Services may be divided into three main categories: the All-India Services, the Union Services, and the State Public Services. Although the Parliament is authorized by the Constitution to create other All-India Services, provided at least two-thirds of the members of the Council of States approve a resolution to this effect, the only All-India Services are those specified in Article 312 of the Constitution, namely the Indian Administrative Service and the Indian Police Service. Union Services include services in various administrative departments of the Government of India, such as the Foreign Service, the Audits and Accounts Service, the Customs and Excise Service, the Defence Accounts Service, the Railway Accounts Service, the Income Tax Service, and the Postal Service. There are also several engineering and ministerial services. Members of the State Public Services are usually appointed by the Governor on the recommendation of the State Public Service Commission. Some of the highest posts in State administration, such as Divisional Commissioners, District Magistrates, Inspectors General of Police and Superintendents of Police may be filled by officers of the I.A.S. or the Indian Police Service.

Responsible for the main task of recruitment, training, and maintaining high standards in the Indian Civil Services is the Union Public Service Commission. This body is the direct successor to the Public Service Commission which was established in 1926, as provided for in the Government of India Act of 1919 and as recommended by a Royal Commission on the Superior Civil Service in India (the Lee Commission). Public Service Commissions had also been set up in the nineteenth century, especially after 1853, when the British East India Company was deprived of its right to make nominations to the Covenanted Civil Service and a system of competitive examinations was first introduced. It is therefore not surprising that the Union Public Service Commission of independent India should follow procedures similar to those which had been developed in the British period under the supervision of similar bodies.

The Constitution of India provided for the establishment of a Union Public Service Commission, consisting of an unspecified number of members to be appointed by the President, and of a Public Service Commission in each State, whose members were to be named by the Governor. There are now eight members of the Union Public Service Commission, including the Chairman. Each member is appointed for a six-year term or until he reaches the age of 65, the compulsory retirement age. He is not eligible for reappointment. To maintain the complete integrity of the Commission, the Constitution states that when he ceases to hold office the Chairman of the Union Public Service Commission "shall be ineligible for further employment either under the Government of India or under the Government of a State," and that other members of the Union Commission shall be similarly ineligible for any office except that of Chairman of the Union or of a State Public Service Commission.

The Commission is an independent statutory body. Its relations with the Government of India are coordinated through the Ministry of Home Affairs, but it deals directly with other ministries and departments. It has a Secretariat of over 500 members, and its office is organized into five branches.[31]

Article 320 of the Constitution specifies a wide variety of duties and functions for the Union Public Service Commission. It is charged with the conduct of examinations for appointment to the services of the Union and of the States; if requested by two or more States, it shall assist those States "in framing and operating schemes for joint recruitment for any services for which candidates possessing special qualifications are required"; it shall be consulted "on all matters relating to methods of recruitment to civil services and for civil posts," on principles to be followed in making appointments, promotions and transfers from one service to another, and on all disciplinary matters and claims affecting members of the civil services; it shall advise on any matter which the President may refer to it; it may be, and in fact has been, given additional functions by the Parliament; and it shall submit an annual report to the President, who shall present it to the Parliament, together with a statement of his reasons for not accepting the advice of the Commission, if such cases have arisen. Almost invariably the advice and recommendations of the Commission have been accepted.

India was fortunate indeed to inherit an administrative system which was characterized by high standards of integrity and efficiency and which gave an increasing number of Indians experience in the conduct of administrative affairs; but, as Dr. Paul Appleby has observed, this system was "designed to serve the relatively simple interests of an occupying power,"[32] and it was not adequate, either in structure or in spirit, for the administration of a vast new country in the interests of the people of that country and not of a foreign power. The major weaknesses of the Indian administrative system are rather generally

[31] See Indian Institute of Public Administration, *The Organisation of the Government of India,* pp. 357–367.

[32] Paul H. Appleby, *Public Administration in India: Report of a Survey* (Delhi, 1953), p. 40.

recognized. They have been pointed out repeatedly by Indian students and practitioners of administration, notably A. D. Gorwala,[33] and by foreign observers, including Dr. Paul Appleby, an American specialist in administration who, at the request of the Government of India, made two detailed surveys of public administration in India and submitted two much-discussed reports. These weaknesses are those of structure and of orientation.

Dr. Appleby, a friendly critic who rated the Government of India "among the dozen or so most advanced governments of the world," stated that his "major over-all concerns" related to constitutional structure, which provides "chiefly for 'co-ordination' rather than for administration," to "the related but more extended diffusion of administrative responsibility," a very major and pervasive weakness, and to "flexibility and future adequacy in administrative conceptions, terminology, structure and practices."[34] He found that "administration" in India was conceived much too narrowly and formally and was "largely negative." He concluded that for all its merits the Indian administrative system was not adequate for the tasks ahead, and he recommended many fundamental changes. "The great achievements of recent years," he stated in his second report in 1956, "have been beyond the capacity of the Indian administrative system. By working key personnel very excessive hours, by giving special attention to a very disproportionate number of transactions, by stubborn persistence of programmatic officials in the face of frustration, great results have been achieved. There is an early limit, however, to what may be done in this fashion. It puts too much reliance on a very small number of individuals, whereas for a much larger achievement reliance must be on a greatly improved organizational performance of systematic character."[35]

One of the features of the Indian civil services which is constantly baffling to foreigners who are not familiar with the traditions and practices of these services is the remarkably limited number of personnel in the top ranks. One would think that a nation of over 400,000,000 people, engaged in the major work of nation-building and development, would require the services of hundreds of thousands of highly trained administrative personnel in its higher services. Instead, the really top civil servants can be numbered in the hundreds.

[33] A. D. Gorwala, *Report on Public Administration* (Delhi, 1951), a report prepared for the Planning Commission.

[34] Appleby, *Public Administration in India*, pp. 8–9.

[35] Paul H. Appleby, *Re-examination of India's Administrative System with Special Reference to Administration of Government's Industrial and Commercial Enterprises* (Delhi, 1956), p. 2.

Most university graduates in India aspire to careers in these top services, which have great prestige and which offer positions of relative security and at least a comparatively good standard of living in a country where other positions are hard to obtain; but few of the many thousands of Indian university-trained people who try to get into the higher civil services are successful. Each year only a handful of persons are taken into the Indian Administrative Service. The result is a great deal of frustration among the educated young Indians and a dearth of top administrative talent in the services. While "big government" suggests the evils of an inflated and entrenched bureaucracy, the fact is that the Government of India is a big government and must become even bigger if it is to discharge the many tasks imposed upon it in the crucial years ahead. For this reason Dr. Appleby warned in his second report:

> It is of the highest importance here that all leaders, in party, parliament and private life understand that the government must grow rapidly in size — in numbers employed and in annual costs — and that this growth will be greater than, not less than, the estimate it is thought acceptable to publish. . . . The needs will be great in both the private and the public sectors, but the public need will be central and primary, limiting the capacity of the government to grow, and therefore limiting its capacity to achieve. In such a condition anything pretending to be precise forward planning is futile and unnecessary except as such planning is done in terms of enlarging the capacity to produce such personnel to an expanding maximum.[36]

In view of the legacy of the past and the tremendous demands that are now placed upon it, it is hardly surprising that, as Dr. Appleby pointed out, "the great achievements of recent years have been beyond the capacity of the Indian administrative system." This same observation could be made about the Government of India generally, including the Parliament, the Ministers, and the top leadership everywhere. The Government has significant achievements to its credit: it has carried on the affairs of the new nation through a difficult decade and a half; it has launched ambitious programs of economic development and social reform; it has maintained its authority and prestige in the face of many divisive forces; it has won respect for India abroad; it has been a working democracy-in-being, and it has given hope to those who want India to move forward in the democratic way. But it has yet to prove that it can gear itself adequately to the tremendous tasks of nation-building.

[36] *Ibid.*, p. 10.

* 7 *

State and Local Government

As the capital of a vast nation of more than 400,000,000 people, the city of New Delhi naturally occupies a uniquely conspicuous and important place in Indian political life. But New Delhi is not India. In many respects, like the capital cities of most states, it is quite unrepresentative of the country of which it is the capital. It is the seat of administration and government, but it not the "real India."

That "real India" is to be found in the countryside, and particularly in the more than 550,000 villages where some 80 per cent of the people live. It is to be found in the districts, the major administrative units of rural India. It is to be found in the great cities — the old Presidential municipalities of Bombay, Madras, and Calcutta; the capitals of the former princely States such as Hyderabad and Mysore and Jaipur; industrial centers such as Kanpur and Ahmedabad and Jamshedpur; the capitals of India States today, such as Lucknow and Patna; the holy cities of the Hindus, such as Banaras (Varanasi) and Allahabad and Hardwar and Nasik and Puri, and of other faiths, such as Amritsar, the holy city of the Sikhs. Except for a cosmopolitan city like Bombay, this "real India" is less modern, less affected by Western ways, more influenced by caste and tradition, than is New Delhi. To the great majority of Indians, mostly illiterate, mostly tradition-bound, and mostly living in villages, New Delhi is far away, in a mental as well as a geographical sense. In fact, to most Indians the very concept of India as a nation is still one that has not been really grasped, and all efforts to inculcate this concept beat against walls of provincialism, casteism, regionalism, and lingualism, and hardly penetrate the little world in which most Indians dwell.

However much New Delhi may dominate the country, administratively and politically speaking, it must work in large measure with and through the various units of State and local government, which have more direct contacts with the masses of the people. In spite of the many unfederal features of the Indian federal system, these units of local government are by no means unimportant, or simply agencies of the national governmental apparatus.

We have already noted the conflicting trends toward centralization and toward decentralization in Indian politics and administration. We have described the anomaly of a strong central government, made even stronger by the authoritarian traditions of India's political past, by the dominance of the Congress Party and the leadership of that Party, by the imperatives of the planned society, and by the general centralizing trends of modern times. This government as noted by observers such as Dr. Paul Appleby, is extraordinarily dependent on the States and on units of local government and often appears to function more as a coordinating body than as a central authority. The long hand of the Centre extends into every village and district in the country. It is extended not only for the things which the Indian people in the past have associated — and to a large degree still associate — with government, such as taxes, police administration, and law and order, but also to help to provide the more positive services of a welfare state to peoples whose standards of life must be revolutionized before they can be regarded as really tolerable. At the same time the people are more familiar with local officials and local governmental units, which deal more directly with problems with which they are most concerned.

In a developing country such as India the problems of government and of administration are exceedingly complex. These problems are both old and new. They include the usual tasks of government — administration, taxation, protection, public services, justice, and the like — and also the new and enlarged tasks of a country seeking not only to raise minimum standards of livelihood in a most distressful land but also to implement ambitious programs of economic development and social welfare. These enlarged tasks fall partly upon more or less conventional forms of government and administration, patterned largely after institutions with which the people of India have been familiar for decades or even for centuries; they also fall upon new institutions, such as Community Development and National Extension Service blocks, or upon revitalized institutions of ancient origin, such as village *panchayats,* which are charged with vital aspects of national planning and development.

In this chapter we shall describe the more conventional forms of State and local government in India, with due attention to the ways in which these forms are being affected by or associated with the new efforts in the development and welfare fields. In Chapter 8 we shall focus our attention on new patterns of government and administration, now in effect or seriously proposed, which are being associated with and which may in time partially supplant the more conventional forms.

The States

The major subdivisions of the Republic of India today are the fifteen States: Assam, Andhra Pradesh, Bihar, Gujerat, Jammu and Kashmir, Kerala, Madhya Pradesh, Madras, Maharashtra, Mysore, Orissa, the Punjab, Rajasthan, Uttar Pradesh, and West Bengal. It is possible that the Naga areas of northeastern India, which are now administered directly by the Central Government through the Governor of Assam, may be created as a sixteenth State. Outside of the State boundaries are the Protectorate of Sikkim, and six centrally administered territories: Delhi, Himachal Pradesh, Manipur, Tripura, the Andaman and Nicobar Islands, and the Laccadive, Minicoy, and Aminidivi Islands. The major subdivisions of the State are the districts, of which there are more than 250 in India. Within the districts, some of which are divided into *talukas* or *tahsils,* the most important subdivision is the village, the basic unit of Indian rural administration, as well as of Indian life. The cities of India are under separate municipal administration.

Federal-State Relations. As in any federal state, special attention should be given to the relations between the Central Government in India and the States. As has been pointed out, the Constitution lists many items on the Concurrent List. In dealing with these items a high degree of cooperation between the Centre and the States is obviously essential. An equally high degree of cooperation is likewise required in financial administration, in joint federal-State planning and in the coordination of programming and execution, in governmental services, and in many other fields of activity. Large numbers of joint federal-State projects are being implemented, and these require the effective cooperation of the States. Various kinds of relationships between the Centre and the States should be examined, particularly political, administrative, legal and constitutional relationships. This is an important field of study, which has not been sufficiently explored.

In the Central Government the Ministry of Home Affairs is charged with direct responsibility for administrative, financial, and economic problems of States, and the Minister for Home Affairs is chairman of each of the five Zonal Councils which were provided for in the States Reorganization Act of 1956; but every Ministry and every other branch of the Central Government has some responsibilities relating to the States. Their responsibilities extend even to matters which are on the State List, such as the vital one of education, and their activities are often far more than advisory and coordinating.

In 1954 the Government of India announced the establishment of a central Council of Local Self-Government, an advisory body with the Central Minister for Health as Chairman and with State Ministers for Local Self-Government and certain heads of village *panchayats* as members. According to the official announcement, "the Council will consider and recommend broad lines of policy, make proposals for legislation laying down patterns of development for the country as a whole, and examine the whole field of possible cooperation in local self-government matters."[1]

Organization of the States, 1947–1956. We have already described the process by which the more than 500 Indian princely States were integrated with the Union of India, most of them even before independence on August 15, 1947, and the process by which these States were subsequently reorganized and for the most part consolidated with each other and with the territories of the Indian Union which formerly comprised British India. These major tasks were carried out by the Ministry of States, created in July, 1947, under the brilliant and forceful direction of Vallabhbhai Patel until his death in 1951. By that time most of the work of integration and consolidation was over, although much still remained to be done in the area of "democratization." In January, 1955, the Ministry of States was merged with the Ministry of Home Affairs. Three of the former princely States — Hyderabad, Mysore, and Jammu and Kashmir — were kept intact, and they became Part B States in the Republic of India when the Constitution went into effect on January 20, 1950. The other five Part B States — Madhya Bharat, Patiala and East Punjab States Union (PEPSU), Rajasthan, Saurashtra, and Travancore-Cochin — were formed by joining together other former princely States, large and small.

In addition to the eight Part B States, the Constitution of 1950 provided for nine Part A States — Assam, Bihar, Bombay, Madhya Pradesh, Madras, Orissa, the Punjab, United Provinces, and West Bengal — corresponding to ten Provinces of British India, and ten Part C States — Ajmer, Bhopal, Bilaspur, Cooch-Behar, Coorg, Delhi, Himachal Pradesh, Kutch, Manipur, and Tripura. The list was amended almost immediately to change the name of the United Provinces to Uttar Pradesh, to omit Cooch-Bihar from the list of Part C States, and to add Vindhya Pradesh to this list. The Andaman and Nicobar Islands were listed in a Part D category. In 1953 the number of States was increased to twenty-eight, when a separate State of Andhra was created out of the upper part of Madras State.

[1] *Indiagram,* No. 543, Sept. 24, 1954.

Part A and Part B States were regarded roughly as of equal status (Jammu and Kashmir was in a rather different status, because of the disagreement with Pakistan over this territory), but Part C States were definitely of lesser status, and were in fact administered by the President of India, through a Chief Commissioner or Lieutenant Governor. Executive power in Part A States was exercised by a Governor, appointed by the President of India; in Part B States the executive head — except in Jammu and Kashmir[2] — was known as a Rakpramukh.

The Reorganization of the States. Thus the Union of India — the Republic of India after 1950 — was a federation of unequal parts, unlike most federations. This arrangement was changed, however, in the States Reorganization Act of 1956 and in the Constitution (Seventh Amendment) Act of 1956, both of which went into effect on November 1, 1956.

The circumstances leading to the political reorganization of India have already been described.[3] The reorganization was occasioned largely by the growing agitation for the creation of linguistic states, and the new map of India is organized mainly on a linguistic basis. The only major exceptions to the linguistic basis of reorganization, after November 1, 1956, were the States of Bombay, which was enlarged and not divided, and the Punjab, where the linguistic situation was complicated by other factors. After the reorganization the Indian Republic consisted of fourteen States of equal legal status — the distinction between Part A, Part B, and Part C States disappeared — and six Union Territories — Delhi, Himachal Pradesh, Manipur, Tripura, the Andaman and Nicobar Islands, and the Laccadive, Minicoy, and Amindivi Islands — which are centrally administered.

On May 1, 1960, yielding at long last to the continuing agitation among both the Marathi- and the Gujerati-speaking peoples of Bombay State, the Government of India divided Bombay into the two States of Gujerat, with a temporary capital at Ahmedabad, and Maharashtra, with its capital in the city of Bombay. This brought the number of Indian States to fifteen. In size these states vary from Madhya Pradesh and Rajasthan, each about 130,000 square miles in area, to Kerala, covering less than 10,000 square miles, and in population from Uttar Pradesh, whose population of approximately 70,000,000 is greater than all but seven nations of the world, to Jammu and Kashmir, which has fewer than 5,000,000 people.

[2] In the latter part of 1952 the son of the former Maharaja of Kashmir, the Yuvraj Karen Singh, was elected as head of the State of Jammu and Kashmir by the Constituent Assembly of that State, under the title of *Sadar-i-Riyasat.*

[3] See above, pp. 106–108. See also *Regionalism versus Provincialism: A Study in Problems of Indian National Unity, Indian Press Digests* Monograph Series No. 4 (Berkeley, Calif., December, 1958).

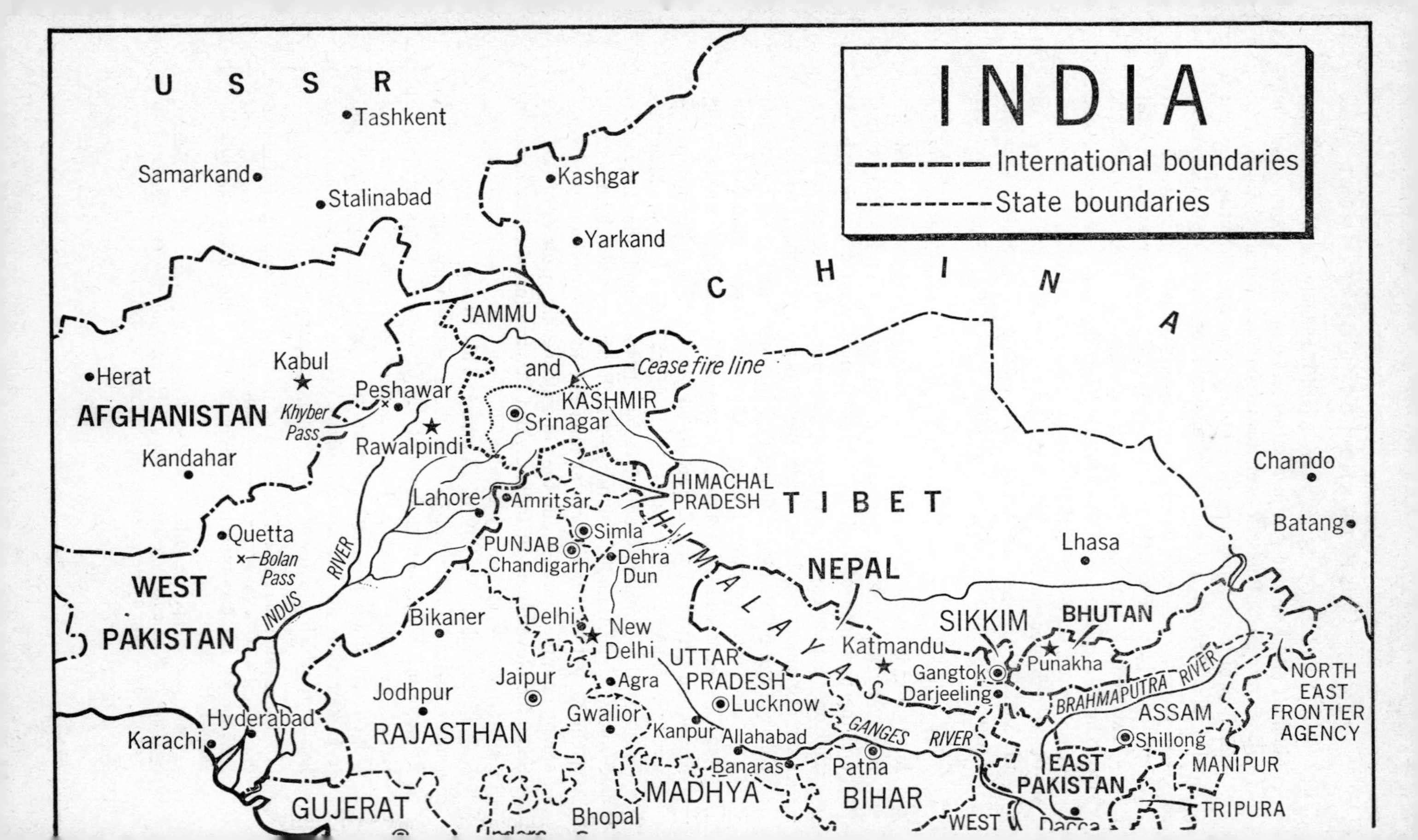
INDIA
International boundaries
State boundaries
U S S R
Tashkent
Samarkand
Stalinabad
Kashgar
Yarkand
C H I N A
JAMMU
and
KASHMIR
Cease fire line
Kabul
Herat
AFGHANISTAN
Peshawar
Khyber Pass
Rawalpindi
Srinagar
Kandahar
Chamdo
HIMACHAL PRADESH
TIBET
Lahore
Amritsar
Batang
Quetta
Bolan Pass
Simla
PUNJAB
Chandigarh
Dehra Dun
Lhasa
RIVER
NEPAL
WEST PAKISTAN
INDUS
HIMALAYAS
Bikaner
Delhi
New Delhi
SIKKIM
BHUTAN
Katmandu
UTTAR PRADESH
Gangtok
Punakha
Darjeeling
BRAHMAPUTRA RIVER
NORTH EAST FRONTIER AGENCY
Jaipur
Jodhpur
Agra
Lucknow
ASSAM
Hyderabad
Gwalior
GANGES RIVER
Karachi
RAJASTHAN
Kanpur
Allahabad
Shillong
Banaras
Patna
EAST PAKISTAN
MANIPUR
GUJERAT
MADHYA
BIHAR
Bhopal
WEST
TRIPURA

Ahmadabad
Baroda
NARMADA
RIVER
Jabalpur
Jamshedpur
BENGAL
Mandalay
Junagadh
PRADESH
Calcutta
Chittagong
BURMA
Nagpur
Cuttack
ORISSA
Bombay
MAHARASHTRA
Bhubaneswara
Poona
ARABIAN
SEA
Rangoon
BAY OF
BENGAL
Hyderabad
ANDHRA
Guntur
PRADESH
Panjim
GOA
MYSORE
Bangalore
Madras
Mysore
Amindivi
Is.
Andaman
Islands
KERALA
MADRAS
Laccadive
Islands
Trivandrum
Minicoy
Nicobar
Islands
CEYLON
Colombo
INDIAN OCEAN

Zonal Councils. The States Reorganization Act of 1956 grouped the new States into five Zonal Councils. The Punjab, Rajasthan, Jammu and Kashmir, and the Union Territories of Delhi and Himachal Pradesh formed the Northern Zone; Uttar Pradesh and Madhya Pradesh were associated in the Central Zone; Bihar, West Bengal, Orissa, Assam, and the Union Territories of Manipur and Tripura comprised the Eastern Zone; Bombay and Mysore formed the Western Zone; and Andhra Pradesh, Madras, and Kerala were grouped together in the Southern Zone. The Zonal Councils are advisory bodies; they "discuss and make recommendations to the Centre with regard to matters of common interest in the field of economic and social planning, border disputes, linguistic minorities, inter-State transport and any matter arising out of the reorganization of States."[4] The central Minister for Home Affairs is chairman of each Zonal Council, whose other members are the Chief Ministers of the member States, who act as Vice-Chairmen by rotation for a period of one year, and two other Ministers of the States. Each Union Territory associated with the Councils is represented by not more than two members, one of whom is the Lieutenant Governor or the Chief Commissioner. A member of the Planning Commission, the Chief Secretaries of the States, and the Development Commissioners or other officers deputed by the States act as advisers to the Councils.

The Zonal Councils could be a means of developing a healthy type of regionalism in the Indian Republic, and important agencies of coordination between the Centre and the States. "A review of the work of the Zonal Councils show that its [*sic*] principal role has been to carry out the program of the Centre in a given policy developed in the nation's capital. Thus the Zonal Councils have discussed the ways and means of implementing the policy of the Centre in matters of food policy, conservation, savings, and water conservation. They have also discussed regional problems affecting the member states including such problems as official state and national languages, border disputes, watershed development, regional hydroelectric power resources, food distribution, and police protection. Provision has also been made for the holding of joint meetings of two or more Zonal Councils wherever two or more regions face common problems."[5] In all probability the Councils will prove to be useful agencies, chiefly for implementing national plans and objectives, without making much of an impact on the government of the country.

[4] "The New Map of India," *The Hindu Weekly*, Nov. 5, 1956.

[5] Benjamin N. Schoenfeld, *Federalism in India* (Washington, D.C., 1960), pp. 17–18. For a rather different interpretation, stressing the importance of the Zonal Councils, see *Regionalism versus Provincialism, Indian Press Digests* Monograph Series No. 4.

The Executive in the States. In structure, if not in power, the government of each State is very similar to the Central Government of India. Parliamentary government exists in the States as well as in the Centre. Executive power is vested nominally in the Governor, appointed by the President of the Indian Republic. The Governor has a considerable amount of discretionary and other power, but he exercises this largely as an agent either of the Central Government or of the Ministry in power in the State. He is usually a distinguished elder statesman, who can discharge his rather perfunctory duties with dignity and who is in a position to exercise what Gandhi called an "all-pervading moral influence." Some Governors, such as C. M. Trevedi in Andhra Pradesh and Sri Prakasa in Madras, have shown how useful a permanent executive, above the battle, can be in times of political instability and crisis. Not all of the Governors are or have been Hindus; among the persons who have given distinguished service in the post of Governor are Professor Gurmukh Nihal Singh, a Sikh, as Governor of Rajasthan, Dr. Zakir Husain, one of India's leading Muslims, as Governor of Bihar, and Dr. H. C. Mookerjee, a Christian, who was Governor of West Bengal. Some students of Indian politics have recommended the abolition of the office of Governor, on the ground that such an official serves no useful purpose and is merely a drain on the treasury; but the predominant opinion, reinforced by the experience in the States since independence, is that there is a need for such a dignitary in each of the Indian States.[6]

The real executive in the States is the Chief Minister, corresponding to the Prime Minister at the Centre. He is appointed by the Governor, but is responsible to the State Legislative Assembly. Some of the most influential of Indian political leaders have served as Chief Ministers, and some promising younger men first gained national recognition in this position. A few years ago five of the best known political leaders of India held the post of Chief Minister: Pandit Pant in Uttar Pradesh, C. Rajagopalachari in Madras, Dr. B. C. Roy in West Bengal, Ravi Shankar Shukla in Madhya Pradesh, and Morarji Desai in Bombay. They were often referred to as "Nehru's five war lords." Today only one of them — Dr. B. C. Roy — is still a Chief Minister, and he will soon be an octogenarian. Pandit Shukla and Pandit Pant are dead, Morarji Desai is Finance Minister in the Central Government, and Rajagopalachari, now in his eighties, after another period of retirement, has emerged as the leader of the new right-wing Swatantra Party. Two Chief Ministers — U. N. Dhebar from Saurashtra and N. Sanjiva Reddy from Andhra Pradesh — have in recent years moved from this position to the presidency of the

[6] See J. P. Suda, *Indian Constitutional Development and National Movement* (Meerut, 1951), pp. 624–628.

Congress Party. Among the younger Chief Ministers who have attracted considerable national attention are Y. B. Chavan, formerly Chief Minister of Bombay State and now Chief Minister of the new State of Maharashtra, and Damodaram Sanjiviah, the youngest Chief Minister, who succeeded Sanjiva Reddy in Andhra Pradesh, who has attracted attention largely because he is the first Harijan (untouchable) ever to become a Chief Minister.

The cabinet of a State is the Council of Ministers, headed by the Chief Minister. Members are appointed by the Governor on the advice of the Chief Minister. Article 164 (2) of the Indian Constitution provides: "The Council of Ministers shall be collectively responsible to the Legislative Assembly of the State." In most States the size of the Council ranges from ten to twelve members, but there is no constitutional limitation in this respect. The members head the most important departments of the State government, but as in the Central Government some department heads may not have cabinet rank. "Finance, general administration, home, food, civil supplies, education, agriculture, forests, medical, health and sanitation, local self-government, public works, legislative, justice, industries and labour, police, jails, excise, registration, information, co-operation, development, are the more important departments found in every State."[7]

State Legislatures. The Constitution of India provided that in each State there should be a Legislative Assembly, chosen by direct election, and consisting of not less than sixty nor more than five hundred members, and that in the States of Bihar, Bombay, Madras, Punjab, Uttar Pradesh, and West Bengal there should also be an Upper House, known as the Legislative Council, chosen by a complicated system of indirect election and nomination, and not exceeding one-fourth of the total number of members of the Legislative Assembly in each of these States, but in no event having less than forty members. One third of its members are elected by local authorities such as District Boards, Municipal Councils, and other public bodies specified by Parliament; one-twelfth by university graduates of at least three years' standing; one-twelfth by teachers of at least three years' experience in educational institutions not lower than secondary schools; one-third by members of the Legislative Assembly from outside its own membership; and one-sixth are nominated by the Governor from among persons who have "special knowledge or practical experience" in such fields as "literature, science, art, co-operative movement or social service." Like the Central Government, those States which have a bicameral legislature have a weak second chamber. Since the Legislative Councils have very limited powers and functions, they are naturally the targets of criticism and attack,

[7] *Ibid.*, p. 629.

although they have in a sense benefited from a degree of anonymity which the central Council of States has not enjoyed. "The Legislative Councils are not intended to be a check upon the Lower Houses but are merely revising and ventilating chambers representative of a variety of interests and experience."[8]

The number of members in the Legislative Assemblies of the States, the source of real authority on most matters on the State level, is prescribed in the Representation of the People Act of 1951, with certain later amendments. Since there is one electoral roll for elections to the House of the People and to the State Legislative Assemblies, each Assembly constituency is an equal unit of a Lok Sabha constituency. Each member of an Assembly represents no more than 75,000 voters. Most of the constituencies are single-member districts, but nearly 600 of them return two members and one returns three. Some seats are reserved in most States for Scheduled Castes and Scheduled Tribes. The size of the Legislative Assemblies varies greatly, from slightly more than 100 members in Assam and Kerala to over 400 in Uttar Pradesh.

The Constitution contains fairly detailed provisions regarding the powers and duties of State Legislatures, the officers (a Speaker and Deputy Speaker preside over a Legislative Assembly, and a Chairman and Deputy Chairman over a Legislative Council), the conduct of business, the disqualifications of members, privileges of members, legislative procedure, procedure in financial matters, and general rules of procedure. The procedures laid down in the Constitution are similar to those for the Union Parliament. Article 210 specifies that "business in the Legislature of a State shall be transacted in the official language or languages of the State or in Hindi or in English." In practice, most of the proceedings in State legislative bodies are now conducted in the prevailing language of the area.

In the State Legislative Assemblies many of the future leaders of the Indian nation are receiving valuable training and experience. Many of these men are different kinds of politicians from the Western-educated elite which thus far has dominated the political life of the country. As has been noted, they are less Westernized, less polished, less at home in English or in the world outside the boundaries of their States, more influenced by considerations of caste and local interests and traditions, but nonetheless probably more representative of the "real India."[9] It remains to be seen how many of these men who move to the Centre will be able to keep their ties and roots in their home constitu-

[8] N. Srinivasan, *Democratic Government in India* (Calcutta, 1954), p. 306.

[9] See W. H. Morris-Jones, "The Exploration of Indian Political Life," *Pacific Affairs,* XXXII (December, 1959), 419.

encies, and how many of them will keep their heads and measure up to the needs of the nation as a whole as they embark warily on the national, and perhaps even the international, scene.

The Judiciary in the States. The highest court in each State is a High Court, consisting of a Chief Justice and "such other Judges as the President may from time to time deem it necessary to appoint." The Chief Justice and the other judges are appointed by the President of the Indian Republic. "The jurisdiction of the High Court extends to all cases under State or federal laws. The extent of its jurisdiction is determined by Parliament in relation to matters in the Union and Concurrent Lists and by the State Legislatures in respect of matters in the State and Concurrent Lists, subject to the provisions of the Constitution. . . . Its jurisdiction extends to civil, criminal and revenue cases and is both original and appellate."[10] Article 227 of the Constitution stipulates that "Every High Court shall have superintendence over all courts and tribunals throughout the territories in relation to which it exercises jurisdiction." District judges are appointed by the Governor of the State in consultation with the High Court.

The High Courts of the Indian States are second in importance only to the Supreme Court of India in the unified judicial system that exists throughout the country. They set the tone of judicial practice in the States, since they constitute the highest courts of record and since they exercise supervision over all lower courts and other judicial agencies and representatives. Some of the outstanding legal minds of India have been or are Chief Justices or Judges of High Courts, and many more have been celebrated Advocates of the High Courts.

The Districts

District Officers. In most of the States of India the district is the major political subdivision. This is of course a direct inheritance from the days of British rule, when the District Officer — variously called the Collector or Deputy Commissioner or District Magistrate — was the kingpin of the administrative system. He is still the most important governmental official in rural India, and his functions have in fact increased; but he is a very different person from the District Officer of British days, who was constantly on the move in his district, in direct touch with the people, the symbol of the kind of benevolent paternalism which existed rather generally in much of the subcontinent in the latter years of British rule. Most of the I.C.S. officers, British or Indian, served much of their apprenticeship in government and administration as District Officers.[11]

[10] Srinivasan, *Democratic Government in India,* p. 316.

[11] See Sir Percival Griffiths, *The British Impact on India* (London, 1952); Philip Woodruff (pseud. for Philip Mason), *The Guardians,* Vol. II of

Today most of the District Officers are members of the Indian Administrative Service, less qualified, on the whole, than the old I.C.S. group, less closely in touch with the people, and much less looked up to by the people under their supervision.[12] Their functions and responsibilities, however, are in some respects even greater than those of the District Officers in the British period. Since 1955 they have been given general responsibility for all development efforts in their districts. This formidable addition to their responsibilities makes sense administratively, for it provides for needed coordination between the usual functions of administration and justice and the new efforts in economic development and social welfare; but it calls for skill and imagination beyond that which most District Officers can reasonably be expected to possess, especially in the light of their background and orientation, and it saddles them with such a variety of duties that they can hardly be expected to discharge any of them adequately. There is much truth in the observation of Hugh Tinker: "The District Officer is the bottleneck of the government process: loaded with new duties, compelled to fill a quasi-political role (like the French prefect) yet still burdened with all his former responsibilities, he is now expected to coordinate and inspire development. . . . The District Officer remains the keystone of the development structure but has been unable to make this his principal concern."[13]

District Boards. In 1951 there were 186 District Boards in the 267 Districts of India. These Boards, like the District Officers, were an inheritance from the British, but, unlike the District Officers, they seldom played the role in rural administration that was expected by their creators. They were composed of members elected on the basis of adult franchise, and also of nominated non-official and official members. They had elected chairmen and vice-chairmen. Their constitution, powers, and functions were laid down in a series of local self-government acts, often dating back to the nineteenth century.

The Men Who Ruled India (New York, 1954); R. Carstairs, *The Little World of an Indian District Officer* (London, 1912); and Hugh Tinker, "Authority and Community in Village India," *Pacific Affairs,* XXXII (December, 1959), 370.

[12] "Today it is probably true to say that the senior district official is more aloof, and out of touch with the general public than was his British predecessor. . . . Much of the British Indian Civil Service tradition has been adopted by the Indian administrators of today, but the legendary British District Officers have bred no Indian successors. . . . The young Indian administrator is well endowed with a sense of public service, but in an abstract rather than a personal sense. His approach is inclined to be clinical. . . . He rejects the relationship of squire and villein which many British officials seemed to cultivate, but he has no new pattern to adopt." Tinker, "Authority and Community in Village India," pp. 369–371.

[13] *Ibid.,* p. 364.

Their main functions were in the fields of education and communications (meaning chiefly roads). They had very limited financial resources. It was hoped, as the Governor of a province of British India said in 1922, that "these bodies . . . will be an admirable school to give the people that training in administration and in business methods and in responsibility which they need to fit them for eventual complete Self-Government."[14]

When "complete Self-Government" came the Boards were continued, but they did not fit in well with the new patterns of administration. In 1957 Professor Bhaskaran of Madras University wrote: "The district board is, therefore, at present an elective agency, with responsibility for public works, health and education activities which are not so expensive or so technical as to be taken over by the state government, and for the provision of the barest local government amenities in areas which do not have a panchayat."[15] Four years previously Chetkar Jha predicted: "The District Boards will be completely useless in years to come. They are likely to succumb to the twin influences of growing provincialisation of some of their more important services and the more ambitious plan of *Gram Panchayats*."[16] The Balvantray Mehta Report, issued in late 1957, referred to "the gradual eclipse of district boards from the social polity."[17]

Most of the States have adopted the recommendations of the Mehta Report for a three-tier system of *panchayats* — village *panchayats, panchayat samitis,* and *zila parishads* — and the former district boards have been abolished, or have in effect survived, as Professor Bhaskaran foresaw, "only as supervisory bodies." Many of their former functions have been taken over by the States, and others have been transferred to the village *panchayats* or to other new agencies, such as *panchayat samitis* or development blocks.

Subdivisions of Districts. The famous Resolution on Local Self-Government, issued with the approval of Lord Ripon in 1882, stated: "The Governor-General in Council considers it is very important that the area of jurisdiction allotted to each Board should in no case be too large. If the plan is to succeed at all, it will be necessary to secure

[14] Quoted in Chetkar Jha, *Indian Local Self-Government* (Patna, 1953), p. 146.

[15] Harold Zink, Arne Wåhlstrand, Feliciano Benvenuti, and R. Bhaskaran, *Rural Local Government in Sweden, Italy and India: A Comparative Study* (London: Stevens & Sons, 1957), p. 65.

[16] Jha, *Indian Local Self-Government,* p. 171.

[17] *Report of the Team for the Study of Community Projects and National Extension Service* (Balvantray G. Mehta, Leader), (New Delhi, 1957), II, 12. This report, in three volumes, was prepared for the Committee on Plan Projects, Government of India, after months of investigation. Hereafter referred to as the *Balvantray Mehta Report.*

among the members both local interest and local knowledge." The Resolution, then, envisaged local boards having jurisdiction over areas much smaller than districts. Such boards were set up in many parts of British India, in subdivisions of districts which were usually called *tahsils* or *talukas*. Some districts are still subdivided into such subdivisions, but today they are declining in numbers and in importance. Some of the *tahsil* officials, the *tahsildars* or the *mamlatdars,* are assigned responsibilities in administering development blocks, in addition to their regular duties, but it is difficult to associate officials in a dying pattern of administration with new patterns of development. The community development block may prove to be a major new unit in rural government. The main units of rural government, however, are still the district and the village. "Experience has demonstrated that between the village or neighbourhood and the district there is no intermediate area that provides a basis for a sense of community."[18]

The Villages

Thus we come to the village, the hope and despair of India today. As Gandhi often pointed out, India lives in its villages, and unless village life can be revitalized the nation as a whole can hardly come alive. The average Indian village is still a most depressing place, particularly for any one who has lived anywhere else. It is a little world of its own. "In a sense each village in India is its own private world, connected in many cases only in an ephemeral way to neighboring villages, the state, and the nation."[19] One of the major objectives of the Five Year Plans, and particularly of the Community Development Program, is to enlist the cooperation of the Indian villager in the work of national development and to improve the quality of his living as well as his living conditions. Only limited progress is being made in either direction, although in time a revolution may indeed sweep the Indian countryside. If this is to come, the villagers themselves must develop a greater sense of participation in the development efforts. Thus far they have been more or less passive recipients of efforts from on high. They need a more vigorous and enlightened leadership. This leadership, as Hugh Tinker has perceived, "would be strengthened if the flight of the educated to the towns could be reversed. . . . But nothing about the village of today makes it any more attractive to the educated; it is still a place to get away from."[20]

[18] Tinker, "Authority and Community in Village India," p. 369.

[19] Richard L. Park, "Administrative Coordination and Economic Development in the Districts of India," an unpublished paper prepared for the Joint Seminar on Commonwealth Studies, Duke University, February 29, 1960, p. 6.

[20] Tinker, "Authority and Community in Village India," p. 374.

In the past the affairs of the village were supervised in a general way by the District Officers and various other officials of the District, and also of the *tahsil* or *taluka,* such as the *tahsildar* or *mamlatdar,* as well as by police officials. Almost every village was in direct charge of a headman or *patil,* usually a person whose authority was derived more from hereditary sources than from legal position. Other officials usually included a village accountant, often known as the *patwari,* and a village policeman, sometime hardly more than a glorified *chowkidar* or watchman.

The Panchayat. The most discussed institution in the Indian village, or groups of villages, at the present time is the *panchayat.* "The word *panchayat* describes form, not purpose — a technique of seeking agreement through consultation, hallowed, according to tradition by divine sanction: *panch men parameswar.* This technique was mainly employed in social or economic organisms . . . but it was also extensively used for the arbitration of both caste and village disputes."[21] *Panchayat* means a council of five, and it usually refers to a village council — which may or may not have five members — which has a great deal to say about the life of the people of the village, in social and religious as well as in economic and political matters. Officially speaking, the *panchayat* is today the lowest — and in a sense the most basic — unit of self-government in India.

The *panchayat* is an institution which existed and which apparently played a rather significant role in many parts of ancient India. Some Indian writers are inclined to glorify this role, and to speak of the ancient *panchayats* as "little village republics" — consciously or unconsciously parroting a much-quoted statement of Sir Charles Metcalfe in 1832 — and as the seedbeds for a democratic tradition in India. Such writers are inclined to see an organic link between the *panchayats* of centuries ago, and the *panchayats* which exist in a growing number of villages today. Actually the link is a tenuous one, for the *panchayat* almost died out as an institution in Indian village life. Hugh Tinker insists that "while the *panchayat* is an ancient institution of unique prestige, it provides no precedent for the village council of today."[22] There is a vast literature on *panchayats,* much of which would partially substantiate and partially refute the validity of Professor Tinker's conclusion.[23]

The British made some efforts to revive the *panchayat,* but with

[21] *Ibid.,* p. 357.

[22] *Ibid.,* p. 358.

[23] See, for example, D. Malaviya, *Village Panchayats in India* (New Delhi, 1956); R. L. Khanna, *Panchayat Raj in India* (Chandigarh, 1956); A. V. Raman Rao, *Structure and Working of Village Panchayats: A Survey Based on Case Studies in Bombay and Madras,* Poona, Gokhale Institute of Politics and Economics, Publication No. 28, 1954.

indifferent success. The Report of the Royal Commission on Decentralization in 1909 stated: "It is most desirable alike in the interests of decentralization and in order to associate the people with the task of administration that an attempt should be made to constitute and develope [*sic*] village panchayats for the administration of local affairs." Gandhi attached great importance to the *panchayat:* "The greater the power of the panchayats," he said, "the better for the people." "To Gandhi perfect panchayat democracy was synonymous with Ram Rajya,"[24] the kind of India to which he aspired. Although this was one matter on which the British authorities and the leaders of the Indian National Congress seemed to agree, the Simon Commission in 1930 was compelled to report that the *panchayat* movement had not made much progress.

When India became independent in 1947 perhaps one-third of the villages of India had *panchayats,* and many of these were in far from flourishing condition. The Congress Government has made a determined effort to promote the creation of *panchayats* and to make them effective units of local government. Article 40 of the Constitution of 1950 declared: "The State shall take steps to organise village *panchayats* and to endow them with such powers and authority as may be necessary to enable them to function as units of self-government." Although this Article appears in Part IV of the Constitution, listing "Directive Principles of State Policy" which are not legally enforceable, all of the States have enacted legislation in the spirit of this constitutional provision, giving legal status to *panchayats,* and the central Parliament has passed a number of acts designed to promote the *panchayat* system. The plan now is not only to spread *panchayats* throughout the villages of India but to make these bodies the main agencies for village administration and cooperation in the Community Development Program and in other phases of the development efforts. The overall objectives are clearly stated in a resolution of the Village Panchayat Committee of the Congress Party: "For the achievement of the objectives laid down in the Constitution, the village panchayats should serve not only as units of Local Self-Government but also as effective institutions for securing social justice and fostering corporate life resulting in fuller employment."[25]

At the beginning of the First Five Year Plan, according to information made available by the Planning Commission, some 83,000 *panchayats* existed in Indian villages. By March 31, 1954, the number had risen to 98,250, covering more than half of the villages of the country. It is hoped that by the end of the Third Five Year Plan, in 1966, all or nearly all of the villages will be embraced in

[24] Khanna, *Panchayat Raj in India,* p. 9.
[25] Quoted in *ibid.,* p. 206.

the *panchayat* system, as well as being full participants in the Community Development Program. Thus an ancient institution, which centuries ago served different needs in a different society, is being revived and remodeled to serve the needs of a modern welfare state.

Many different kinds of bodies called *panchayats* have existed, and many still exist, in India. There are little *panchayats,* in small villages, and large *panchayats,* representing a number of villages.[26] There is the large, multi-purpose *panchayat,* the *panchayat raj.* There are *panchayats* with primarily judicial functions, such as the *gram, adalati,* and *nyaya panchayats.* There are statutory *panchayats* that are legally recognized units of local self-government, and informal *panchayats* that often have greater status and prestige among the villagers. These two types of *panchayats* may exist in the same village; one is readily identifiable and legally constituted, whereas the other, more closely related to "the power structure of the village," may be difficult to analyze, or even to identify. "The statutory *panchayats* that have been established by law since the 1930's, and increasingly since 1937, do not take into account the informal *panchayat* system that has been relatively effective as a stabilizing element in village India's past. Officials may assume that the statutory body has supplanted the informal; but the facts seem to indicate that the two co-exist, with the statutory body more often than not being manipulated simply as the recording office for decisions actually made informally (and, incidentally, illegally) by the older, officially unrecognized, *panchayat* system."[27]

The revival of the *panchayats,* their extension to most of the villages of India, their legal recognition as basic administrative units of government, and their association with the Community Development Program and other efforts at rural uplift, are significant new departures in Indian politics and administration, and they may indeed mark the revitalization of rural India and the beginnings of a true popular awakening. If the Indian village comes to life, and if the villager really gains a sense of participation in a cooperative enterprise of social re-

[26] "Little panchayats constituted for small villages are generally swayed by narrower considerations and sometimes dominated by caste interests which are toned down in a bigger body, comprising a number of villages inhabited by practically all castes. Membership in such a body infuses a wider outlook and a sense of responsibility which transcends narrow and parochial considerations." *Balvantray Mehta Report,* II, 3. "The trend towards a larger unit appears to predominate. . . . According to the *Fifth Evaluation Report,* the average population of each *panchayat* circle in a sample survey was 2,600." Tinker, "Authority and Community in Village India," pp. 361, footnote 26. See also *Fifth Evaluation Report* of the Programme Evaluation Organisation, Planning Commission, Government of India (New Delhi, 1958).

[27] Park, "Administrative Coordination and Economic Development in the Districts of India," p. 9.

juvenation and nation-building, then a revolution will truly have come to the Indian countryside, and to India as a whole. In this gigantic enterprise the *panchayat* could play a central role.

There is little evidence to date, however, that these hopes are being realized. *Panchayats* are being introduced into most of the villages of India, but most of them are not functioning satisfactorily. In late 1957 the Balvantray Mehta team reported that "the available information indicates that possibly not more than 10 per cent of the total number of *panchayats* are functioning effectively." Some of the reasons for this poor and disappointing record are suggested in the Report: "The number of panchayats which are torn by factions or in which squabbles are rampant is large"; "panchayat elections have resulted in creating or aggravating factional rivalries in about one-third of the villages in which there was a contest"; "caste becomes a political division of society at the same time it is losing its position as a ritual division"; "the economically weaker sections have as yet little voice in the affairs of the panchayat."[28]

If imposed upon a village by statute the *panchayat* may find little acceptance among the villagers themselves. If it fits in with local customs and practices, it is likely to reflect the social conservatism of the village, its caste and factional composition, its mental isolationism. In either case the *panchayat* is hardly a suitable instrument for social, economic, and political change. Its relations to representatives and agencies of the "new look" in economic and social development — the village level worker (the *Gram Sevak*), the development block, etc. — are still undetermined, and apparently vary greatly from area to area. If the three-tier system of *panchayats* proposed by the Balvantray Mehta team, and already being put into effect in many of the Indian States, proves to be practical, the village *panchayat,* linked with the *panchayat samiti* and the *zila parisad,* which are in a sense larger *panchayats,* may still play the administrative and social role envisioned for it by those who are planning the new India.

The Cities

Between one-fifth and one-sixth of the people of India live in urban areas. In 1951 there were 72 cities in India of over 100,000 population. Five had over 1,000,000 people; these were Calcutta, Bombay, Madras, Delhi-New Delhi, and Hyderabad. More than 5,500,000 people now live in the metropolitan areas of Calcutta and over 4,000,000 in Bombay; Delhi, New Delhi, and Madras have around 2,000,000 each; the population of Ahmedabad exceeds 1,000,000, and Bangalore and Kanpur are nearly as large.

There is a considerable similarity in the pattern of municipal gov-

[28] *Balvantray Mehta Report,* II, 1, 2, 7, 18.

ernment throughout India. Large cities have corporations, smaller cities of 10,000 population or more are municipalities, and smaller and less developed urban areas are either Notified Areas or Town Areas. The cities of India are generally under the supervision and control of the State Governments, although under the State Municipality Acts and under the charters granted by the States they have a considerable measure of autonomy.

In a special category are the old Presidency municipalities of Calcutta, Bombay, and Madras. These cities have been Corporations for many years.[29] After independence this status was redefined by special legislation in the States in which they are located, and they were associated more closely with the evolving pattern of municipal government under general State supervision. All three great Corporations are governed by a Municipal Council, ranging in size from slightly more than 80 members in the cases of Calcutta and Madras to nearly 125 members in the case of Bombay City. These members are elected by adult franchise. They in turn choose a President or Mayor. Each Corporation also has a Municipal Commissioner, appointed by the State government, who is the chief executive officer.

The government of most of the other Corporations of India is modelled along similar lines. In most cases the members of the Municipal Council range between 20 and 100. In some States a few Council members are appointed or co-opted or otherwise nominated, but the trend is toward Councils made up only of elected members. Smaller municipalities are also usually governed by Municipal Councils, with less autonomy and fewer financial resources.

The functions of Indian municipalities are spelled out in State municipality acts and other measures. Some are obligatory, while others are optional. "Important obligatory functions relate to the construction and maintenance of roads, conservancy, lighting, abatement of public nuisances, regulation of dangerous and offensive trades, water-supply, drainage, hospitals and dispensaries, vaccination, public markets, sanitation, education and fire protection, etc." Optional functions "generally relate to laying out new streets, reclamation of unhealthy localities, acquisition of land, public parks, gardens, museums, lunatic asylums, rest-houses, poor houses, dairies, baths, public utilities like water, electricity and transport, fairs and exhibitions."[30] Many additional functions may also be given to municipalities, although some authorities advise against this.

[29] Madras since 1688, and Calcutta and Bombay since 1726. See Hugh Tinker, *The Foundations of Local Self-Government in India, Pakistan and Burma* (London, 1954), pp. 25–26.

[30] Jha, *Indian Local Self-Government,* pp. 40–41.

It is clear that Indian municipalities are overburdened with functions and poorly equipped to undertake even essential duties. The reasons for this state of affairs are many, but for the most part they revolve around inadequacy of funds and problems of personnel. Indian municipalities have authority to levy a wide range of rates and taxes. Other sources of income are fees, grants-in-aid, and loans. Taxation is by far the chief source of income. There are usually two general taxes, both on property — a tax on owners of property and a tax on occupiers of property. Water rates are another important source of tax revenue. The total amount of money available to municipalities, however, is very small in relation to the functions and services they are expected to perform. An even more serious problem is the low standard of performance and even of integrity in municipal administration. Chetkar Jha has suggested that four factors are primarily responsible for this unfortunate state of affairs: (1) "the absorption of the elected personnel in administrative details"; (2) the "absence of a proper division of responsibility between the whole council and committees"; (3) the "absence of an honest and competent staff"; and (4) the "absence of a right system of financial administration."[31]

Substantial parts of the area covered by some Indian cities, and some of the functions normally devolving on municipal authorities, may be vested in the control of semi-autonomous bodies, usually created by special State legislation or under the supervision of a Central Government agency. Among these semi-autonomous bodies are improvement trusts, for city planning and development, and port trusts in the port cities. Cantonments may cover large areas within city limits, and these areas, so important in British days, are of course under the control of the defense authorities, with only limited responsibility to the municipal administrations.

Is the Machinery of State and Local Government Adequate?

Even a brief survey of State and local government in India suggests the importance of giving due attention to this subject, and some of the anomalies that arise from what Selig Harrison has called the peculiar "imbalance of the Union."[32] Most of our attention has been focused on the Central Government, which of course speaks for India as a whole in world affairs and which in many respects dominates the country in an administrative and political sense. On the other hand, as we have seen, there are many signs that the Centre is dependent,

[31] *Ibid.*, p. 66.

[32] Selig S. Harrison, *India: The Most Dangerous Decades* (Princeton, N.J., 1960), p. 303.

to a degree almost unprecedented in other federations, upon the State and local authorities, and upon the people generally, for the implementation of its basic plans and policies and in some respects seems to function more in a coordinating than in a governing capacity. The strong tendencies toward centralization in India are for the most part self-evident and self-explanatory; the equally strong trends toward decentralization and toward regionalism and localism are perhaps less self-evident and self-explanatory, but they seem to be growing rather than diminishing. To the masses of the Indian people New Delhi is far away, and they are inclined to be suspicious of what goes on in British-built piles of this "un-Indian" city. But they are often interested in what goes on in the States, sometimes to a greater extent than in their own local affairs; "public interest in state politics is keener than in national or local politics, and keener and more sustained in local politics than in national politics."[33]

Administratively speaking, State governments are functioning effectively. Politically, the record is more spotty. Now that the fight for essentially linguistic States has been fought and won — an outstanding and rare instance of the victory of regional and local pressures over the wishes of the top leaders of the Government and the Congress Party — it is hoped that within their new boundaries the Indian States can prove to be effective units; but many scars remain from this historic battle, which was in a sense a victory of emotion over reason, of regional and local pressures over administrative stability.

Some kind of incipient revolution seems to be going on in the Indian countryside, as the impact of the twentieth century and of the "revolution of rising expectations" meets the barriers of social conservatism and localism, and as the efforts at national planning and development gradually penetrate the areas where the masses of the Indian people live. This incipient revolution raises questions of the suitability of old patterns of administration, such as those in the district involving the District Officers and the District Boards, in the *talukas* and *tahsils,* and in the villages. Moreover, new agencies are being introduced into rural India, and old ones are being revived and adapted to new needs. Many of the new agencies are basic ingredients of the Community Development Program and other aspects of development planning and social welfare programs under the Five Year Plans. They have introduced new units, such as the development block, and new types of government servants, notably the *Gram Sevak,* the village level worker, and the Block Development Officers, into the district, the *taluka,* and the village.

[33] Zink, Wåhlstrand, Benvenuti, and Bhaskaran, *Rural Local Government in Sweden, Italy and India,* p. 112.

In the villages themselves the old customs and patterns endure, along with the old prejudices and superstitions; but the villagers are inevitably affected by such direct onslaughts on their time-honored ways as the attacks on untouchability and the caste system as a whole and the efforts to associate them with larger units of government and administration and to give them a feeling of participation in a nation-wide effort at development and change. In this connection the emphasis on the revival and adaptation of the *panchayats,* and their spread to virtually every village, or groups of villages, throughout India, has great significance, both politically and psychologically. Unhappily, many of these changes are not working well, and one wonders whether, even if they can in time "catch fire," the results will be as revolutionary as the times seem to demand.

In the Indian municipalities, which are more immediately responsive to social and political changes — and which in fact do much to bring about these changes — the agencies of government and administration are fairly well established, although they are subject to many kinds of criticism and do not seem to be functioning very effectively. The great cities of India are centers of life and movement; however unrepresentative they may be of the "real India," they exert an almost fatal attraction on the more enterprising villagers. In a sense, almost every Indian, whether he lives in Calcutta or Bombay or Delhi or Lucknow, or in a remote and tiny village, is a villager at heart; almost certainly he has roots in a village, and thinks of this village as his home. Thus there are special, and often not fully perceived, links between rural and urban India. This condition may be one of the factors which give to India a greater basic unity than those who are so disturbed by the obvious divisions and diversities are accustomed to see.

While much depends on greater vitality in local and municipal administration than now exists, the general patterns of administration and the special powers of the States and the Central Government tend to stifle these basic units of local government. "District boards, urban municipalities and village *panchayats* are not subject to the jurisdiction of each other, but are rather independent units, each directly controlled by the state government through a hierarchy of civil servants headed by a state official called a director or inspector who reports to the secretary of the Local Government Ministry" in the State. "The tradition of centralism in the country makes the local body more a kind of administrative agent of the state government, subject to the same conditions of discipline as its paid employees, rather than a governmental authority with some exclusive jurisdiction or initiative of its own." This administrative dominance is accentuated by the financial limitations under which almost all local bodies have to operate. To some extent the States of India suffer under the same limitations. "All local bodies have only one-third of the income of the state governments and all state governments together have less than three-fourths of the resources of the central government."[34]

The great changes that are occurring in India today impose new demands on the instrumentalities and officials of State and local administration. Old agencies are being forced to take on additional duties and responsibilities, and new agencies are being created. All kinds of problems of coordination and overlapping jurisdiction arise from this evolving situation. Can the organs of State and local government, which have not been functioning very well in discharging their regular duties and responsibilities, be adapted to meet the new needs and opportunities? Certainly if a new India is to be created, it will have to have its roots in the village and districts and cities, and here the local bodies and State governments will either be agencies of change or bottlenecks too narrow to permit the entrance of vitalizing forces into those areas where most of the people of India dwell.

[34] *Ibid.*, pp. 80, 81, 95.

* 8 *

The Politics of Planning

"India . . . has embarked on an experiment in democratic p' ,ing which is perhaps larger and more complex than any in the ,dern world. Some have called it a fateful experiment. . . . W , is on trial . . . is, in the last analysis, whether democracy ca' ,lve the problems of mass poverty. It is a trial perhaps never be' , made in such an atmosphere of urgency."[1] The stakes in India', ,eat experiment are high. They are much more than economic ,kes; indeed, they are essentially the stakes of human and national ,vival.

Approaches to Planning

As in every great experiment, the chances for ,ccess or failure of India's efforts cannot be evaluated realistically. ,dia is at once one of the most depressing and one of the most e ,ting countries in the world, and it is easy to find grounds for eithe ,essimism or optimism, depending partly on what one happens to see ,d even more on what he is looking for or expects to see.

How is India's "experiment in demo' ,ic planning" progressing? The sober answer is that it is not progr ,ng well — at least not well enough. As India's planners settle dow' , a more realistic basis for the formulation and implementation of th ,evelopment programs, the gap between needs and fulfilment grows ,er larger. India has to accomplish so much to "break through th ,arrier," to use Nehru's words, to sound economic growth, and it is ,fact having great difficulty in making relatively modest gains. Bec ,e of the low living conditions of its people and the pressure of a g' ,ing population, it has, to paraphrase the words of the Red Queen, ,un so fast in order to stay where it is, and staying where it is is nc ,nough. Its modest successes — modest in relation to need and not ,elation to available resources — contrast

[1] Planning Commission, ,overnment of India, *The New India: Progress Through Democracy* (New York, 1958), pp. 2, 4.

unfavorably with the apparently more spectacular rates of development of Communist China, and thus raise questions in many minds, in India and elsewhere, whether the path to economic progress in underdeveloped lands leads inescapably to totalitarianism.

"There seems to be general agreement," noted a team of American agricultural specialists, who visited India in early 1959 at the request of the Union Ministries of Food and Agriculture and Community Development and Co-operation, under the sponsorship of the Ford Foundation, "that the major problems in India lie not so much in basic idea or philosophy of the programmes but in implementation."[2] This may be true with respect to those articulate Indians who have helped to shape the development programs, and there is particular value in concentrating at this time on problems of implementation. But one should not forget that there is as yet no basic agreement in India even on ideas, objectives, and philosophy. What kind of India do the people of India want? What are the objectives of Indian society? India, it may be said, has not yet made peace with the twentieth century. It is not even certain that Indians wish to do so. Do they want to modernize? Do they really want fundamental changes? How real is the Indian "revolution"? There is clearly what may be called an "inner struggle" in India, at various levels, involving conflicting viewpoints, often in the same minds, on fundamentals.

Many Indians do not accept the basic approach of those who are governing India today. They may favor other ways of social and political organization and polity. Some favor the Gandhian way, from which, they insist, Nehru and his associates in the present Government of India have departed. This would involve a conscious effort to resist many of the consequences of modernization, to create a simple *sarvodaya* society with a maximum of decentralization and an emphasis on satisfying basic human wants, not on creating new wants. Others favor some kind of communal approach, with a return to traditional ways, perhaps seeking the establishment of a kind of Hindu Raj in more or less modern dress. Still others favor the Communist way, perhaps on the China model, with such adaptations as would be necessary to fit the Indian scene. Others speak vaguely of a partyless democracy, quite different from any Western form.

Even within the ranks of those who support the broad lines of policy laid down by the leaders of the Government of India, there are many political differences regarding major aspects of national planning. These concern such questions as the relative merits of

[2] *Report on India's Food Crisis and Steps to Meet It,* by the Agricultural Production Team sponsored by the Ford Foundation (New Delhi, April, 1959). This report was issued by the Ministry of Food and Agriculture of the Government of India.

small-scale and large-scale industries, the relative emphasis on agricultural and industrial development, the relative value of public and private investment, the relative role of the public and private sectors, the role of foreign capital, the desirability or undesirability of foreign aid, and many other basic issues.

Before considering some of the problems of implementing India's development efforts, we should examine briefly the economic philosophy which motivates India's leaders.

The "Socialist Pattern of Society." The proclaimed objective of the Government of India is the establishment of a "socialist pattern of society." This objective has been proclaimed in one way or another for many years. It was stated quite specifically in a famous resolution adopted at the Annual Session of the Congress Party at Avadi in January, 1955, which declared that "planning should take place with the view to the establishment of a socialistic pattern of society, where the principal means of production are under social ownership and control, production is progressively speeded up and there is equitable distribution of the national wealth."

The term, "socialist pattern of society" — the word "socialistic" in the Avadi resolution was soon replaced by "socialist" — expresses India's concept of the welfare state. It is a rather nebulous concept, which has never been rigidly defined. It seems to embrace a mild degree of Marxism, a considerable amount of Gandhism, including emphasis on nonviolent means and peaceful change, and ideas of social and economic equalitarianism.[3] Nehru and other Indian leaders boast that their whole approach is pragmatic, and nowhere does this seem to be more true than in the approach to economic planning. "What do we mean when we say 'socialist pattern' of life?", asked Nehru when he presented the Second Five Year Plan to the Indian Parliament; "surely we mean a society in which there is social cohesion without classes, equality of opportunity and the possibility for everyone to have a good life." The text of the Second Plan itself was hardly more specific: "The accent of the socialist pattern is on the attainment of positive goals; the raising of living standards; the enlargements of opportunities for all, the promotion of enterprise among the disadvantaged classes and the creation of a sense of partnership among all sections of the community."[4]

There has always been an irritating and baffling vagueness about most varieties of socialism that have flourished in the Indian scene. No socialist party has been able to formulate a specific statement of its

[3] See *Indian Approaches to a Socialist Society, Indian Press Digests* Monograph Series No. 2 (Berkeley, Calif., 1956).

[4] Planning Commission, Government of India, *Second Five Year Plan* (New Delhi, 1956), p. 24.

ideological and economic views, and the ideas which are subsumed under the term, "socialist pattern of society," would surely be accepted by many who do not regard themselves as socialists at all. In India almost everyone thinks of himself as a socialist, and believes that the path of democratic socialism is the only path to true democracy. Yet it is certainly true, as Professor William Lockwood has observed, that India "preaches more socialism than it practices," and that many critics of the "socialist pattern of society" are alienated by the term and not by the goals which it embraces.[5]

In some respects India is one of the least socialist of countries. "India has, in fact," states Professor J. K. Galbraith, "superimposed a smallish socialized sector atop what, no doubt, is the world's greatest example of functioning anarchy."[6] Most of the instruments of production are still in private hands, and most of the income is produced by the private sector. Yet many of the leaders of India hold socialist views, are distrustful of the profit motive, suspect private businessmen, and favor the growing intervention of the state in the economic life of the country.

A summary of the First Five Year Plan, issued by the Planning Commission in December, 1952, when the Plan was "finalised," contained the following statement: "In a planned economy, the distinction between the public and the private sector is one of emphasis. The two sectors are and must function as parts of a single organism." The summary also stated: "Private enterprise functions largely within the conditions created by the State."[7] According to spokesmen of the Government of India these conditions are favorable to the "private sector," and to foreign private investment. In support of their claim they point to the Industrial Policy Resolutions, issued by the Government in 1948 and again in 1956, and to the major role which is assigned to the private sector in the Five Year Plans. During the course of the First Five Year Plan (1951–1956) about as much was invested in the private sector as in the public sector, including contributions of both federal and state governments and foreign grants and loans. The total in each case was approximately four billion dollars. The Second Five Year Plan (1956–1961), as revised, called for an expenditure of somewhat over ten billion dollars in the public sector, divided about equally between the central government and the States, and of half that amount in the private sector. Actually, the

[5] William W. Lockwood, "'The Socialistic Society': India and Japan," *Foreign Affairs,* XXXVII (October, 1958), 130.

[6] J. K. Galbraith, "Rival Economic Theories in India," *Foreign Affairs,* XXXVI (July, 1958), 590.

[7] Planning Commission, Government of India, *The First Five Year Plan* (New Delhi, 1952), p. 9.

amounts expended in each sector fell short of planned objectives by some 20 per cent. The Third Five Year Plan (1961–1966) envisages an investment in the public sector of over fifteen billion dollars, and in the private sector of $8.4 billion.

The Government is placing a great deal of emphasis on various kinds of cooperatives, which presumably would tend to give India the character of a mixed economy rather than of a wholly socialist society. In a famous resolution adopted at the Nagpur session of the Congress Party in January, 1959, the Congress went on record in favor of service cooperatives and village cooperatives. The exact outlines of the kinds of cooperatives which are envisioned have not yet been made clear, and the Congress Party and the Government have been notably slow in pushing this new departure in the Indian political and social environment. At a public meeting in Bhopal in November, 1960, Nehru declared that he hoped to see a cooperative society, as well as a *panchayat* and a school, in every Indian village, for in his opinion all three were "absolutely necessary for the all-round progress of Rural Areas and for making people stand on their own legs."

Foreign businessmen who have been engaged in making loans or in carrying on business operations in India have often spoken of the different views of the role of the private sector and of the opportunities for private enterprise which are reflected by influential people in India. Nehru himself has often criticized Indian private businessmen, sometimes with good reason, and he has made no secret of his belief that the great tasks of national development in a country like India must be carried out under strict control of the state.

While it is still true that well over 90 per cent of the total gross national product is contributed by the private sector, this percentage is bound to decrease as the steel mills, the multi-purpose river valley projects, and other major projects in the public sector begin to operate. In any event, the private sector will continue to be circumscribed by Government orientation and policies and it will be expected to develop in ways which will contribute most directly to the overall development program. Frank Moraes has clearly perceived the future trend:

> What the Indian Government aims at is a mixed economy combining the three elements of public enterprise, private enterprise, and in-between cooperative enterprise on the lines of Scandinavian countries such as Sweden. In this type of mixed economy the balance must inevitably be tilted in favor of the government, with the area of the private sector progressively shrinking. . . . The likelihood is that as the Plans develop, the private sector's share will progressively decrease.[8]

[8] Frank Moraes, *India Today* (New York, 1960), p. 183.

Democratic Planning. "The central objective of planning in India," stated the Planning Commission at the beginning of the First Five Year Plan, "is to raise the standard of living of the people and to open out to them opportunities for a richer and more varied life." Nehru believes that this "central objective" can only be achieved in the democratic way. "We have definitely accepted the democratic process," he told delegates to the annual session of the Congress Party in 1957, "because we think that in the final analysis it promotes the growth of human beings and of society."

At a time when various patterns of authoritarianism seem to be the prevailing political forms in most of the underdeveloped countries, the conscious and strong dedication of India to the democratic way is a source of inspiration and hope. If India can show, not only that democracy is compatible with planning on a large scale, but that democratic planning can provide masses of people with a richer and more varied life without the appalling human costs of totalitarianism, the prospects for democracy in the world as a whole will be vastly brighter. If India fails in its great experiment in democratic planning, its failure will be a blow to hopes for freedom everywhere.

Objectives of the Five Year Plans

India has had considerable experience in economic planning, and has shown a marked aptitude for it. Even before independence a series of economic plans had been drawn up, by the British Government, by the Indian National Congress, or by private business organizations or individuals. As early as 1938 the Indian National Congress appointed a Planning Committee. India now has had a decade of experience in coordinated economic planning since independence; it has in fact carried economic planning farther than perhaps any other non-totalitarian country.

In spite of all the delays, cut-backs, and frustrations, India's record in economic planning has been impressive. In 1956 Dr. Paul Appleby, after a second look at India's administrative system, expressed the view that "India has solved better than any other country known to this writer the problem of national planning."[9]

The planned progress for the two decades, 1956–1976, is indicated in the following table prepared by the Planning Commission.[10]

[9] Paul H. Appleby, *Re-examination of India's Administrative System with Special Reference to Administration of Government's Industrial and Commercial Enterprises* (New Delhi, 1956), p. 31. This report was issued by the Organisation & Methods Division of the Cabinet Secretariat, Government of India.

[10] This chart is taken from *India News,* Jan. 26, 1959, p. 5. It is adapted from a table which was published in *The New India,* p. 29.

Twenty Years of Growth: 1956–76

	AT THE END OF		
	1st Plan 1955–56	*2nd Plan* 1960–61	*3rd Plan* 1965–66
National Income (in millions of dollars)	22,680	28,308	36,246
Total Net Investment (in millions of dollars) (Total for entire Plan period)	6,510	13,020	20,790
Rate of Investment (as percentage of national income)	7.3	10.7	13.7
Population (millions)	384	408	434
Capital-output Ratio (over the Plan period)	1.8:1	2.3:1	2.6:1
Per Capita Income (in dollars)	59.01	69.51	83.16

	AT THE END OF		
	4th Plan 1970–71	*5th Plan* 1975–76	*% Increase* 1956 to 1976
National Income (in millions of dollars)	45,528	57,267	152.5
Total Net Investment (in millions of dollars) (Total for entire Plan period)	31,080	43,470	576.7
Rate of Investment (as percentage of national income)	16.0	17.0	132.9
Population (millions)	465	500	30.2
Capital-output Ratio (over the Plan period)	3.4:1	3.7:1	——
Per Capita Income (in dollars)	97.88	114.66	93.9

(All at 1952–53 Prices)

These figures suggest an impressive planning effort; but even if they are translated into reality, India will still be a poor and underdeveloped country. The per capita income will be only about $115 by 1975–76, an amount already exceeded in some thirty underdeveloped countries; and since the estimates of population are clearly too low, the per capita income will probably be even less than $115 fifteen years hence.

In an address to the All-Indian Congress Committee in January, 1957, Prime Minister Nehru said: "If in the course of these five years, we achieve what we have laid down in our Second Five Year Plan, it will be a great victory — one of the greatest that India has won. . . . We will have crossed that dangerous barrier which separates an underdeveloped country from a developing country, and once we have done that, it will be easier and faster going." The full objectives of the Second Plan were not realized, but even if they had been

India would still have been on the wrong side of "that dangerous barrier which separates an underdeveloped country from a developing country." An announced objective of the Third Plan is the rapid advancement of the national economy to a stage when it can become "self-sustaining"; but again it is doubtful that even a full realization of the planned targets would bring India to the level of self-sustaining growth. In fact, unless the goals set for 1975–76 are substantially exceeded, India will probably not be able to cross "that dangerous barrier" to which Nehru referred in another fifteen years.[11]

In the opinion of Walt W. Rostow, whose concept of "the stages of economic growth" has attracted worldwide attention, India may already be considered to be in its "take-off" period; if so, it is in a very early stage. It has not yet reached the stage of real self-sustaining growth, and, unless the economic progress can be stepped up it offers little prospect of reaching this stage for the foreseeable future. Wilfred Malenbaum has called attention to the gap "between plan and performance in the case of India's first two five-year programs," and he has insisted that "if India's development outlook is to be favorable, there must be changes either in the type of plan or in the degree of accomplishment — or perhaps, both in some measure."[12]

The broad objective of the First Five Year Plan was "to lay the

[11] In November, 1960, two prominent Indian officials predicted that if the targets which have been set for their country by the economic planners are realized, India would reach the "take-off point to self-sustaining growth" in approximately ten years. Addressing the Economic Club in New York on November 15th Ambassador B. K. Nehru, India's Commissioner General for Economic Affairs, said that if India's development efforts were successful, "we should at the end of ten years be in a stage of development where, though we will still remain incredibly poor, it will not be necessary for us any further to rely on Government-to-Government assistance for our continued growth at a satisfactory rate." Quoted in *Indiagram,* No. 47, Nov. 25, 1960. On the same day, at a Ministerial Meeting of the Colombo Plan Conference in Tokyo, Shrimati Tarakeshwari Sinha, Union Deputy Minister of Finance, said that "a beginning has already been made in setting India on the path of self-sustaining growth," and that "India would be able to develop without any extraordinary form of external assistance within the next ten or eleven years." Quoted in *ibid.* Ambassador Nehru estimated that a sum of approximately 50 billion dollars would have to be invested in the Indian economy in the next decade if these still modest goals were to be attained. He thought that "in spite of our extreme poverty, and in spite of all the limitations of a Democratic System, where sacrifices have to be made by consent and cannot be imposed, we will be able to produce from within the country no less than $40 billion." This would call for foreign assistance at the rate of about one billion dollars a year for at least ten years.

[12] Wilfred Malenbaum, "Leadership Tasks in India's Economy," a paper prepared for a Seminar at the Commonwealth Studies Center, Duke University, April, 1960, pp. 1, 8–9.

foundations on which a more progressive and diversified economy could be built up." More than two-thirds of the total expenditure in the public sector of somewhat over four billion dollars were devoted to agriculture and community development, irrigation and power projects, and transport and communications. Less than 10 per cent went for industrial development. In general, the goals of the First Plan were met, and in some instances they were substantially exceeded. The principal objective of the Second Plan was "to secure a more rapid growth of the national economy and to increase the country's productive potential in a way that will make possible accelerated development in succeeding plan periods." Four objectives were enunciated as of prime importance: (1) a "sizeable increase" in national income; (2) "rapid industrialisation with particular emphasis on the development of basic and heavy industries"; (3) "a large expansion of employment opportunities"; and (4) "reduction of inequalities in income and wealth and a more even distribution of economic power."

The Second Plan ran into serious difficulties and midway in the Plan period the targets had to be reduced. It is estimated that when the Second Plan was completed in late March, 1961, it fell short of its targets by about 30 per cent. The unemployment picture was darker at the end of the Plan than at the beginning, and not much progress had been made in reducing "inequalities in income and wealth." Because of a series of unforeseen circumstances, India's need for foreign exchange during the Second Plan period was greater than was anticipated — for example, serious droughts forced India to use precious foreign exchange to import far more food than was planned — and greater reliance than was intended had to be placed on international financial assistance and deficit financing. The expenditures in the public sector during the period of the Second Plan were nevertheless more than twice as great as during the First Plan.

While the targets set in the Third Plan are more than double those of the Second, they do not envisage the kind of "accelerated development" that was apparently contemplated when India embarked on "the difficult and tremendous journey" of economic growth in the Second Plan. A report issued by the Government of India in July, 1960, stated that the total investment contemplated under the Third Plan was $23.625 billion, of which $15.225 billion would be expended in the public sector and $8.4 billion in the private sector. The report estimated the total foreign exchange requirements during the period of the Third Plan as $6.3 billion. It also indicated a much greater concentration on industrial development than in the first two Plans. Of the total investment in the public sector of more than $15 billion, 56.9 per cent would go to industry, 23.1 per cent to agriculture, community development, and irrigation, and 17.2 per cent to social services.[13] The final version of the Third Plan, presented to Parliament in August, 1961, raised the estimated cost of the Plan to $24.3 billion. This was accompanied by a startling official estimate that the population of India was expected to increase by 187,000,000 in the next fifteen years; and the Plan itself contained the solemn warning that the objective of stabilized population growth "must be at the very center of planned development."

Political Problems and Aspects of Planning

Any political scientist who seeks to understand the mainsprings of actions and the major trends and developments in post-independence India must give special attention to the politics of planning; and he will have to turn to specialists in other disciplines for interpretation of matters of fundamental importance to the experiment in national planning. Some important problems — such as financing, foreign exchange, foreign assistance, savings, investment, and tax policies, food production, unemployment and underemployment, the most effective means of mobilizing scarce resources — can best be treated by the economist. Others — such as planning and social change, population problems, questions of status and structure, problems of communalism, caste, and factions — belong more in the domains of the anthropologist and the sociologist. All of these problems are of interest to the political scientist, for they all have political implications, and they can be dealt with satisfactorily only with the right kind of political policies and leadership.

Three major clusters of political problems — or problems with major political aspects — in relation to the development efforts may be singled out for special attention. These are problems arising from the inadequacies of the Indian administrative system, from the nature of the Indian political system, and from the difficulties of enlisting the cooperation of the people in the work of economic development and national revitalization. Here we shall confine our discussion to these three major clusters of political problems, although obviously many other basic problems facing India today have major political aspects and directly affect the development program. One thinks immediately of such problems as unemployment and underemployment, food production, population growth, divisive tendencies in Indian

[13] See "Indian 5-Year Plan Needs 4.6 Billion in Foreign Aid," dispatch from New Delhi, July 5, 1960, in the *New York Times,* July 6, 1960. Actually the total foreign exchange requirements during the period of the Third Plan will run to about $7 billion; nearly $5.5 billion will be needed to finance projects under the Plan, over $1 billion for repayment of foreign exchange credits advanced over the past ten years, and some 630 million to meet private sector requirements for foreign exchange.

life — regional, linguistic, caste and other divisions — and pressures impinging upon India from the outside.

Problems of Administrative Reorganization and Reform. After a searching examination of the Indian administrative system, Dr. Paul Appleby rated the Government of India as one of the most advanced governments, perhaps the most advanced, in any underdeveloped nation. Yet Dr. Appleby pointed out that "the very system that justified classifying the Indian government among the few that are most advanced was conceived in pre-revolutionary terms," and he indicated that the administrative structure which had been developed impressively in British days has grave defects for a large developing nation. The administrative system, he found, was too rigid and too authoritarian; instead of being geared for action responsibilities, it put a premium on excessive attention to detail and unwillingness to make decisions or to accept responsibility. "There are too many forms of class, rank and prerogative consciousness, too much insistence on too-uniform concentration of communication in formal channels, too much cross-reference including too many reviews of administrative papers by legal officers, too much control of detail, too much preoccupation with 'saving' rupees and too little with larger effectiveness."[14] "Perhaps nowhere else," he asserted, "have so many systematic barriers been erected to prevent the accomplishment of that which it has been determined should be done." At the outset of the Second Five Year Plan he warned that "full success of the Plan . . . turns rather exclusively on administrative reform to make the government as an organism equal to its identified goals." If India wished to realize broad goals it must have an administrative structure and administrative outlook which would be adequate for the task. "Will the people and the Parliament," he asked, "be sufficiently willing to pay enough and to give through delegation sufficient scope for the discretion and wisdom providing the kind of public service of performance necessary for administrative effectiveness?"[15]

Most students of public administration, Indian and foreign, who have examined India's administrative system and outlook in the light of present and future needs have voiced similar criticisms of the existing system and have advanced various proposals for administrative reform.[16] Now that India has embarked on "that difficult and

[14] Paul H. Appleby, *Public Administration in India: Report of a Survey* (New Delhi, 1953), pp. 8, 9, 21. This report was issued by the Cabinet Secretariat, Government of India.

[15] Appleby, *Re-examination of India's Administrative System,* pp. 17, 49.

[16] In his fascinating book on the Etawah project in India, Albert Mayer states: "But by far the most doubtful and maybe baffling problem is this: that while within our project we have developed something which works

tremendous journey" of economic development and nation-building, it must gear its administrative machinery for the task and it must develop an administrative climate which will be conducive to planned change, carried out efficiently and, let us hope, in a democratic way.

If such an administrative climate is to be developed, special attention must be given to the planning process and the organization of planning, to the organization of local government and its adaptation to development activities, to the administration of the Community Development Program and the National Extension Service, and to efforts to revive the *panchayats* as basic units of local government and administration and to develop a system of village cooperatives. All of these involve fundamental problems of administrative reorganization and reform.

The Planning Commission. The central agency for planning in India is the Planning Commission. Established early in 1950, shortly after the Constitution of India entered into effect, and working under the general guidance of the provision in the Constitution for promoting the general welfare by securing political, economic, and social justice, the tasks of the Planning Commission are "to assess the nation's resources, draw up a plan to use them with proper priorities and allocation, determine the conditions, machinery and adjustments needed to make the plan succeed; appraise the progress of the plan from time to time and make any recommendations necessary to facilitate it."[17]

The Chairman of the Commission is the Prime Minister himself. There are seven other members including a Deputy Chairman and the Ministers for Planning, Defense, and Finance, and an excellent staff of about 250 persons. The staff and the Commission work closely with the Parliament, the Finance Ministry, the Cabinet Secretariat, and the State governments. Once a plan is formulated, it is submitted

within itself, unlocking some new strengths, it exists within an over-all administrative system where its direct methods and unlocked action are still unknown. Our system is basically alien to theirs, which is very much a system of checks and balances, delays, refinements, and decisions passing through many hands. In the routine administrative system, a sense of problem and urgency are second-hand. We hitherto existed within it by dint of strenuous special effort and high-level attention to pry things open — efforts and attention which cannot be expected to continue when such enterprises multiply." Albert Mayer and Associates, with McKim Marriott and Richard L. Park, *Pilot Project, India* (University of California Press, 1958), p. 92. See also D. R. Gadgil, "Prospects for the Second Five Year Plan Period," *India Quarterly*, XIII (January–March, 1957), 5–23.

[17] *The New India*, p. 66. See Chapter V, "How India Plans," pp. 64–75. For a detailed description of the organization of the Planning Commission and its affiliated agencies see the Indian Institute of Public Administration, *The Organisation of the Government of India* (Bombay, 1958), pp. 342–353.

to the National Development Council composed of the Chief Ministers of the States and the members of the Planning Commission. Nehru is also Chairman of the National Development Council, which is playing an increasingly significant role in national planning.

The Planning Commission has advisers on program administration in the States, who help in the evaluation of the progress of the plans and in making recommendations for more effective implementation. Through its Research Programmes Committee the Commission benefits from, and occasionally sponsors, studies and reports by a large number of private and public organizations and institutes, including various ministries, Indian universities, the Indian Statistical Institute, the Central Statistical Organization, State statistical bureaus, the National Sample Survey, the Agricultural Credit Department of the Reserve Bank, the National Council of Applied Economic Research, the International Bank for Reconstruction and Development and other United Nations agencies, and the Ford Foundation.

Within the Planning Commission's framework the Programme Evaluation Organization issues frequent reports on the progress of the rural development programs. An important supplement to the reports of the Programme Evaluation Organization was the three-volume report in late 1957 of the Balvantray Mehta Committee, appointed by the Committee on Plan Projects to study the Community Development Program and the National Extension Service. The Home Minister is Chairman of the Committee on Plan Projects, and the other members are the Ministers of Finance and Planning and two Chief Ministers of States nominated by the Prime Minister. In addition to the Balvantray Mehta Committee, the Committee on Plan Projects has set up study teams on "Irrigation and Power" and on "Building Projects." To associate officials and non-officials of the country with the work of national planning, and to enlist the cooperation of the people generally, a Co-ordination Committee for Public Co-operation was established in 1952, with the Chairman and Deputy Chairman of the Planning Commission as the chief officers. "The Committee represents the top leadership of various groups in the country and is primarily concerned with matters of general policy and direction in relation to public co-operation."[18]

The Planning Commission is an advisory body, not a line agency. The administration and implementation of the development program is the responsibility of the Centre and the States. There is no doubt, however, that the Planning Commission has extraordinary influence in India, and that it carries on many activities which are more than advisory in nature. While there is widespread agreement that the Commission has functioned in an impressive way, it has been criticized

[18] *Ibid.*, p. 353.

for exceeding its functions and for failure to enlist the cooperation of local governmental units and officials and of the people generally. K. M. Munshi, a veteran Indian political leader, stated flatly at a public meeting in New Delhi in 1959: "Parliament, in fact, does not govern the country. . . . The nominated super-cabinet, the Planning Commission, does the supervision, control and direction of the Government of India, and owes no responsibility to Parliament."[19]

One of the sharpest criticisms of the Planning Commission was voiced by an eminent Indian economist, Professor D. R. Gadgil, Director of the Gokhale Institute of Economics and Politics at Poona. In a lecture at the Harold Laski Institute of Political Science in Ahmedabad in 1958 Professor Gadgil stated:

> The main functions set down in the 1950 resolution establishing the Planning Commission were to assess resources, formulate the plan, define its stages, appraise progress and make related recommendations on policy and administration. Examination of events since 1955 shows that barring the theoretical formulation, the Planning Commission has failed in almost every respect. . . . The root of the failure lies in the process by which the Planning Commission, essentially only an Advisory body, has come to mix itself with the actual process of the formation of public policies even in matters other than development. . . . It is the power complex of the Planning Commission or its members, their natural desire to exercise power and patronage like Ministers that are chiefly responsible for the neglect by the Commission of its main functions and for a needless extension of its activities over many irrelevant fields. The misdirection has been helped largely by membership of the Prime Minister and the Finance Minister of the Planning Commission which appears to have invested the Planning Commission and its decisions with an unnatural kind of prestige and importance.[20]

Nehru has admitted that the Planning Commission has not performed all of its many functions satisfactorily, but he has denied all charges that the Commission was becoming a kind of super-cabinet, without detracting in any way from the important role which it is playing in the whole field of national planning. "Essentially," he pointed out in a statement in the Rajya Sabha on September 6, 1960, "it had advisory functions but it might be that in certain circumstances its advice was too important to be by-passed."

[19] Quoted in "The Super-Cabinet," *The Radical Humanist,* XXIII (Dec. 6, 1959), 571.

[20] D. R. Gadgil, *Indian Planning and the Planning Commission* (Ahmedabad, 1958). For a more favorable commentary on the role and work of the Planning Commission see Appleby, *Re-examination of India's Administrative System,* pp. 31–32.

Balvantray Mehta Report and Panchayati Raj. The Balvantray Mehta Committee, after a comprehensive study of local government in rural areas, strongly recommended the democratic decentralization of Indian administration. It proposed a three-tier system of local government, with extensive responsibilities for community development, to be vested in three locally-elected bodies: a directly-elected *panchayat* at the village level, a *panchayat samiti* (assembly) within each development block, and a *zila parishad* (district committee) at the district level, composed of the chairmen of the *panchayat samitis* within the district.[21] This system is generally referred to as *panchayati raj* (government by *panchayats*).

The Balvantray Mehta Report has had a profound impact on Indian thinking about rural administration and democratic reorganization, and it has already led to the introduction of *panchayati raj* in Rajasthan, Andhra, Mysore, Madras, Kerala, Assam, and other Indian states. "Indeed, with the exceptions of Bombay and West Bengal, all Indian states seem to be moving towards a similar form of administrative reorganization."[22] It is still too early to evaluate the prospects of success for these new experiments in democratic decentralization. Potentially, they are of the greatest significance, and if, by happy chance, they should prove to be generally successful, they might go far toward "rooting democracy firmly in India." However, it would be wise to suspend judgment on the outcome of these latest experiments until they have been tested over a longer period of time.

Some observers have predicted that this new three-tier system of local government will greatly reduce the powers and influence of the District Collectors, and that the Collectors, the symbol and embodiment of governmental authority in the past, may even be on the way

[21] See *Report of the Team for the Study of Community Projects and National Extension Service* (Balvantray G. Mehta, Leader), New Delhi, Committee on Plan Projects, Government of India, 1957. Vols. I and II (November, 1957); Vol. III (Parts I and II) (December, 1957).

[22] Richard L. Park, "Administrative Coordination and Economic Development in the Districts of India," a paper prepared for a Seminar at the Commonwealth Studies Center, Duke University, February, 1960, p. 25. See also P. K. Chaudhuri, "Decentralisation or Delegation of Power? The Rajasthan Panchayat Samitis and Zila Parishad Act, 1959," *The Economic Weekly* (Bombay), Oct. 3, 1959; "Panchayat Raj in Madras," *The Hindu Weekly Review,* Dec. 7, 1959, p. 13; "Decentralisation: The Report and After," *Link* (New Delhi), Nov. 15, 1959, pp. 20–21; P. C. Chaudhuri, "A Year of Panchayati Raj," *The Economic Weekly,* Twelfth Annual Number, XIII (Feb. 4, 1961), 137–142; Rajni Kothari, "Panchayati Raj: a Reassessment," *The Economic Weekly,* XIII (May 13, 1961), 754–760; and "India to Spur Rural Democracy as Key to Swifter Development," dispatch from Paul Grimes from New Delhi, dated July 10, 1961, in *New York Times,* July 11, 1961.

out. The views of Richard L. Park on this point are most interesting: "Will this alteration of older patterns of administration really take hold, and will the *samitis* and *parishads* be able to integrate piecemeal plans into coordinated programs, or will the ubiquitous Collector, sure of his skills, simply manipulate the new bodies as he controlled district and municipal boards in the past? We do not know as yet, but the signs are strong that the Collectorate is fading away in its power as the people try their hands at the coordinating tasks."[23] In all probability, however, the Collector will be around for a long time; in fact, his services will be necessary until and unless the development block, "a new unit of action and administration," becomes an integrated "social system," as two American observers of India's development efforts have predicted,[24] until and unless the *panchayats,* the *panchayat samitis,* and the *zila parishads* really perform the functions envisioned for them by the Balvantray Mehta Committee.

The Community Development Program and National Extension Service. On October 2, 1952, the anniversary of Mahatma Gandhi's birthday, the Community Development Program was officially launched in India. This Program has been the most publicized aspect of India's development efforts. Less public attention was attracted by the inauguration of the National Extension Service in 1953, but this came to be "regarded as one of the most significant achievements of the First Plan years."[25] In 1955 Nehru himself said: "I think that the most significant development of these years has been in the domain of Community Projects and the National Extension Service. . . . It means a social revolution in our ways of life and work which is creeping gradually but surely over the vast land of India."[26]

Under the general supervision of a Central Committee and a Central Ministry for Community Development, and similar committees and ministries in each of the States, the community projects are multipurpose efforts in rural areas. Groups of roughly a hundred villages are associated in "development blocks," the basic units of development. By the end of the First Five Year Plan 1200 blocks — about one-fourth of which were intensive Community Development blocks, with the larger number being less intensive National Extension Service blocks — had been established, reaching about one-fourth of the people of rural India. The goal was to cover all of India by the end of the

[23] Park, "Administrative Coordination and Economic Development," p. 28.

[24] Howard W. Beers and Douglas Ensminger, "The Development Block as a Social System?", *The Indian Journal of Public Administration,* V (April–June, 1959), 135–152.

[25] *The New India,* p. 170.

[26] Address at the Fourth Development Commissioners' Conference, Simla, May, 1955; quoted in *The New India,* pp. 178–179.

Second Plan, but because of unforeseen difficulties this goal has been postponed for two to three years. By the end of the Third Five Year Plan in 1966 it is hoped that all of the villages of India will be integrated into the intensive Community Development scheme.

The Community Development Program is at once one of the most exciting and one of the most discouraging features of economic and social planning in India. In spite of glowing reports of substantial and indeed revolutionary progress in this field, the program has bogged down badly, and its entire future is in jeopardy. It has been very difficult to enlist the participation of the people in the program, or to give them a sense of real identity with it, and these have been the basic objectives of the entire effort. It has been difficult to recruit and train properly qualified persons to serve in the key positions of block development officers and village level workers (*Gram Sevak*). It has been difficult to provide the proper co-ordination and direction for the program, whether on the national and State levels or in the districts. The Balvantry Mehta Report made devastating criticisms of the program, and its recommendations for democratic decentralization of administration in India in effect proposed a different structure of organization and popular participation in rural India.

Most recent reports on the Community Development Program and the National Extension Service have been quite critical and discouraging. The seventh evaluation report of the Programme Evaluation Organization of the Planning Commission, issued in the summer of 1960, stated that there were "lights and shades in the picture of the C. D. Programme in actual operation. The shades, however, predominate and one gathers the impression of an inadequately co-ordinated endeavour, governmental rather than popular in character and sustained more by hope than achievement."[27]

S. K. Dey, Minister for Community Development, has recalled that "the slogan which was inscribed on the banner of the pioneers" of the Community Development Program was "Destination Man." "The implications were never clearly analysed, . . but it was generally understood that the focus was on human growth and not on material development." For all the shortcomings of the Community Development Program, Dey believes that the fundamental approach is sound, and that there are grounds for hope: "Happily, there are some still in India whose faith in community development remains undimmed. They are to be found in all walks of life. . . . They have been privileged to see the first faint stirrings of the human spirit which can be evoked under sensitive ministration. . . . The human factor will still remain crucial. . . . There can be sustained response

[27] Quoted in "Crucial Factors in Community Development," *The Radical Humanist,* XXIV (July 24, 1960), 355.

only when people feel the urge within themselves. Community development is the only way in which that urge can be awakened."[28]

Panchayats and Village Cooperatives. In addition to its efforts to spread the Community Development Program and the National Extension Service all over India the Government is also placing a great deal of emphasis, at the grass roots level, on the widespread organization of village *panchayats* and village cooperatives, with extensive responsibilities for development work and certain other activities. Speaking at Ernakulam in Kerala on January 18, 1960, Prime Minister Nehru said that the steps which the Government of India was taking all over the country to give powers to *panchayats* and to establish village cooperatives were of revolutionary importance as a means of bringing masses of people into the administrative structure in rural areas and thereby of laying the bases of real democratic self-government.

The efforts of the Government of India to implement Article 40 of the Constitution, which called for the creation of village *panchayats* "as units of self-government," have already been described. These efforts have been impressive. They have led all the States to pass *panchayat* acts, and *panchayats* have been established for more than half of the villages of India; but there are ample grounds for Hugh Tinker's conclusion that "in general, the *panchayat* experiment has shown the same discouraging refusal to 'get off the ground' as before independence." Professor Tinker is doubtless justified in believing that "their poor performance stems directly from the circumstances of rural life."[29] Indian villages are still relatively static social groups, riddled by factional and caste divisions, tradition-bound and resistant to change, suspicious of government in any form, desirous of resisting all alien influences. It is possible, nevertheless, that *panchayats* may provide the vehicles for associating villagers with national development, and people with government.

The cooperative movement has been strong in India for more than half a century, especially since the passage of the Cooperative Credit Society Act of 1904. "In 1919 cooperation became a subject for action by the States, under the control of an elected Minister. . . . By 1950–51, the eve of the First Plan, there were 181,000 cooperative societies," mostly rural credit societies.[30] The First Five Year Plan called the cooperative form of organization "an indispensable instrument of planned economic activity in a democracy." Thousands of cooperatives have been formed since the First Plan was inaugurated.

[28] S. K. Dey, "The Crisis in Community Development," *The Radical Humanist,* XXIV (Jan. 10, 1960), 17–18, 24.

[29] High Tinker, "Authority and Community in Village India," *Pacific Affairs,* XXXII (December, 1959), 361.

[30] *The New India,* pp. 202–203.

At its sixty-fourth annual meeting, held at Nagpur in January, 1959, the Indian National Congress endorsed a far-reaching resolution regarding cooperatives, which declared:

> The future agrarian pattern should be that of cooperative joint farming in which the land shall be pooled for joint cultivation, the farmers continuing to retain their property rights and getting a share from the common produce in proportion to their land. Further those who actually work on the land, whether they own the land or not will get a share in proportion to the work put in by them on joint farms. . . . As a first step prior to the institution of joint farming, service cooperatives should be completed within a period of three years; even within this period, however, wherever possible and when generally agreed to by the farmers, joint cultivation may be started.

Nehru himself attaches great importance to this resolution, and he envisages village cooperatives as a means of economic organization of village India, comparable in importance to the *panchayats* as the main units of political organization. "We should cover every village as a co-operative," he has said. "We are launching out, in this way, in new directions outside the scope of our old administrative apparatus and we want to give far greater power to panchayats and to the village co-operatives than they have today, knowing that they may misuse it, make mistakes, and the like."[31]

The Nagpur Resolution of 1959 for greater emphasis on village cooperatives has provoked a great deal of criticism and opposition within India. The Swatantra Party was formed largely to fight the tendencies toward the abolition of private property and the collectivist tendencies which were ascribed to it. Nehru has indignantly denied the sweeping charges of the leaders of the Swantantra Party and of others who oppose the Nagpur Resolution approach, and he has undertaken a campaign of national education regarding the real objectives of the Resolution and the role of village cooperatives in the New India which he is trying to create; but while he has had some success in arousing popular interest and in counteracting some of the extreme charges against the program for village cooperatives on a massive scale, the objectives of the Nagpur Resolution remain largely unfulfilled. It is significant that the resolutions of the annual sessions of the Congress and of the A.I.C.C. in 1960 and 1961 contained only passing references to these objectives.

Problems of Centralization and Decentralization. In implementing

[31] "Towards a Dynamic Administration," address at the Indian Institute of Public Administration, New Delhi, April 25, 1959; in *The Indian Journal of Public Administration,* V (April–June, 1959), 131–132.

economic planning in India the political system itself, with its evolving patterns and its great dependence on personal leadership, presents a number of serious problems. Among these are the tendencies toward centralization, on the one hand, and toward decentralization, on the other, in a rather peculiar federal system, and the problem of leadership at all levels.

In all democratic countries the increasing concentration of power, authority, and functions is a matter of deep concern. This is true even in federal states, where presumably the constituent units of the federation have special authority as well. In India the concentration of authority seems to be particularly obvious. There is today a strong and pervasive tendency to look to the Central Government whenever difficulties arise in the "private sector" or in the States or in local units of government. The dominant position of the Congress Party and of Nehru in the country generally has reinforced this tendency. Moreover, there is widespread acceptance of the view that without strong direction from the Centre India cannot hope to deal effectively with its vast problems, carry out its comprehensive experiment in national planning, and establish a "socialist pattern of society."

In October, 1959, the Union Minister of Industries, Manubhai Shah, went so far as to state publicly that "the Centre is becoming a steam roller and the States appear to be in a pitiable position." Shah insisted that the Government of India was not responsible for this trend. "It is not that the Central Government wanted to corner as much power and authority for itself. The social and economic compulsions are creating a situation which the Government of India has to accept willy-nilly."[32] Critics of the Government and the Congress Party would share Shah's alarm over the growing centralization of power, but they would probably blame the Government, and even more the Congress Party, for this trend.

As has been noted, Dr. Paul Appleby is concerned not so much with the growing power of the Central Government in India as with what he regards as "its extraordinary national dependence upon the States for a large part of its administration."[33] "No other large and important national government," in his opinion, "is so dependent as India on theoretically subordinate but actually rather distinct units responsible to a different political control, for so much of the administration of what are recognized as national programs of great importance to the nation."[34] Few observers would go as far as Appleby in this regard, but the experience to date with the implementation of the development

[32] Quoted in "Devolution of Power & Democracy," *The Radical Humanist,* XXIII (Nov. 1, 1959), 511.

[33] Appleby, *Re-examination of India's Administrative System,"* p. 47.

[34] Appleby, *Public Administration in India,* p. 21.

programs has indicated that his concern is justified. Generally speaking, the States have not provided the resources or carried out the tasks assigned to them in the Five Year Plans, and the Central Government has been unable to hold them to greater accountability.

Authority is also concentrated in the States at the expense of local units of government and at the expense of individual initiative and autonomy. This may be due, as Shah stated, to "reluctance to take responsibility at the lower level," but, whatever the cause, it calls attention to one of the most serious failings in India's development efforts. The Balvantray Mehta Report, as has been indicated, recommended a reversal of the tendency to centralization, and the adoption, as a deliberate policy of the Government, of a program of decentralization, designed to give real substance and vitality to local units of government and to enlist the cooperation of the people more effectively, in ways that are meaningful to them.

Leadership and National Development. Leadership is important in any country, and particularly so in an underdeveloped country which has recently embarked on an independent existence. When the masses of the people are still relatively inert and when the tasks of nation-building are so gigantic, a large measure of paternalism is probably essential. In the development field, as in all other areas of national endeavor, India has benefited greatly from the quality and orientation of its top leaders.

Here as elsewhere Nehru has played the leading role. Although he is in no sense an economist, he has assumed direct supervision and control over India's whole development effort. The economic philosophy motivating the development planning, the priorities assigned in the Five Year Plans, and many of the unique features of the Plans are determined in large measure by him. He has done far more than any one else to explain the Plans to the people and to mobilize popular support, to the extent that it has been mobilized, behind the great experiment in nation-building.

Nehru is an active chairman of the Planning Commission and of the National Development Council, which from time to time reviews the progress of the national plans and makes recommendations to the Central and State Governments. The Ministers for Finance, Planning, and Defense also are members of both bodies. Unusually able men have served in these posts.

India has no dearth of trained and competent economists, and many of the best of them have served on the staff of the Planning Commission, on the Programme Evaluation Organisation, on study teams appointed by the Committee on Plan Projects, or in other capacities. Thus Indian economists have had a major share in the development of the Five Year Plans. Of particular importance has been the role of Professor P. C. Mahalanobis, Director of the Indian Statistical Institute in Calcutta. He has served as chief adviser on planning to the Prime Minister, and has been one of India's chief planners. He is now a member of the Planning Commission. In his several capacities he has had a great influence — some of his critics would say too great an influence — on India's approach to planning, in determining long-range planning goals, and in the actual formulation of at least the Second Five Year Plan.

For the implementation of the national plans the Central Government inevitably has to rely to a great extent on State and local units of government. All too often the leadership at State and local levels has been lacking in understanding, initiative, and imagination. This has greatly handicapped the development efforts. Although some of the ablest of the Congress Party leaders have devoted most of their time to the affairs of their States, and although the Chief Ministers of all the States are members of the National Development Council and the Zonal Councils and participate in the work of planning and development in many other ways, the States have in fact been bottlenecks, as far as the implementation of the Five Year Plans has been concerned.

In the districts the District Officers or Collectors have generally been able men, but they have invariably been civil servants and at best benevolent paternalists rather than leaders of the people. In the villages leadership has been largely on a factional or caste basis. Generally speaking, neither the District Collector nor the village headman has been an effective leader, except in a paternal and custodial sense. New types of leaders in rural India are needed for the implementation of the experiments in the regeneration of the country which are the warp and the woof of the development programs. One of the main problems in implementing the Community Development and National Extension Service programs has been that of finding the right kind of leaders to serve as block development officers and village level workers, and even more of finding the kinds of leaders in the villages who can and will respond to the challenge of the new programs and who can enlist the participation of the people in them.

Problems of Popular Participation and Identification. Underlying all the problems of implementing economic planning in India is how to secure the active cooperation of the people and identify them with the great effort in "the building up of India, taking this country and its millions of people forward." The eventual success or failure of India's total national effort may revolve around this problem. It is at once the most challenging and the most discouraging aspect of the entire development effort. "The participation of the people is of the very essence of the programme," stated the Planning Commission in a summary of the First Five Year Plan. "Unless people feel that the program is theirs and value it as a practical contribution to their own welfare, no substantial results will be gained."[35]

To what extent have popular participation and identification been achieved? Optimistic observers, including most Government spokesmen, have often referred to the great revolution that is under way throughout India as the plans progress, to the "awakening of the countryside." "The revolutionary character" of the development programs, according to a popular work on *The New India,* issued under the aegis of the Planning Commission, "lies precisely in that it has succeeded in awakening this participation and organizing it on a national scale."[36] Few candid observers of the Indian scene can find impressive evidence of widespread awakening or mass identification.[37] It is probably too much to expect that the people of India, living in mental and geographical isolation in a stratified society, accustomed to having decisions imposed on them from above, without any experience in effective cooperation in national efforts, would respond to another and greater program which has come to them from the far-away centers of power in New Delhi. With the possible exception of the mass response to Gandhi's appeals and teachings, and to a more limited degree to Vinoba Bhave's Bhoodan Yagna movement, no movement has "succeeded in awakening" widespread popular participation and "organizing it on a national scale." Thus India's planners today are confronted with an inescapable dilemma: they have almost no prospects of securing effective popular initiative and participation in national development programs, yet their programs cannot possibly succeed without such initiative and participation.

[35] Planning Commission, Government of India, *First Five Year Plan* (New Delhi, 1952), p. 223.

[36] *The New India,* p. 171.

[37] The seventh report of the Programme Evaluation Organisation of the Planning Commission contained the following observation: "Peoples' attitudes and reactions in most of the Community Development Blocks are not yet generally favourable to the success and growth of the Community Development Programme. The majority of the villages do not regard it as their own programme and seem to rely mainly on the Government for effecting the development of rural areas. The basic philosophy and approach of the Community Development Programme are, therefore, inadequately subscribed to by the people."

* 9 *

The Party System

Experience with Political Parties in Asia

With the possible exceptions of Japan, the Philippines, and Israel, no effective democratic party system in the Western sense has emerged anywhere in Asia. The very idea of parties is strange and even unacceptable to many Asians; it conforms neither with their traditional ways of looking at things and of doing things nor with their concepts of how political life in their countries should be organized to meet the needs of a changing, yet basically static, society. As they look at the present state and activities of political parties in most Western countries, they are not impressed; and they reason that if parties are functioning so unsatisfactorily in the countries of the West, where the tradition of parties is deeply rooted and where literate and economically fortunate peoples have had long experience with party systems, it would be folly to expect that parties could be successfully grafted onto the institutions of Asian peoples.

Only a few Asian political parties date back to the nineteenth century; most of them arose as "umbrella" organizations in the latter days of the struggle for independence from the ruling colonial powers, and then carried on as the dominant parties after independence. "An independence movement," as Richard L. Park has observed, "is not the best breeding ground for political parties in the Western sense. In the search for unity in opposition to the ruling imperial power, the Asian nationalist movements exerted every effort to bring all factions together into one independence-bound organization. . . . After independence, as was natural, these movements tended to break down, with groups of minority views leaving the parent body to form new political groupings."[1] Generally speaking, these dominant political

[1] Richard L. Park, "Problems of Political Development," in Philip W. Thayer, ed., *Nationalism and Progress in Free Asia* (Baltimore: The Johns Hopkins Press, 1956), p. 103.

groupings, which were both more and less than political parties, performed a useful service, not only in the independence struggle but in the years of trial and difficulty which followed its success.

In some respects new countries with a dominant national political organization fared better than those in which the pattern of political activity was more diffuse. There may be considerable merit in Professor Park's contention that "a well-organized political party system might have hindered the relative stability. . . . Much of the success of the legislative and planning programs in these countries can be traced to the large, disciplined majorities held by the party in power in the respective parliaments. The hard test of parliamentary government, of course, will come when this situation no longer prevails."[2]

In most Asian countries which adopted the parliamentary system, at least in form, the hard test has already come. In some, as in Pakistan, the leaders now in power have turned away from the system itself; in others, as in Burma, after a transitory period of military rule a second test of parliamentary democracy is being made; in still others, as in Indonesia, parties still exist, but largely on sufferance, and they occupy a subordinate place in the new national front system of "guided democracy." Most of the umbrella organizations that headed the independence movements have either disappeared or have fallen on evil days. The Muslim League in Pakistan virtually disintegrated by 1954, and although it seemed to be experiencing a mild revival just prior to the "revolution" of October, 1958, it is today, along with all other political parties, one of the unlamented casualties of the new order in Pakistan. The Indonesian Nationalist Party is still one of the three or four most important political organizations in Indonesia, but today it is associated, along with all other parties, in a subordinate capacity with Sukarno's "guided democracy." The AFPFL in Burma, the party of Aung San and then of U Nu, split up into two factions, a "clean" AFPFL, headed by U Nu, and a "stable" AFPFL, headed by Ba Swe and Kyaw Nyein. The Kuomintang has long since been superseded by the Communists on the Chinese mainland. Only in India does the party of independence still dominate the political life of the country, and, as we shall see, the Congress Party of today is a far cry from the Indian National Congress of the Gandhian era, and its future, after Nehru goes, is very much in doubt.

The Nature of Political Parties in India

Since the Congress Party has fared better than any other Asian nationalist-movement-turned-political-party, the "hard test of parliamentary government," to use Professor Park's phrase, has been post-

[2] *Ibid.*, p. 104.

poned. There are manifold signs, however, that the "hard test" is at hand; they are to be found in growing criticisms of the Congress, in the internal divisions, which, while not new, are becoming more serious, in the admitted failings of its leadership, especially on State and local levels, in the growing political opposition to it in the States and municipalities and local areas, in the dissatisfaction with its economic and social achievements, in the rise of regional and linguistic and communal pressures which challenge the basic tenets of national unity and the secular state, in the failure of the Congress to train a new generation of leaders to replace the "tall leaders," most of whom are well along in years, and in the inevitable crises which will beset the party when the tallest of all the "tall leaders," Nehru himself, now in his early seventies, passes from the scene.

For all these reasons India can no longer be correctly described as a "one-party state"; but there is still some truth to such a characterization as far as the national scene is concerned. In spite of growing criticisms and dissatisfactions, the Congress is still as dominant on the national scene as it ever was, in terms of its hold on the Government of the country if not on the loyalty of the citizens. In the second general elections the Congress polled an even higher percentage of the popular vote than it did in the first, and it increased its already top-heavy membership in the Lok Sabha. After the 1957 elections the Congress had 365 seats in the Lok Sabha, whereas the next largest party — the Communists — had 30, and the entire non-Congress membership, including Independents, numbered only about 135.

This lop-sided dominance of the Congress Party may have provided the kind of political stability which India needed in the early years of independence, as Professor Park has suggested, but it has thus far prevented a healthy party system from emerging. The situation is made even worse by the weakness of the Praja Socialist Party and other Socialist parties, which presumably could provide the nucleus of an effective democratic opposition, and by the challenge of the Communist Party, which would use the ballot box and its representation in the Parliament to destroy the institutions of democracy, and of communal groups with political representation, which in their own way are equally determined enemies of secular democracy.

Another major barrier to the development of a healthy party system in India is posed by those who do not believe in parties at all. This group includes many people who are influential in Indian political life and many more who are influential in Indian society. Many of these people look upon parties as undesirable organizations, and they would substitute for them other means for permitting popular expression and for implementing the peoples' will. Often they derive their ideas from Gandhi, and from the Mahatma's ideas of the *sarvodaya* society. Such ideas are being propagated today by two of the most influential people on the Indian scene, both long-time followers of Gandhi, Acharya Vinoba Bhave, in his Bhoodan Yagna movement, and Jayaprakash Nayayan, through his support of the Bhoodan movement and through his frequent writings and public pronouncements on political matters. Jayaprakash, or J. P. — as everyone calls him — advocates a "partyless democracy." He has written and spoken in favor of such a system on many occasions, but he has never been able to formulate a specific statement of precisely what a system of "partyless democracy" would involve, how it would differ from a democratic system in which parties existed, and how it would meet the needs of a vast nation trying to cope with the problems of the modern world and to develop the basis for a healthy national life.[3] Many Indians feel, as did M. N. Roy, and as do his followers, the Radical Humanists, that the people are too backward to become politically conscious and discriminating members of any party; hence, a different approach to the participation of the individual in social and political life is held to be necessary.[4]

Although many Indians profess to believe in "partyless democracy," parties have mushroomed in great profusion in the years since independence. Most of the major parties originated within, and not outside, the Indian National Congress; among them were the Congress Socialist Party, which became the nucleus of the Praja Socialist Party, and even the Communist Party, which was not expelled from the Congress until 1945. Prominent leaders of the major opposition parties were once active workers in the Congress ranks. Scores of so-called parties contested the general elections of 1951–52 and 1957. In the present Lok Sabha some twenty-five parties are represented, although only the Congress has any significant representation, and only two other parties, the Communists and the PSP, have more than fifteen members. Most parties are really local or at most regional groupings,

[3] See, for example, Jayaprakash Narayan, "Towards a Fuller Democracy," *The Radical Humanist,* XXII (June 15 and 22, 1958), 281–282, 288, 295–296. In the latter part of 1959 Narayan circulated a paper entitled "A Plea for Reconstruction of Indian Polity," in which he elaborated briefly on his ideas on partyless politics. He has been working for the past two years or more on a book, in which he will develop his thesis of partyless government.

[4] The pages of *The Radical Humanist,* the organ of the Radical Humanist movement, frequently contain articles on this theme. See, for example, M. N. Roy, "Opening of a New Chapter in Indian History," *The Radical Humanist,* May 25, 1958, and Ellen Roy, "Indian Party Politics," *The Radical Humanist,* July 24, 1955. See also M. N. Roy, *Power, Parties and Politics* (Calcutta, 1960).

often hardly more than the followers of some leader. Such groupings spring up and disappear quickly, or merge with similar groups, or move in and out of "electoral arrangements," sometimes of a weird character. In India, as elsewhere, politics makes strange bedfellows.

In a statement issued on March 18, 1953, in connection with his talks with Jayaprakash Narayan regarding the bases of closer cooperation between the Congress and the PSP, Prime Minister Nehru made an interesting comment on the party situation in India:

> The parties, as they exist in India today, apart from the Congress, may be divided into four groups. There are certain political parties with an economic ideology. There is the Communist Party with the allied organisations. There are the various communal parties under different names but essentially following a narrow communal ideology, and there are a number of local parties and groups having only a provincial or even narrower appeal.[5]

It will be convenient to discuss the political parties of India with Nehru's classification in mind. In the first group will be included the major political parties which not only have an economic ideology — for presumably most of the parties profess some economic tenets — but also those parties which are truly dedicated to the preservation of a democratic secular state. Thus the Congress itself belongs in this category, along with the PSP and the Socialist Party, and probably the new Swatantra Party as well.

The Congress Party

We have already traced the evolution of the Indian National Congress from its founding in 1885 until its emergence as the dominant political party in an independent India. Three main periods in the history of the Congress prior to 1947 may be discerned. During the first period, from 1885 to about 1907, the objective of the Congress was not independence for India but cooperation with the British and mild pressure on the foreign rulers to give greater political representation to Indians. In these years the Congress was under the control of Western-educated moderates, men like Dadabhai Naoroji, Surendranath Banerjea, Pherozshah Mehta, and especially G. K. Gokhale. From about 1907 until the end of World War I the Congress was split between the moderates and the more extreme and militant elements, led by Bal Gangadhar Tilak, Aurobindo Ghose (until he retired from politics), Bepin Chandra Pal, and Lala Lajpat Rai. Tilak and his associates raised the cry of *swaraj* and *swadeshi,* advocated resistance to the British instead of cooperation with them, and harked back to the ancient Hindu past for their ideology and inspiration. The extremists

[5] *The Hindustan Times,* March 19, 1953.

introduced new vigor into the nationalist movement, and attracted a larger following than the moderates ever could.

With the death of Gokhale in 1915 and of Tilak in 1920, with new forces entering the Indian scene, and above all with the entry of Gandhi into the political life of the country, after a long sojourn in South Africa, the Gandhian period of the nationalist movement began. Under the influence of Gandhi the Congress adopted new techniques of nonviolent noncooperation or civil disobedience which gave a new kind of militancy to the national movement and brought it nearer to the masses. The new militancy was reflected in various civil disobedience campaigns and in the noncooperation of the Congress with the British during the period of World War II, because the British would not grant immediately the demands for *swaraj,* which by the late thirties had come to mean complete independence.

With better organization, more widespread popular support, and the magic influence of Mahatma Gandhi, the Congress became a truly national movement. As long as it was the main organization for independence, it could include in its ranks people of very diverse backgrounds and interests, and it could function as an umbrella organization without serious political indigestion. There were, however, marked divergencies within the top leadership of the Congress. In the Gandhian era a kind of right wing and left wing split developed. The right wing was led by more conservatively inclined Congressmen, such as Motilal Nehru and Vallabhbhai Patel, while the left wing was led by younger spokesmen of such diverse viewpoints as Subhas Chandra Bose (who later left the Congress to form his own party, the Forward Bloc, and then collaborated with the Nazis and the Japanese during World War II), Jawaharlal Nehru, more radically minded than his father, especially before he assumed the responsibilities of political office, and Jayaprakash Narayan, a founder of the Congress Socialist Party and still one of the most influential Socialists in India. Over all of these divergent groupings and all of these individuals of such different viewpoints was Gandhi, a kind of super-leader who was at times not even officially a member of the Congress at all, whose views were *sui generis,* not easily categorized as either left or right wing. In some respects Gandhi was more conservative than most conservatives, and in others he was more radical than most radicals. Thus it was not surprising that, as Robert Crane has written, "From the time of the first civil disobedience campaign the internal history of the Congress was the reconciliation of a multitude of special interests and different points of view."[6]

[6] Robert I. Crane, "Leadership of the Congress Party," in Richard L. Park and Irene Tinker, eds., *Leadership and Political Institutions in India* (Princeton, N.J., 1959), p. 181.

After independence the Congress had to play a very different role. It ceased to be a national movement, a unifying omnibus organization which could embrace almost any Indian who wanted his country to be free, and became instead a political party, which was at the same time the government of independent India and a social and propaganda agency. This inevitably meant that it could no longer command the support of many of its former followers, and that its internal divisions and factions could no longer be sublimated in the interests of the national struggle. Even after August, 1947, however, it retained some of its former mystique and influence. It was still the party of Gandhi and of Nehru, the organization that had led India to freedom, and it still tried to be all things to all men. Gandhi suggested that since its main objective had been achieved the Congress should disband and should be reformed as a Lok Sevak Sangh, a kind of social service organization. He did not think that it should continue "as a propaganda vehicle and parliamentary machine." His advice, of course, was not followed, and his assassination so soon after independence removed from the scene the most unifying influence of all. Many former members of the Congress left, either individually or in groups; some were expelled, or were forced out by changes in Congress policy.

With Gandhi's death, Nehru emerged as clearly the leading figure on the Indian stage. Only Vallabhbhai Patel, much more conservatively inclined, could hold his own with Nehru, who dominated the party, the government, and Indian political life generally. As long as Patel was alive, Nehru had a top co-worker with great administrative ability and iron will. Although the two men disagreed on many points, they complemented each other too effectively to lead to a final parting of the ways. In any event, Gandhi's death made their cooperation for the governance of the new nation all the more necessary. The Nehru-Patel duumvirate was a most effective one. Since Patel's death in 1951 no one of equal stature has emerged, either to challenge or to buttress Nehru's role.

The most serious challenge to Nehru's control of the Congress came in 1950, when Purshottamdas Tandon, a representative of the conservative wing in the Congress, with more than a marked flavor of communalism, was elected President of the Congress, with the support of Patel, over Acharya Kripalani, who was backed by Nehru. Nehru made this a test of his position in the party, much as Gandhi had done when Subhas Chandra Bose was elected President of the Congress, against his wishes, in 1936. By resigning from the Congress Working Committee Nehru forced Tandon to resign the Congress presidency — as Bose had in effect been forced to do in 1937. Since 1951 Nehru's position in the party has remained supreme, although from time to time some of his associates have complained publicly of his policies, or his dictatorial methods, or his failure to groom a successor, or the stifling effect of his overall dominance of the party.

After the Tandon crisis Nehru himself assumed the post of President of the Congress, a position which he had previously held more than twenty years before (in succession to his father, Motilal Nehru). He held this position for some four years, although he repeatedly stated that in his judgment the offices of Congress President and Prime Minister sould not be held by the same man. When he finally yielded the party presidency, it was to a hand-picked successor, U. N. Dhebar, who was not at all prominent in the higher circles of the party or of the Government. In 1959 Dhebar was succeeded by Indira Gandhi, Nehru's daughter, hostess, and inseparable companion. Although her father stated that he was not happy with this arrangement, he obviously did little to prevent it. Mrs. Gandhi's successor in 1959 was N. Sanjiva Reddy, a relatively young and inexperienced Chief Minister of Andhra Pradesh, who was not a leader of national reputation. Thus whether he has held the position of Congress President or not, Nehru has been the unquestioned leader of the Party as well as of the nation.

The Congress Party is the only political group in the nation with a truly all-India organization. Its lowest organizational unit is the local committee in a village or town or city ward. The line of organization extends from the local committee to other committees in larger subdivisions of the States, to the Pradesh (State) Committees, and from the Pradesh Committees to the central party apparatus, headed by the All-India Congress Committee and the Working Committee. Theoretically the annual sessions of the Congress, usually held in January, are the supreme policy-making bodies, but in practice, while they are highly publicized and bring together the top leaders of the party and thousands of party representatives, they are something in the nature of party rallies.[7] The delegates and others who attend listen to interminable speeches by Nehru and other party leaders and to numerous reports from party committees, and they endorse, usually without much debate, large numbers of resolutions, formulated or at least approved by the Party's high command.

Another important central agency of the Party is the Congress Parliamentary Party, which has its own offices and organization. Since

[7] For details regarding the organization of the Congress see three mimeographed papers by Susanne Rudolph, issued by the Center for International Studies, Massachusetts Institute of Technology, in 1955. The titles of these papers are: *The Action Arm of the Indian National Congress: The Pradesh Congress Committee; The All-India Congress Committee and the Annual Congress Session; The Working Committee of the Indian Congress Party: Its Forms, Organization, and Personnel.*

the Congress is so dominant in the Parliament, many of the major decisions are taken not so much on the floor of the Lok Sabha as in the closed meetings of the members of the Congress Parliamentary Party; but the decisions invariably reflect the more basic decisions that have been made by Nehru, with the support of the Working Committee of the Party and/or the AICC. Furthermore, Nehru and many other top leaders of the Party are also members of the Congress Parliamentary Party. The whole question of the relationship between the Congress Parliamentary Party and the regular agencies of the party machinery deserves more detailed investigation.[8] It is in a sense a phase of the larger question of the relationship between the Government of India and the Congress Party, a relationship which is bound to change with the passing of Nehru and with the growing importance of the Indian Parliament. At the present time it would certainly seem that the Party is more influential than the Government, and that most of the basic decisions are made in the higher agencies of the Party. To the extent that the decisions are made by Nehru himself, it is difficult to determine whether he is acting as Prime Minister or as party leader or as Lord High Everything. He wears many hats and sits in many seats, but whatever hat he wears or whatever seat he occupies, he is India's supreme decision-maker.[9]

The AICC is a fairly sizable body, elected by the Pradesh Congress Committees, and consisting of one-eighth of the members of each of these Committees. It meets irregularly, usually more than once a year. The Working Committee, a smaller body which meets more frequently, is the most important agency in the Congress structure. Most of the top leaders of the party are members of the Working Committee. It is composed of the President of the Congress and twenty members chosen by the President from the members of the AICC. Very often it includes members of the Congress Parliamentary Party, and members of the Cabinet. Nehru, who of course is always a member, relies heavily upon this Committee for advice and support. The basic policies of the Congress, and therefore of the country, are usually formulated or approved in the Working Committee before they are placed before the agencies of the Party which technically have a larger policy-making authority, the AICC and the annual session. Thus the Working Com-

[8] See W. H. Morris-Jones, *Parliament in India* (Philadelphia, 1957), pp. 185–199; and Norman D. Palmer and Irene Tinker, "Decision Making in the Indian Parliament," in Park and Tinker, eds., *Leadership and Political Institutions in India,* pp. 129–134.

[9] "The major decisions in India have not been made at the parliamentary level nor by the party in power but by a small group within that party. In the case of the Congress this is the Working Committee, which is dominated, . . . not by the Congress president but by the prime minister." Frank Moraes, *India Today* (New York, 1960), p. 163.

mittee is not only the executive of the Congress but is a kind of shadow cabinet, with more real power and influence than the regular Cabinet.

For a political organization which has dominated the political life of the country, the Congress has a rather small membership — only about 6,000,000 "primary" members and fewer than 100,000 "active" members. An active member, according to the Party Constitution, must "wear khadi, be a teetotaller, oppose untouchability, favor equality of opportunity, believe in intercommunal unity, perform 'constructive' activity, pay Rs. 1 annually and collect another Rs. 10 for Congress." Any one who accepts the objectives of the Congress and who pays a few *naye paise* annually as a membership fee may become a "primary" member.

Considering the heterogeneous character of the Congress from its inception, it is hardly surprising that its stated objectives are rather nebulous and comprehensive. Undoubtedly the Congress as a party has tried, consciously or unconsciously, to preserve a good deal of the national character and catholicity of views which it possessed when it was a national movement for independence. Economically, its ideology is rather clear, but this reflects the prevailing orientation in Indian thinking and practice generally toward a high degree of State initiative and control. Even here, however, the Congress reflects its mixed heritage and the varied strands of thought which are subsumed under the Indian varieties of socialism. The economic ideology of the Congress has been evolved from three or four main currents of modern Indian thought. These include the Gandhian ideal of the *sarvodaya* society, with emphasis on service, social welfare, decentralization, cottage industries, and village self-sufficiency; the continuance of a system of free enterprise, even in a "socialist" state, which is reflected in the fact that well over 90 per cent of the productivity of the country is contributed by the "private sector"; socialist ideas of state ownership and control of the instruments of production; and a variety of other socialist views, Marxist or non-Marxist in character. The main trend, however, with certain lip service to Gandhian ideals, has been toward the welfare state, with a strong socialist flavor. Long before the Avadi resolution of 1955 the Congress was in favor of "the socialist pattern of society," although there was never complete agreement on the precise outlines and prerequisites for the "socialist pattern." Under Nehru's leadership the Congress has followed a markedly left-of-centre course, with considerable concessions to the "private sector," on the one hand, and with occasional experiments which are more reminiscent of an authoritarian than of a democratic state, on the other.

This socialist bent of the Congress has tended to undermine the parties which call themselves socialist, including the Praja Socialist Party, and the Communists, who find that they alienate possible supporters by too extreme policies and by too obvious kow-towing to the international party line and who hope to increase their power through the ballot box and through the espousal of a form of "socialism" of their own. There is much truth in Nehru's claim, made in 1958, that "The broad approach of the average Congressman was all along socialistic. Some of our Provincial Congress Committees passed resolutions precisely in terms of socialism even twenty-seven years ago." Hence, to the consternation of both the Socialist and Communist parties, the Congress is as closely identified with "socialism" as they are. "*The* socialist party of India is not the Communist Party or the Socialist Party but the Congress Party; it cornered socialism decades ago. The great socialist efforts in India since independence — the Five-Year Plans and the development programs — were conceived and carried out, or are being carried out, by the Congress."[10]

If the most obvious fact about the Indian political scene today is the continued dominance of the Congress Party, the next most important, if not next most obvious, fact is that all is not well with the Congress, that it is losing the support of the intellectuals and is losing touch with the masses of the people.

> Even with a comfortable majority in Parliament and in most of the State Assemblies, the Congress holds the reins of power in nervous hands to-day. A sense of what Mr. Nehru has called "inner failure" seems to have overtaken it. On the one hand ugly manifestations of ambition and power-lust, love of ostentation in public life, hankering after office, personal rivalries — all these point to the lack of integrity and idealism in most Congressmen to-day, and thus lower it in the estimate of the people. Factions inside the organisation, rivalries among various caste and communal groups, sectional pressures have all been contributing to its internal weakness and consequent decay. . . . Everywhere a process of disintegration has set in, resulting from the scramble for the loaves and fishes of office. On the other hand, pre-occupation with these petty jealousies and rivalries makes it impossible for the party to give attention to the more urgent task before it — which is to provide the people with an emotional and intellectual leadership. Consequently it has no grip over the situation to-day. New forces have arisen in the country, social and intellectual — there are new problems and new tasks; but Congressmen with their mentality and outlook of the pre-independence days are failing to live up to them.[11]

[10] George Bailey, "Pandit Nehru's One-Party Democracy," *The Reporter*, Nov. 13, 1958, p. 31.

[11] "The Ballot Box: A Pointer," *The Radical Humanist*, XXI (May 19, 1957), 247.

Criticism of this sort has been heard very often in recent years, and some of the severest criticisms have been made by Congressmen themselves. No one has been more outspoken than Nehru. In 1957 he told the Congress M.P.'s: "The Congress Party is weak and getting weaker. . . . Our strong point is the past. Unless we get out of our present rut, the Congress Party is doomed." A few months later, at a meeting of the AICC, he put his finger on one of the most serious weaknesses of the party when he declared that "if the Congress was losing respect and regard in the eyes of the people and getting a bad name, it was because of the inefficient functioning of the Congress Committees at the city, district and provincial levels." On another occasion he said: "We started mass movements 34 years ago. . . . Another type of movement comes and we are left behind. . . . we become out of date. The speed of youth, mind and body goes from us organisationally and we go on struggling, trying to catch up with something which is ahead of us." "The Congress," said its leading spokesman, now comprises people who "repeat phrases and ideas, and have lost the capacity to think afresh." Hence they were haunted by a sense of "inner failure."

The Congress has been in power so long that it almost inevitably has become sluggish. Moreover, it is blamed for everything that goes wrong or that is disliked, for whatever reason. It has been put on the defensive on a number of issues of domestic and foreign policy — the failure of the Second Five Year Plan to achieve its original objectives, the disappointing results of the Community Development Program, the slow rates of growth and industrial progress as compared with Communist China, the handling of the linguistic states issue, the rather hesitant policy of the Government of India in response to the Chinese moves in Tibet and along India's Himalayan frontiers. Some of this criticism is hardly justified, and partakes of the usual kind of criticism of the "ins" by the "outs"; but there can be no doubt that the Congress is itself responsible for much of its loss of support and prestige. This loss is not so obvious at the Centre, but it is very obvious in some of the States and on local levels. In the general elections of 1957 its showing on the national level was even better than in 1951–52, but it lost a total of more than 200 seats in State Assemblies, and it suffered greatly in Bombay State, usually one of its strongholds, where it ran afoul of the coalition tactics of the opposition parties and of the agitation for separate States of Maharashtra and Gujerat. In several municipal elections since 1957 the Congress has fared rather badly. There are growing evidences that it is losing support among members of the middle class and industrial workers, as well as among the masses of the people in the countryside. As long as Nehru is around, this loss of support will probably not prove to be too serious, but once his unifying influence and great prestige are no longer available the Congress may well be in for rough times. Nehru, now in his seventies, cannot carry for many more years the heavy burdens which he has borne for more than a generation. Hence the questions which irritate him so much are often asked nevertheless: After Nehru, who? After Nehru, what?

In the opinion of Frank Moraes, "a group rather than an individual will in all likelihood direct the government after Nehru's demission." Moraes predicts that one of two groups will come to power: a conservative group headed by Dr. Rajendra Prasad, Morarji Desai, and S. K. Patil, with Desai as the most likely successor to Nehru as Prime Minister but with the possibility that a "dark horse" like Lal Bahadur Shastri, Pandit Pant's successor as Home Minister, who is eight years younger than Desai, might be chosen; or a coalition of a left-wing Congress group and the Socialists, probably with Jayaprakash Narayan as Prime Minister, with the support of men like Asoka Mehta and Kripalani and the moral encouragement of Bhave. Moraes believes that the latter is the more likely possibility, and that it would probably lead to a split of the Congress into two parties, "thereby," he thinks, "fostering the growth of a stable party system in the country."[12]

While no obvious successor to Nehru is in sight, there is no dearth of able leaders who might fill the office of Prime Minister with distinction, once they are out from under the encompassing mantle of Nehru's great prestige. "There are a good many able young men in the top echelons of the party . . . who are, as it were, being groomed en masse for leadership. These men are unknown to the general public either within or outside India — obscured by and all but inaudible behind the strongest 'cult of personality' in the world today. But they are there."[13]

The more important question is "After Nehru, what?" Can the Congress Party hold together and retain its nationwide strength when its great leader goes? If the Party loses its hold on the Indian scene, what will take its place — a democratically oriented political organization, or a nondemocratic organization of either a communalist or Communist orientation? Will the new nation be able to hold together and continue its major efforts in economic development and social uplift if Congress loses its hold and no strong successor replaces it?

It is much too soon to write off the Congress as a losing cause. In the past the party has weathered many crises, and it may be able to regain something of its former vigor and resiliency. As *The Eastern Economist* pointed out in July, 1960, "it would be foolish to ignore

[12] Moraes, *India Today,* pp. 222–231.
[13] George Bailey, "Pandit Nehru's One-Party Democracy," p. 32.

the fact that Congress leadership, weak and disorderly as it often appears, has a remarkable capacity of rising to the occasion in times of stress."[14]

The future of democracy in India does not necessarily depend upon the continuance in power of the Congress Party — indeed some would argue that the prospects for democracy will be slight as long as a single party is all-powerful. But in view of the gravity of the problems facing the country and the lack of any effective democratic opposition, there are grounds for apprehension as well as for hope in the passing of the organization which has been the main channel of political activity in India for more than three-quarters of a century. "One of the ironies of the Indian political scene is that an effective democratic opposition seems to be out of the question as long as the Congress exists in its present form, while at the same time the disintegration of the Congress might have adverse effects on the entire prospects for democracy in India."[15]

Socialist Parties

Between the Congress Party, which has proclaimed its dedication to "the socialist pattern of society", and the Communist Party, which espouses its own brand of socialism, the Praja Socialist Party, the major Socialist party outside of the Congress, is trying to find a more influential place in the Indian political arena. In these efforts it is experiencing serious difficulties. "Inconsistencies and indecisiveness are still apparent among the leaders over certain matters of ideology, parliamentary strategy, and program. They are unable to agree on whether or not the party needs an ideology, what constitutes an ideology, and whether it should be Marxian, Gandhian, some synthesis of both, or a pragmatic search for a new doctrine of democratic socialism relevant to India. . . . The party's crises have been those of the national leadership: the party's inability to communicate effectively with the secondary echelons and the membership concerning the changes desired in ideology, organization, and strategy; its failure to assess correctly and adhere consistently to a given role in Indian politics; and its failure to maintain its own cohesion in the face of public adversity and party rebellion."[16]

Three stages in the history of organized Socialist parties in India may

[14] *The Eastern Economist,* July 15, 1960.

[15] Norman D. Palmer, "Political Parties in India," in George McT. Kahin, ed., *Major Governments of Asia* (Ithaca, N.Y., 1958), pp. 313–314.

[16] Thomas A. Rusch, "Dynamics of Socialist Leadership in India," in Park and Tinker, eds., *Leadership and Political Institutions in India,* pp. 204, 208.

be distinguished: (1) from 1934 to 1948, when the Congress Socialist Party functioned within the Congress organization; (2) from 1948 to 1952, when the independent Socialist Party, composed largely of former members of the Congress Socialist Party, tried unsuccessfully to develop the basis of an effective democratic opposition to the Congress; and (3) since 1952, a period of further coalescence and further splits, with the PSP as the most important Socialist party.

Ideologically speaking, the leaders of Indian socialism were from the beginning, as Thomas A. Rusch has observed, "divided by three amorphous and overlapping tendencies: Marxism, social democracy of the British Labor Party type, and a democratic socialism tempered by Gandhian concepts and the use of nonviolent civil disobedience techniques for nationalist and class struggle." In 1934 a small group of young Congress members, mostly from North India, organized the Congress Socialist Party within the Congress. "Though a majority . . . were non-Marxists, the most influential were the Marxists."[17] Neither Gandhi nor Nehru was identified with this group, but both of them showed a great deal of sympathy with its aims and objectives. Gandhi, in particular, tried to act as a moderator between the members of the Congress Socialist Party and the more conservatively-inclined Congressmen, led by Vallabhbhai Patel. The Socialist leaders refused to participate in Congress ministries which functioned in most of the Provinces of British India in 1937–39, and in the Constituent Assembly which was elected in 1946. In 1947 the word "Congress" was dropped from the name of the party-within-a-party, and the decision was made to recruit non-Congressmen as members.

In 1948, after Gandhi's assassination, the Patel group in the Congress was instrumental in securing a resolution of the AICC which outlawed political parties within the Congress ranks. This action forced the Socialists to choose between giving up their organized status within the Congress or to leave the parent organization. The latter course was decided upon at the Nasik congress in March, 1948, and for the first time a significant independent Socialist party came into being. Some of the former supporters stayed within the Congress, while others went over to the Communists.

The Socialist Party proclaimed the ideological goal of a "democratic socialist" society. "The organizational goal was to fashion a democratically structured, mass membership party controlled and financed by its members." A stern test of the success of its popular appeal came in the first general elections, and the results were disappointing. "In place of the expected second-rank status in India's legislative bodies, the socialists achieved only third place in terms of seats won, though

[17] *Ibid.*, p. 189.

they were second in terms of popular votes. They were forced to accept the defeat of all their national leaders and the election of only one fourth of the seats anticipated."[18]

One of the results of the post-mortems that followed the elections of 1951–52 was the merger of the Socialist Party with the Kisan Mazdoor Praja Party, which had been formed by dissatisfied Congressmen led by Acharya Kripalani just before the elections and which had fared even more badly than the Socialists in the voting. "The KMPP was interested in practical parliamentary activity and Gandhian village constructive work, thereby complementing the Socialist Party leadership's interest in urban trade union, intellectual and agitational activities."[19] The new party was called thc Praja Socialist Party. In the spring of 1943 its best-known member, Jayaprakash Narayan, held a series of talks and exchanged some correspondence with Nehru, at the Prime Minister's request, with the object of exploring possible bases of cooperation between the Congress and the PSP. These exchanges did not lead to any specific agreement, but they aroused widespread interest and speculation.

The PSP experienced the same difficulties and differences as had all previous Socialist parties. It suffered two blows in 1954, when Acharya Narendra Deva, a highly respected elder statesman who as chairman helped to hold the party together, died and when its best-known leader, Jayaprakash Narayan, announced his retirement from active politics. The top leaders differed publicly over the proper relationship between the Party's high command and the Socialist ministry which in 1954–55 held power precariously as a minority government in the State of Travancore-Cochin (now Kerala).

Not surprisingly, the PSP showed less strength in the second general elections in 1957 than had the Socialist Party and the KMPP in the first general elections five years before; but it did not fare as badly as was generally predicted, and since 1957 it has scored some limited electoral successes in by-elections and local elections.

Of the outstanding leaders of the Congress Socialist Party at the time of its founding in 1934, three — Jayaprakash Narayan, Asoka Mehta, and Rammanohar Lohia — are still prominently identified with Socialist parties today; but they differ on many questions of theory and practice, and each has taken an individualistic path that has not made for Socialist unity. In 1954, as has been noted, Jayaprakash announced that he was retiring from politics, and would devote the rest of his life to the Bhoodan Yagna movement. He has been remarkably active in politics and remarkably outspoken on political questions

[18] *Ibid.*, pp. 200, 202.
[19] *Ibid.*, p. 203.

for one who has presumably turned his back on politics, but it remains to be seen whether from his semi-detached position he will move away from or toward a more active role in political life. He is still regarded as a possible successor to Nehru. He is the one Socialist leader who seems to command a mass following. "Publicly, he is still the symbol of the party and speaks for it, whether in an official capacity or not." The slender, bearded Asoka Mehta, one of the leading Socialist theoreticians, is a man of great integrity and dedication who is very influential in the inner circles of the Socialist movement and who is an unusually able parliamentarian, but he does not have a mass appeal and his views are so close to those of the Congress left wing that many observers have predicted that he might lead the right-wing members of the PSP back into the Congress Party. Rammanohar Lohia deviated so emphatically from the position of the majority of the leaders of the PSP that in 1955 he was expelled, and proceeded to form his own Socialist Party. In 1960 Acharya Kripalani, another important former leader and its first chairman, resigned from the PSP and presumably now is following a more independent course in Indian political and social life.

The older leadership of the independent Socialist movement in India has long since been weakened by deaths, defections, and ideological and personal differences. "Party leadership," as Thomas Rauch has pointed out, "is shifting its focus of action away from the non-parliamentary, agitational, and intellectual leaders of previous phases in favor of a growing group of practical, parliamentary men who are beginning to wield more influence."[20] The PSP is not even holding its own in national and State elections, except in a few States; but it has not disintegrated, and in time, with better organization, better financing, more coherent programs, and a greater identifiability, the new and emerging leaders may be in a position to take advantage of any weakening of the Congress after Nehru goes. They must build for the future, for in the past no independent Socialist political organization has been able to make much of an impact by itself.

The Swatantra Party

In 1959 the first democratically oriented conservative party of any importance in India came into being. The decision to organize it was taken at a meeting in Madras in early June, and the new party, named the Swatantra (Freedom) Party, was formally inaugurated at a convention in Bombay in August. The formation of the new party, it was reported, was hastened because of the opposition to the resolution in favor of farming cooperatives adopted by the Congress Party

[20] Rusch, "Dynamics of Socialist Leadership in India," p. 208.

at its annual meeting in Nagpur in the previous January. A report of the conclusions arrived at in the course of the June meeting in Madras contained the following statement of the new party's aims and beliefs:

> We are of the opinion that social justice and welfare can be reached more certainly and properly in other ways than through techniques of so-called Socialism. . . . Social justice and welfare should not be brought about by violence or State compulsion . . . but must be brought into being by the spread of the doctrine of trusteeship as suggested by Gandhiji. . . . The educational activities of government, direct and indirect, should be such as to emphasize the moral obligations of those who possess wealth to hold it in trust for society, and a doctrine of life based on that moral obligation as distinguished from seeking to establish a socialistic structure based on legislative sanctions involving expropriation and loss of incentive for the individual to work and increasing dependence on the State and its officials in every walk of life.[21]

The Swatantra Party is conservative in its economic and social views, very anti-Communist, and is opposed to many of the policies and to the socialist orientation of the Congress. It emphasizes the freedom of the individual, the importance of private enterprise, the ancient concept of *dharma,* and the principle of trusteeship, in the Gandhian sense. In foreign affairs it favors cooperation with Pakistan in the defense of the subcontinent.

One of the main promoters of the Swatantra Party was M. R. Masani, once a prominent founder-member of the Congress Socialist Party who has been critical of Congress and Socialist policies for many years. Masani has an important public relations position with the Tata industrial enterprises, the best known of all private concerns in India. A smooth, polished, Western-educated man of the world, he was elected to the Lok Sabha in the general elections of 1957 as a candidate of the leading tribal party, the Jharkand Party! The President of the Swatantra Party is Professor N. G. Ranga, a peasant leader from Madras, who was once General Secretary of the Indian National Congress. Another prominent member of the new party is K. M. Munshi, a distinguished scholar-politician, at one time a leading figure in the Congress Party and a former Governor of Uttar Pradesh.

But the stellar attraction in the Swatantra Party is Chakravarti Rajagopalachari — fortunately known as just C. R. or Rajaji — who was an intimate associate of Gandhi and the first — and last — Indian Governor-General of the Dominion of India. He is now a wizened old

[21] Quoted in Ellen Roy, "A Closer Look at the Swatantra Party," *The Radical Humanist,* Feb. 14, 1960, pp. 77–78.

man in his eighties, but there is still magic in his name. "C. R. is acutely aware of his messianic role. He speaks to people as a biblical leader come to *his* people."[22] "After Gandhi is dead," he has said, "we have socialism. Socialism is now preached boldly because there is no Gandhi to answer it. I say the same things as Gandhi said. . . . If Gandhi had been alive or Vallabhbhai Patel had been alive I would not have had to do all this work."[23] He charges that the Congress has "in effect accepted communistic principles." In particular he regards the experiment in cooperative farming announced in the Nagpur resolution of the Congress in 1959 as "the royal road to communism." The Swatantra Party, he proclaims, is "dedicated to saving India from the dangers of totalitarianism."[24]

The party to which Rajaji has given his blessing and which brought him out of retirement into active political life once more has attracted a great deal of attention, and it has gained the support of influential businessmen and others who have little taste for socialism or who welcome the appearance of a noncommunal conservative opposition and alternative to the Congress. It has also, paradoxically, been welcomed by many who are more liberally inclined, who are attracted by the appeals of the new party to the Gandhian tradition or to ancient Indian ideals, or who for any other reason are not satisfied with existing Indian political parties. Jayaprakash Narayan has welcomed the Swatantra Party as a "balancing factor between conservatism and radicalism," and he has appeared on the same platform with Swatantra leaders, although he says he has no intention of joining the new party. The party hopes to gain the moral support, at least, of Vinoba Bhave. Even Nehru has professed to be happy over the formation of the Swatantra Party, and he was most cordial to Rajaji when the venerable statesman came to Delhi in the spring of 1960 to promote the interests of the new movement; but Nehru has also denounced Swatantra as "a reactionary party, drawing into its fold various types of vested interests," and he has declared that if India "follows the policies of the Swatantra Party, India will be doomed."

The Swatantra Party has already attracted more support than most political observers predicted, and it will probably be around for some time. It may well become the nucleus for a conservative opposition to existing policies of the Government. If the Congress Party itself should ever split up into conservative and socialist wings, the Swatantra

[22] Suyash Chander Malik, "The Mixed Potion of Swatantra," *The Radical Humanist,* May 22, 1960, p. 251.

[23] Address at Kakinda, Feb. 28, 1960; quoted in *ibid.,* pp. 251–252.

[24] Quoted in Ashwini Kumari, "Indian Statesman, Friend of Gandhi, Forms Party to Challenge Congress," *The Washington Post,* Aug. 29, 1960.

Party might win the support of many conservative Congressmen, or it might merge with this group to form a really effective conservative party. It may serve as a catalytic agent, presaging a realignment of Indian political groupings. In view of the growing radicalisation of Indian politics, however, it is doubtful that any political organization openly opposed to socialism in any form will gather much momentum.

Communal Parties

"Communalism" is a term that is frequently used in any description of Indian politics and society. It refers to the strong ethnocentrism which characterizes many Indian social, religious, caste, ethnic, racial, linguistic, and other groups, and to the frictions which often develop within and between these groups. To Nehru and other advocates of communal harmony and the secular state communalism is one of the greatest evils in Indian society today. The greatest of all communal problems over the years has been the Hindu-Muslim problem, and communalism is often used with reference to this main problem. A great variety of communal organizations exist in India. These "represent homogeneous political units only in the sense that each is concerned with the prerogatives of a single segment of Indian society — they are pressure groups seeking to secure for the cultural unit they represent a larger measure of prestige, power, wealth, and predominance of cultural patterns."[25]

The most important of the many Hindu communal organizations is the Rashtriya Swayamsevak Sangh (RSS). This RSS has great political influence, but it is not a political party. Rather it "is a tightly knit, disciplined, hierarchical organization seeking to incorporate larger and larger segments of the public within its ranks. Its primary aim is to establish within its own group a model of a revitalized Hindu society and eventually to secure the adoption of this cultural form in the whole country."[26] It is organized along semi-military and hierarchical lines. The basic units are the cells. Deliberative councils composed of elected and appointed members exist on State levels and at the Centre. The inner core consists of a group of Organizers who devote their lives to the service of the RSS. At the apex is the leader, known as the Sar Sanghchalak, a lifetime post which is passed along from one Sar Sanghchalak to another. Only two men have held this post, the founder of the RSS, Dr. Keshav Hedgewar, and his successor, Madhav Rao Golwalkar.

The RSS is a militant Hindu organization that is much more

[25] Richard D. Lambert, "Hindu Communal Groups in Indian Politics," in Park and Tinker, eds., *Leadership and Political Institutions in India,* p. 211.

[26] *Ibid.,* p. 215.

influential and much better disciplined than any Hindu communal political party. It has given various kinds of encouragement and support to Hindu parties, especially to the Hindu Mahasabha. Only three of these parties, the Hindu Mahasabha, the Ram Rajya Parishad, and the Bharatiya Jan Sangh, have had any political importance, and of these only the Jan Sangh has polled enough votes to be recognized as a national party. The Hindu Mahasabha and the RSS, under the leadership of Dr. Shyama Prasad Mookerjee and Golwalkar, respectively, prospered in the mid-1940's, when the Congress leaders were in jail and when the Muslim League, supported by various more militant Muslim organizations, was also gaining strength. After Gandhi's assassination in January, 1948, by a Maharashtrian Brahman who had had some affiliation with both Hindu communal organizations, the RSS was outlawed for several months, and the Mahasabha, still under Mookerjee's leadership, suspended political activity until the furor had died down. The Ram Rajya Parishad has some strength in Rajasthan and in a few other North Indian States. It is the most reactionary of the Hindu communal parties. Its goal is "an Indian India."

The Jan Sangh was formed in 1951 by Dr. Shyama Prasad Mookerjee, who left the Hindu Mahasabha after Gandhi's murder and who for a time held a post in the Cabinet of the Central Government. Dr. Mookerjee insisted that the Jan Sangh was not a communal party at all. It "drew its support from refugees, remnants of former princely power, others favoring a stronger policy toward Pakistan, and various groups with conservative economic interests,"[27] and it was also associated with the RSS. Dr. Mookerjee seemed to be working for a coalition of conservatively-oriented parties in the Indian Parliament, with the Jan Sangh as the central co-ordinating group. As long as he was alive, he exerted a powerful influence on Indian politics, far beyond the electoral strength of the Jan Sangh. He was one of the ablest parliamentarians and orators of modern India. After he died in Srinagar in June, 1953, the prospects of an anti-Congress rightist coalition faded, and the Jan Sangh became almost leaderless. Nevertheless, it is the most important of the Hindu communal parties.

None of these parties has fared well on the national scene. In the first general elections the Hindu Mahasabha won four seats in the House of the People, and the Jan Sangh and the Ram Rajya Parishad each won three. Only the Jan Sangh polled more than three per cent of the total popular vote, and thereby gained recognition as a national party. In the 1957 general elections the Hindu Mahasabha elected only two members to the Lok Sabha and the Ram Rajya Parishad was not able to return a single representative. Both parties also suffered losses in the elections to State Assemblies, winning only eight and twenty-two

[27] *Ibid.*, p. 222.

seats, respectively, mostly in Madhya Pradesh and Rajasthan. The Jan Sangh, however, for all its troubles of leadership and organization, increased its representation in the Lok Sabha from three to four seats and in State Assemblies from thirty-four to forty-six. Since 1957 it has been surprisingly successful in some municipal elections, especially in Uttar Pradesh, normally a Congress stronghold.

"The strength of the Hindu communal organizations, however, lies outside the elective assemblies. . . . Their importance comes from the catalytic function that they play in exacerbating tensions and divisive forces already present in the society."[28] As such they are major threats to the unity of India, for they operate largely beneath the surface and they have roots deep in traditional Indian society.

Many non-Hindu communal groups have some political influence in India, usually in opposition to Hindu communalism; but since they are largely concentrated in certain local, State, or at most regional areas of the country, they will be considered under the heading of local and regional parties.

The Communist Party of India

Before independence the Communist Party of India never made much headway in its efforts to infiltrate the nationalist movement or to appeal to the masses of the people. Since 1947 it has passed through a number of tactical phases, usually in delayed response to shifts in the international Communist line, and it has experienced its share of successes and failures.[29] By following essentially neo-Maoist tactics since the early 1950's, by emphasizing the policy of collaboration with socialist and even with "bourgeois" groups, and by professing a policy of constitutionalism and relying on the ballot box to gain political strength, the CPI has won numerous electoral victories. It has also suffered some serious electoral reverses, notably in Andhra in 1955. Many Indians are understandably concerned because the leading opposition to the Congress in the Lok Sabha is a nondemocratic party which is linked with a political conspiracy — a party which is trying to use the methods and freedoms of democracy to destroy both democracy and freedom.

Communists now sit in all or nearly all of the State Legislative

[28] *Ibid.*, p. 224.

[29] For the history of the Communist Party of India and its relations with the international Communist movement and with the Soviet Union, see the following excellent studies: M. R. Masani, *The Communist Party of India: A Short History* (London, 1954); John H. Kautsky, *Moscow and the Communist Party of India: A Study in Postwar Evolution of Communist Strategy* (Cambridge, Mass., and New York, 1956); Gene D. Overstreet and Marshall Windmiller, *Communism in India* (Berkeley, Calif., 1958); and David N. Druhe, *Soviet Russia and Indian Communism* (New York, 1959).

Assemblies, and they are particularly strong in West Bengal, Andhra, and Kerala. In Kerala a Communist Government was in power from April, 1957, to July, 1959 — the first significant experience which any non-Communist state has had with a Communist regime in office in one of its constituent units. While the party has appreciable strength at the Centre, its roots are in the States and local areas of the country, where it is playing down international and ideological issues and basing its appeal on local and regional interests and grievances.

Of all the Communist parties of the world the CPI is one of the most undisciplined and mixed up. The Indian Communists, in the opinion of the late Ellen Roy, wife of the most famous of all Indian Communists, M. N. Roy, "are no different from other Communists, except that they have to their credit probably more mistakes, more turnabouts and somersaults than Communists elsewhere."[30] The party has had a number of able leaders, but it has been weakened by personal and ideological differences, and no single leader has emerged.

> It has been customary to think of the leadership of the CPI as divided into three factions crudely labeled "rightist," "leftist" and "centrist." The rightist faction, led by former General Secretary P. C. Joshi, has favored close cooperation with other left-wing parties at all levels, primary emphasis on legal tactics and a moderate attitude toward the Nehru Government. The leftist faction, presumably led by B. T. Ranadive (also a former General Secretary), has attacked the leadership of other left-wing parties and tried to lure away their rank and file members. It has supported extra-legal tactics and has a noticeable penchant for violent forms of struggle. Its attitude toward the Nehru Government has been one of uncompromising opposition.
>
> In inner-Party debate each of these two factions charges the other with the usual deviations of Communist literature — the leftists accuse the rightists of "reformism" and the rightists accuse the leftists of "left sectarianism." The centrist group, led by the present General Secretary, Ajoy Ghosh, has functioned as a peace-maker between the other two and has attempted to keep CPI policy in line with world Communist strategy as expressed by the pronouncements of Soviet statesmen and theoreticians.
>
> It should be emphasized, however, that these factional groupings are by no means clear-cut, for Party members may take a leftist position on one issue and a rightist position on another.[31]

Generally speaking, the major shifts in the position of the CPI

[30] Ellen Roy, "Indian Party Politics," *The Radical Humanist,* July 24, 1955, p. 356.

[31] Marshall Windmiller, "Indian Communism and the New Soviet Line," *Pacific Affairs,* XXIX (December, 1956), 350.

have been from a leftist to a rightist to a leftist and then to a Maoist or neo-Maoist strategy. These shifts have been occasioned largely by directives from Moscow, conveyed in various ways: by direct orders, by CPI leaders who have visited Moscow, through the Comintern while that organization was in existence, for many years through the British Communist Party and through individual representatives of that Party, such as Harry Pollitt or R. Palme Dutt, and through other channels. In recent years the instructions have apparently come, often after long delays, directly from Moscow, although there is some evidence that some directives have come via Peking.

The major problems of strategy confronting the CPI have been to decide who is the principal enemy, what classes should be accepted as allies, what kinds of alliance should be formed with those classes, what should be the attitude toward the Congress Party and toward Nehru himself, what position should be taken toward Communist China — a question which has caused considerable soul-searching and bitter intra-party debates since the Chinese Communist suppression of the revolt in Tibet and the moves along India's Himalayan frontiers. The rightist strategy regards imperialism and feudalism as the main enemies, and favors a "united front from above," that is, alliance with labor and bourgeoisie groups and anti-imperialist parties. The leftist strategy regards capitalism and the bourgeoisie as the main enemies, and favors a "united front from below," by alliances with workers, peasants, and petty bourgeoisie. The Maoist or neo-Maoist strategy combines both "right" and "left" strategies by directing its attack against imperialism and feudalism but also by seeking to form a united front "from below."[32]

The CPI has generally conformed to the international party line, although often only after considerable delay and internal feuding. The Party followed the "left" strategy laid down at the Sixth World Congress of the Comintern in 1928. It avoided alignment with the Indian National Congress and had considerable success in infiltrating the All-India Trade Union Congress. In 1935, after some delay, it changed to a "right" strategy in accordance with the decisions of the Seventh World Congress of the Comintern, and it followed the Comintern directives "to work within the National Congress and the national revolutionary organizations affiliated with it, maintaining at the same time their complete independence and organizational independence." It had little success in influencing the top leadership of the Congress, but it did manage to place some of its representatives on the Executive Committee of the Congress Socialist Party.

[32] For a brilliant analysis of the strategies followed by the international Communist movement at different periods see Kautsky, *Moscow and the Communist Party of India,* Chapters 1 and 7.

After the outbreak of World War II the CPI reverted to a "left" strategy, denouncing the British as warmongers and branding the war as "the great imperialist war"; but when the Nazis attacked the Soviet Union in June, 1941, the CPI followed the example of Communist parties everywhere and executed a speedy flip-flop in its policy. Resuming a "right" strategy, it now supported the war effort. This action revealed how fundamentally the Party diverged from the mainstream of Indian nationalism. While it regained its legal status — which it had lost in 1929 — it became increasingly alienated from the Congress and the Indian people at large. After the war it was expelled from the Congress. It has never fully recovered from the stigma of its wartime gyrations of policy, and from its belated support of the British war effort, at a time when the Congress was refusing to cooperate with the British on any terms short of immediate independence.

Until 1947 the CPI followed what has been described as "a bewildered 'right' course," but by 1946 it was obvious that the dominant group in the Party, led by the General Secretary, P. C. Joshi, was under considerable pressure from a group within the party led by B. T. Ranadive to change to a more militant course. A series of events and statements in 1947 and 1948 indicated a hardening of Soviet and international Communist policy, and this shift in the international party line led the CPI to change over to a "left" strategy. Ranadive became General Secretary, and the most militant period in the history of the CPI began. The Party denounced Nehru as "a representative of the bourgeoisie, which is now collaborating with imperialism," organized guerrilla units in various parts of the country, and launched a wave of terrorism and strikes. The scenes of greatest violence were in the Telengana district of the State of Hyderabad (now a part of Andhra Pradesh), where for some months peasant uprisings, which had started even before 1948, threatened to develop into incipient civil war under the encouragement of the Communists. It was at this time and in this place, incidentally, that a follower of Gandhi and in a sense the Mahatma's "spiritual heir," Vinoba Bhave, launched a crusade of sacrificial land-giving which soon developed into the Bhoodan Yagna movement. This movement helped to divert support from the Communists, although from time to time the Communists have tried to use it for their own ends.

Their experience in Telengana convinced the Communists of Andhra that the "Chinese elements of strategy," notably guerrilla warfare and reliance on the peasantry, were the most suitable for India. At about the same time, however, Ranadive was criticizing Mao Tse-tung, whom he called "a reformist and reactionary." This was in direct violation of the Moscow line. An editorial in the Cominform publication in January, 1950, asked all colonial and dependent countries to espouse the Chinese way. In June, 1950, Ranadive was replaced as General Secretary by C. Rajeshwar Rao of Andhra, an advocate of the "Chinese path."

Abandoning its policy of violence and unsparing criticism of Nehru and the Congress Party, the CPI entered the general elections of 1951–52 as an organized political group, and it received enough votes to gain recognition as a national party. Although it got less than half the votes polled by the Socialist and KMPP parties, by concentrating its efforts in areas where it had the greatest strength it emerged as the major opposition group to the Congress in the House of the People, and it scored some notable successes in elections to the Legislative Assemblies in Madras, Hyderabad, and Travancore-Cochin. It capitalized on and encouraged the agitation for a separate Telegu-speaking State of Andhra, and when this State was created in 1953 it gained a strong representation in the Legislative Assembly. For a time it hoped to be able to oust the Congress Ministry, but in elections in Andhra in March, 1955, it suffered an overwhelming reverse. This reverse was due in part to internal dissension within the Communist ranks in Andhra and in the top circles of the CPI, and to effective tactics of the Congress and other opposition parties; but it was also due in part to the "New Look" in the Soviet Union following the death of Stalin, which was reflected in increasing emphasis on Soviet-Indian friendship and in public endorsements of India's neutralist policy.

After the Andhra debacle the CPI attempted to reconcile the new Communist line toward Indian foreign policy with its own opposition to the Government's domestic policies. A resolution passed by the Central Committee in June, 1955, declared: "Although the foreign policy of the Government of India has undergone a welcome change in recent years, no such change has taken place in the internal policies. These policies, on the contrary, continue to be in the main reactionary and undemocratic." Ajoy Ghosh, who became General Secretary of the CPI in 1951, attended the historic Twentieth Congress of the CPSU in Moscow in the spring of 1956. His contacts with the leaders of international communism strengthened his support of the group in the CPI which favored an alliance between the Party and "that section of the national bourgeoisie which is still opposing imperialism." In spite of the opposition of the Ranadive group in the CPI, which advocated a tougher line generally, the Fourth Congress of the CPI, held in Palghat in April, 1956, adopted "the strategy of lending support to the Government's domestic and foreign policies while striving to build up a united front in co-operation with all other opposition groups." This strategy was effectively employed in the second general elections in February–March, 1957, in which the CPI, by electoral coalitions and other means, more than doubled its strength in the country, won spectacular successes in Kerala, West Bengal, and Bombay, and obtained representation in every Legislative Assembly.

In Kerala the Communists won more seats than the Congress, and, in April, 1957, with the support of five Independents, were able to form the first Communist government in any major non-Communist state. This Communist regime, a unique experiment which attracted world-wide attention, lasted until July 31, 1959, when, under conditions of increasing disorder, the Central Government stepped in and President's rule was proclaimed.[33] While it was therefore far from being a pronounced success, it could claim that its work was hampered by the obstructionist tactics of those opposed to it.

In April, 1958, at an Extraordinary Party Congress in the holy city of the Sikhs, Amritsar, the CPI adopted a new program and a new constitution, designed to put the party into power by parliamentary means. The preamble to the new party constitution clearly affirmed the means by which the CPI hoped to achieve its main goal: "The Communist Party of India strives to unite and lead all patriotic and democratic forces in the country in the struggle for defence and consolidation of national freedom." All references to the inevitability of revolution and the dictatorship of the proletariat were dropped, although the preamble stated that the CPI "works out its policies by applying the theory of Marxism-Leninism to the realities of the Indian situation," and "organises itself in accordance with the principles of democratic centralism."

In the revised party organization the main organs were the All-India Party Congress, "the supreme organ of the Party for the whole country," which "shall be convened by the National Council ordinarily once every two years"; the National Council of 101 members — the successor to the Central Committee — to be elected by the Party Congress; the Central Executive Committee — formerly the Political Bureau — which now consists of 25 members; the Central Control Commission, elected by the Party Congress; and the Secretariat, headed by the General Secretary. Similar organs exist on State, district, and local levels. The "primary unit of the Party" is the Party Branch, divided into Groups, with the General Body as "the highest organ of the primary unit." The constitution emphasized the necessity for "strict adherence to Party discipline," but it also provided for "inner-Party discussion" as "a regular feature of Party life."

[33] See Marshall Windmiller, "Constitutional Communism in India," *Pacific Affairs,* XXXI (March, 1958), 22–35; Benjamin N. Schoenfeld, "Kerala in Crisis," *Pacific Affairs,* XXXII (September, 1959), 236–248; Gene D. Overstreet, "The Communists and India," *Foreign Policy Bulletin,* Nov. 1, 1959, pp. 29–31; and Selig S. Harrison, *India: The Most Dangerous Decades* (Princeton, N.J., 1960), pp. 193–199.

Since 1958 the CPI has lost considerable prestige and support. In part this has been due to a renewal of internal dissensions, involving personal rivalries and differences regarding strategy and tactics, but the main reasons have apparently been the failure — or at least the frustration — of the Communist regime in Kerala and, even more important, the actions of the Chinese Communists in Tibet and along India's Himalayan frontiers — actions which have provoked great indignation and apprehension in India and which have confronted the CPI with some grave dilemmas. The top leadership of the CPI was openly divided on the proper approach to adopt with reference to the aggressive Chinese Communist moves. The militant wing apparently favored public support of these moves, even though this position would clearly be unpopular in India; another group seemed to favor complete endorsement of the position taken by the Government of India; whereas a third sought some compromise position, which would not involve strong criticism of the actions of the leading Asian Communist state and which would stress the importance of resolving all Sino-Indian differences by negotiation. The third group seemed to prevail at a meeting of the National Council of the CPI in Meerut in November, 1959. The Council was reported as having expressed "complete lack of faith in the slogan of Left Unity adopted at Amritsar," and as having advocated "closer links with the democratic forces working within the Congress under Mr. Nehru's leadership."[34]

Nehru's firm stand in his talks with the Premier of Communist China, Chou Enlai, on border issues and other developments in late 1959 and early 1960 created further differences within the leadership of the CPI. The extremists within the Party, still led by Ranadive, expressed concern over India's growing dependence on Western economic aid, while a more moderate group, led by E. M. S. Namboodiripad, former Chief Minister of Kerala and now Chairman of the CPI, and S. A. Dange, long a prominent figure of the Party and the leader of the Communist group in the Lok Sabha, supported the Government's approach to economic planning and argued that Western aid was balanced in part by the assistance from the Soviet Union and the Communist states of Eastern Europe.

Thus the CPI entered the 1960's in the same confused state that had characterized it from the beginning, with the handicaps of divided leadership, the absence of a single dominant leader, the stigma of the "failure" of the Communist government in Kerala, the dilemmas created by the Chinese moves in Tibet and along the Sino-Indian borders, and what seemed to be a growing recognition in the country as a whole that the Communist tactics of working within the democratic

[34] "CPI Disillusioned with Left Unity?", *The Radical Humanist,* Nov. 22, 1959.

system were "Trojan horse" tactics at best. It was still following a policy of apparent cooperation with the Congress at the Centre and strong opposition to the Congress at State and local levels, where questions of national and international moment were of less importance than more immediate issues. As Marshall Windmiller has pointed out, the CPI believes, perhaps quite rightly, "that real power exists primarily at the state level and that control of a mass following either in a particular region or in a trade union organization is more important than holding national office."[35] If the Congress organization on the local levels continues to deteriorate while that of the CPI becomes more solidly entrenched, the future prospects for communism in India may be much brighter than they appear at the present time.

Regional and Local Parties

Only the four parties which are officially recognized as national parties — the Congress, the Communist Party, the PSP, and the Jan Sangh — are truly all-India parties, and of these only the Congress has strength in all parts of the country. On State and local levels a very different picture emerges. In addition to the national parties a plethora of other so-called parties exists. Some of these are of great significance in the localized areas of strength; some, indeed, can give the Congress stiff competition in these areas. They usually are built around a few leading personalities and emphasize communal, caste, or sectional interests and loyalties. Special mention may be made of other communal parties, other left-wing socialist parties, tribal parties, certain electoral coalitions, and a major conservative party in Orissa.

The communal parties or organizations which have been discussed at some length — the RSS, the Jan Sangh, the Hindu Mahasabha, and the Ram Rajya Parishad — arc orthodox Hindu groupings, with a strong Brahman influence. There are many other communal groupings, some representing or largely supported by lower-caste Hindus or even by untouchables and others which are non-Hindu in character. The leading party of India's untouchables is the Scheduled Castes Federation. This party has been in existence for many years. Its leader, until his death in 1957, was Dr. B. R. Ambedkar, the most famous of India's untouchables. Its main strength has been among the Mahar untouchables of Maharashtra. It has had a small representation in both the Lok Sabha and the Rajya Sabha, but it has never been a truly national party. Its aim is to gain for India's untouchables a status equal to or at least approaching that of the caste Hindus, socially, economically, and politically. Obviously, however, it will be a long time before the nearly 60,000,000 untouchables of India will be able to emerge from the lowly position to which their ancestors

[35] Windmiller, "Indian Communism and the New Soviet Line," p. 361.

were confined for centuries by the rigidities of the Hindu caste system.

In the Tamil-speaking areas of South India — chiefly in the State of Madras — the Dravidian movement has won considerable popular support. This movement "is essentially a social protest of the Tamil masses against Brahmans and even elite non-Brahmans at the top of the caste hierarchy" and "a channel for protest against alleged north Indian economic imperialism. Indeed, as an alliance of aggrieved Tamil castes, the movement typifies the political potential of regional caste groups united behind a catch-all slogan against a 'foreign' scapegoat." It has taken political expression in the "Blackshirt" movement, "composed of two kindred groups, the Dravida Kazagham or Dravidian Federation, and the Dravida Munnetra Kazagham or Dravidian Progressive Federation." The Dravida Kazagham was founded in 1945 by E. V. Ramaswami Naicker, whom his followers know as Periyar or Great Sage. Naicker left the Indian National Congress in 1922, and for the next two decades and more he supported the efforts of the Justice Party in obtaining greater non-Brahman representation in governmental agencies and in schools. Now in his eighties, he has been forced to take a back seat in favor of a former lieutenant, C. N. Annadurai, who seceded from the Dravida Kazagham in 1949 and founded the Dravida Munnetra Kazagham. At times both Naicker and Annadurai flirted with the Communists, and even entered into electoral alliances with them, but in the 1957 general elections the DMK had considerable strength of its own, and the Communists, without DMK support, fared badly in Tamilnad. The anti-Brahman, even anti-Hindu, and anti-North and anti-Aryan position of the DMK, and its demand for a separate Dravidistan, appeal powerfully to the non-Brahman people of Tamilnad. "Dravidian propagandist A. S. Venu has explicitly claimed that it is the Dravidistan demand which gives his movement its unique position in Tamilnad, relegating other anti-Congress parties to insignificance."[36]

The most important of the non-Hindu communal parties is the Shiromani Akali Dal, the major Sikh political — and social — organization. Its best known leader is Master Tara Singh, one of the most colorful personalities in India today. Master Tara Singh often follows his own penchants, and members of the Akali Dal do not always walk in his meandering path. This major Sikh party is of course strongest in the Punjab, where most of the Sikhs of India live. It has a few members in the Indian Parliament. The Deputy Speaker of the Lok Sabha is a former President of the party. It represents the claims of the Sikhs for a separate Sikh state and it champions their claims for an honored role in the country as a whole.

After partition most of the Muslims who remained in the Union of

[36] Harrison, *India: The Most Dangerous Decades,* pp. 122, 124, 188.

India, including most of those who had supported the Muslim League for many years, left the League and entered into other political groupings. In Pakistan the League was the dominant party for some years, occupying a position comparable to the Congress Party in India; but in India it ceased to have any great political significance. There is still, however, an all-Indian Muslim League, and it still has some strength in the South, chiefly in parts of Madras and in the northern part of Kerala. It attracted some prominence in the elections in Kerala in the spring of 1960, for it entered an electoral coalition against the Communists, and was in fact the third most important group in the coalition, after the Congress and the PSP.

Many extreme left-wing socialist parties exist in India. Some of these are hardly distinguishable from Communist-front and fellow-traveler organizations, but others are able to preserve a distinction between their socialism and the Communist variety. Foremost among these groups is the Peasants' and Workers' Party, which has some strength in the West and South of India, mainly in Maharashtra.

Best known of the many tribal parties is the Jharkhand Party, which draws its main support from tribal groups in the State of Bihar. Its President is Jaipal Singh, himself a tribal from Bihar, who holds an M.A. with honors from Oxford. The first Indian to win an Oxford Blue, captain of a world champion Indian hockey team, formerly a Senior Headmaster at Achimota College in the Gold Coast (now Ghana), Vice-Principal of Rajkumar College in Raipur (a college for princes), a member of the cabinet of the Maharaja of Bikaner, one of the best-dressed men in India and one of its finest orators, and a member of the Lok Sabha, Jaipal Singh has devoted his talents and energies in recent years to the cause of the scheduled tribes of India. For some years he was President of the All-India Adivasis Mahasabha, and he has served in the same capacity with the Jharkhand Party, which he founded in 1945.

Along the borders of India and Burma, in the frontier areas of eastern Assam, live several thousand Naga tribesmen. The Naga areas are directly administered by the Central Government of India, and the Governor of Assam is designated as its representative in dealings with the Nagas. The Nagas do not have any well-organized political parties, but they do have some organizations which assert their claims either for complete independence or for a separate Naga state in the Indian Republic. In 1960 it was announced that the Indian Government had accepted in principle the demand for a separate Naga state as one of the constituent units of the Republic of India.

Innumerable electoral coalitions and arrangements were entered into by minor parties — and sometimes even by major parties as well — in each of the two nation-wide general elections, and in almost all of the other elections that have been held in India. Most of these are arrangements of convenience, and do not survive long after the voting occurs. The most common form is an election arrangement among parties to the left or right of the Congress for the purpose of defeating Congress candidates and electing agreed-upon candidates instead. Occasionally the Congress itself has entered into such agreements, as in the Andhra elections in 1955 and in the Kerala elections in 1960, in each case to defeat a strong challenge by the Communists through the use of the ballot box.

Two unusually important and durable coalitions came into existence in what was then Bombay State shortly before the general elections in 1957, for the express purpose of supporting the demands for separate linguistic states in Maharashtra and Gujerat and of defeating the Congress candidates by opposing them with a single slate. In Maharashtra the coalition was known as the Samyukta Maharashtra Samiti, and in Gujerat as the Mahagujerat Janata Parishad. Each coalition was a strange one indeed, uniting for the time being and for a clearly understood purpose political parties and groups as widely divergent as Hindu communal parties, the PSP, the Peasants' and Workers' Party, and the CPI. Each elected some members of the Lok Sabha and each scored striking successes in elections to the Bombay Legislative Assembly. Needless to say, the CPI benefited particularly from these electoral arrangements. Thanks to the coalition support, and to astute bargaining and pressures in selecting and placing its candidates, it elected several members to the Lok Sabha — one, the well-known veteran Communist, S. A. Dange, from a constituency in Bombay City by the largest plurality of any candidate for the Lok Sabha in all of India — and it increased its representation in the State Assembly from one to eighteen. Both of these coalitions refused to accept the decision of the Congress Party not to divide Bombay State, but instead to preserve and enlarge it, and by their successful tactics and unremitting agitation they were undoubtedly instrumental in forcing Nehru, the Congress high command, and the Indian Government to reverse their decision and to create, in May, 1960, the separate states of Maharashtra and Gujerat. Now that this major piece of political surgery has been accomplished, the *raison d'être* of the two highly successful electoral arrangements in former Bombay State seems to have disappeared. Possibly they will find other grounds for continuing the peculiar associations which have proved to be so effective in the past and which have presented the Congress with a major challenge in a part of the country which has been one of its chief strongholds.

In Orissa the Congress Party is faced with formidable opposition from the Ganatantra Parishad, a conservative coalition dominated by landlords and Maharajas. This coalition has won almost as many seats in the Legislative Assembly of Orissa as has the Congress. It is an outstanding example of a party which has great appeal in one Indian State and no significance at all in any other area.

What Future for Political Parties in India?

The general outlines of the party system in India are relatively clear, although they present some very contradictory tendencies. A healthy party system has not emerged, and there seems little likelihood that it will emerge in the forseeable future. The Congress Party has remained so dominant nationally that India is often described as a one-party state. It has nearly four-fifths of the membership in the Lok Sabha, and the largest opposition party, the CPI, can muster only about thirty members. On the state and local levels, however, a very different picture emerges. In many States the Congress is faced with really formidable opposition, and, more important, in villages and other local areas it is losing a great deal of "grass roots" support. Selig Harrison has called attention to the paradox of a party which seems to be as strongly entrenched at the Centre as it ever was and which, at the same time, seems to be losing ground in the States and districts and villages of India:

> The possibility of divergence on a multiplying scale between the national party in power and an assortment of ruling state parties now looms unmistakably on the Indian political horizon. Not only did more regional political groupings, and more potent ones, emerge in 1957, but their emergence occurred at the expense of national parties. Thus the great issue before Indian leaders is whether the present Constitution, drafted at a time when a national party system seemed to be in the making, will be adequate to a new time in which the interplay of national parties makes way for the new contest between the central power and regionally based political forces.[37]

Political scientists throughout the world are divided in their opinions of the importance of parties in a democracy, but the fact remains that parties do exist, and play vital roles, in all modern democratic states, and indeed in most states, whatever their ideological orientation. If India is to survive as a state moving generally in the democratic direction, it must evolve a healthier party system or develop some effective alternatives to parties, i. e., a system of "partyless politics" which Jayaprakash Narayan and others believe to be both possible and necessary.

[37] *Ibid.*, p. 246.

* 10 *

Elections and Electoral Procedures

Since most of the people of India not only had had no experience in the electoral process, but also were illiterate and in other respects seemingly unprepared to play a responsible role as free citizens in a democratic society, the decision of the Constituent Assembly and the Government of India to give every adult Indian, male or female, the privilege of the franchise, under a system of universal and direct suffrage, was, as has been noted, a truly momentous one. It was, as the Election Commission later characterized it, "an act of faith — faith in the common man of India and in his practical common sense."[1]

India's "Act of Faith"

Part XV (Articles 324–329) of the Indian Constitution dealt with the subject of elections. It provided for adult suffrage, giving the vote to every citizen of India who was not less than 21 years of age, except those who were mentally unsound or who had been found guilty of criminal or corrupt practices; it decreed that there should be "one general electoral roll for every territorial constituency for election to either House of Parliament or to the House or either House of the Legislature of a State"; it created an Election Commission charged with "the superintendence, direction and control of the preparation of the electoral rolls" and with the conduct of all elections to Parliament, to the State Legislatures, and to the offices of President and Vice-President of the Indian Union; and it empowered the central Parliament and the State Legislatures, within their respective spheres, to make provision "with respect to all matters relating

[1] Government of India, Election Commission, *Report on the First General Elections in India, 1951–52* (New Delhi, 1955), I, 10.

to . . . elections to either House of Parliament or to the House or either House of the Legislature of a State including preparation of electoral rolls, the delimitation of constituencies and all other matters necessary for securing the due constitution of such House or Houses."

Under the Government of India Act of 1935, which was in effect India's constitution until it was superseded by the Constitution of 1950, separate electorates or reserved seats were provided for no fewer than fifteen different categories of voters. The question of separate electorates had been a highly controversial one for many years, especially after the British granted the Muslim requests for a separate status in elections as early as 1909. Gandhi and the leaders of the Indian National Congress generally were opposed to separate electorates, in principle and in practice. The framers of the Indian Constitution would have none of them. Article 325 of the Constitution stated that "no person shall be eligible for inclusion . . . in any special electoral roll . . . on grounds only of religion, race, caste, sex or any of them." Articles 330 and 332, however, provided for reserved seats in the House of the People and in every State Assembly in Part A and Part B States for "Scheduled Castes," meaning untouchables, and "Scheduled Tribes." These seats were to be filled by representatives of these "backward" groups, but not by a system of separate electorates. Instead, all voters in the constituencies affected were to vote for these representatives. Hence, in such constituencies two members — or three, in at least one Lok Sabha constituency — are elected by all the eligible voters who exercise their franchise.

The only other special arrangement for particular groups in the Constitution related to the Anglo-Indian community. Article 331 empowered the President of the Union of India, if he decided that this community was not adequately represented in the House of the People, to nominate not more than two members to the House.

According to the Constitution, both the provisions for reserved seats for Scheduled Castes and Tribes and for the nomination of representatives of the Anglo-Indian community were to "cease to have effect" after ten years. They have, however, been renewed for another ten-year period.

Because of this "act of faith" India became the great testing ground of the adaptability and workability of universal adult suffrage in free and secret elections in underdeveloped countries, whose peoples are mostly illiterate, tradition-bound, unaccustomed to the idea as well as the practice of voting, and unfamiliar with the ways and tenets of democracy. In most of the newly independent countries universal suffrage has not been given a fair test, if it has been tried at all, and even in cases where reasonably free elections have been held, the results have seldom been encouraging.[2]

In India the principle of giving every adult Indian the ballot was accepted in the Constituent Assembly with remarkably little opposition. During the campaign preceding the first general elections in 1951–52 Prime Minister Nehru made a passing observation that perhaps indirect elections would have been more suited to India's needs and conditions, but attempts to read disillusionment with the system of direct elections in the Prime Minister's offhand remark were discouraged by Nehru himself, who claimed that his comment had been misinterpreted. Second thoughts on the wisdom of the decision in favor of direct, secret elections have doubtless been occasioned by the unhappy experience with such elections in neighboring Asian countries and, above all, by the considerable success of the Indian Communists in their efforts to use the ballot box for their own ends, which are clearly not in consonance with the basic goals of democratic India. There has, however, been relatively little open objection in India to the principle of direct elections, and the Indian experience with elections in the years following the adoption of the Constitution has on the whole been an encouraging one.

Two nationwide general elections — the world's largest democratic elections — have been held, and a third is scheduled for early 1962. While there were many examples of minor violations and a great deal of evidence of a lack of understanding of the purposes and procedures of voting, the two general elections that have been held were impressive demonstrations of the ability of a largely illiterate people to exercise the franchise wisely. The conduct and results of the several State elections that have been held since 1950 have not always been so satisfactory or encouraging, but these too have usually been carried out without major incidents or acts of violence.

Preparations for First General Elections

In April, 1950, the Constituent Assembly, still functioning as the Indian Parliament, passed the first electoral law, dealing with the registration and qualifications of the voters. Even before that date the Election Commission, headed by the able Sukumar Sen as Chief Election Commissioner, began to prepare for the first general elections. This was in itself a tremendous task, and there was considerable urgency about it, especially since the elections were originally scheduled for the spring of 1950. They were actually held in the winter of 1951–52. By that time over 173 million voters had been registered by more than 1,600 registrars, mainly on the basis of a house-to-house canvass

[2] See T. E. Smith, *Elections in Developing Countries* (New York, 1960).

throughout the country. There were special problems arising from linguistic complications, the difficulty of obtaining accurate names in a country where varying practices are followed in this respect and where many people are known by the same designation, the ambiguous status of hundreds of thousands of refugees from Pakistan, and the virtual impossibility of obtaining reliable information in "backward" areas. In the preliminary rolls some 4,000,000 women were registered simply as the "wife of —" or "daughter of —." When the registration officials, upon instructions from Sukumar Sen, tried to get the proper names of these women, 2,800,000 of them refused to give such information, and were accordingly struck off the rolls.

Another difficult task was the delimitation of the constituencies. This was accomplished only after lengthy deliberation and debate, chiefly because the Election Commission had to work with advisory committees, each consisting of seven members of Parliament. Eventually 3,772 constituencies were demarcated, 489 for the Lok Sabha and 3,283 for the State Assemblies. In the Part A and Part B States each M.P. would therefore represent some 720,000 persons. For administrative convenience each Lok Sabha constituency in a State contained the same number of State Legislative constituencies. In addition to the general seats, 477 seats were assigned to Scheduled Castes and 192 to Scheduled Tribes, on the basis of population, thus creating a number of double-member constituencies.

In order to make the procedures of voting as simple as possible and to instruct the voters in these procedures, a great deal of advance preparation was obviously necessary. Because of the shortage of election officials and some special problems of geography and climate, the voting was scheduled at different times in different places, extending over a period of some four months, from October 25, 1951, to February 21, 1952, although most of the voters went to the polls in January, 1952. Only government employees, including thousands of teachers, were used as election officials. Some 900,000 officials were required to supervise the actual voting.

To obviate some of the problems created by the illiteracy of perhaps 80 per cent of the voters, the use of symbols and the multiple ballot box scheme were employed. Each of the many parties was assigned a symbol, either by the national Election Commission or by a State Election Commission. Fourteen of the larger parties were recognized as national parties, and each was assigned a symbol for its exclusive use throughout the country. The symbols could not have special political or religious significance; thus no party was allowed to use a picture of Gandhi, or a cow, or the charka wheel (which appears on the Indian flag), or a hammer and sickle. Some of the parties, however, benefited greatly from the symbols assigned to them. The Congress Party, for example, obtained approval for a pair of bullocks as its symbol, and this suggested all kinds of favorable connotations. Many Indians could be persuaded that they should certainly not vote against bullocks, which symbolized the source of their livelihood, their main source of power and transportation, and perhaps even their religious faith as well. While the Communists could not use the hammer and sickle, they did obtain approval for a sickle and an ear of corn, a very appealing symbol to the Indian farmer.

Since at least 80 parties contested the elections (including individually oriented groups the figure was over 190), since each polling booth had to contain as many ballot boxes as there were candidates of different parties, some 2,600,000 ballot boxes were required, and 620,000,000 ballot papers were printed. It was estimated that the paper which was required for election purposes amounted to 170 tons. More than 200,000 polling booths and stations were set up in every part of the country. This large number was necessary because of the decisions that each polling station could effectively accommodate a relatively small number of voters — approximately 1,000 — and that there should be a polling station or booth within walking distance of virtually every eligible voter.[3] This latter decision posed major problems of logistics, especially in areas where distances were great and voters were few. Voters came to the polls on foot, by bullock carts, on bicycles, by public conveyance, and by almost every conceivable means of transportation. Parties and candidates were forbidden to provide any form of transportation to the voters, for obvious reasons.

The First General Elections, 1951–52

India's first general elections were held for 489 seats in the House of the People (for twelve of these seats Congress candidates ran unopposed) and for approximately 3,300 seats in State Legislative Assemblies.[4] Nearly 17,500 candidates ran — or perhaps one should

[3] At one polling booth in Orissa no voters at all showed up on election day. The officials at the booth reported that the only visitors had been an elephant and two panthers! "The Indian Experience with Democratic Elections: Results and Procedures (1951–1956)," *Indian Press Digests* Monograph Series, No. 3 (December, 1956), p. 5.

[4] For details regarding India's first general elections see *ibid;* Government of India, Election Commission, *Report on the First General Elections in India, 1951–52* (2 vols., New Delhi, 1955); S. V. Kogekar and Richard L. Park, eds., *Reports on the Indian General Elections, 1951–52* (Bombay, 1956); Edward R. O'Connor, *India and Democracy — A Study of the 1951–52 General Elections and Their Political Impact* (unpublished doctoral

say stood — for these seats. More than one-third of these ran as Independents; only 240 were women. The Congress contested every constituency, but it was the only party to do so. The Socialists entered candidates in some 1,500 constituencies, which proved to be unwise in view of their relatively limited resources and their lack of support in many of the constituencies which they contested. The Communist Party concentrated its efforts in some 500 constituencies where its strength was greatest, and as a result it was more successful in electing its candidates than were the Socialists, even though its popular vote was well below the total votes cast for Socialist Party candidates.

Quite understandably, campaigning in India was characterized by a variety of familiar techniques, such as speeches and meetings, ceaseless travel by the candidates, more or less effective party organization for campaign purposes, handshaking and house-to-house canvassing, extensive use of placards and posters, partisan appeals and profuse promises. Certain techniques of campaigning extensively employed in Western countries were either not available or were used quite sparingly. The radio, for example, was not a significant factor in the campaign, and of course India had no television. Parties were not allowed to use the facilities of All-India Radio, the only radio network in the country. The radio was used to instruct voters in voting procedures and to urge them to exercise their privilege and right of the franchise. The election manifestoes of the parties were read over the radio from time to time. Some of the parties and candidates were quite ingenious in developing novel election techniques, and in reaching voters in remote areas. Many of the placards and posters reflected real ingenuity; they usually appealed to local pride or prejudice. In cities, towns, and even in many villages loudspeakers mounted on jeeps blared forth the messages of particular parties and candidates in an almost unceasing babel of sound. Truckloads of shouting young people, most of whom were obviously well below the voting age, cruised through the streets and along the highways. Mobs followed candidates through the streets or massed outside of party headquarters. Even elephants and camels were used in electioneering work.

It is difficult to isolate the real issues in the election. In a sense there were no real national issues, except those arising from dif-

---

dissertation, Notre Dame University, 1954); Irene Tinker and Mil Walker, "The First General Elections in India and Indonesia," *Far Eastern Survey,* XXV, (July, 1956), 97–110; Richard L. Park, "Indian Election Results," *Far Eastern Survey,* XXI (May 7, 1952), 61–70; Taya Zinklin, "The Indian General Elections," *The World Today,* VIII (May, 1952), pp. 181–192, and Ela Sen, "The Indian General Election and After," *The Asiatic Review,* XLVIII (April, 1952), 115–125. Many of the comments on the first general elections are based on first-hand investigations and impressions of the author, who was in India in 1952–53.

ferences in party allegiance or support of different personalities. Broadly speaking, in the voting for members of the House of the People, the voters were either voting for or against the Congress. Naturally the magic of Nehru's name, and the memories of Gandhi, were great sources of strength for the Congress; whereas the Congress was vulnerable because over the years it had alienated many people for one reason or another, or because, as the party in power, it could be blamed by almost anyone who was frustrated or unhappy with his lot in life. Very often the issues in the campaign were described as those of food and freedom. In the elections for members of the State Assemblies local issues and grievances were predominant. These varied from State to State, and indeed from constituency to constituency.

On the whole, India's first nationwide elections went off well, and were an encouraging demonstration that masses of voters, mostly illiterate, could act with dignity and with a fair measure of judgment in selecting those who would represent them in the central Parliament and the State Assemblies. The actual process of voting was simplified as much as possible, but even then it was a new and strange experience for most of the voters — an experience at once frightening and exhilarating. Very often long lines queued in front of the polling places, usually divided into two lines, one for men, the other for women. This division was almost invariably the case in rural areas. In the cities, however, single lines were common, and in almost every instance people of many different religions and castes, including even the lowly untouchables, stood in the same line together. After having his name checked on the election roll and receiving a ballot, and after an official placed a drop of indelible ink on his hand, to ensure against anyone's voting more than once, the voter normally cast a ballot in a curtained area for a candidate for the State Assembly, and then received another ballot, which he thereupon cast for his choice for the House of the People. In double-member constituencies the voter cast two votes in each instance instead of one. This was a source of some confusion, and accounted for many of the 1,635,000 votes which were invalidated. Many other voters left their ballots on top of the ballot boxes, or on the floor in the booth, instead of dropping them into the ballot boxes, and hence their votes too were thrown out as invalid.

Most of the people took their electoral responsibilities seriously. The turnout of voters was impressive, except in a few parts of the country, as in most of Rajasthan. Of the 176,000,000 eligible voters, 88,600,000, or slightly more than 50 per cent, actually voted, and nearly 106,000,000 valid votes were cast.

It is of course impossible to determine what considerations motivated the Indian people in their exercise of their new democratic privilege of the franchise. Undoubtedly bloc voting, on a village, caste, association, or sectional basis, was fairly widespread. Apparently many villagers, in particular, voted as the headman or the village elders instructed them to do, and many women voted in accordance with their husbands' instructions. Doubtless many voted for the symbols rather than for the parties. This often led to invalid practices, such as the extreme example of a man who wanted to vote for the tree — the symbol of the Socialist Party — and who took his ballot out of the polling place and deposited it atop a tree. Some voters, especially women, appeared to regard the process of voting as a ritual or as a religious ceremony. Occasionally they worshipped the ballot box, and left some kind of offering beside it, or on top of it, or even in it. On the whole, however, the people, with some diffidence and hesitation, followed the proper procedures, and seemed to vote with discretion. The numerous cases of invalid voting, and the few cases of attempted use of fraudulent methods, such as impersonation or voting more than once, were exceptions to the generally efficient conduct of the election. For this considerable credit must go to the Election Commission for the careful preparations which it made for the elections, and to the army of nearly a million election officials and police who supervised the actual voting, but the main credit must go to the people themselves, who rose to the occasion in a truly impressive way.

The results of the elections for members of the House of the People were as follows:[5]

Party	*Seats Contested*	*Seats Won*	*Total Vote*	*% of Total Vote*
Congress Party	479	362	47,588,000	45.0
Socialist Party	255	12	11,129,000	10.5
KMPP	137	9	6,147,000	5.8
Bharatiya Jan Sangh	94	3	3,180,000	3.0
CPI and Allies	70	27	5,723,000	5.4
Ram Rajya Parishad	57	3	2,014,000	1.9
Scheduled Castes Federation	32	2	2,438,000	2.3
Hindu Mahasabha	30	4	954,000	0.9
Other Parties	194	30	11,023,000	10.4
Independents	453	37	15,792,000	14.9

Thus the Congress Party, while polling less than half the votes cast for members of the House of the People, won nearly 75 per cent of the seats, and continued to be dominant at the Centre. The next largest group consisted of the 27 Communists and their allies. While the So-

[5] These figures are based chiefly on "Election Results in India, 1951–1952," Appendix II, in W. Norman Brown, *The United States and India and Pakistan* (Cambridge, Mass., 1953), pp. 285–290. The statistics of the first general elections vary slightly in different reports. The most voluminous compilation is contained in Vol. II of the Election Commission's *Report on the First General Elections in India.*

cialist Party polled about twice as many votes as the Communists, it won only 12 seats. The reasons for this have already been suggested: the Socialists spread themselves too thin, whereas the Communists concentrated on fewer constituencies where they had appreciable strength. No other party got enough members to be of any real significance, although two others, the KMPP (which shortly after the elections merged with the Socialists to form the Praja Socialist Party) and the Jan Sangh, received more than 3 per cent of the total vote and therefore retained their status as recognized national parties. Large numbers of Independents contested the election, and while many of these were among the nearly 9,200 candidates for Parliament and the State Assemblies who forfeited their deposits because they did not receive one-sixth of the total votes cast in their constituencies, 37 Independents were elected to the House of the People.

For the State Assemblies the results were not markedly different, except in a few States. In total votes cast the Congress fared almost as well in the States as on the national level, gaining nearly 45 per cent of the total votes and about 2,250 of the approximately 3,300 seats. The Socialists and KMPP together won 205 seats. No other party had much success on an all-India level, although the CPI won 62 seats in the Madras Assembly, 34 seats in the Assembly of Travancore-Cochin, 28 in the West Bengal Assembly, and a few seats in other State Assemblies. The Congress won a clear majority of seats in all of the States except Orissa, where the Ganatantra Parishad scored some successes, in PEPSU (Patiala and East Punjab States Union), where Sikh political groups were strong, in Travancore-Cochin, where the Communists scored heavily, and in Madras, where Communists in the Andhra area and pro-Dravidian groups in Tamiland represented a formidable opposition. In Rajasthan the Congress had a bare majority, and in West Bengal the Congress majority was achieved largely by solid support in the rural areas, against the strong Communist opposition in the city of Calcutta.

Despite many gloomy predictions, the prospects for democracy in India seemed brighter after the general elections than they had before. The elections were a major event in India's experience as an independent state, and the fact that they were run off in good order, over a period of several weeks, and that so many of the eligible voters had actually participated augured well for the future.

Leaders of the Congress Party were alarmed, and rightly so, because, in spite of their overwhelming successes in electing candidates to both the House of the People and the State Assemblies, less than half of the voters had cast their ballots for Congress candidates, and there were disturbing signs of a trend away from the Congress in many parts of the country. Particularly disturbing, also, were the signs that the CPI had considerable support, and that on local levels many political groups or alliances which championed ideas inimical to the unity of the nation had attracted so many votes. An encouraging result was that the Hindu communalist parties had on the whole fared so badly. The large number of Independents who were successful in their campaigns indicated that many thousands of Indian voters were unwilling to throw their support to any party.

State Elections and States Reorganization, 1954–56

Between 1952 and 1955 by-elections were held in many parts of India for seats in both the House of the People and State Assemblies which had been vacated because of death or resignation or other reasons, and important elections were held in three of the States — in PEPSU and Travancore-Cochin in 1954, and in Andhra in 1955. All three State elections were necessitated by the failure of the Congress Party to maintain a working majority in the State Assembly. In PEPSU and Andhra the situation had become so unstable that President's rule, under the emergency provisions of the Constitution of India, had been imposed.

In PEPSU the State-wide elections held early in 1954 helped to clarify the atmosphere, for the Congress won a clear majority of seats in the State Assembly, and the new Congress Ministry proved to be both more efficient and more honest than the Congress Government that had ruled uneasily before President's rule was proclaimed.

In the elections in Travancore-Cochin in 1952 the Congress won only 45 of the 117 seats, and the Congress Ministry found itself unable to function effectively in the face of the opposition of the Communists and other left-wing groups in a State where economic conditions were among the worst in India. Unlike the outcome in PEPSU, the elections of 1954 in Travancore-Cochin did nothing to clear the political atmosphere. Even though top Congress leaders toured the State — Nehru himself spent six days there, and was well received — the Congress was unable to increase its membership in the State Assembly. The opposition leftist parties agreed to run only one candidate in each constituency against the Congress candidate, so that straight contests were fought in all of the constituencies. Of the 117 legislative seats the Congress won 45, the Communists 29, and the PSP 18. Since the Congress Party could not carry on by itself, and since the last thing it wanted was a Communist government in the State, it reluctantly threw its support to the PSP, which thereupon organized a government under its leader, P. T. Pillai, a former Congress Chief Minister, who had no love for his former party. The minority government of the PSP continued in office, if not in power, until the spring of 1956, when President's rule was imposed. This was the situation in Kerala — as the former State of Travancore-Cochin, with slightly different boundaries, was called after the States' reorganization went into effect in November, 1956 — at the time of the second general elections a year later, which brought into office the first Communist government in any Indian State.

When the new State of Andhra was created in October, 1953, a Congress government was installed, even though the Congress did not have a majority in the State Assembly. In November, 1954, the Communists, who held almost as many seats in the Assembly as did the Congress, was able to bring down the Congress Ministry, but it was not given a chance to form a government itself. Instead, the Central Government assumed direct control, under President's rule, until new elections could be held. There seemed to be every prospect that Andhra would become India's first Communist-ruled State. It had long been a center of Communist strength. This time, however, the Congress mobilized its biggest guns, and did not underestimate the gravity of the challenge. It had considerable success in working with minor parties and independent candidates to form a united front against the Communists.

The result was the most exciting and most hotly contested electoral contest in the history of independent India. The voting took place over a five-day period in late February, 1955, and the outcome was an overwhelming debacle for the Communists. The Congress and its allies gained a decisive majority of 196 seats in the new State Assembly, while the Communists were reduced to a feeble minority. Even the leader and deputy leader of the Communist Party in Andhra were defeated.[6] Since 1955 the Communists have never regained the political strength in Telegu-speaking areas which they had in the troubled years when the new State of Andhra was born.

Before the second general elections were held a major feat of political surgery was carried out in India by the reorganization of the Indian States, and the reduction of their number from 29 to 14. This reorganization became effective on November 1, 1956, only a few weeks before the second elections were scheduled to be held. After the Congress Ministry yielded on the issue of the creation of a new State of Andhra, thus giving the Telegu-speaking peoples a State of their own, the linguistic demands in other areas could hardly be denied.

[6] For a summary of the results of the Andhra elections of 1955, see A. M. Rosenthal, "India Reds Routed in Andhra Voting," dispatch from New Delhi, March 2, 1955, in the *New York Times,* March 3, 1955. For background information, see Selig S. Harrison, *India: The Most Dangerous Decades* (Princeton, N.J., 1960), pp. 237–245.

Once Nehru and his associates were convinced that this was the case, they tried to evolve some pattern of reorganization which would be generally acceptable to the linguistically oriented peoples of the South, in particular, without destroying the bases of Indian unity; and they were anxious to effect the unavoidable reorganization soon enough so that it would not interfere with the second general elections or with the prospects of the Congress Party in those elections. In this effort they were largely successful. Linguistic issues were not decisive factors in the general elections, with the notable exception of Bombay State and to a lesser degree of the Punjab — the only parts of India, be it noted, where linguistic demands had not been largely satisfied by the reorganization of the States.

The Second General Elections, 1957

Whereas the first general elections were extended over a period of nearly four months, with most of the voting in January, 1952, the second general elections were confined — except for a few remote areas where special problems existed — to a period of three weeks, from February 24 to March 14, 1957.[7] With the experience of the first nationwide elections, many by-elections, and three State elections behind it, the Election Commission was able to prepare for the second general elections with greater ease and dispatch than for the first all-Indian elections, even though the number of eligible voters had increased by nearly 20,000,000. The 2,600,000 ballot boxes which had been assembled for the first general elections were available for the second, so that only an additional 500,000 were required. Nearly one million government officials, including teachers and police, were needed to supervise the voting, but many of those who were recruited for the task had served in 1951–52 and thus were generally familiar this time with their duties. It was still a gigantic task, however, to

[7] For the background of the second general elections see S. L. Poplai, ed., *National Politics and 1957 Elections in India* (Delhi, 1957); note especially the excellent bibliography which is included as Appendix "C" (pp. 169–172). For the details of the second general elections see John R. Roach, "India's 1957 Elections," *Far Eastern Survey,* XXVI (May, 1957), 65–78; Bodh Raj Sharma, "Some Reflections on the Second General Elections in India," *The Indian Journal of Political Science,* XIX (January–March, 1958), 73–77; "India's Second General Elections," *The World Today,* XIII (June, 1957), 232–241; Phillips Talbot, "The Second General Elections: Voting in the States," a report, dated Bombay, April 28, 1957, issued by the American Universities Field Staff; "Analysis of Election Results," *India News,* April 15, 1957. The author was in India during the entire period of the second general elections. Some of the comments and impressions which are summarized here are based on notes which he made during and immediately after the elections.

hold "the world's largest election," and the Election Commission and all of the people who were involved had their hands full.

In 1957 the Indian people voted with more confidence and, presumably, with greater understanding and judgment than they had in 1951–52. Many of the fears and suspicions which had kept thousands of eligible voters from registering properly, or from casting valid ballots, were removed by 1957. Most of the women who had refused to give their own names now understood why this personal concession was necessary, and were at last convinced that this was not a betrayal of confidence to which their husbands alone should be privy. Voters who had previously placed ballots outside instead of inside the ballot boxes, or who had stuffed the boxes with flowers or grass as votary offerings, now generally understood what the boxes symbolized and where they were expected to deposit their ballots.

To be sure, there were still a fair number of cases of attempted impersonation and other irregularities, and more of misunderstanding. One voter, for example, started to weep when the drop of indelible ink was placed on his hand at the polling booth, for he thought he had been "vaccinated." A woman would not cast her vote when the polling officials could not show her "the burning lamp," which was the symbol of the Jan Sangh Party. As in 1951–52, many instances could be cited of quixotic voting behavior, and of strange methods of deciding for whom to vote.

Even more than in 1951–52 the second general election was an election without issues, as far as national politics was concerned. Except for the communalist parties and the Communists, most of the parties which had any pretensions to functioning on a nationwide basis were agreed on basic approaches to national and international issues, and the regional and local parties had little interest in such issues. Most of the voters and parties were concerned with local issues and grievances, and on this level a number of issues did exist. Some of these centered more on differences in personalities than on issues, but a number of rather influential local parties or alliances, such as the Ganatantra Parishad in Orissa, the Dravida Munnetra Kazagham in Madras, and, above all, the Samyukta Maharashtra Samiti and the Mahagujerat Parishad in Bombay, took positions which were opposed to the official policies of the Congress in certain fundamental respects. Writing shortly after the second elections an American political scientist who had observed the elections remarked:

> The campaign was rich in clichés and rigorous in avoiding issues. . . . In India this is, at least in part, the result of a general attitude which seems to prevail where government, administration and public

> policy are concerned. The attitude is one of uncritical, unexamined acceptance of the correctness of the decisions of those who govern. . . . [There is] a certain lack of reality in Indian politics in that the public concern with politics is rarely with anything fundamental.[8]

As in 1951–52, electoral alliances and arrangements were formed in a few States, often composed of heterogeneous elements whose only apparent bond of unity was the desire to defeat Congress candidates. The most elaborate of these alliances were those in West Bengal and in Bombay State. In West Bengal there were no fewer than three separate electoral arrangements: (1) the United Election Committee, composed of the five main leftist parties, the Communists, the PSP, the Revolutionary Socialists, the Forward Bloc, and the Marxist Forward Bloc; (2) the United Left Front, composed of eight other small leftist parties; and (3) the United Democratic People's Front, composed of a coalition within a coalition called the National Democratic Party (the Hindu Mahasabha, the Jan Sangh, and the Ram Rajya Parishad), plus a section of the Revolutionary Communist Party of India and some dissident Congressmen.

Shortly before the voting was held in Bombay State *The Times of India* predicted confidently: "National and economic issues rather than regional or linguistic appeals will sway the vote with the great mass of the electorate in the new composite State of Bombay in the coming general elections." No prediction could have been more wrong. As Phillips Talbot observed, "The voters of Bombay entered this election campaign in the wake of an unprecedented, protracted emotional jag over group loyalties based on regional cultures and languages."[9] On the linguistic issue virtually all the opposition parties in Maharashtra joined in a united front called the Samyukta Maharashtra Samiti; and in the Gujerat section of Bombay State some of the parties joined in a looser and less inclusive anti-Congress arrangement which was called the Mahagujerat Janata Parishad.

Within some of the parties considerable divergence of opinion developed over the wisdom and desirability of entering into electoral arrangements with other groups which were hardly ideological bedfellows. In the Punjab, where linguistic and religious issues were fairly significant, the major Sikh political organization, the Akali Dal, agreed to support Congress candidates. The best-known leader of the Akali Dal, Master Tara Singh, repudiated this agreement on the eve of the

[8] Roach, "India's 1957 Elections," p. 76.

[9] Talbot, "The Second General Elections: Voting in the States"; and Poplai, ed., *National Politics and 1957 Elections in India,* p. 19.

voting, but most of the members of his party refused to follow his advice. A heated debate raged within the top circles of the PSP regarding the question of entering into electoral arrangements with the Communists. Jayaprakash Narayan favored such arrangements, on the ground that this was the only way to build up an effective opposition to the Congress. Ashoka Mehta, however, was strongly opposed, on the ground that entering into alliances with the Communists was playing into the hands of a group which was basically opposed to the democratic system. The compromise which the PSP reached was strictly a pragmatic one. The Party took a stand in opposition to these arrangements with the Communists, but also authorized them in certain cases, if the local leaders deemed them to be necessary. As a result, in some States, notably in Bombay State, the PSP did join with the Communists and often with other parties in anti-Congress arrangements.

The second general elections did not change the political complexion of India, either on the national or on the State levels; but some of the results were unexpected and even startling. The Congress gained a few seats in the Lok Sabha, as the House of the People was then called, but lost 300 to 400 seats in the State Legislative Assemblies. Its heaviest losses in popular votes as well as in seats in the Assemblies were in Kerala and Uttar Pradesh. In Bombay, Bihar and West Bengal it also lost a number of Assembly seats, even though its percentage of the popular vote increased. So effective were the coalition tactics of the opposition, and so strong was the anti-Congress feeling on the linguistic issue, that six State ministers and three Central Ministers — the Labor Minister, the Minister for Legal Affairs, and the Deputy Minister for Rehabilitation — were defeated in Maharashtra and Gujerat. N. V. Gadgil, a veteran Congress leader and former Cabinet minister, was beaten in the city of Poona. The Congress markedly increased its percentage of the total vote in Assam, Madras, the Punjab, and Rajasthan, as well as in West Bengal and the Telegana district of Andhra. It still retained a clear majority in every Indian State, except in Kerala and Orissa.

The CPI retained about the same number of members in the Lok Sabha, but greatly increased its percentage of the total vote and won substantially more seats in the State Assemblies. It won striking successes in Kerala, West Bengal, and Bombay. In Uttar Pradesh it increased its strength from one in 1952 to nine, and it placed at least one member in every other State Assembly. In Kerala its popular vote was less than that of the Congress, but it won 60 seats as compared with 43 for the Congress, and with the help of five Independents whom it had supported it had a narrow majority in the Kerala Assembly.

Soon after the results of the election were known, the Communists were invited to form a Government in Kerala, with E. M. S. Namboodiripad as Chief Minister.

The PSP received a considerably lower percentage of the popular vote than had the Socialists and the KMPP in 1951–52, but it retained the same number of seats in the Lok Sabha. It lost a few seats in the elections for members of the State Assemblies, despite some unexpected gains in West Bengal. The Hindu Mahasabha lost two of its four seats in the Lok Sabha; its President, N. C. Chatterjee, and its General Secretary, V. G. Deshpande, were defeated. The Ram Rajya Parishad was unable to elect a single candidate to the national Parliament, and it placed very few in any of the State Assemblies. The number of Independents in the Lok Sabha was also less than before.

In their own localities, and only there, a number of local parties or groupings scored impressive victories. Notable among these were the Ganatantra Parishad in Orissa, the Dravida Munnetra Kazhagam in Madras, the Jharkhand Party in Bihar, and, as has been noted, the Samyukta Maharashtra Samiti and the Mahagujerat Parishad in the Maharashtra and Gujerat sections of Bombay State, respectively.

In December, 1957, the Election Commission released provisional figures of the results of the second general elections earlier in the same year. The total number of eligible voters was announced as 199,519,188, and the number of valid votes cast as 120,822,487. As in 1951–52, about half of the eligible voters cast their ballots. Two votes were cast by voters in the 91 double-member Lok Sabha constituencies and in the 584 double-member State Assembly constituencies. For the elections to the Lok Sabha the announced results were as follows:[10]

Party	*Seats Won*	*Total Vote*	*% of Total Vote*
Congress Party	369	57,579,948	47.66
PSP	21	12,508,754	10.35
CPI	27	10,753,995	8.90
Bharatiya Jan Sangh	4	7,193,267	5.96
Independents and Other Parties	73	32,786,523	27.11

Speculating on the results of the second general elections a writer in the *Radical Humanist* found two tendencies which stood out above all others:

> First, the prestige and strength of the Congress is steadily declining. It has lost its hold in urban-industrial areas, and more particularly over the middle class. . . . Secondly, there is no powerful democratic alternative to the Congress. The P.S.P. does not show the vigour

[10] "General Elections, 1957: Provisional Polling Figures," *India News*, Dec. 15, 1957.

and confidence of rising opposition. It cannot hope to compete with the C.P.I. in discipline and organization, in militancy and skilful utilising of the mass moods. . . . Meanwhile the "shift in the mass mood toward radicalisation" will continue, and the C.P.I. with its militant organisation, effective techniques of manipulating mass-psychology and an alluring radical programme appears on the horizon of the Indian political scene as the most potent threat to democracy and freedom. . . . The C.P.I. is therefore the only party which has emerged out of the elections with confidence in its own strength, and that its strength is steadily growing is evident from the facts. . . . If the elections have any lesson to offer, it is that the future of democracy in this country is dark, because appreciation of its values is lamentably lacking.[11]

Caste and Politics

Another rather alarming trend, strongly illustrated in the second general elections, was the mounting evidence that the tactics of the political parties and the general nature of election campaigns were accentuating, rather than minimizing, caste and communal differences and prejudices. A great deal of attention is given to caste and communal considerations by India's politicians, including, in spite of their professions to the contrary, the political tacticians of the Congress and of the CPI. The politics of Andhra, for example, can be explained to a considerable degree on caste lines. Generally speaking, the two largest non-Brahman caste groups in Andhra, the Kammas and the Reddis, while they were united in demanding a separate Andhra State, "emerged as rivals for the limited political and economic spoils that were available to them in the multilingual confusion of Madras caste groups."[12] The Kammas controlled the Communist Party in Andhra, while the Reddis dominated the Congress organization in that State. The rivalry of these two landowning castes or subcastes is a longstanding one. In the Gujerat and Maharashtra sections of Bombay State during the second general elections the two great anti-Congress electoral alliances paid a great deal of attention to caste considerations, and the Congress itself was not far behind in this respect.

It may seem anomalous that the Communists should also be caste-minded, but in India they certainly have been. Kerala provides convincing proof of this fact. "The success of the Kerala Communist Party as the first regional Communist Party in India to capture control of a state government," observes Selig Harrison, "can be explained,

[11] "The Ballot Box: A Pointer," *The Radical Humanist,* XXI (May 19, 1957), 248.

[12] Harrison, *India: The Most Dangerous Decades,* p. 111.

above all, by its ability to manipulate politically strategic caste lobbies within linguistic boundaries . . . as in Andhra, the Kerala Communists were able to transform economic despair into a legislative majority because their footing on regional caste ground, notably among the numerous Ezhavas, provided the necessary margin of bloc strength in the necessary number of constituencies."[13]

Reflecting on the role of caste in Indian politics, Harrison wrote:

> Political competition in a representative system was bound to give casteism "a new lease on life," as Vinoba Bhave put it, if only because the single-member constituency inherently favors — barring gerrymandering — any social group in any country which happens to live in close proximity in a particular locality. The political role of caste is widely conceded in the Indian press, and invariably, the most perplexing election surprises become crystal-clear when the caste factors in a constituency come to light. But the strength of caste in Indian political life is not the diffused strength of scattered local caste factions, each organized to elect its own single member of a state assembly or Parliament. It is because caste lobbies function coherently on the basis of entire linguistic regions . . . that caste assumed such irrepressible importance.[14]

The Election in Kerala in 1960

The main event in India's electoral history between the second and third general elections was the election in Kerala in February, 1960. With the possible exception of the election in Andhra in 1955, this was the most bitterly contested and the most highly publicized State election in the history of independent India. In July, 1959, after a long period of indecision and because of reports of growing troubles in the State, the Government of India intervened in the deteriorating situation, and the Communist government of Kerala was superseded by President's rule, until new elections could be held. Determined not to be outmaneuvered this time by the Communists, the Congress took the initiative in forming a Triple Alliance with the PSP and the Muslim League (which still had some strength in that part of India), and it conducted a vigorous electoral campaign, with Nehru and other top leaders participating. As a result of these tactics, of the changing views of the voters regarding the Communists, and other more basic factors, the Triple Alliance emerged with 94 of the 127 seats in the Kerala Assembly. The Congress alone won 63 seats, while the PSP won 20, and the Muslim League 11. Before the voting the Congress

[13] *Ibid.*, p. 193.
[14] *Ibid.*, p. 109.

had 43 seats and the PSP had 9. Communist membership in the Assembly plummeted from 60 to 26 (plus three Communist-supported Independents).[15]

With some justification the results of the Kerala election of February, 1960, were widely hailed as a resounding Communist setback, and the changed composition of the State Assembly seemed to justify this interpretation. A more careful examination of the results, and especially of the general situation in Kerala, would lead to a less optimistic view. The Communists in Kerala actually increased their popular vote substantially over the figures in 1957; in fact, their popular vote was even greater than that of the Congress. The substantially improved position of the Congress in Kerala, therefore, could not be attributed to any lessening of support for the Communists, or any marked increase of support for the Congress, but rather to more effective electoral tactics on the part of the Congress and to certain other relatively ephemeral factors. The coalition government which has been in power in Kerala since the elections, with the Congress, of course, the main element in the coalition, has experienced considerable difficulties, and it is quite possible that any serious failure in government and administration by a Congress or Congress-dominated Ministry might give the Communists a second chance in Kerala.

India's Experience with Elections: An Appraisal

Measured by one of the severest tests — the holding of free, direct, general elections — democracy in India has worked. Some very serious abuses have come to light, however, both on the procedural and on the substantive side.

Procedurally speaking, the nomination procedures, the use of the multiple ballot box technique, the delays in disposing of cases of alleged election frauds, and other matters have raised serious problems. Steps have been taken, however, to deal more efficiently with them. After the second general elections, for example, the Election Commission announced that in every future election, as far as possible — with some concessions to the more backward areas — ballot papers would be substituted for the multiple ballot boxes. The ballot papers will contain the names of all contesting candidates in each constituency, along with facsimiles of their respective symbols. A voter will mark his ballot in secret, but will insert it in a ballot box within the view

[15] "Final Tally and Party Positions in Kerala Elections," *Indiagram*, Feb. 19, 1960. For an account of the conditions in Kerala which led to the overthrow of the Communist Government in July, 1959, and to the elections in that State in February, 1960, see Benjamin N. Schoenfeld, "Kerala in Crisis," *Pacific Affairs*, XXXII (September, 1959), 235–248.

of the presiding officer and others in the polling station. This procedure will be quicker, less complicated, and less expensive, and it will remove many difficulties which have been experienced in previous elections, such as tampering with the ballot boxes, the failure of some voters to insert their ballot papers into the boxes, the carrying away of ballot papers instead of inserting them in the boxes, and other practices arising out of deliberate fraud or ignorance. It will speed up not only the voting on election day but also the counting of the ballots afterward. On the other hand, this procedure, obviously patterned after the prevailing election practices in Western democracies, may be too sophisticated for the masses of the Indian electorate to understand.

The limited experience with ballot papers to date, especially in the Kerala elections of 1960, has been rather encouraging. They will be given a more thorough testing in the third general elections, in 1962.

Many of the substantive problems arising from India's electoral experience have been mentioned, such as the multitude of problems stemming from the illiteracy and inexperience of the ordinary Indian voter, his predilection for voting in accordance with instructions from some recognized authority, often based on caste or communal ties, his almost exclusive concentration on local issues, the deliberate tactics of most of the parties to capitalize on caste and other divisions in Indian society, and the basic problem of obtaining some kind of national consensus out of the congeries of regional, local, caste, and communal groupings that constitute India today.

* 11 *

Foreign Relations

In power-political terms India today is a rather weak state, but it is obviously playing a large role in world affairs. The explanation for this paradoxical situation is to be sought in the uniqueness of India's position and outlook. Economically and militarily India is far from being a major power, and it faces serious political and social problems which threaten its national unity and its cultural cohesiveness; but at the same time it has great present influence and even greater potential power. It is the most populous of the non-Communist nations of the world. It is the largest and probably the most important of the underdeveloped countries in an age when "the revolution of rising expectations" in underdeveloped areas is one of the most potent forces in international relations. It is still perhaps the single most influential member of the Asian-African Group in the United Nations, although its relative influence has declined with the emergence of many new states and the rise of other centers of influence and power in Asia and Africa. Its past connections with Great Britain and its present associations through the Commonwealth and the sterling area give India an added importance in world affairs.

India is the leading nation in the "uncommitted world," a position which gives it a far greater influence than it would have if it were closely associated with either of the great "power blocs." Thus the importance of India in world affairs is enhanced by the nature of the existing world struggle and by India's unique and somewhat detached position with respect to that struggle.

Its foreign policy has been variously described as one of "neutrality," "nonalignment," or "independence." Most Indian spokesmen prefer to describe India's foreign policy as an independent one, a policy based on the consideration of each issue on its own merits.[1] Indians like

[1] In the first statement which he made when he became Member for External Affairs in the Interim Government in September, 1946, Nehru

to feel that their past traditions of tolerance, the influence of their great leader, Mahatma Gandhi, and their policy of nonalignment or independence place them in a favorable position to play a mediating and conciliatory role in international relations, to contribute to the lessening of international tensions and to the development of a "climate of peace." Without claiming any special moral superiority over other peoples, most Indians seem to feel that their country can contribute greatly to improving the standards of diplomatic behavior and to "sweetening" international relations. Hence India conceives that it has an active role to play in the world; and there are indeed few issues of importance on which it does not express an opinion or advance a recommendation.

Factors Shaping India's Foreign Policy

In a basic sense the foreign policy of India is determined by precisely the same factors that shape the foreign policy of any country. Some of these factors are tangible, such as geographic and economic and demographic factors, while others are intangible, such as morale and

---

said: "In the sphere of foreign affairs, India will follow an independent policy, keeping away from power politics of groupings aligned against the other." In an address to the United Nations General Assembly, on October 17, 1960, V. K. Krishna Menon, Nehru's chief adviser on foreign policy, declared: "We are not a neutral country. . . . We want it understood that we do not welcome this appellation of being called a neutral, or neutralist, whatever it means. . . . We are not neutral in regard to war or peace. We are not neutral in regard to domination by imperialist or other countries. We are not neutral with regard to ethical values. We are not neutral with regard to the greatest economic and social problems that may arise. Neutrality is a concept that arises only in war. . . . Even that expression 'positive neutrality' is a contradiction in terms. There can no more be positive neutrality than there can be a vegetarian tiger. Therefore, our position is that we are an unaligned and uncommitted nation in relation to the cold war. . . . We do not belong to one camp or another." Fifteenth Session, General Assembly, United Nations, *Provisional Verbatim Record of the Nine Hundred and Sixth Plenary Meeting,* 17 October, 1960 (A/PV.906, 17 October 1960), pp. 44–46. M. S. Rajan argues that even though Nehru and other Indian spokesmen frequently call India, as did Krishna Menon, "an unaligned and uncommitted nation," the only proper adjective to use in describing India's foreign policy is "independent." "Indian Foreign Policy in Action, 1954–56," *India Quarterly,* XVI (July–September, 1960), 229. In his biography of Nehru, Michael Brecher has an illuminating comment on this subject: "The term to describe Indian foreign policy has undergone frequent change. It began with 'neutrality' or 'dynamic neutrality', later became 'neutralism' and then 'non-alignment'. Nehru prefers the phrase 'positive policy for peace', he told the author in New Delhi on 13 June 1956." Michael Brecher, *Nehru: A Political Biography* (London: Oxford University Press, 1959), p. 563, n. 2.

leadership. In India's case three factors deserve special emphasis, namely geographical and strategic position, historical experience, involving traditional patterns and foreign impact, and domestic forces and pressures.

A glance at a map will be a sufficient reminder that India occupies a position of great geographic and strategic importance, in a local, regional, and global sense.[2] In 1903 Lord Curzon, then Governor-General of India, predicted that the geographical position of India would more and more push it into the forefront of international affairs. In 1948 Nehru spoke of India as the pivotal center of South, Southeast, and Western Asia.

Flanked by the world's highest mountains on the north and by the Indian Ocean and its vast reaches, the Arabian Sea and the Bay of Bengal, on the south, east, and west, the western frontiers of India border on West Pakistan while to the east Indian territory almost surrounds East Pakistan and extends to the frontiers of Burma. India has something like 3,500 miles of seacoast and 8,200 miles of land frontier, if all the borders with Pakistan are included. Because of its strained relations with its sister nation of the subcontinent, India is faced with a security problem in its own front yard; yet ironically Pakistan has sometimes been called India's first line of defense, for India has to rely largely upon Pakistan for the defense of those parts of the subcontinent in the Northwest Frontier area which were the traditional avenues of entry by one invader after another across the centuries. Recent activities of the Chinese Communists have reminded India that it has other security problems along its Himalayan frontier. Including Nepal, Sikkim, and Bhutan, as well as Ladakh and the Northeast Frontier area within India's strategic frontiers, India has more than 1,500 miles of frontier with Communist China — the longest frontier of any non-Communist state with a Communist state; and in the northern part of Kashmir it is separated from Soviet territory by only a few miles. India has a vital security interest in Nepal and Bhutan, and many of its policies attest to this fact. Sikkim, between Nepal and Bhutan, is a protectorate of India.[3]

India is also deeply concerned with the control of the Indian Ocean region, but for the moment at least it has no major fears from this quarter. While the Indian Navy is weak, effective control of the Indian Ocean is in the hands of states with which India is on friendly terms.

[2] See P. P. Karan, "India's Role in Geopolitics," *India Quarterly,* IX (April–June, 1953), 160–169; K. M. Panikkar, *India and the Indian Ocean* (London, 1945).

[3] See Leo E. Rose, "Sino-Indian Rivalry and the Himalayan Border States," *Orbis,* V (Summer, 1961), pp. 199–215.

The long, rich, and complicated historical experience of the Indian people has done much to condition Indian attitudes and outlook. Some knowledge of this experience, extending over many centuries, is essential for an understanding of the contemporary Indian scene as well as of India's past. In analyzing India's behavior in foreign as well as in domestic affairs, it is well to remember, as Nehru wrote in *The Discovery of India,* that "we are very old, and trackless centuries whisper in our ears."[4]

The predominant civilization of India has always been the Hindu, although in more recent centuries the Muslims and later the British have made a great impact. Some of the characteristics and practices of Hindu civilization have a very noticeable influence on Indian attitudes and policies today. Among these may be mentioned a kind of otherworldy attitude toward life and an emphasis on nonmaterial factors, and a spirit of tolerance, detachment, mediation, and compromise which perhaps is best exemplified in Buddhism, which is, after all, an offshoot of Hinduism.

The British remained in India for more than three hundred years, and for well over a century, through direct and indirect rule, they were in effective control of virtually the entire subcontinent. While much can be said about British contributions to India, and while Indians reacted favorably to the way in which the British left in 1947, the many decades of Western "imperialism" left deep scars. They account in large measure for the sensitivity of independent India to any evidences, real or imagined, of imperialism and colonialism, of racial superiority and discrimination, of Western manipulation, of disregard of the interests and wishes of the newly independent nations of Asia and Africa.

It would be interesting to speculate on the extent to which India's present policy of nonalignment and its emphasis on the "middle way" in world affairs can be traced to ancient roots. Or are they rather attributable to the teachings and example of Gandhi? Or can they be explained largely by the practical assessment of India's present leaders of the wisest course for India to follow in world affairs?

Foreign Policy of the Indian National Congress Before Independence

In the position taken by the Indian National Congress on many issues of international import during the sixty-two years of its existence prior to independence may be found the immediate roots of the foreign policy of independent India. This is particularly true after World War I, when the Congress became more articulate and outspoken in its views, when Mahatma Gandhi gave a unique twist to the work

[4] Jawaharlal Nehru, *The Discovery of India* (New York, 1946), p. 144.

of the Congress, and when the organization developed a kind of foreign office of its own, with Nehru in charge.

A study of the resolutions passed by the Indian National Congress will reveal that the Congress took a deep interest in certain external questions from its inception, and that it based its position on certain fundamental principles which still shape the foreign policy of India today.[5] A resolution passed at the first session of the Congress in 1885 deprecated the annexation of Upper Burma by the British. In 1892 the Congress objected to "the military activity going on beyond the natural lines of the defences of this country, in pursuance of the Imperial policy of Great Britain in its relation with some of the Great Powers of Europe." Increasingly the Congress objected to the use of India as a base for political maneuvering or military moves against surrounding areas such as Tibet, Burma, Afghanistan, and Persia. A resolution of 1904 asserted that an expedition to Tibet was "but part of a general forward policy, which . . . threatens to involve India in foreign entanglements." "This resolution," states Dr. N. V. Rajkumar, a "Foreign Secretary" of the Indian National Congress who compiled the major resolutions of the Congress relating to foreign affairs, "was perhaps the earliest expression of India's dislike of getting involved in unnecessary foreign entanglements and favouring a neutral stand on matters that did not concern her."

During World War I the Congress passed several resolutions of loyalty to the British and of support for the use of Indian troops in the war effort. After the War it began to take a more active interest and a more independent line on foreign issues. It was intensely interested in the Khilafat question.[6] In 1920 it sent "a message of sympathy to the Irish people in their struggle for independence." The meeting of the All-India Congress Committee in Delhi in 1921 was "a landmark in the history of India's foreign relations." For the first time the Congress passed a general resolution on foreign policy, which included the statement that "the present Government of India in no

[5] All of the Congress resolutions cited in this section are given in full in N. V. Rajkumar, ed., *The Background of India's Foreign Policy* (New Delhi, 1952).

[6] In 1920 "a new issue blazed across the Indian horizon and stirred the emotions of the Muslim community — the *Khilafat* agitation. It was a curious but none the less significant political phenomenon, with highly charged spiritual overtones relating to the Khaliphate, the highest religious office in the Islamic world. The defeat of Turkey in the first world war caused genuine disquiet among many Indian Muslims. More particularly, the Allied decision to dismember the Ottoman Empire and to disband the office of Khaliph aroused anger and hostility. . . . The result was the creation of a powerful politico-religious movement. . . . More important, this episode led to an alliance between the Congress and the Muslims. . . . Gandhi correctly perceived the measure of Muslim feeling." Brecher, *Nehru,* p. 67.

way represent Indian opinion." "This resolution," explains Rajkumar, "is important in as much as it was the first significant declaration on the part of nationalist India that its interests in the field of foreign policy were diametrically opposed to those of Britain. It further laid down the bases of an independent India's foreign policy. An analysis of this historic declaration would show that the fundamental principles guiding Free India's foreign policy today can be traced back to it." The Congress Session in Madras in 1927 passed a resolution of protest against the use of Indian troops in China, Mesopotamia, and Persia and deplored the "extensive war preparations which the British Government is carrying on in India." Nearly thirty years later Nehru stated that the foundations of India's foreign policy had been laid down at the Madras session of the Congress in 1927.

A resolution of the Congress in 1925 authorized the AICC to open a Foreign Department under it "to look after the interests of Indians abroad and to carry on educative propaganda in the country regarding their position in the British Empire and foreign countries." Three years later, after another reminder from the annual session of the Congress, the AICC did set up a Foreign Department, with Jawaharlal Nehru at its head. From that time to the present day Nehru has been the major voice of India in foreign affairs. This is a record unparalleled among the leading democratic statesmen of the twentieth century. It helps to explain the remarkable consistency in Indian foreign policy, and serves as a reminder that that policy had evolved in most of its fundamentals well before 1947.

The 1928 Congress session at Calcutta sent its greetings to the peoples of Egypt, Syria, Palestine, and Iraq "in their struggle for emancipation from the grip of Western imperialism" and authorized the appointment of a representative to the Second World Congress of the League Against Imperialism, to be held in 1929. "These resolutions," states Rajkumar, "gave the first indication that India's national leaders were thinking in terms of a Pan-Asian movement to resist European imperialism."

In many resolutions in the late 1930's the Congress condemned the aggressive acts of the Nazis and Fascists, but it also declared that it would not be a party to "imperialist war." At the Tripura session in 1939 the Congress strongly disapproved of British foreign policy and dissociated itself from it. "In the opinion of the Congress, it is urgently necessary for India to direct her own foreign policy as an independent nation, thereby keeping aloof from both imperialism and fascism, and pursuing her path of peace and freedom." When the war came the Working Committee of the Congress, in a lengthy resolution, stated the attitude of the Congress toward the war: "The issue of war and peace for India must be decided by the Indian people. . . . Their sympathy is entirely on the side of democracy and freedom. But India cannot associate herself in a war said to be for democratic freedom when that very freedom is denied to her." The Congress ministries in the provinces resigned in protest against British policy, and the Congress refused to support the war effort. Under the influence of Gandhi organized non-violence was advocated as an alternative to war. The "Quit India" resolution of August marked the final parting of the ways, and thereafter, as Rajkumar notes, "the Congress went into the wilderness for the duration of the war."

With the release of most of its leaders early in 1945, the Congress resumed its demands for Indian independence and it spoke out strongly for the freedom of all countries and "the elimination of all traces of imperialist control by whatever name it may be called." While it welcomed the formation of the United Nations, from the outset it expressed certain major points of dissatisfaction with the kind of organization that had been formed. A resolution of the Working Committee of the Congress in July, 1945, raised two major objections: one against the dominant role of the Great Powers in the new organization to the extent that "they are placed above and beyond the law they have themselves helped in framing," with the consequence that "the position allotted to the smaller nations in the Charter is one lacking all effectiveness," the other against the "vague and unsatisfactory" declaration in the Charter regarding non-self-governing territories, instead of "a full and frank recognition of national independence." In subsequent resolutions in 1945 and 1946 the Working Committee voiced apprehensions regarding the consequences of the atomic bomb and the growing tensions in international relations, "resulting in open recrimination between the Great Powers and attempts on their part to secure or hold on to colonial areas and vantage points and create satellite states." The Congress was especially concerned over the many evidences that "the imperialist powers are again engaged in the old contest for dominion over others." It demanded the end of foreign domination over the countries of Asia and Africa, and it expressed its strong sympathy and support for the independence movements in Indonesia, Indo-China, and elsewhere. It was particularly insistent on the early granting of independence for India. A resolution of the Working Committee in March, 1946, declared: "India still remains the crux of the problem of Asian freedom and on the independence of India depends the freedom of many countries and the peace of the world."

Basic Principles of India's Foreign Policy

Shortly after India became an independent nation, the Congress called attention to the importance of the freedom struggle in shaping the foreign policy of free India, and it stated the basic principles of that policy:

> The foreign policy of India must necessarily be based on the principles that have guided the Congress in past years. The principles are the promotion of world peace, the freedom of all nations, racial equality and the ending of imperialism and colonialism. In particular, the Congress is interested in the freedom of the nations and peoples of Asia and Africa who have suffered under various forms of colonialism for many generations.

Thus the foreign policy of India today can be explained in large part by the historical experience and attitudes of the Indian people, and is rooted in the policies which were established by the Indian National Congress during the long years of the independence struggle. "It is well to remember," said Nehru in 1955, "that our foreign policy is not a sudden growth but a natural outcome of our thinking for many years past." In a famous letter to the Presidents of the Pradesh Congress Committees in July, 1954, Nehru stated that India's foreign policy

> must be in keeping with the traditional background and temper of the country. . . . What is our background, leaving out the distant past, although it is important? This background has been conditioned by our struggle for freedom under Gandhiji's leadership which taught us peaceful methods and tolerance; friendship with other nations but at the same time independence of action. Inevitably it was opposed to colonialism or domination of one country by another. It was based on democracy and freedom of the individual and social progress aiming at a society where there was no exploitation by one class over another and where present inequalities, social or economic, were gradually removed. The basis of the action was always peaceful. Our present foreign policy flows from that background and naturally works for world peace and avoidance of war.

In developing these principles Nehru placed particular emphasis on "nonalignment with the great power groups," on opposition to colonialism, and on the necessity of peaceful co-existence and of creating a climate of peace. "Peace," he argued, "can only be preserved by methods of peace. A war-like approach to peace is a contradiction in terms. . . . Peace cannot live in an atmosphere of constant preparation for war and threat of war."

Concluding his letter Nehru stated: "The major fact is that we are following not a passive or merely neutral policy, but a dynamic policy which is based on certain definite principles and objectives as well as certain methods. We try not to forget the means in search for our ends. . . . It must be recognized . . . that any policy that is realistic must take into consideration the profound changes in the relationships of forces in Asia and the world."

In an address at Columbia University on October 17, 1949, Nehru summed up the main objectives of Indian foreign policy in a single sentence. "The main objectives of that policy are: the pursuit of peace, not through alignment with any major power or group of powers but through an independent approach to each controversial or disputed issue, the liberation of subject peoples, the maintenance of freedom, both national and individual, the elimination of racial discrimination and the elimination of want, disease and ignorance, which afflict the greater part of the world's population."

The Panchsheel. Nehru and other Indian spokesmen have attached great importance to the enunciation and endorsement of rather nebulous principles of peace, especially the *Panch Shila,* or *Panchsheel.* The now-famous five principles of peace were first enunciated in specific form in the Sino-Indian treaty on Tibet in April, 1954, and were restated in the joint declaration issued by Nehru and Chou En-lai at the end of the visit of the Chinese Premier to India in June of the same year. Since then they have been referred to in many subsequent joint statements and pronouncements by Indian spokesmen, and they have come to be symbolic of India's views and approaches in world affairs. The words *Panch Shila* are derived from Sanskrit, and mean the five foundations or the five principles. Nehru heard the words "in an entirely different context" when he was in Indonesia in 1955, and he immediately suggested that they would be "a suitable description of the five principles of international behaviour to which we had subscribed."[7]

As stated in the Sino-Indian Treaty and the Nehru–Chou En-lai declaration of 1954, the five principles were: (1) mutual respect for

[7] A remarkable explanation of the origin and development of the idea of the *Panch Shila* or *Panchsheel* was given by Nehru in a letter to Professor Russell H. Fifield of the University of Michigan, dated June 4, 1957. The text of this letter is printed in Russell H. Fifield, *The Diplomacy of Southeast Asia: 1945–1958* (New York, 1958), pp. 510–511. Nehru first used the term *Panch Shila* at a State banquet given to him by the Prime Minister of Indonesia in Djakarta, on September 23, 1954. Apparently "the credit for calling these principles, for the first time in public, as *Pancha Sila* (or the five bases of conduct which India had consistently preached and attempted to follow in her international relations) should go to K. M. Panikkar, who used it in a broadcast talk over the All India Radio on 28 July 1954. He was commenting on the Nehru-Chou joint statement." M. S. Rajan, "Indian Foreign Policy in Action, 1954–56," p. 224, n. 77.

each other's territorial integrity and sovereignty; (2) nonaggression; (3) noninterference in each other's internal affairs; (4) equality and mutual benefit; and (5) peaceful co-existence. While even Nehru himself has admitted that "there is nothing wonderful about the *Panchsheel*" and that "no one could disagree with them," they have real meaning for him. In his view they are deeply rooted in Indian tradition and experience, and they have a definite bearing on India's desire to maintain an independent position in world affairs and at the same time to cooperate with other nations in the interests of world peace. At a civic reception in Calcutta for Bulganin and Khrushchev on November 30, 1955, the Indian Prime Minister explained the relationship of the *Panchsheel* to India's foreign policy:

> India does not propose to join any camp or alliance. But we wish to cooperate with all in the quest for peace and security and human betterment. . . . Peaceful coexistence is not a new idea for us in India. It has been our way of life and is as old as our thought and culture. . . . From this it has naturally followed that we should keep ourselves free from military and like alliances and have not joined any of the great power groups that dominate the world today. It is in no spirit of pride or arrogance that we pursue our independent policy. We could not do otherwise unless we were false to everything India has stood for in the past and stands for today. We welcome association and friendship with all and the flow of thought and ideas of all kinds, but we reserve the right to choose our own path. That is the essence of "Panch Shila." . . . These principles form the basis of our relations with other nations. If Panch Shila were fully and sincerely accepted by all countries, then peace would be assured to everyone and cooperation would follow.

Spokesmen of all nations tend to be rather nebulous when attempting to enunciate principles of foreign policy, and they inevitably open themselves to the criticisms that they do not seem to have clear-cut policies and that the actual policies of their countries bear little relation to their professions. Indian spokesmen are often subject to this kind of criticism. But while their words are vague, and perhaps at times a bit irritating and naive, many of India's foreign policies are quite specific and realistic. This is especially the case with regard to those issues, like colonialism and racialism, on which Indians feel deeply, and to those issues which are of most immediate concern to them.

Relations with Pakistan

Many of these issues center around India's unsatisfactory relations with its neighbor in the subcontinent, Pakistan. Indeed, as A. M.

Rosenthal has stated, "a good part of India's foreign policy is based on Pakistan."[8] Pakistan is at once India's "first line of defense" and closest neighbor, and at the same time the source or the object of India's deepest concerns in foreign affairs. In fact, in view of the past relationships of the people who now inhabit the two countries and in view of their inescapable intimacy, the relations between India and Pakistan might well be treated as aspects of domestic rather than of foreign policies.

In their attitudes toward each other India and Pakistan are handicapped by a communal past, the tragedy of partition, and a long series of issues which have caused friction between them since independence. Feelings of suspicion and distrust have been exacerbated by differences on a long list of specific issues, notably settlement of property claims of persons who were forced to move from one country to the other and abandon much of their property in so doing, disposition of stores and assets after partition, trade relations, exchange and currency difficulties, differing attitudes and policies in foreign affairs, the canal waters dispute, and the Kashmir question.

Of the many specific issues in dispute between India and Pakistan the most vexing have been those relating to canal waters and to Kashmir. In 1960, after years of intermittent negotiation, India and Pakistan, through the good offices of the International Bank for Reconstruction and Development (the World Bank), reached an agreement on the use of the waters of the Indus River system; but the Kashmir question seems to be as far from solution as ever, and it remains the major issue in Indo-Pakistan relations.

The Canal Waters Question. Whereas most of East Pakistan has too much water and experiences frequent and devastating floods, large parts of West Pakistan get too little water and are dependent on the rather uncertain supplies which are made available through some half dozen of the rivers which make up the Indus River system, the vital artery of West Pakistan. Three of these rivers — the Jhelum, the Chenab, and the Indus itself — rise either in Tibet or in remote parts of Kashmir, but three others — the Beas, the Ravi, and the Sutlej — flow through northwest India into West Pakistan, and can therefore be diverted for India's uses. "Rainfall is scanty in the plains area, and without the rivers and the irrigation system, the plains of the Indus basin would be desert. But, with the system of irrigation developed over the last hundred years, the rivers support a population of about 40 million people in Pakistan and about 10 million in India — ap-

[8] A. M. Rosenthal, "India Sees Her Role as Power for Peace," dispatch from New Delhi, dated Sept. 22, 1956; in the *New York Times,* Sept. 23, 1956.

proximately one-tenth of the combined population of the two countries."[9]

As a consequence of partition the question of the use of the waters of these rivers, whose annual flow is twice that of the Nile, became crucial for Pakistan, but for some years no progress was made in resolving this life-or-death issue. In 1951 David Lilienthal, former Chairman of the Tennessee Valley Authority, suggested a solution, involving the working out of a comprehensive engineering plan for the use of the waters of the Indus River system and financial assistance by the World Bank. In March, 1952, both India and Pakistan accepted an offer of good offices from the President of the Bank. Representatives of the two countries negotiated intermittently for many months, in Washington and elsewhere,[10] but not until the spring of 1959 was agreement reached on the main issues in dispute. The drafting of the treaty required further negotiations, over a period of a year and a half. Finally, on September 19, 1960, the Indus Waters Treaty was signed in Karachi by Prime Minister Nehru, President Mohammad Ayub Khan, and W. A. B. Iliff, Vice-President of the World Bank. Subject to certain exceptions, the treaty allocated the waters of the eastern rivers — the Ravi, the Beas, and the Sutlej — for the use of India, and of the three western rivers — the Indus, the Jhelum, and the Chenab — for the use of Pakistan. Simultaneously an international financial agreement was signed by representatives of Australia, Canada, West Germany, New Zealand, Pakistan, the United Kingdom, the United States, and the World Bank. This agreement created the Indus Basin Development Fund of about $900 million to finance the construction of irrigation and other works in Pakistan provided for in the Indus Waters Treaty. Approximately $640 million is to be supplied by the participating governments, $174 million by India under the Indus Waters Treaty, and $80 million by a World Bank loan to Pakistan.

The Kashmir Question. Prime Minister Nehru hailed the signing of these agreements as "a unique occasion," and he expressed the hope "that this will bring prosperity to a vast number of the people on both sides and will increase the goodwill and friendship for India and Pakistan." Many people in India and elsewhere hoped that the agreement on the canal waters issue, and the improved relations between India and Pakistan which this symbolized, might make it possible for the two countries to reach some amicable understanding regarding the even more complicated and much more highly publicized question of Kashmir.

[9] "Indus Waters Treaty," *Pakistan News Digest,* VIII (Oct. 1, 1960), 6.

[10] See Eugene Black "The Indus: A Moral for Nations," *New York Times Magazine,* Dec. 11, 1960. Mr. Black is President of the World Bank.

Here the disagreements between India and Pakistan have been complete, from the beginning of the dispute shortly after the two countries began their independent existence.[11] They have not even been able to agree on the facts of the dispute, not to mention the proper interpretation of these facts. The Indian position is based on the "fact" of the accession of the Maharaja of Kashmir to India in 1947, the "fact" of Pakistani aggression in Kashmir, the "fact" of the manifest desire of the post-partition governments of that part of Kashmir on the Indian side of the cease-fire line to associate Kashmir with India. Indian spokesmen point out that India brought the question before the Security Council of the United Nations early in 1948, and they criticize the Security Council, and especially the United States and Britain which are permanent members, for allowing Pakistan to befog the issue and for taking an unduly critical position with regard to the Indian claims ever since. They have been maintaining for some years, certainly since 1952, that "the accession of Kashmir to India is complete in law and in fact," and they seem to imply that, in spite of the contrary views of Pakistan, the Security Council, and vocal segments of world public opinion, the Kashmir issue is in fact settled. Presumably they are willing to settle for effective Indian control of the Valley of Kashmir and of other parts of the former princely State on the Indian side of the cease-fire line, while at the same time they have not abandoned at least their theoretical claims to all of Jammu and Kashmir.

When Pakistanis call attention to India's pledge to hold a plebiscite in Kashmir as soon as conditions had settled down, in order to determine the wishes of the inhabitants as to their political future, Indians argue that this "pledge" was contingent on certain preconditions that have not been realized, that the offer was not a standing one, and that a plebiscite is no longer feasible or desirable in the light of developments during the past twelve years. They also maintain that the present government in Kashmir represents the popular will, and that a plebiscite would only tend to raise old issues and divisions and might produce communal tensions between Hindus and Muslims, not only in Kashmir but throughout India. To the Pakistani contention that the majority of the people, who are Muslims, are living in a police state and would much prefer to be a part of Pakistan, Indians empha-

[11] For details of the complicated developments in and relating to Kashmir since 1947 see Michael Brecher, *The Struggle for Kashmir* (New York, 1953); Josef Korbel, *Danger in Kashmir* (Princeton, N.J., 1954); Lord Birdwood, *Two Nations and Kashmir* (London, 1956); and J. B. Das Gupta, *Indo-Pakistan Relations, 1947–1955* (Amsterdam, 1958), Chapters III and IV.

size the concept of the secular state and point to the many millions of Muslims who are living peacefully within the Republic of India.

Since India will probably never agree to hold a plebiscite in Kashmir and since Pakistan is not strong enough to force India to hold such a plebiscite, the situation in Kashmir will in all probability remain as it is at present, a festering sore as far as Pakistan is concerned and a settled issue from the Indian point of view. Basic agreement and a general improvement in relations of India and Pakistan might make the Kashmir question less of a thorn in Indo-Pakistan relations, but, on the other hand, one might argue that a general improvement in these relations will be impossible until agreement is reached on Kashmir.

In the meantime, the Kashmir dispute is perhaps the major issue exacerbating Indo-Pakistan relations, and it is one of the major issues in dispute between two non-Communist nations. The fact that India and Pakistan have so much in common, geographically, historically, racially, and culturally, that they are fellow-members of the Commonwealth, the Colombo Plan group, the "Colombo Powers," and other associations, and that their mutual suspicion and hostility impose additional burdens upon them at a time when they need to devote all their limited resources to purposes of national development, makes the present state of their relations all the more tragic. Moreover, the existence of a major dispute between two of the most important nations along the periphery of the Communist-dominated world, involving a strategically important territory deep in Asia and close to both Russian and Chinese territories, creates a situation of weakness in an already vulnerable part of the world. The dispute also raises embarrassing problems for Western states, particularly Britain and the United States, which would like to be on close terms with both India and Pakistan. This goal is made more difficult by the inclination of both of these South Asian countries to test the attitudes of other states by the position which they take on the Kashmir issue and by the dissatisfaction which both have expressed, for different reasons, with the position taken by the United Nations, and especially by Britain and the United States, on Kashmir.

Relations with Other Non-Communist States of Asia

India is also especially concerned with its relations with other near neighbors, which, in spite of certain sources of friction, are much happier than its relations with Pakistan. Quite understandably, India has shown a special interest in the Himalayan states of Nepal and Bhutan, which lie between it and Tibet, now under the direct control of Communist China, and which form a part of India's strategic Himalayan frontier. Indian troops have from time to time entered

Nepal, and Indian advisers have been conspicuous in that country. India has been rather jealous of any other countries which have shown a special interest in Nepal. This jealousy and concern were manifest toward Britain and the United States, and they are now directed toward Communist China and the Soviet Union. Nehru's rather arduous visit to Bhutan in late 1958 was evidence of the gradual and partial emergence of that isolated state into the modern world and of India's special ties with Bhutan, at a time when India is troubled over the possibility of penetration of the area from the north by agents of the Chinese Communists.

Leaders of India and Ceylon have worked hard to accentuate the positive in the relations of their two countries, but these relations have been strained by the differences arising from the treatment of the Tamil-speaking people of Ceylon, some of whom emigrated from India long ago while others are relatively recent arrivals whose status is still uncertain.

Geographic and historical ties with Burma have always been close. Until 1935, in fact, Burma was associated with India, under the general supervision of the British Viceroy. Burma achieved independence a few months after India, but unlike the larger state it chose to opt out of the Commonwealth. Economic and political bonds between free India and Burma have been numerous, and the natural friendship of the two countries has been deepened by the personal friendship of Nehru and U Nu, who has been Prime Minister of Burma during most of the years since independence. Major differences have arisen over Burmese treatment of the large Indian minorities in Burma. Burmans resent the privileged position which many Indians have managed to achieve in the economic life of Burma, and India has shown a special concern for persons of Indian origin in Burma, even though it has urged these people to give their primary loyalties to the state in which they live and work. The attitude of India toward persons of Indian origin in Ceylon and Burma is typical of its general attitude towards the millions of Indians overseas, in many parts of the world.

India has shown a special interest in the other countries of Southeast Asia, where in the past Indian cultural and political influence has been so strong. It has supported the independence struggles in Indonesia and Indochina. Its relations with Thailand and the Philippines have been less cordial and less close. It has muted its conventional views on colonialism in Malaya and Singapore, where large numbers of Indians live in plural societies composed largely of Chinese and Malays.

In the Far East and the Middle East, too, India has special interests and concerns. India, China, and Japan form what is sometimes called the Asian triangle. It is clear that the relative evolution and mutual relations of these three most important Asian states are of special significance in world affairs. Communist China exercises an almost hypnotic influence on India, which does not even recognize the existence of the Nationalist regime on Formosa and which is a leading champion of Communist China in the councils of the nations. The visit of the President of India to Japan in late 1958 was symbolic of the growing awareness of the two most important non-Communist states of Asia of each other. Actually relations between India and Japan have been rather distant, and their growing contacts are somewhat affected by rivalries in trade and in influence in Southeast Asia and other parts of the continent.

India has been generally more successful than its Muslim neighbor, Pakistan, in its relations with the Muslim states of the Middle East. Possibly its special interest in Afghanistan and its special efforts to cultivate the spokesmen of Arab nationalism, including Nasser himself, are prompted in part by a desire to counteract Pakistani influence in this part of the world; but these attitudes may also be explained by other basic considerations of Indian foreign policy.

The *U.S. News and World Report* once carried a bold headline on its outside front cover: "NEHRU DOESN'T SPEAK FOR ASIA." The statement was attributed to former Senator William F. Knowland of California. On this point, if on few others, the Prime Minister of India might well agree with the former Senator from California, for he has often disclaimed any desire to be regarded as "the voice of Asia" or any interest on the part of India in becoming a leader of Asian countries. Whatever his motives, however, he has repeatedly spoken as a champion of Asian views and attitudes, and he has been by no means averse to taking the initiative in any aspects of international relations of particular concern to Asia. Again and again he has criticized the Western powers for their past and present policies regarding Asia, and he has warned that the rest of the world should recognize that great changes have occurred in Asia and that Asia will have to be reckoned with in the future.

India sponsored two of the major Asian conferences in the postwar period, namely the Asian Relations Conference in 1947 and the conference on Indonesia in 1949, and it was one of the sponsors of the greatest of all Asian conferences, that at Bandung in April, 1955. While in a sense Chou En-lai and not Nehru was the "star" of the Bandung Conference, the Indian Prime Minister was certainly one of the major luminaries at this meeting, which was hailed in India as marking a new era for Asia in world affairs. India has been in fact a leader in most of the Asian associations in which she has participated — the "Colombo Powers," the Colombo Plan countries, the Economic Commission for

Asia and the Far East, and many other more specialized organizations — and she was the prime mover in the loose association of Asian and African members of the United Nations which is now referred to as the Asian-African or the Afro-Asian Group.

Relations with Communist China

Because of the vast size, large and rapidly expanding populations, economic growth and unlimited potentials of the two Asian giants, the relations between India and China will do much to shape the future of Asia and indeed of the world. The Communist leaders of China and the democratic leaders of India are trying to deal with essentially similar problems of political unity and stability, economic development, and social uplift in fundamentally different ways, and much will depend on their comparative success or failure. If China under communism makes great economic progress and is able to demonstrate convincingly that Communist techniques, however ruthless, do produce results in terms of individual living standards and national strength, while at the same time the Indian experiment in economic and political development and social change does not produce sufficiently convincing results, the prospects for democracy in Asia and in the world will be dim indeed, whereas the attractive power of the Asian brand of communism centering in Peking will vastly increase. In this sense there is, in spite of all the protestations in India to the contrary, a fundamental rivalry between democratic India and Communist China, with very high stakes at issue. The leaders of India are probably well aware of this basic test, but at the same time they appear to believe that they are on the right path, and that an increasingly powerful India can co-exist with an increasingly powerful China, whatever the differences in the ideological outlook of the Chinese leaders or whatever their success in progress through "brute reason" and regimentation.

Until 1959 official relations between India and China were generally close and friendly, and there were few major disagreements between them. Nehru and his associates were markedly conciliatory in their approach to Communist China — "nobody on earth," observed Vincent Sheean, "has tried harder to make friends with the Chinese than Jawaharlal has"[12] — and public opinion generally was favorably disposed toward the Communist regime in China. The actions of the Chinese Communists in Tibet and along the Indo-Chinese borders in 1959 hit India like an icy blast from the high Himalayas, and seemed to provoke a marked change in public moods and attitudes, as well as in

[12] Vincent Sheean, *Nehru: The Years of Power* (New York: Random House, 1960), p. 185. For a brief summary of Indo-Chinese relations in recent years see Brecher, *Nehru,* pp. 588–592.

official policy. It is still too early to determine whether the Chinese actions and the Indian reactions to them foreshadowed a basic change in Indo-Chinese relations, or in Indian foreign policy as a whole.

India has been the leading champion of the claims of Communist China for admission to the United Nations and for its "rightful place" in world affairs. It has been outspokenly critical of the China policies of the United States, which, in its view, have been mainly responsible for propping up "the so-called Kuomintang regime on Formosa" and for keeping the Communist Government of China out of the UN. Nehru and other Indian leaders have visited China since 1949, and have been warmly welcomed, while Chou En-lai and other leaders of Communist China have visited India and have usually received equally warm receptions. The one outstanding case of a rather cool reception in India of a leading Chinese Communist official came in April, 1960, when Chou En-lai visited New Delhi to discuss current disagreements with Nehru. Contacts between India and China have been increasing, on both official and unofficial levels (if any contacts with a Communist state can truly be described as "unofficial"). As has been indicated, the statement of the famous "five principles of peace" — the *Panchsheel* — was first made in a Sino-Indian treaty on Tibet and in the Nehru–Chou En-lai declaration of 1954; and spokesmen of Communist China have often referred to these principles.

Until 1959, at least, the prevailing climate of opinion in India was markedly sympathetic toward the "New China." Chinese Communist literature was available in India, in large quantities and at very low prices. A number of Indian organizations helped to promote the favorable climate regarding China. The great majority of members of these organizations were non-Communists who were nevertheless so favorably disposed toward the New China that they tended to become Chinese apologists and defenders; or perhaps it would be fairer to state that they were so impressed with the apparent progress of China under Communist control and so indignant at what they regarded as insulting treatment by outside powers of a fellow-Asian nation that they tended to accept a roseate picture of actual conditions in the New China and to overlook the human and social costs of whatever progress was being made.

Most of the books on Communist China published in India have been written by admirers of the new regime. A few books by trained observers who have seen something of China both before and after the Communist takeover have, however, been sharply critical.

For all the professions of friendship and brotherhood, it is not difficult to find evidences of open differences and fundamental rivalry between the two great Asian states. Undoubtedly the low point in Sino-Indian relations prior to 1959 came in the fall of 1950, when

Chinese Communist troops moved into Tibet. India's protest against this action led to an exchange of blunt notes, without giving India any satisfaction. Nehru himself admitted in the House of the People in early December that the events in Tibet had come as a "surprise" and a "shock" to him. Two years later another low point in Sino-Indian relations was reached when an Indian formula to resolve the prisoner exchange issue in Korea, which was introduced in the Political Committee of the General Assembly of the United Nations in early November, 1952, and approved by the Committee in December, was scathingly rejected by the U.S.S.R. and Communist China. The Chinese note of rejection labeled the proposal as "unfair" and "illegal," as couched in "sly terms to deceive world opinion" and to "facilitate" the forcible retention of the war prisoners in Korea. The Indian delegation, the note declared, had "already entered the Anglo-American camp."

Even before 1959 the presence of Chinese Communist forces along the borders of India, and of Nepal and Bhutan, which India regards as falling within its security zone, and the increased Chinese activities along the Himalayan frontier were viewed by India with many misgivings. India repeatedly protested to the Chinese Government because Chinese maps still showed parts of Assam and Kashmir as belonging to China. The battle of the maps was an indication of India's great sensitivity to any real or alleged violations of her northern territories and of her acute security consciousness.

In 1959 relations with China took a sudden and unexpected turn for the worse, and cast doubts on the whole course of India's foreign policy. In March a widespread rebellion in Tibet against the Chinese was ruthlessly suppressed by Chinese Communist troops. Shortly afterward the young Dalai Lama himself, and some 13,000 other Tibetans, escaped from Tibet and arrived in India. Nehru responded rather mildly to Chinese Communist charges that Indian "expansionists" and "interventionists" were behind the revolt in Tibet, that the "command center" of the rebels was in the Indian border town of Kalimpong, and that the Dalai Lama was being held in India "under duress"; but he did not deny asylum to the Tibetan spiritual leader, and he gradually adopted a stronger line toward the Chinese regime.

In August the occupation of the frontier post of Longju in India's Northeast Frontier Agency by Chinese Communist troops, which was followed by a whole series of border incidents, aroused strong anti-Chinese feelings in India, and strong criticisms of the foreign policy of India, especially toward China.[13] Nehru called the Chinese occupation of Longju a "clear case of aggression," and he announced

[13] For an account of the Sino-Indian border dispute in late 1959 and the Indian reactions to it see *Indian Affairs Record* (New Delhi), V (December, 1959), 279–288.

his firm intention "to defend our borders and to strengthen them and thus to protect the integrity of India"; but he also recalled the long friendship between India and China, and he indicated that "the door is always open to accommodation." When Parliament met in November Nehru defended himself vigorously against criticisms that he did not take the Chinese challenge seriously enough. On November 27th, speaking in the Lok Sabha, he said:

> In fact, if I may say so, it became for me one of those peak events of history when a plunge has to be taken in some direction which may have powerful and far-reaching effects not only on our country but on Asia and even the world. . . . We are dealing . . . not with a small or casual matter but with a matter of the utmost significance to the present and future of India and Asia. . . . It has made tremendous differences . . . not only to the Government's present relations with China but also to what may happen in the future.[14]

At about the same time, in a note to Chou En-lai, Nehru declared that "the cause of the recent troubles is action taken from your side of the border," and he warned the Chinese Premier that "the relations between our two countries are likely to grow worse." He left no doubt of his unhappiness over recent Chinese actions. He stated flatly that India would not only defend its own borders, but would regard "any aggression" against Nepal or Bhutan as aggression against India.

In the fall of 1959 the Government of India issued two White Papers on the crisis with China, consisting of the texts of the exchanges of notes and memoranda with China over border issues and related matters. Two more White Papers were issued in 1960, in March and November. These White Papers clearly revealed that the Indian Government had protested in the strongest terms against the Chinese violations of the Sino-Indian frontiers, and that, as Nehru said in the Lok Sabha in April, 1960, after talks with Chou En-lai, India and China "always came up against the hard rock of a different set of facts." These differences were highlighted in two very divergent reports, released in December, 1960, after several weeks of negotiations between Indian and Chinese representatives.[15]

How serious is this current crisis in Sino-Indian relations? Has it resulted in a complete reversal of opinion and mood, as well as of policy, in India toward the Communist regime in China? How has it

[14] Quoted in *The Hindu* (Madras), Nov. 28, 1959.

[15] *Report of the Officials of the Governments of India and the People's Republic of China on the Boundary Question* (New Delhi, 1961).

affected Indian foreign policy generally? Many observers in India and in the West are convinced that the crisis is a watershed in the history of India's foreign relations and orientation. Vincent Sheean, a sympathetic Western observer who has had close contacts with Gandhi as well as with Nehru and many other leaders of modern India and who knows India well, expressed this view eloquently in his recent biography of Nehru:

> A bitterness has been created which obliterates other distinctions and unites those who otherwise have few points of agreement. Jawaharlal's incredible skill, his immense prestige and the love the people bear him have all been hard pressed these last months because he alone, very often, seems to stand for peace with China at almost any cost. When he is forced to speak out against the pretensions of Peking (particularly on boundaries) he is cheered to the echo; and when he advises moderation, patience and restraint, his own followers are restive and ill at ease. It has been a development fraught with misery, and the end is not yet.
>
> Politically speaking, the India-China relationship of the late summer and autumn of 1959 seems very nearly to dominate the mind of India. It certainly dominates every other consideration in foreign affairs. . . . The passionate resentment against China which inhabits the very air of India today is a political reality of the greatest importance. It flows in upon almost every other consideration, even the most distant; it pervades the intellectual and emotional climate of the hour. It has required every resource of Nehru's personal supremacy to ride out this storm without disaster, and it casts the chilliest and most somber fog over the future.[16]

Other observers, on the other hand, believe that the shock effects of the Chinese actions in 1959 have already begun to wear off, and that Nehru's policies, which have been less forceful than vocal segments of Indian public opinion have demanded, have been justified. Nehru himself has insisted that, far from revealing the "failure" of the basic approach of India in world affairs, the crisis with China has provided a fresh opportunity to demonstrate the fundamental soundness and "rightness" of that policy. In recent months he has repeatedly reaffirmed the intention of the Government of India to continue to follow an "independent" foreign policy, and he has rejected all suggestions that India should reorient its policy and should cooperate more closely with other non-Communist countries, including Pakistan, in mutual defense measures and other matters of policy.

In all probability Indian attitudes toward China can never be the same as they were before 1959; but this does not mean that the

[16] Sheean, *Nehru*, pp. 186–187.

attitudes have fundamentally changed, or that as a result of the Chinese actions Indian foreign policy is likely to change in its fundamentals. The answer to the question of the future relations between the two Asian giants seems to rest in Peking; for most Indians still want to be friends with China, if the Chinese regime will not make this impossible.

Attitudes Toward the Soviet Union and Communism

Indians are favorably disposed toward China not because but in spite of the Communist orientation of its leadership. The same comment may be made about Indian attitudes toward the Soviet Union, the head center of world communism. Indians are not very familiar with what is happening in the Soviet Union, and, as in China, they are inclined to ignore the seamier aspects of the Soviet experiment in Russia. They are profoundly impressed by Russia's obvious economic progress. Within the short span of less than half a century an underdeveloped country has risen to the position of one of the two greatest industrial and military powers in the world, far overshadowing such once-great powers as Britain and France. Many Indians think that the Soviet experience offers a model for them to follow. They are also impressed by the apparent absence of racial and color consciousness in the multinational U.S.S.R., and by the treatment of minority groups; by the flattering attention which the Russian Communists pay to Asia and Asians; by the Soviet encouragement of their independence struggles and their opposition to imperialism, "capitalism," and racialism; and by the Soviet propaganda "offensives" in the era of the "new look" — peace "offensives," economic "offensives," anti-imperial and anti-capitalist "offensives," and cultural "offensives." They do not accept the thesis of a Soviet-Communist threat, nor do they recognize the existence of a Soviet form of imperialism.

Until Stalin's death in 1953 — an event which was officially mourned in India — India's relations with the Soviet Union were confined almost exclusively to the official level; but in the more open and relaxed period of the "new look" India has been wooed more directly and more ardently by the Soviet suitor and the Indian response has been quite cordial. The visit of Bulganin and Khrushchev to India in December, 1955, was a high point in the new cordiality. The top Russian leaders used Indian platforms to attack Western policies, as well as to support Indian views; and Nehru shared the platform with them on several occasions, although he reaffirmed in the presence of the Soviet leaders the determination of India to follow a policy of nonalignment. The Soviet Union gained a great deal of good will in India by a public espousal of the Indian position on Kashmir and

Goa, two issues dear to the heart of official and unofficial India. Large numbers of Indians go regularly to the Soviet Union for educational, professional, or official reasons, and cultural missions are often sent from one country to the other. India has concluded a number of trade agreements with Russia, and Russia has extended economic assistance to India on liberal loan terms. Perhaps the major Soviet effort at economic assistance in the non-Communist world is the assistance which is being given in loans, materials, and technicians to building a steel mill at Bhilai in Madhya Pradesh.[17]

As long as India holds out successfully against Communist pressures from the outside and from within it will be a major barrier to what John Gunther has called "the Communist gamble for the world." In this sense, then, India is a major opponent of the Communist world. Western critics, however, argue that India is showing altogether too much sympathy for the Communists; that it is "neutral" on the Communist side; that it is a great source of weakness and not of strength against the Communist drive; that India often becomes an apologist for the Communists; that Nehru himself often plays the Communist game and lends an air of respectability and gives acceptance to the Communists and to Communist policies. It is probably true, as A. M. Rosenthal has contended, that "the total effects of Indian foreign policy must be more pleasing to Moscow and Peking than to Washington and London."[18] Even if this is the case, however, Indians do not plead guilty to the charge of "guilt by association."

In many basic ways the Indian view of the national and world situation differs fundamentally from the prevailing view in either Washington or Moscow.[19] To most Indians communism, if it is regarded as a threat at all, is only one, and by no means the most dangerous, of the many dangers and problems that beset them; and quite naturally they give priority to the dangers and problems which seem most pressing to them. Notable among these are communalism, colonialism, and racism. In an oft-quoted statement in the course of an address in the Rajya Sabha (the Indian Council of States) in August, 1954, Nehru declared: "We talk about the crisis of our time and many people do it in different ways. Probably in the United

[17] See Wilfred Malenbaum, *East and West in India's Development* (a report prepared for the National Planning Association, 1959), pp. 38–44; Joseph S. Berliner, *Soviet Economic Aid* (New York, 1958), especially Chapter VIII ("Greeks Bearing Gifts?"); G. N. S. Raghavan, *India and Russia* (a report prepared for the Center for International Studies, Massachusetts Institute of Technology, 1957).

[18] Rosenthal, "India Sees Her Role as Power for Peace."

[19] See Rajan, "Indian Foreign Policy in Action, 1954–56," pp. 229–236; N. D. Palmer, "India's Outlook on Foreign Affairs," *Current History,* XXX (February, 1956), 65–72.

States the crisis of the time is supposed to be communism versus anti-communism. Maybe so to some extent. Well, the crisis of the time in Asia is colonialism versus anti-colonialism."

Indian Interests in Africa

As the largest and probably the most influential of the newly independent states of the so-called underdeveloped world, India regards itself as a champion of other peoples struggling to attain political independence and to raise their standards of life. For this reason, among many others, it has shown a special concern for developments in Africa as well as in Asia. Its spokesmen have taken a leading part in the discussions of the Moroccan, Tunisian, and Algerian questions in the General Assembly of the United Nations. In the Trusteeship Council the Indian representatives have been particularly assiduous in scrutinizing the reports of the trust powers and in considering petitions of native peoples and reports of visiting missions; and they have urged the trust powers to prepare the trust territories under their supervision for independence in the near future and to set definite dates for independence.[20]

Indians rejoiced when Ghana became independent and associated itself with the Commonwealth. The seventeen-day official visit to India in December, 1958, of the Prime Minister of Ghana, Dr. Kwame Nkrumah, attracted widespread interest in India. His visit, stated an Indian reporter, "has started a process which may vitally affect Afro-Asian politics." The warm reception which Dr. Nkrumah received was hailed by Nehru as "an expression of India's greeting to the new awakening in Africa."

The Indian Prime Minister, at a civic reception for Dr. Nkrumah in the historic Red Fort in Delhi, urged the Indian community in Africa to develop friendship and good will toward the African people and to conduct themselves in a manner that would reflect credit on India. Relatively few persons of Indian origin live in Ghana, but several hundred thousand live in East and South Africa. India has always taken a special interest in Indians overseas, while at the same time its leaders have advised the Indians living in other countries to identify themselves with the countries in which they are living.

Gandhi spent many years in South Africa, and he first developed there his techniques of *satyagraha* in his efforts to defend his fellow-Indians from all kinds of oppression and discrimination by the ruling whites in that part of Africa. India has seen to it that the question of

[20] See *India and the United Nations,* a report of a Study Group of the Indian Council of World Affairs (New York, 1957), Chapters 4 and 5; Ross N. Berkes and Mohinder S. Bedi, *The Diplomacy of India* (Stanford, Calif., 1958), pp. 175–196.

"the treatment of persons of Indian origin in the Union of South Africa" has been almost continually on the agenda of the UN General Assembly. In spite of the protests of the Union of South Africa, the General Assembly has passed resolution after resolution in support of the Indian views on this question. Because of this issue relations between India and South Africa, once fellow-members of the Commonwealth, could hardly be worse. Even without the presence of many thousands of persons of Indian origin in the Union, India would be a leading critic of the policies of apartheid in South Africa; but the large numbers of Indians there and the long history of past mistreatment and continuing discrimination of these people give India very special reasons for her continuing hostility to the present South African regime.

India, Britain, and the Commonwealth

In spite of bitter memories of the past and strong anti-imperial sentiments and policies, the prevailing Indian attitudes toward Britain and toward Englishmen are remarkably good. India has benefited from its continued associations with Britain in the sterling area and the Colombo Plan organization. It chose to remain in the Commonwealth, and an Englishman, Lord Mountbatten, was the first Governor-General of the Indian Dominion. Even after India became a Republic in January, 1950, it maintained its membership in the Commonwealth, under a formula worked out at a Commonwealth conference in the preceding year. Under this formula the sovereign of England ceased to be at the same time the emperor of India, but the Republic of India recognized the English sovereign as the symbolic head of the Commonwealth.

It may seem ironical that India should belong to an association which numbers among its members the Western nation which ruled India for so many decades and the neighboring nation in the subcontinent with which India is on rather uneasy terms; but the advantages of remaining within the Commonwealth are many, and in the new Commonwealth, heavily focused on Asia, India has a prominent place.[21]

In India itself, as has been noted, there was a good deal of opposition to the continuance of the Commonwealth tie, but it is difficult to assess the various strands of unofficial Indian opinion on this question. A

[21] See James W. Mahoney, *India in the Commonwealth* (unpublished doctoral dissertation, Fletcher School of Law and Diplomacy, 1956); M. S. Rajan, "India and the Commonwealth," *India Quarterly,* XVI (January–March, 1960), 31–50; B. N. Rau, *India's Constitution in the Making* (Bombay, 1960), Chapters 22 and 23; Brecher, *Nehru,* pp. 579–581. See also above, pp. 100–102.

real crisis developed in the latter part of 1956, as a consequence of the British military action in Egypt and the vigorous Indian opposition to it. This action "led to a widespread and strong disapproval in India of the Commonwealth connexion. . . . And such was the state of public feeling in India at the time that even the governing Congress Party would have probably supported the demand" for leaving the Commonwealth "but for the well-known and strong views of the Prime Minister on the subject. The Government was firmly opposed to any such precipitate action, though . . . even Mr. Nehru was compelled to state publicly that they did not consider the connexion so sacrosanct or irrevocable that it could not be terminated at any time in the future."[22]

Curiously enough, the widespread criticism in India of the Commonwealth tie which followed Britain's actions in the Suez Canal area in 1956 — actions which were taken without consultation with any Commonwealth Government — led to a deeper understanding and perhaps even a more general support in India of the Commonwealth association.

> The significant result of this reappraisal was not merely a reaffirmation of India's continued membership of the Commonwealth — which was perhaps never seriously in doubt — but the fact that it was done after a public debate which clarified or underlined the real nature of the Commonwealth and the reasons for India's membership in it in the minds of millions of Indian people. Such a public discussion on the Commonwealth issue was unprecedented in Indian public life — even compared to the 1949 debate on continuing Commonwealth membership after becoming a Republic. Henceforth, it could be said with some assurance that the approval of the Commonwealth connexion in India was very much more broad-based than it had ever been, especially outside official circles, and a connexion that only a greater calamity than that of British military action against Egypt could compel the Government of India to terminate.[23]

Relations with the United States

Prior to independence very few Americans had direct contact with India, and most of these were traders, missionaries, and consular officials.[24] Americans took considerable interest in the Indian struggle for independence. This interest was enhanced by occasional visits to

[22] Rajan, "India and the Commonwealth," pp. 32, 36–37, 47.
[23] *Ibid.*, p. 32.
[24] See E. R. Schmidt, *American Relations with South Asia, 1900–1940* (unpublished doctoral dissertation, University of Pennsylvania, 1955).

the United States of outstanding Indian leaders, notably Vivekananda in the 1890's and Rabindranath Tagore on five occasions between 1912 and 1930. Gandhi captured the hearts and imagination of the American people, as he did of people in many other parts of the world. Nehru was well-known in America well before 1947, although he did not visit the United States until 1949. The American image of India was a mixed one, formed by conflicting impressions of Gandhi and Maharajas, the Taj Mahal and the burning ghats at Benares, glamor and the terrible economic and social conditions pictured so vividly in Katherine Mayo's best-selling shocker, *Mother India.*[25] The Indian image of America was equally mixed, reflecting a confused kaleidoscope of pictures of vast material progress and exploitative capitalism, of the Declaration of Independence and Abraham Lincoln and racial discrimination in the South and imperialism in Latin America, of gratitude for the American interest in India's independence struggle and resentment at the picture of Indian life presented in *Mother India.*

As long as India was under British control the official policy of the United States was largely a stand-offish one. This became less true during World War II. Thousands of American GI's were stationed in India — most of them in rather undesirable places such as Karachi and Calcutta and the jungles of Assam — and the Roosevelt administration, convinced that the tough British policy toward the Indian National Congress was interfering with the objectives of the combined war effort in Asia and was sowing the seeds of later troubles, showed enough interest in the situation in India to alarm the British and to gain the lasting appreciation of the Indian leaders and people. The Johnson and Phillips mission to India during the war were warmly welcomed by the Indians and frigidly tolerated by the British, and Roosevelt's mild suggestion to Churchill for greater concessions to India provoked indignant reactions from the man who later said that he had not become His Majesty's First Minister to preside over the liquidation of the British Empire.[26]

Since the end of the war Indians and Americans have got to know each other better, on both official and unofficial levels, at a time when both countries have occupied a conspicuous place in world affairs.[27]

[25] See Harold R. Isaacs, *Scratches on Our Minds: American Images of China and India* (New York, 1958), pp. 239–378.

[26] See *ibid.*, p. 300.

[27] For commentaries on Indo-American relations since World War II see L. K. Rosinger, *India and the United States: Political and Economic Relations* (New York, 1950); Phillips Talbot and S. L. Poplai, *India and America* (New York, 1958); Selig S. Harrison, ed., *India and the United States* (New York, 1961); N. D. Palmer, "Ups and Downs in Indo-American Relations," *The Annals* of the American Academy of Political and Social

These closer contacts have not erased the great areas of ignorance and misunderstanding of the past; they have even added new tensions arising from differences in approaches and in policies. But fundamentally the relations between India and the United States have been good, based as they are on shared objectives and on mutual friendship and respect. "Our two republics," said Nehru in a radio and television address to the American people in December, 1956, during his second visit to the United States, "share a common faith in democratic institutions and the democratic way of life, and are dedicated to the cause of peace and freedom." "What is important," he stated nearly a year later, "is the basic approach between one country and another. In regard to that I am quite convinced that the basic approach of India and the United States, in spite of often hard criticism on either side, is a friendly approach, is an appreciative approach, an approach with a desire to understand and improve relations with each other." The most thorough study of Indian-American relations that has yet been made — based on two years of discussions by thirty-four Indian and American specialists and written by an Indian and an American — reached this conclusion: "Despite the differences of approach and of policy that have so far troubled Indian-American relations and that may for some time continue to do so, this study has shown that the mutual interests of India and the United States far outweigh the differences, that it is strongly in the interests of both India and the United States for the two countries to cooperate effectively on important world problems, and that the mutual advantage of cooperation is being increasingly recognized in both countries as their policy interests touch at a growing number of points."[28]

In the January, 1954 issue of *Foreign Affairs* an Indian writer who signed himself simply as "P," later identified as the well-known scholar-diplomat, K. M. Panikkar, warned that "there is a growing difference between South Asian opinion and the United States in matters affecting world policy." On three issues, in particular, the differences are great and disturbing. These issues are: (1) approaches to peace, (2) the seriousness and reality of the Soviet-Communist threat, and (3) policies toward Communist China.[29]

Science, CCXCIV (July, 1954), 113–123; "The United States and India," *Current History,* XXVIII (January, 1955), 43–50; "India and the United States: Maturing Relations," *Current History,* XXXVI (March, 1959), 129–134.

[28] Talbot and Poplai, *India and America,* p. 193.

[29] "P," "Middle Ground Between America and Russia: An Indian View," *Foreign Affairs,* XXXII (January, 1954), 259–269. See also Taya Zinkin, "Indian Foreign Policy: An Interpretation of Attitudes," *World Politics,* VII (January, 1955), 179–208.

Americans are just as interested in peace as Indians, although many Indians do not appear to accept this assumption. Reluctantly, and only after sincere efforts to cooperate with the Soviet Union, the United States has been forced to conclude that in this dangerous world it must keep its defenses strong and must negotiate from strength and not from weakness. It has therefore placed emphasis upon national security and collective security arrangements, of which NATO is the outstanding example. This policy has been viewed with real alarm in India. Nehru has repeatedly criticized the reliance on collective security arrangements, which in his judgment have created "insecurity, uncertainty, and instability," and have heightened rather than lessened international tensions. He has been particularly critical of SEATO, which he insists has "no reality" and which has increased the danger of Asian involvement in the power struggle between the two rival giants of the contemporary world. He has been quite bitter about Pakistan's adherence to SEATO, on the ground that this has brought the cold war to the very gates of India. In 1954 he said that there were "two approaches to the question of war and peace": to consider war inevitable and to prepare for it; or the course he chose to follow, to consider that war "must be avoided if not at all costs, almost at all costs." Thus Indian spokesmen are fearful that the security policies of the United States tend to increase the danger of nuclear war and mutual destruction, and they therefore question the basic approach of the United States to the problem of war and peace. "The great difference between America and India," wrote the veteran Indian leader and former Governor-General of India, C. Rajagopalachari, in the *Hindustan Times* of March 3, 1955, "is that the means America is adopting for establishing peace on earth do not appeal to India."

Few Americans need to be convinced of the reality and seriousness of the Soviet-Communist threat; most Indians seem either not to recognize this threat at all or to assign it a relatively low priority in their list of present problems and dangers. This difference in viewpoint helps to explain many of the differences in the foreign policies of the United States and India. It springs from a basic difference in both internal and external position, as well as in general outlook. India is a relatively weak nation, beset by a multitude of internal problems which are so pressing that they tax the resources of the country and the energies of its leaders. It cannot afford to antagonize the Communist giants of the Soviet Union and China. The United States is the most powerful nation of the non-Communist world, and therefore is inescapably the major bulwark of defense of that world against the further encroachments of the Soviet Union or of international communism. It is quite natural, therefore, that the United States should be more directly concerned than India with the problem of resisting the Soviet-Communist pressures and should be inclined, out of sheer necessity, to give less attention to other and perhaps in the long run more important problems of international life.

India and the United States have been poles apart in their attitudes toward Communist China. India is the leading advocate of a conciliatory approach to the regime which now controls the destinies of more than one-fifth of the human race, and it favors the full acceptance of that regime in the councils of the nations. The United States, on the other hand, is the leading advocate of the nonrecognition of Communist China, and the leading supporter of the Nationalist Government of China, which India does not recognize at all. Indian leaders are outspoken in their criticism of United States China policy, which they regard as based on an inexcusable refusal to face "the facts of life" and as being in effect a barrier to international cooperation and virtually an insult to a fellow-Asian people. Actually India is more apprehensive than it will admit regarding Communist China's internal and external policies, whereas opinion in the United States regarding the China policy is much more divided and much more flexible than official pronouncements would suggest. In view of the harder Indian attitude toward Communist China since early 1959 and the more flexible attitude of the United States under the Kennedy administration, the differences between the two countries over China policy seem to be less serious than they have been in the past.

Against a background of general agreement on objectives and fundamentals of national policy and of frequent disagreements and misunderstandings on specific issues, relations between the United States and India have, as Robert Trumbull once stated, gone up and down like a yo-yo in the postwar years. At all times there has been a strong undercurrent of common interests and mutual good will, but this has often been tempered by mutual recriminations and mutual criticisms regarding both the general approach to foreign policy and regarding specific issues. Many influential Americans have been outspokenly critical of India's "neutralist" orientation, which they interpret as neutralism in favor of the Communists, and of Nehru himself. Nehru's chief foreign policy spokesman, V. K. Krishna Menon, has been one of the least popular of foreign diplomats in the United States. Indians have been equally critical of America's cold war mentality and approach to world problems, and they have been appalled by the views of such prominent American politicians as former Senator Knowland, and highly critical of the late American Secretary of State, John Foster Dulles. On the other hand, both countries have been well served by their ambassadors. Special credit for improvement in Indo-American relations should go to Chester Bowles, who during his service of eighteen months as American Ambassador to India endeared himself to the Indian people in a unique way, and to G. L. Mehta and M. C. Chagla, who during their service as Indian Ambassadors to the United States were indefatigable in making contacts with Americans of all walks of life and in interpreting their country to Americans.

Late in 1949 Nehru made his first "voyage of discovery" to the United States. Unfortunately it was more of a voyage of disenchantment, for himself and for his American hosts. "By any standards this first visit to America was a failure. Nehru came away empty-handed. American leaders were not over-impressed with him, primarily because of his refusal to 'stand up and be counted.' And he was decidedly unhappy at his experience."[30] His second visit, however, seven years later, was another story. India and the United States had learned to understand each other better, and Indian reactions to the United States stand on the Anglo-French-Israeli military intervention in Suez a few weeks before had been most favorable. Nehru was warmly received in New York, Washington, and wherever he went, and he made a very favorable impression upon American officials and, through the medium of television, upon the American people generally.

Three years later President Eisenhower, on the first visit which an American President had ever made to Asia while in office, returned the visit of the Indian Prime Minister. He came at an opportune time, while the Indian Government and people were still smarting from the actions of the Chinese Communists in Tibet and along the India-China borders; but while it was generally expected that "Ike" would be warmly welcomed, Indians still speak wonderingly of the nature of the reception which he actually received. New Delhi, accustomed to welcoming world leaders of all types and orientation, staged a welcome which was described as exceeding any other in modern Indian history. In Delhi the American President addressed perhaps the largest crowd that had ever assembled in the shadow of the nation's capital. Nehru and Eisenhower seemed to get along famously, and the Eisenhower smile, very much in evidence, was infectious. Eisenhower himself was profoundly moved by his experience in India. Undoubtedly his visit marked a high point in Indo-American relations.

The ups and downs in Indo-American relations can be traced in reactions to specific issues. Indians responded very favorably to such American acts or policies as the substantial wheat loan to India at a time of dire need in 1951 (although India's gratitude was somewhat lessened by the long debate on the wheat loan question in the United

[30] Brecher, *Nehru*, pp. 419–420.

States Congress and by some of the critical comments that were made during that debate), the American policies in the Suez crisis in 1956, the warm reception extended to Nehru when he visited the United States in late 1956, and the substantial American economic assistance to India in recent years. On the other hand, Indians reacted very unfavorably to a variety of American acts and policies, notably American arms aid to Pakistan, the American sponsorship of various security arrangements, notably SEATO, and the whole gamut of America's China policy. India has been generally unhappy with the position of the United States on the Kashmir question, with the sending of American troops to Lebanon in 1958, and with many evidences of racial discrimination in the United States.

As the two countries have become more accustomed to their new position in world affairs and to the realities of international life, and as they have got to know each other better, there have been many evidences of a growing appreciation of each other's problems and aspirations and of maturing relations. Tangible evidence of the deep interest in India's struggle to deal with its basic economic and social problems and to survive as a democratic state was afforded by the economic assistance which the United States has extended to free India. The amount of that assistance now exceeds two billion dollars, including the 1951 wheat loan, development assistance loans, technical assistance grants, and the provision of substantial quantities of surplus agricultural commodities under Public Law 480. Sympathetic American reactions to India's needs for foreign assistance in financing its Five Year Plans have also been reflected in a growing appreciation of what President John F. Kennedy described as "our stake in the survival of free government in India." "A strong, democratic India," declared John Sherman Cooper, former U.S. Ambassador to India, in 1957, "is in accord with our national security, and is in harmony with our goal of sovereign, democratic nations." India and the United States are both vital bastions of the free world, and a growing appreciation of the things which both countries have in common has ushered in a new and more promising era in Indo-American relations.

SELECTED BIBLIOGRAPHY

Bibliographies

Government and Politics of India and Pakistan, 1885–1955; a Bibliography of Works in Western Languages, compiled by Patrick Wilson. Modern India Project Bibliographical Study No. 2, Institute of East Asiatic Studies, Univ. of Calif., 1956. Lists over 5,000 works.

South Asia: A Selected Bibliography on India, Pakistan, Ceylon, compiled by Patrick Wilson. New York, 1957.

General and Historical

Basham, A. L. *The Wonder That Was India: A Survey of the Culture of the Sub-Continent Before the Coming of the Muslims.* London, 1954. One of the best one-volume surveys of Indian history, culture, and institutions during the Hindu period.

Brown, W. Norman. *The United States and India and Pakistan.* Cambridge, Mass., 1953. An excellent brief interpretation of Indian history, culture, and politics. Contains a good bibliography.

Majumdar, R. C., general editor. *The History and Culture of the Indian People.* Bombay, 1951– . This series, to be published in ten vols., will undoubtedly be the standard reference work on Indian history and culture. Six vols. have already been published: Vol. I, *The Vedic Age;* Vol. II, *The Age of Imperial Unity;* Vol. III, *The Classical Age;* Vol. IV, *The Age of Imperial Kanauj;* Vol. V, *The Struggle for Empire;* Vol. VI, *The Delhi Sultanate.*

Majumdar, R. C., H. C. Raychaudhuri and Kalikinkar Datta. *An Advanced History of India.* London, 1950.

Moreland, W. H. and Atul Chandra Chatterjee. *A Short History of India.* 3rd edition, London, 1953.

Nehru, Jawaharlal. *The Discovery of India.* New York, 1946. *Must* reading for anyone interested in India or in Nehru.

O'Malley, L. S. S., ed. *Modern India and the West, a Study of the Interaction of Their Civilizations.* London, 1941.

Radhakrishnan, S. *The Hindu View of Life.* London, 1927.

Radhakrishnan, S. *Indian Philosophy.* 2 vols., New York, 1922–27.

Riencourt, Amaury de. *The Soul of India.* New York, 1960. A thoughtful and challenging interpretation.

Sources of Indian Tradition, compiled by Wm. Theodore de Bary, Stephen Hay, Royal Weiler, and Andrew Yarrow. New York, 1958. An invaluable book of source readings, carefully selected and edited.

Spear, Percival. *India, Pakistan, and the West.* 2nd edition, London, 1952.

Wallbank, T. Walter. *A Short History of India and Pakistan.* New York, 1958. A convenient pocketbook edition, somewhat abridged, of the same author's *India in the New Era* (Chicago, 1951).

Zimmer, Heinrich. *Philosophies of India.* New York, 1951. A more recent edition of a classic work.

Biographies and Autobiographies

Azad, Maulana Abul Kalam. *India Wins Freedom: An Autobiographical Narrative*. Calcutta, 1959. Provocative comments by India's leading Muslim. Text by Humayun Kabir.

Brecher, Michael. *Nehru: A Political Biography*. London, 1959. An excellent "life-and-times" biography.

Bolitho, Hector. *Jinnah: Creator of Pakistan*. London, 1954.

Chaudhuri, Nirad C. *The Autobiography of an Unknown Indian*. New York, 1951. An Indian classic.

Fischer, Louis. *Gandhi: His Life and Message for the World*. New York, 1954. A paperback book.

Gandhi, M. K. *An Autobiography, or the Story of My Experiments with Truth*. 2nd edition, Ahmedabad, 1940. The first edition was published in 1927.

Moraes, Frank. *Jawaharlal Nehru*. New York, 1956.

Nehru, Jawaharlal. *Toward Freedom: The Autobiography of Jawaharlal Nehru*. New York, 1941. Also available in a paperback edition (Boston, 1958).

Tendulkar, D. G. *Mahatma: Life of Mohandas Karamchand Gandhi*. 8 vols. Bombay, 1951–1954.

Tennyson, Hallam. *India's Walking Saint: The Story of Vinoba Bhave*. Garden City, N.Y., 1955.

Government and Politics in the Pre-British Period

Altekar, A. S. *State and Government in Ancient India*. Benares, 1949.

Brown, D. Mackenzie. *The White Umbrella: Indian Political Thought from Manu to Gandhi*. Berkeley, Calif., 1953. Part I, "Ancient Political Thought," contains a brief commentary on "The Nature of Indian Thought" and excerpts from four classics of the Hindu period: the *Manusamhita,* the *Santiparvan* of the *Mahabharata,* Kautilya's *Arthasastra,* and the *Sukraniti*. Part II, "Modern Political Thought," has a brief note on "The Indian Renaissance" and excerpts from the writings of four of the great figures of modern India: Vivekananda, Tagore, Aurobindo Ghose, and Gandhi.

Goshal, U. N. *A History of Hindu Political Theories — From the Earliest Times to the End of the First Quarter of the Seventeenth Century A.D.* 2nd edition, London, 1927. A widely-known work, first published in 1923.

Jayaswal, K. P. *Hindu Polity — A Constitutional History of India in Hindu Times*. Calcutta, 1924. Describes "republican institutions" in ancient India.

Kautilya. *Arthasastra*. Trans. by R. Shamasastry. 4th edition, Mysore, 1951. An Indian political classic.

Prasad, Beni. *The State in Ancient India — A Study in the Structure and Practical Working of Political Institutions in North India in Ancient Times*. Allahabad, 1928.

Sarkar, Sir Jadunath. *The Mughal Administration*. 3rd edition, Calcutta, 1935.

Sharma, Sri Ram. *Mughal Government and Administration.* Bombay, 1951.

Sherwani, H. K. *Studies in Muslim Political Thought and Administration.* 2nd edition, Lahore, 1945.

Srivastava, A. L. *The Mughal Empire, 1526–1803.* 2nd edition, Agra, 1957. Emphasizes administrative and social aspects of Mogul rule.

Government and Politics in the British Period

Banerjee, A. C., ed. *Indian Constitutional Documents, 1758–1945.* 2 vols. Calcutta, 1945–1946.

Birdwood, Lord. *A Continent Experiments.* London, 1946. Describes the last years of British rule in India.

Campbell-Johnson, Alan. *Mission with Mountbatten.* London, 1951.

Coupland, Sir Reginald. *The Indian Problem: Report on the Constitutional Problem in India.* London, 1944. Three vols. in one: Vol. I, *The Indian Problem, 1833–1935;* Vol. II, *Indian Politics, 1936–1942;* Vol. III, *The Future of India.*

Coupland, Sir Reginald. *India: A Re-statement.* London, 1945.

Dodwell, H. H. F., ed. *The Indian Empire, 1858–1919, with Chapters on the Development of Administration, 1818–58* (Vol. VI of *The Cambridge History of India*). Cambridge, 1932.

Furber, Holden. *John Company at Work: A Study of European Expansion in India in the Late Eighteenth Century.* Cambridge, Mass., 1948.

Griffiths, Sir Percival. *The British Impact on India.* London, 1952.

Keith, A. B. *A Constitutional History of India, 1600–1935.* 2nd edition, London, 1926.

Menon, V. P. *The Transfer of Power in India.* Princeton, N.J., 1957.

Proceedings of the Round Table Conference (3 sessions, 1931–32). Cmd. 3378, 3997, 4238.

Report on Indian Constitutional Reforms (the Montagu-Chelmsford Report), 1918. Cmd. 9109.

Report of the Indian Statutory Commission (the Simon Commission), 1930. Cmd. 3568–9.

Singh, Gurmukh Nihal. *Landmarks in Indian Constitutional and National Development.* Vol. I: 1600–1919. 3rd edition, Delhi, 1952.

Suda, J. P. *Indian Constitutional Development and National Movement.* Meerut, 1951.

Thompson, Edward, and G. T. Garrett. *Rise and Fulfilment of British Rule in India.* London, 1934.

Tinker, Hugh R. *The Foundations of Local Self-Government in India, Pakistan, and Burma.* London, 1954.

Woodruff, Philip (pseud. for Philip Mason). *The Men Who Ruled India.* Vol. I, *The Founders of Modern India.* London, 1953. Vol. II, *The Guardians.* London, 1954.

The Nationalist Movement

Andrews, C. F., and G. Mookerji. *The Rise and Growth of the Congress in India.* London, 1938.

Banerjea, Surendranath. *A Nation in the Making: Being the Reminiscences of Fifty Years of Public Life.* London, 1925.

Bondurant, Joan. *Conquest of Violence; the Gandhian Philosophy of Conflict.* Princeton, N.J., 1958. An unusually perceptive interpretation.

Buch, M. A. *Rise and Growth of Indian Militant Nationalism.* Baroda, 1940.

Desai, A. R. *Social Background of Indian Nationalism.* Bombay, 1948. A valuable historical and sociological analysis.

Lajpat Rai, Lala. *Young India: An Interpretation and a History of the Nationalist Movement from Within.* New York, 1916.

Lovett, Sir Harrington Verney. *A History of the Indian Nationalist Movement.* London, 1920.

Mukherjee, Haridas and Uma. *The Growth of Nationalism in India, 1857–1905.* Calcutta, 1957.

Pal, Bipin Chandra. *The Spirit of Indian Nationalism.* London, 1910.

Sitaramayya, P. B. *The History of the Indian National Congress (1885–1935).* Allahabad, 1935. The standard official history, by a leading member of the Congress.

Sitaramayya, P. B. *The Nationalist Movement in India.* Bombay, 1950.

Smith, William R. *Nationalism and Reform in India.* New Haven, 1938.

India Since Independence: General

Birdwood, Lord. *India and Pakistan: A Continent Decides.* New York, 1954. Deals with both domestic and foreign policy; eight chapters on Kashmir.

Dean, Vera M. *New Patterns of Democracy in India.* Cambridge, Mass., 1959.

Griffiths, Percival. *Modern India.* New York, 1957. A comprehensive general survey, with some historical chapters.

Harrison, Selig S. *India: The Most Dangerous Decades.* Princeton, N.J., 1960. Emphasizes the divisive factors in Indian society and politics.

Lyon, Jean. *Just Half a World Away: My Search for the New India.* New York, 1954. Penetrating observations by an American journalist.

Menon, V. P. *The Story of the Integration of the Indian States.* New York, 1956. The definitive work, by Vallabhbhai Patel's right-hand man in the States Ministry.

Moraes, Frank. *India Today.* New York, 1960. A good general survey by a well-known Indian journalist. Contains several historical chapters.

Palmer, N. D. "India," five chapters on Indian government and politics in George McT. Kahin, ed., *Major Governments of Asia* (Ithaca, N.Y., 1958).

Park, Richard L., and Irene Tinker, eds. *Leadership and Political Institutions in India.* Princeton, N.J., 1959. Important papers by Indian and American scholars on Indian leaders, politics, parties, planning, village life and organization, and other themes.

Parton, Margaret. *The Leaf and the Flame.* New York, 1959. Personal reflections on the Indian scene, by an able American journalist.

Report of the States Reorganization Commission, 1955.

Smith, Donald. *Nehru and Democracy: The Political Thought of an Asian Democrat.* Calcutta, 1958.

White Paper on Indian States, 1950.

The Constitutional System

Constituent Assembly Debates, 1946–49. Twelve vols.

Provisional Parliament Debates, 1950–52.

House of the People (Lok Sabha) Debates, 1952– .

Council of States Debates, 1952– .

Alexandrowicz, C. H. *Constitutional Developments in India.* London, 1957.

Basu, D. D. *Commentary on the Constitution of India.* 2 vols. 3rd edition, Calcutta, 1955.

Douglas, William O. *We the Judges: Studies in American and Indian Constitutional Law from Marshall to Mukerji.* Garden City, N.Y., 1956.

Gledhill, Alan. *The Republic of India: The Development of Its Laws and Constitution.* London, 1951.

Indian Institute of Public Administration. *The Organisation of the Government of India.* Bombay, 1958. A very useful manual.

Jennings, Sir Ivor. *Some Characteristics of the Indian Constitution.* Madras, 1953.

Joshi, G. N. *The Constitution of India.* 3rd edition, London, 1954.

Lal, A. B., ed. *The Indian Parliament.* Allahabad, 1956.

Majumdar, B., ed. *Problems of Public Administration in India.* Patna, 1954. A collection of papers by many authors.

Morris-Jones, W. H. *Parliament in India.* Philadelphia, 1957. A first-class study.

Pylee, M. V. *Constitutional Government in India.* Bombay, 1960. One of the best of the commentaries on the Indian Constitution. Detailed bibliography.

Rau, B. N. *India's Constitution in the Making,* edited by B. Shiva Rao. Bombay, 1960. Selections from the papers of a distinguished Indian who was Constitutional Adviser to the Constituent Assembly through all the stages of the drafting of the Indian Constitution.

Sharma, M. P. *Local Self-Government in India.* 2nd edition, Bombay, 1951.

Srinivasan, N. *Democratic Government in India.* Calcutta, 1954.

Political Parties and Elections

Curran, J. A., Jr. *Militant Hinduism in Indian Politics: A Study of the R.S.S.* New York, 1951.

"The Indian Experience with Democratic Elections," *Indian Press Digests* Monograph Series No. 3. Berkeley, Calif., December, 1956. Summaries of results of the first general elections and by-elections and State elections between 1952 and 1957.

Kautsky, John H. *Moscow and the Communist Party of India: A Study in the Postwar Evolution of Communist Strategy.* Cambridge, Mass., and New York, 1956.

Kogekar, S. V., and Richard L. Park, eds. *Reports on the Indian General Elections, 1951–52.* Bombay, 1956. A State-by-State report on the first general elections.

Lakhanpal, P. S. *History of the Congress Socialist Party.* Lahore, 1946.

Lal Bahadur. *The Muslim League: Its History, Activities, and Achievements.* Agra, 1954.

Mehta, Asoka. *The Political Mind of India.* Bombay, 1952. Analysis of the first general elections by a prominent Indian Socialist.

Masani, M. R. *The Communist Party of India: A Short History.* London, 1954.

Overstreet, Gene D., and Marshall Windmiller. *Communism in India.* Berkeley, Calif., 1959. The most comprehensive treatment of the subject.

Poplai, S. L., ed. *National Politics and 1957 Elections in India.* Delhi, 1957. Contains policy statements, election manifestoes, and an article on "Parties Between the Elections."

Prakash, Indra. *A Review of the History and Work of the Hindu Mahasabha and the Hindu Sanghatan Movement.* New Delhi, 1952.

Rajkumar, N. V. *Indian Political Parties.* New Delhi, 1948.

Rajkumar, N. V., ed. *The Pilgrimage and After: The Story of How the Congress Fought and Won the General Elections.* New Delhi, 1952.

Report on the First General Elections in India, 1951–52. 2 vols. Vol. I: General. Vol. II: Statistical. New Delhi, 1955. Issued by the Election Commission.

Rudolph, Susanne H. *The Action Arm of the Indian National Congress: The Pradesh Congress Committee. The All-India Congress Committee and the Annual Congress Session. The Working Committee of the Indian Congress Party: Its Forms, Organization, and Personnel.* Cambridge, Mass., 1955. Three detailed studies (mimeograph), prepared for the Center for International Studies, Massachusetts Institute of Technology.

Sharma, Bodh Raj. *Report on Elections in the Punjab.* Jullundur, 1952.

Venkatarangaiya, M. *The General Election in the City of Bombay, 1952.* Bombay, 1953.

Weiner, Myron. *Party Politics in India: The Development of a Multi-Party System.* Princeton, N.J., 1957.

Economic Planning and Development

Chandra, J. G. *India's Socialist Pattern of Society.* Delhi, 1956.

Gadgil, D. R. *Economic Policy and Development.* New York, 1955.

Economic Development with Stability: A Report to the Government of India by a Mission of the International Monetary Fund. Washington, D.C., 1953.

Malenbaum, Wilfred. *East and West in India's Development.* A report prepared for the National Planning Association in 1959.

Malenbaum, Wilfred. *Prospects for Indian Development.* London, 1961. A realistic and comprehensive analysis by an American economist.

Mayer, Albert, and Associates, in collaboration with McKim Marriott and Richard L. Park. *Pilot Project, India.* Berkeley, Calif., 1958. An absorbing case study of the Etawah Project in Uttar Pradesh, which became a kind of "model" for the Community Development Program.

Ministry of Food and Agriculture, Government of India. *Report on India's Food Crisis and Steps to Meet It.* New Delhi, April, 1959.

Planning Commission, Government of India.

First Five Year Plan. People's edition. January, 1953.

Second Five Year Plan: A Draft Outline. February, 1956.

Panel of Economists, *Papers Relating to the Formulation of the Second Five Year Plan.* 1955.

Programme Evaluation Organization, *Evaluation Report on Working of Community Projects and N. E. S. Blocks.* 1956. One of a series of evaluation reports.

The New India: Progress Through Democracy. New York, 1958. A valuable popular interpretation of "the underlying approach and main features of India's economic and social programs," prepared at the request of the Planning Commission by a special study group, including two representatives of the Ford Foundation. Written largely by Jean Joyce of the Ford Foundation.

Subramania Ayyar, C. S. *Planning the Indian Welfare State: A Study of the Constitutional Aspects of India's First Five-Year Plan.* Madras, 1954.

Vakil, C. N., and P. R. Brahmanda. *Planning for an Expanding Economy: Accumulation, Employment, and Technical Progress in Underdeveloped Countries.* Bombay, 1956.

Woytinsky, W. S. *India, the Awakening Giant.* New York, 1957.

Foreign Relations

Berkes, Ross N., and Mohinder S. Bedi. *The Diplomacy of India.* Stanford, Calif., 1958. A study, based largely on UN documents, of "Indian Foreign Policy in the United Nations."

Birdwood, Lord. *Two Nations and Kashmir.* London, 1956.

Bowles, Chester. *Ambassador's Report.* New York, 1954.

Brecher, Michael. *Indian Foreign Policy to 1951.* New York, 1958.

Das Gupta, J. B. *Indo-Pakistan Relations (1947–1955).* Amsterdam, 1958.

Foreign Policy of India: Texts of Documents, 1947–58. New Delhi, 1958. Issued by the Lok Sabha Secretariat.

Gupta, Karunakar. *India's Foreign Policy in Defence of the National Interest.* Calcutta, 1956.

Harrison, Selig S., ed. *India and the United States.* New York, 1961.

India and the United Nations. (National Studies on International Organization series, sponsored by the Carnegie Endowment for International Peace.) New York, 1957. Report of a study group of the Indian Council of World Affairs.

The Indian Year Book of International Affairs. Annual volumes, beginning in 1952, published under the auspices of the Indian Study Group on International Law and Affairs, Madras University (Professor C. H. Alexandrowicz, editor). Articles by Indian and foreign scholars.

Jain, Girilal. *India Meets China in Nepal.* Bombay, 1959. *Panchsheela and After.* New York, 1960. Both volumes deal largely with Sino-Indian relations in the context of the uprising in Tibet in 1959.

Karunakaran, K. P. *India in World Affairs, August 1947–January 1950.* Calcutta, 1952. *India in World Affairs, 1950–1953.* Calcutta, 1958. The first of a series of volumes, issued under the auspices of the Indian Council of World Affairs. The third volume, by M. S. Rajan, will cover the period 1954–1956.

Kundra, J. C. *Indian Foreign Policy, 1947–1954: A Study of Relations with the Western Bloc.* Groningen, 1955. A solid and objective study.

Levi, Werner. *Free India in Asia.* Minneapolis, 1952.

Moraes, Frank. *Revolt in Tibet.* New York, 1960.

Panchsheel, Its Meaning and History. New Delhi, 1958. Issued by the Lok Sabha Secretariat.

Rajkumar, N. V., ed. *The Background of India's Foreign Policy*. New Delhi, 1952. Issued by the All-India Congress Committee. A useful compilation of the resolutions of the Indian National Congress on foreign policy and international affairs, from 1885 to 1952.

Rosinger, L. K. *India and the United States: Political and Economic Relations.* New York, 1950.

Sundaram, Lanka. *India in World Politics: A Historical Analysis and Appraisal.* Delhi, 1944.

Talbot, Phillips, and S. L. Poplai. *India and America.* New York, 1958. Based on discussions and exchanges of views of two study groups, one set up by the Council on Foreign Relations in New York, the other by the Indian Council of World Affairs in New Delhi.

INDEX